Reimagining Characters with Unreal Engine's MetaHuman Creator

Elevate your films with cinema-quality character designs and motion capture animation

Brian Rossney

<packt>

BIRMINGHAM—MUMBAI

Reimagining Characters with Unreal Engine's MetaHuman Creator

Group Product Manager: Rohit Rajkumar

Publishing Product Manager: Vaideeshwari Muralikrishnan

Senior Editor: Hayden Edwards

Technical Editor: Simran Ali

Copy Editor: Safis Editing

Project Coordinator: Sonam Pandey

Proofreader: Safis Editing

Indexer: Manju Arasan

Production Designer: Joshua Misquitta

Marketing Coordinators: Teny Thomas and Nivedita Pandey

First published: January 2023

Production reference: 1071222

Published by Packt Publishing Ltd.

Livery Place

35 Livery Street

Birmingham

B3 2PB, UK.

ISBN 978-1-80181-772-1

`www.packt.com`

To my mother, Gaby, for her relentless inspiration. To my wife, Kenia, and my two children, Eoin and Isabella, for their encouragement, support, and understanding. To all the folks at Media House for their never-ending motivation. And, last but not least, to all my great friends who have been checking in on the book's progress and spoiling me with their encouraging words.

– Brian Rossney

Foreword

I have known and worked with Brian Rossney for the best part of a decade.

Our paths crossed when Brian and I worked on TV commercials, with Brian as the Director and myself as Director of Photography. What was unusual about Brian was that he had an innate ability to direct, that was equally complemented by a comprehensive grasp of all aspects of post-production and visual effects.

Brian's hard-won experience and passion in this field goes back over 20 years. Primarily working in commercials and dramas, he has produced countless excellent visual effects, 3D environments, and digital doubles. These skills, along with the ability to transfer information about the subject to others, was quickly recognized, and it came as no surprise that he was hired to teach advanced video production at Dublin City University.

As a Director of Photography on feature films and episodic television, I've grown accustomed to seeing pre-visualization. But seeing what was possible with Brian's guidance and the Unreal Engine, particularly in terms of lighting and animation, was an eye opener. On one film, Brian created pre-visualizations in 3D for every shot. Then he progressed to using the Unreal Engine for his own work, creating an impressive short film titled *Apetito* which maximized the technology.

Simultaneously ILM and Disney began utilizing the Unreal Engine for their *The Mandalorian* series!

The Unreal Engine is most definitely a filmmaker's tool, with the required skills seemingly out of reach for most. However, *Reimagining Characters with Unreal Engine's MetaHuman Creator* allows artists to animate realistic characters in an easy-to-follow fashion, without being bogged down by boring techno garble.

The book is designed for professionals and hobbyists who don't have time to learn about all the technology behind the magic, but want to get to work on their projects quicky. This is why Brian's book is an effective reference – it gradually introduces you to key concepts surrounding digital characters, along with how to use and navigate around Unreal Engine's MetaHuman Creator.

On top of this, he collates the most efficient ways of working, particularly in terms of getting MetaHumans to work with Mixamo animation libraries or bespoke body motion capture through DeepMotion.

Users who have an iPhone can also create highly realistic facial capture to use on their characters, or alternatively can use their webcam and Faceware technology. Both methods are provided with step-by-step breakdowns of how they are accomplished.

Brian never intended to write the definitive guide to every aspect of MetaHumans or all things relating to Motion Capture. However, he did intend to write a book where readers can get results fast, without having to rely on multiple sources of information. Having completed all of the research for you, the outcome is within these pages.

So, get up and running with creating your own highly realistic digital characters and animations for your film project – something that, until now, was only imaginable for huge animation and film studios - without all the stress and heartache.

Happy filmmaking!

Ciaran Kavanagh

ISC IATSE 669

Contributors

About the author

Brian Rossney is a creative director and VFX supervisor at Rossney Pictures. With 22 years of experience working in the film and TV industry, Brian specializes in post-production and digital visual effects. He has produced commercials and TV opening sequences using 3D animation tools and 3D node-based compositing applications. With a thorough understanding of the VFX and 3D animation pipeline and live-action film producing and directing, Brian has lectured at Dublin City University and Galway Film Centre, and has worked as a VFX supervisor for Hallmark and Maravista. He is also the creator of two short films – they are called *Apetito*, using Unreal Engine, and *1976*, using Unreal Engine and MetaHuman Creator.

I'd like to thank my very patient editor, Hayden Edwards.

About the reviewer

Emilio Ferrari is a motion capture supervisor and the CEO of Raised by Monsters (a preproduction studio based on Unreal Engine). He works closely with the Unreal Engine department to develop tools that facilitate a smooth transfer between the mocap stage and engine. In addition to managing the mocap stage, he also leads research and development efforts focused on finding ways to blend VFX, film, and Unreal Engine through playable tools.

Emilio is currently working on the development of the book *Digital Filmmaking with Unreal Engine 5*, which focuses on cinematography and storytelling with Unreal Engine.

Table of Contents

Part 2: Exploring Blueprints, Body Motion Capture, and Retargeting

3

Diving into the MetaHuman Blueprint 85

4

Retargeting Animations 103

5

Retargeting Animations with Mixamo 135

6

Adding Motion Capture with DeepMotion 165

Part 3: Exploring the Level Sequencer, Facial Motion Capture, and Rendering

7

Using the Level Sequencer 195

8

Using an iPhone for Facial Motion Capture 217

9

Using Faceware for Facial Motion Capture 237

10

Blending Animations and Advanced Rendering with the Level Sequencer 269

Preface

Technology and art have always gone hand in hand. In recent years, we have seen technology evolve rapidly, and for many of us, the advancements are hard to keep track of. The technology behind movies is no different.

I grew up in the 1980s when all film technology was analog. An incredibly inspiring film for me was *Clash of the Titans* (1981). Learning that the visual effects animation was created by just one person, Ray Harryhausen, amazed me. Fast-forward to the 2000s, and there are now teams consisting of hundreds of visual effects artists and animators, with several companies working on one single film title.

With Unreal Engine and MetaHuman Creator, things have seemingly gone full circle. Gone are the days when cinema-quality animation and VFX tools were exclusive to large and wealthy studios. With a reasonably powered computer, even a laptop, people can now make their own films. There are no boundaries and no excuses. We are at the exciting dawn of a new era, where we will see new Ray Harryhausens emerge.

Who this book is for

This book is written by a filmmaker for filmmakers. To understand some of the more difficult concepts introduced in the book, you should have a reasonable understanding of the filmmaking process, particularly 3D animation. If you've dabbled with 3D character animation and have read at least one book on the subject, you should have no problem understanding anything written in the book. If you don't have any prior learning, don't worry – you can still progress to the end without getting stuck.

Ultimately, this is a step-by-step guide on how to create an animated MetaHuman with Unreal. It covers various techniques that you can apply to your own ideas and designs.

What this book covers

In *Chapter 1, Getting Started with Unreal*, you will learn what Unreal is, what a MetaHuman is, and how to set up Unreal Engine on your computer.

In *Chapter 2, Creating Characters in the MetaHuman Interface*, we will examine all the major features of the Metahuman Creator Interface, how to edit a MetaHuman, and also how to download and export your own MetaHuman.

In *Chapter 3, Diving into the MetaHuman Blueprint*, we will learn what a Blueprint is and how to use them in relation to MetaHumans.

In *Chapter 4, Retargeting Animations*, we will learn all about IK Rigs, IK Chains, and the IK Retargeter.

In *Chapter 5, Retargeting Animations with Mixamo*, we learn how to retarget animation with Mixamo animation assets.

In *Chapter 6, Adding Motion Capture with DeepMotion*, similar to the previous chapter, we will learn about markerless motion capture using DeepMotion and how we can retarget DeepMotion-acquired motion capture data onto a MetaHuman.

In *Chapter 7, Using the Level Sequencer*, we will learn about the Level Sequencer and how we can use it to control our MetaHuman character.

In *Chapter 8, Using an iPhone for Facial Motion Capture*, we will learn how to install the Live Link app and use an iPhone to capture facial capture live and directly into Unreal Engine.

In *Chapter 9, Using Faceware for Facial Motion Capture*, as an alternative to the last chapter, we will look at how we can use a simple webcam to get an equally high standard of facial motion capture utilizing the Faceware software.

In *Chapter 10, Blending Animations and Advanced Rendering with the Level Sequencer*, we will look at how we can use multiple motion capture clips inside a Level Sequencer. This chapter will also introduce some advanced rendering concepts using the Level Sequencer, such as Post Process Volumes.

In *Chapter 11, Using the Mesh to MetaHuman Plugin*, as a bonus, you will learn about a new plugin that allows users to adapt their own 3D scans for their MetaHumans to be based on.

To get the most out of this book

To get the most out of this book, a basic understanding of concepts from the 3D animation industry such as meshes, video timelines, motion capture, and keyframes is required. Some experience with 3D applications such as Maya, 3ds Max, Houdini, Blender, Cinema 4D, or Modo would be an advantage.

It is recommended that you familiarize yourself with the results of motion capture and 3D animation by watching behind-the-scenes clips from VFX movies such as Avatar, Pirates of the Caribbean, and The Avengers.

Software/hardware covered in the book	Operating system requirements
Unreal Engine version 5.01 or above	Windows or macOS
iPhone X or above	iOS
Faceware software	
Live Link	
Kiri Engine	

You will need a fast internet connection and a lot of hard drive space. A MetaHuman character when downloaded will easily take up about 4 GB of hard drive space, and an Unreal Engine project with a simple MetaHuman scene could take up to around 50 GB of hard drive space. Additionally, a high-spec graphics card such as an NVIDIA RTX 3000 series is recommended.

Also, take a look at the writer's YouTube channel for tips and tricks regarding all aspects of Unreal Engine and MetaHumans relating to this book as soon as they become available: `https://bit.ly/3Fv9u18`.

Download the color images

We also provide a PDF file that has color images of the screenshots and diagrams used in this book. You can download it here: `https://packt.link/5RXwo`.

Conventions used

Bold: Indicates a new term, an important word, or words that you see on screen. For instance, words in menus or dialog boxes appear in **bold**. Here is an example: "Select **System info** from the **Administration** panel."

> **Tips or important notes**
> Appear like this.

Get in touch

Feedback from our readers is always welcome.

General feedback: If you have questions about any aspect of this book, email us at `customercare@packtpub.com` and mention the book title in the subject of your message.

Errata: Although we have taken every care to ensure the accuracy of our content, mistakes do happen. If you have found a mistake in this book, we would be grateful if you would report this to us. Please visit `www.packtpub.com/support/errata` and fill in the form.

Piracy: If you come across any illegal copies of our works in any form on the internet, we would be grateful if you would provide us with the location address or website name. Please contact us at `copyright@packt.com` with a link to the material.

If you are interested in becoming an author: If there is a topic that you have expertise in and you are interested in either writing or contributing to a book, please visit `authors.packtpub.com`

Share your thoughts

Once you've read *Reimagining Characters with Unreal Engine's MetaHuman Creator*, we'd love to hear your thoughts! Scan the QR code below to go straight to the Amazon review page for this book and share your feedback.

`https://packt.link/r/1-801-81772-3`

Your review is important to us and the tech community and will help us make sure we're delivering excellent quality content.

Download a free PDF copy of this book

Thanks for purchasing this book!

Do you like to read on the go but are unable to carry your print books everywhere?

Is your eBook purchase not compatible with the device of your choice?

Don't worry, now with every Packt book you get a DRM-free PDF version of that book at no cost.

Read anywhere, any place, on any device. Search, copy, and paste code from your favorite technical books directly into your application.

The perks don't stop there, you can get exclusive access to discounts, newsletters, and great free content in your inbox daily!

Follow these simple steps to get the benefits:

1. Scan the QR code or visit the link below:

   `https://packt.link/free-ebook/9781801817721`

2. Submit your proof of purchase
3. That's it! We'll send your free PDF and other benefits to your email directly

Part 1: Creating a Character

In *Part 1* of this book, you will learn about the key prerequisites you need to know, such as installing Unreal Engine and Quixel Bridge. Then, you will learn all there is to know about the MetaHuman Creator, including how to create your character and how to bring it into Unreal Engine.

This part includes the following chapters:

- *Chapter 1, Getting Started with Unreal*
- *Chapter 2, Creating Characters in the MetaHuman Interface*

1

Getting Started with Unreal

In the first chapter of this book, you will learn about what Unreal Engine is, what it is used for, and how you can start working with it. You will then learn how to set up an account with Epic Games and download Unreal Engine, before using the same account details to download Bridge, which is the application needed to start creating MetaHuman characters.

Overall, you will become proficient in installing and setting up these applications on a Windows machine.

So, we will cover the following topics:

- What is Unreal Engine?
- What are MetaHumans?
- Setting up Unreal Engine and the MetaHuman Creator

Technical requirements

Before we get started, I must remind you that this book is about extremely high-quality 3D characters so it's important you understand this before setting up Unreal and risk being disappointed because of technical issues. This is because Unreal Engine, like any 3D graphics tool, requires a powerful machine; much of this power comes from the graphics cards.

As a result, if you want to enjoy the real-time experience of working in Unreal, you'll need a computer that can handle the best settings and display a MetaHuman character in real time. Otherwise, you'll experience a very sluggish machine with a tendency to crash a lot, and nobody wants this. To complete this chapter, you will need an internet connection and the minimum hardware specifications that Epic Games recommends:

- Windows 10 64-bit
- 64 GB RAM
- 256 GB SSD (OS drive)

- 2 TB SSD (data drive)
- NVIDIA GeForce GTX 970
- 10-Core Xeon E5-2643 @ 3.4 GHz

The screen grabs you will see in the pages of this book are from my own machine, which is configured as follows:

- Windows 10 64-bit
- 256 GB RAM
- 1 TB GB SSD (OS drive)
- 4 TB SSD (data drive)
- NVIDIA GeForce RTX 3090
- 20-Core i9 10-900k @ 3.7 GHz

If you're a devoted Mac user, you're just not going to have as good an experience as you would have compared to a Windows user. Much of this is to do with Epic Games putting more time into developing the engine for use on Windows. This isn't to say it's not available on Mac but many of the features, particularly rendering features to achieve photorealism, are not available on Mac machines, most notably Direct X 12 and Ray Tracing Cores on the NVIDIA RTX series of GPU cards.

I'd also like to point out that there are solutions out there that will allow you to test on powerful machines. For the most part, they will get you through all the chapters of this book, except for live facial motion capture and any live body motion capture that may be featured. Therefore, if you're on a budget, I suggest you look at some cloud computing solutions such as the following: `paperspace.com`.

> **Note**
>
> On a cloud machine, you still won't be able to do any live motion capture, as this requires a direct interface or shared network with your machine. However, you could take advantage of the higher specification of the cloud machine for experimenting with render and lighting settings.

At this point, you may be getting needlessly worried. However, I personally tried using the tools mentioned in this book on a lower-spec machine and for the most part, I was able to work through it using very low render settings. However, I was just not able to do any live motion capture at all. Instead, I was only able to rely on library motion capture – so if you plan to learn now and invest in a newer, faster machine later, this book is certainly still for you.

What is Unreal?

Put simply, **Unreal Engine** is a game engine. There are many other game engines out there, but Unreal Engine is one of two that are the leading ones in the field of game development, the other being Unity. Had the people of Unity come up with MetaHumans, this book would have a slightly different title!

Unreal Engine is an incredibly powerful tool used for displaying graphics in real time. It was originally built for a PC-based first-person shooter game called Unreal and developed by Epic Games in the mid to late 1990s. In its earlier years, Unreal Engine was capable of rendering frames at rates as high as 60 fps on the CPU, giving the user a real-time experience.

However, there were many limitations, such as the frame size, limits on how many triangles could be displayed at any given time, and the complexity of the math behind the lighting. The end results were graphics that were not photorealistic but were a significant improvement on other game engines.

As GPUs improved over time, so did Unreal, as it was able to migrate a lot of its mathematical computations over to the GPU. As a result, the engine was able to rely on hardware that was specifically designed to calculate 3D rendering faster, and many features were developed to introduce photorealistic lighting solutions that were previously only available on traditional CPU path-traced solutions found in film and TV.

Path-traced or ray-traced rendering solutions involved very complex mathematics that would trace photons from the pixel of the final render through the CGI camera and around the scene. This tracing was incredibly time-consuming and required a lot of processing power just to deliver a single image. Therefore, conveying a sense of motion or real time was impossible for photorealism.

Because of very recent innovations, Unreal Engine is now being used to generate photorealistic renders in real time and we can see the result of that in Disney's The Mandalorian. The company behind the real-time environments, StageCraft Industrial and Light & Magic, worked together to create LED backgrounds that displayed the output of scenes within Unreal Engine. In addition to supplying a photorealistic background, the LED backgrounds would also light the real actors, adding even more realism.

I expect that if you are a complete newbie to all of this, you may be scratching your head thinking: *What does a game engine like Unreal do?* More generally, it is a software application designed for building games that render graphics in real time. For games, Unreal is used for the creation of the following:

- User functions
- Game logic
- Environment design
- Animation
- Real-time rendering of what the user sees

Be it input from a mouse click, an Xbox controller button, or an Oculus headset, this user input affects how and when characters move and what is being displayed at any given time.

Ultimately, this book is about getting you up and running with your own characters and animating them how you want them to be animated even if you don't have an art background or character animation background. Exciting stuff? I think so.

Next, let's think a little more about how we are going to create those characters.

What are MetaHumans?

MetaHumans are very complex characters that have the capability of looking photorealistic and moving realistically. They are templates to be edited by users and artists. The editing of the character templates takes place on a web browser and allows the user to see their character design being displayed in extreme realism.

A lot of the development of MetaHuman Creator is around real-time rendering. Typically, the shading of skin for CGI characters involves a substantial amount of CPU processing, particularly for high-detail areas, such as subtle reflections, pores, and tiny hairs or fuzz. The MetaHuman skin shaders are designed to work in real time within Unreal Engine by harnessing recent technological hardware advances, such as real-time ray-tracing in NVIDIA RTX cards.

In addition to photorealistic skin shaders, MetaHumans have a network of bones and blend shapes that allow for incredibly intricate and powerful facial puppeteering, as well as the ability to be combined with facial and body motion capture, all in real time within Unreal.

Now that you have a good understanding of Unreal Engine and MetaHumans, we will get the software up and running on your system so you can start using Unreal in the next chapter.

Setting up Unreal and the MetaHuman Creator

Before we can start using Unreal Engine and MetaHumans, we need to do some setup. In upcoming sections, we will do the following:

- Create an Unreal account
- Download and install Unreal Engine 5
- Launch Unreal Engine 5
- Install Quixel Bridge
- Boot up MetaHuman Creator

So, let's get started.

Creating an Epic account

To get started with Unreal, the first thing you need to do is create an Epic account. To do this, follow these instructions:

1. First navigate to the Epic Games website: `https://www.epicgames.com/`.

> **Note**
>
> Depending on your region, don't be surprised if the URL changes to something like the following: `https://www.epicgames.com/store/en-US/` (you're still in the right place).

2. Once on the Epic Games website, you can navigate to the Unreal Engine link. Alternatively, just use the following URL: `https://www.unrealengine.com/`.
3. In the right-hand corner, click **Sign In** (even though you don't have sign-in credentials, you must still click on this).
4. You'll see a list of ways you can sign in, including using your email account with a bespoke password or just simply linking other social media or gaming credentials to Epic Games. Assuming this is your first account and you're not signed in, select **Don't have an Epic Games account? Sign Up**:

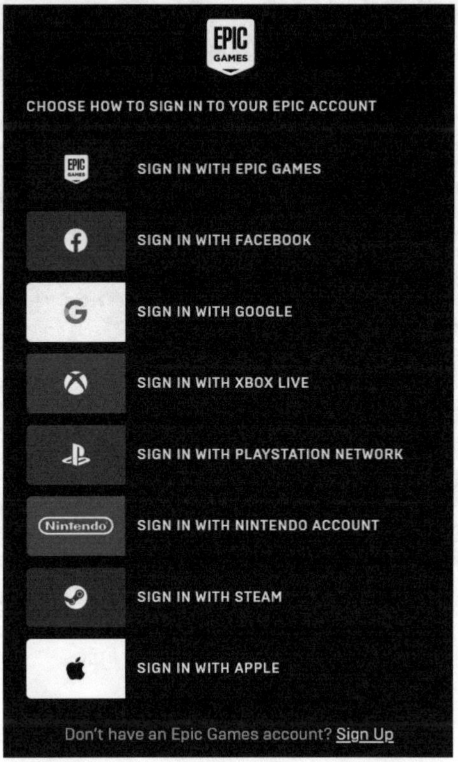

Figure 1.1: Different sign-in methods

5. On the next page, you will be asked for your name, surname, username, and email, and to designate a password for your email. You can opt to receive additional emails, but you will need to read the terms and conditions and tick that you have done so.

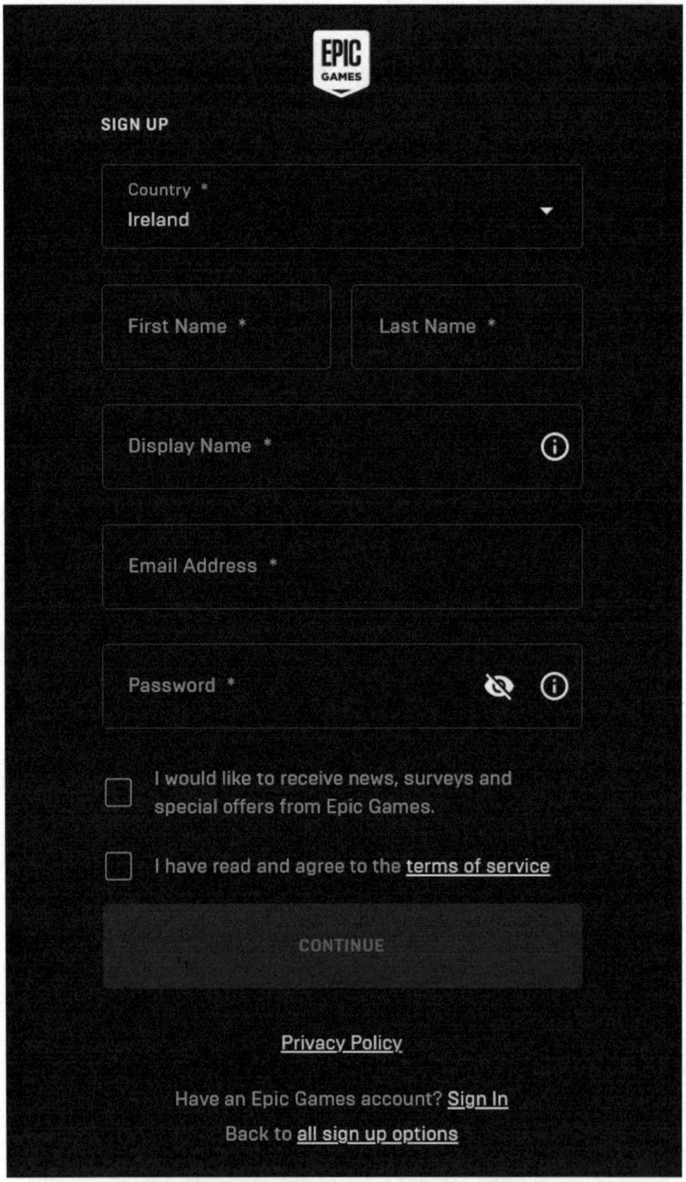

Figure 1.2: Signing up for Epic

6. Once you have done this, a link will be sent to your designated email for verification. When you click on this link, you'll have successfully created an account. You'll need to be logged in whenever you plan to use the engine.

Next, we need to download and install Unreal Engine 5.

Downloading and installing Unreal Engine 5

Using your Unreal account, we need to download and install Unreal Engine 5. The application you are about to install is the Epic Games Launcher. This is where you install the engine and gain access to other features related to the engine, such as updates, plug-ins, scripts, models, and a host of many other assets. To do this, follow these steps:

1. Once you have successfully signed in to Epic, you'll see a page like this (the page may vary, as the screenshot is the latest marketing material from Epic at the time of print):

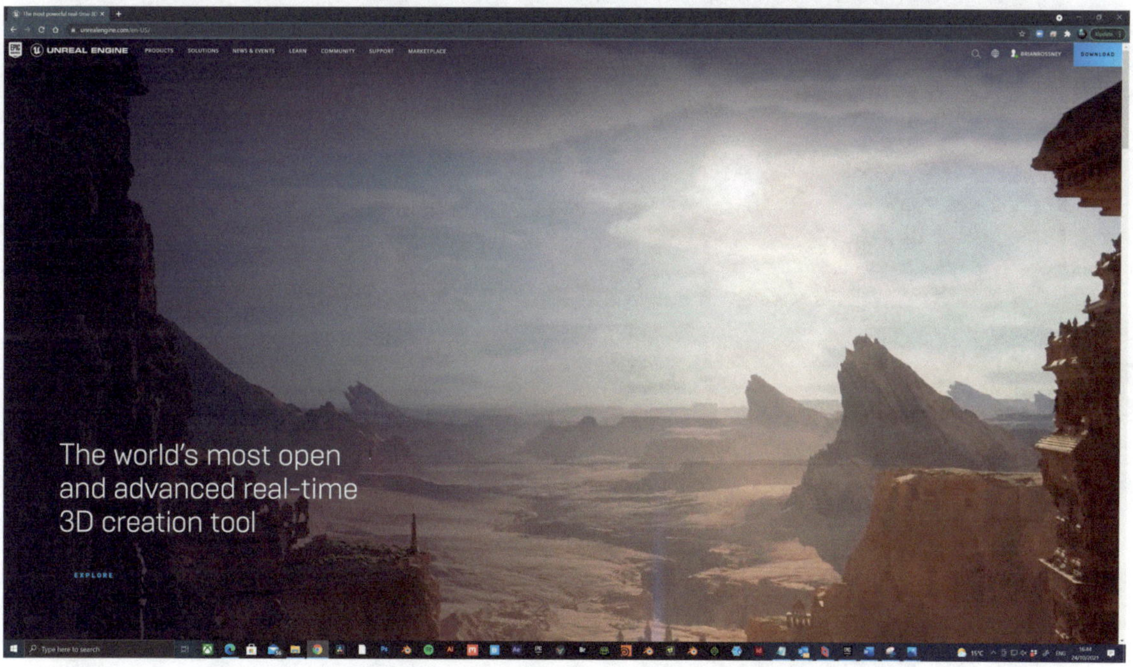

Figure 1.3: Epic splash screen

   In the top right corner, you will see your name, as well as the **Download** button. Click this to take you to the following page:

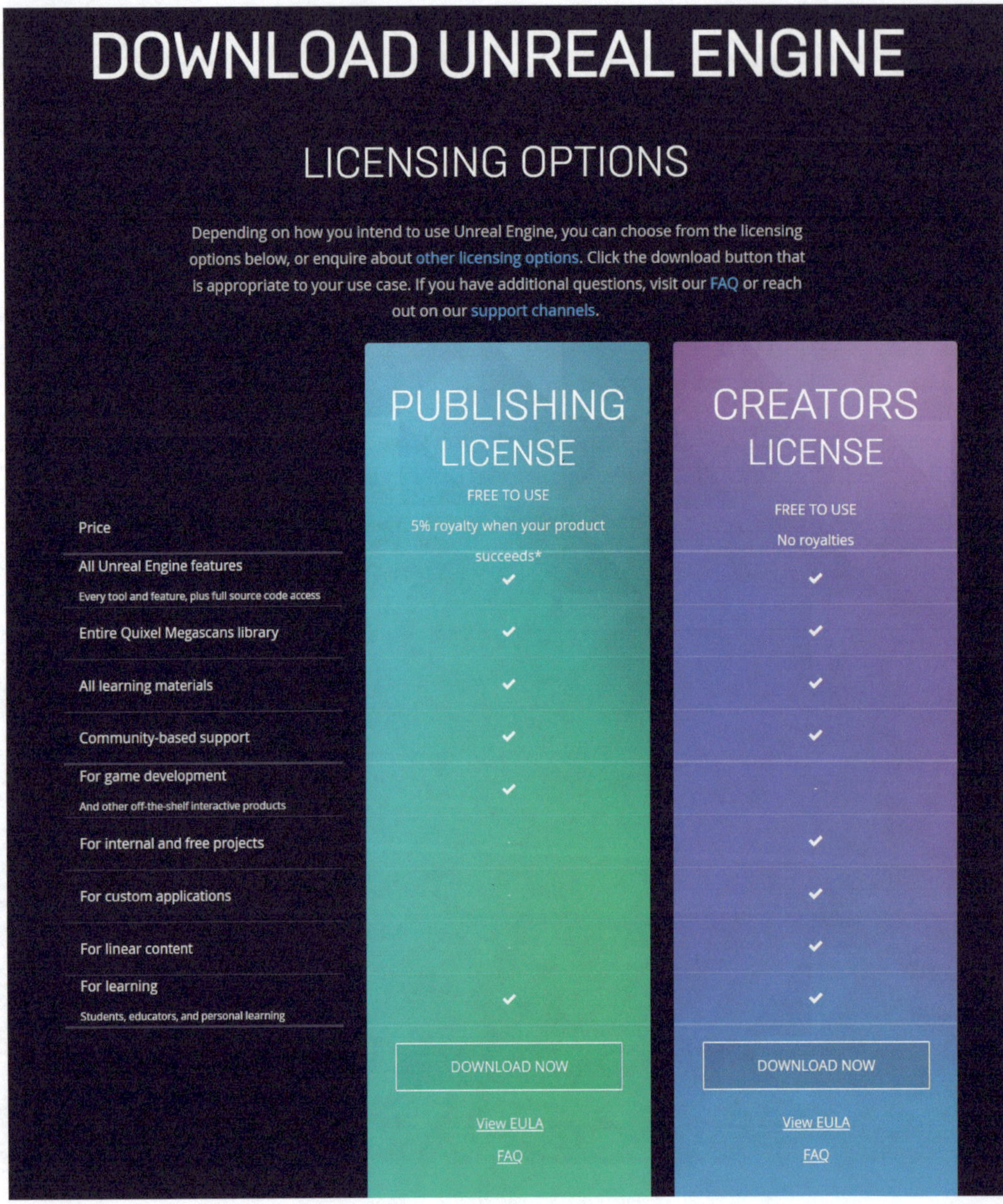

Figure 1.4: Licensing options

For the purpose of this book, we'll assume you're in the film and animation business and not the game development business. The column on the left is a **Publishing License** agreement for game developers where a percentage of sales profits go to Epic Games. You just need to concern yourself with the column on the right: **Creators License**. In most cases, the readers of this book will fall under **Students, educators, and personal learning**. However, professionals delivering **linear content**, such as film and animation, fall under the **Creators License** option.

2. When you've read through the details and have had a look at the EULA license agreement, hit the **DOWNLOAD NOW** button under **Creators License**.
3. Now, choose where you want to download the installer, which will be called something similar to `EpicInstaller013.0.0.enterprise.msi`. It's a Windows installer package and can be saved anywhere on your machine. You only need this file for the installation process.

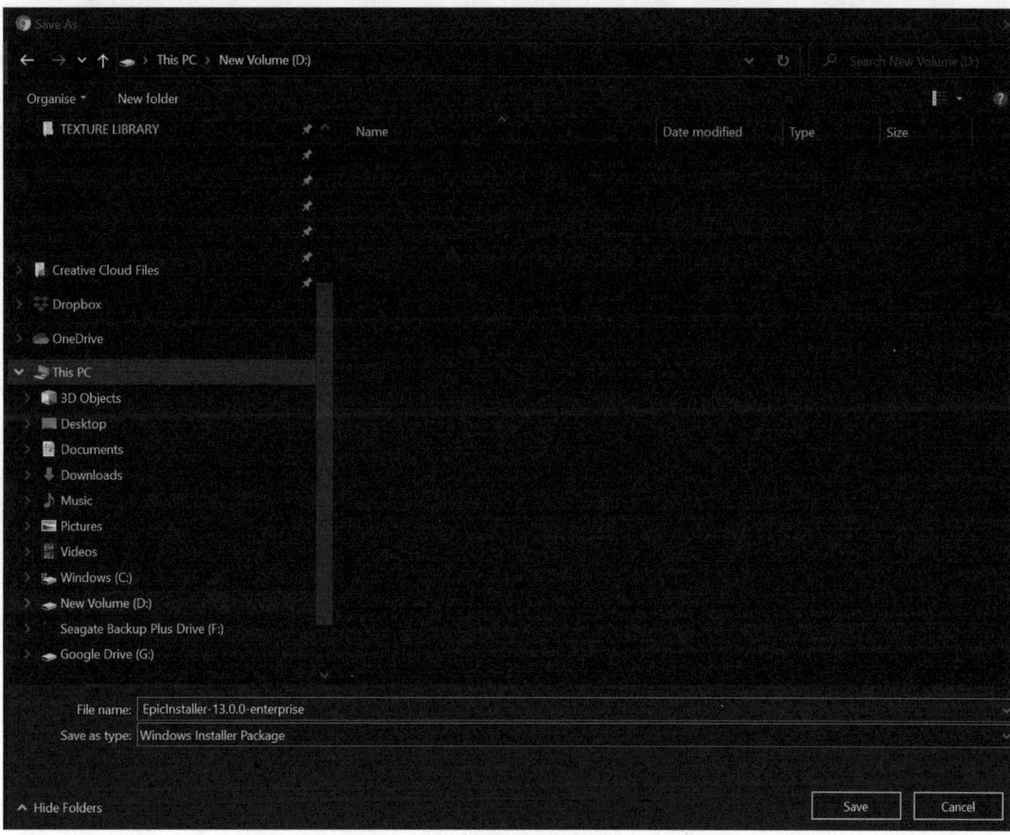

Figure 1.5: Downloading the installer

When you have found a suitable place, hit **Save**.

4. Once downloaded, double-click the file and it will run:

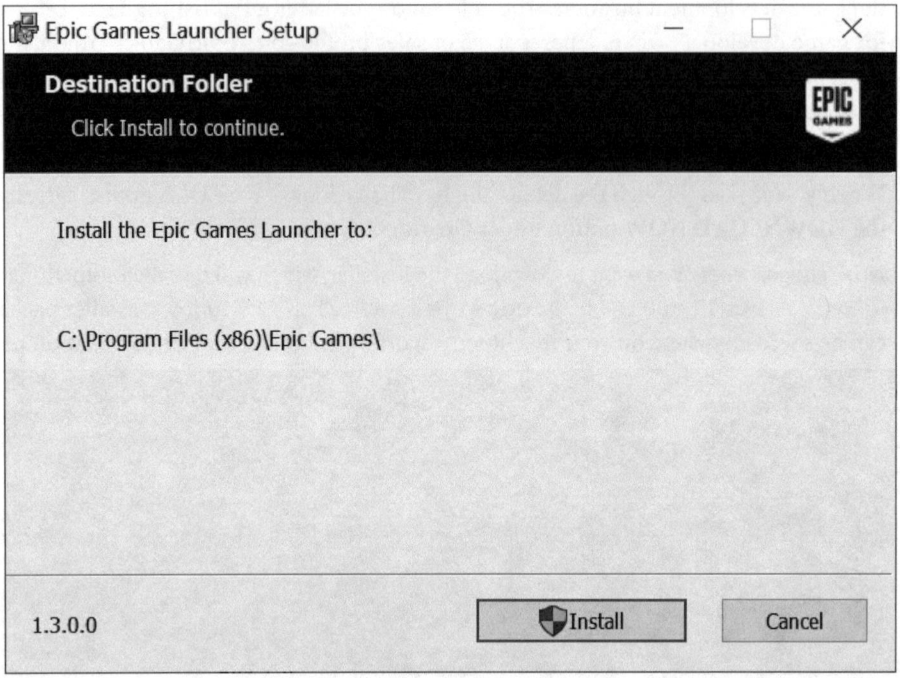

Figure 1.6: The Epic Games Launcher

5. Now, you can click **Install**.

When the installer has finished, you'll see an icon titled **Epic Games Launcher** on your desktop. Clicking on this will open the Launcher (note that it could take a few minutes to open the first time). Typically, it doesn't open fullscreen but when it does, it looks something like this:

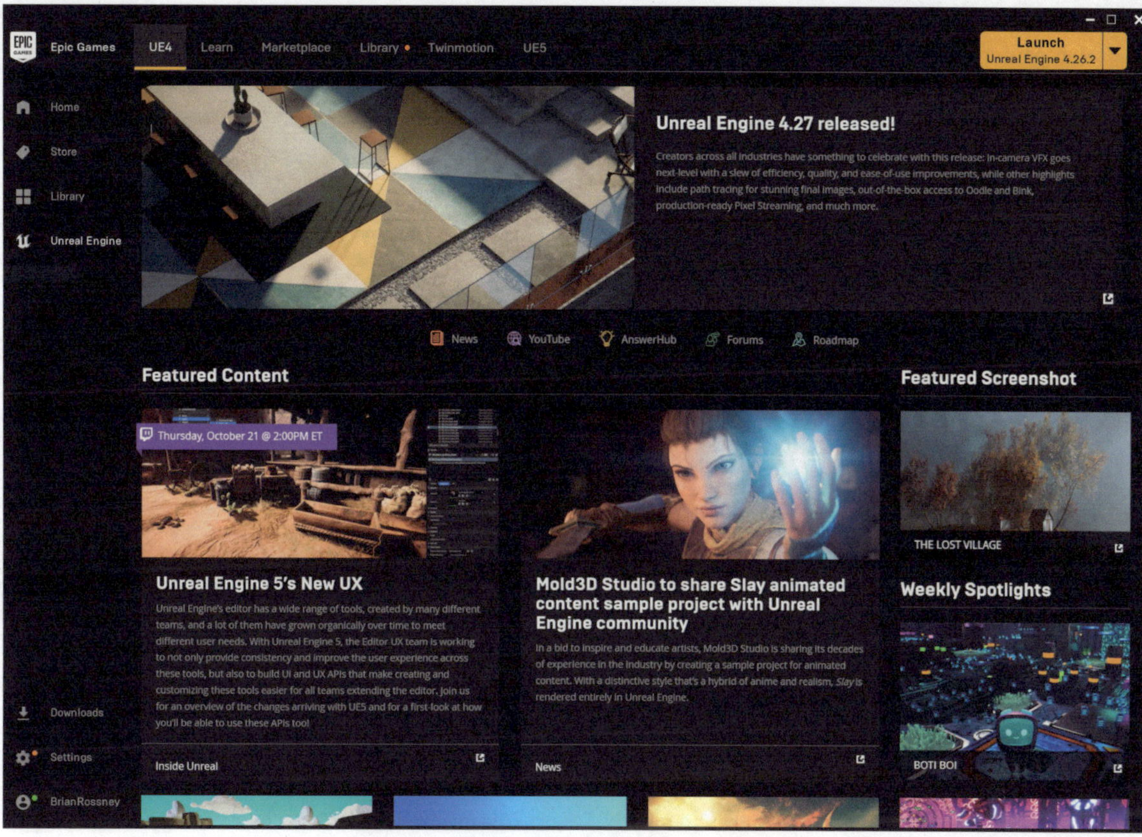

Figure 1.7: The Epic Games Launcher application

From here, you'll see a few tabs running along the top to the right of the Epic Games icon. Most notably, we have the following:

- **UE4**: For blogs, UE4 version updates, and general news
- **Learn**: Opens the learning center, where you can watch tutorials and download sample projects
- **Marketplace**: Where you can buy models, environments, and characters designed to work in Unreal Engine
- **Library**: Used to find content that you have saved, purchased, or installed
- **Twinmotion**: An architectural pre-visualization application, with assets and presets designed specifically for architectural real-time pre-visualization
- **UE5**: Where you will install UE5 from

From **UE5**, click **Download UE5**, and the installer starts installing immediately. You will see this happening either in the **UE5** tab or it may flip over to the **Library** tab and show you the progress of this download.

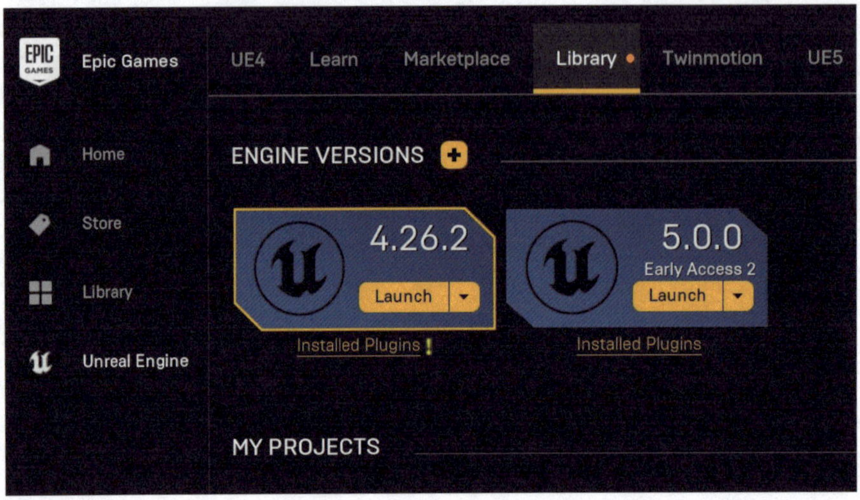

Figure 1.8: Engine versions

The installation does take a while, so you may want to come back to this.

> **Note**
>
> At the time of writing, UE5 is only under Early Access. This means that it's not technically supported for any production and the new features exclusive to this release are deemed experimental.

In the next section, we will launch UE5!

Launching UE5

After you have followed all of the previous instructions and the installer has finished installing, you will see **Launch** appear; this indicates that Unreal Engine is ready to go.

When you have clicked **Launch** (making sure you have selected UE 5.0), you may receive pop-up dialog boxes such as the following: **The Megascans Plugin was designed for build 4.27.0. Attempt to load it anyway?** Messages such as this are precautionary because not everything has been tested to work with UE5 at the time of writing. However, as I have tested them with the Early Access edition, I know they are safe and stable, so it is okay to select **Yes**.

Next, you'll see a small splash screen as Unreal Engine initializes. This could take a few minutes the first time it runs. Eventually, it will lead to the following interface:

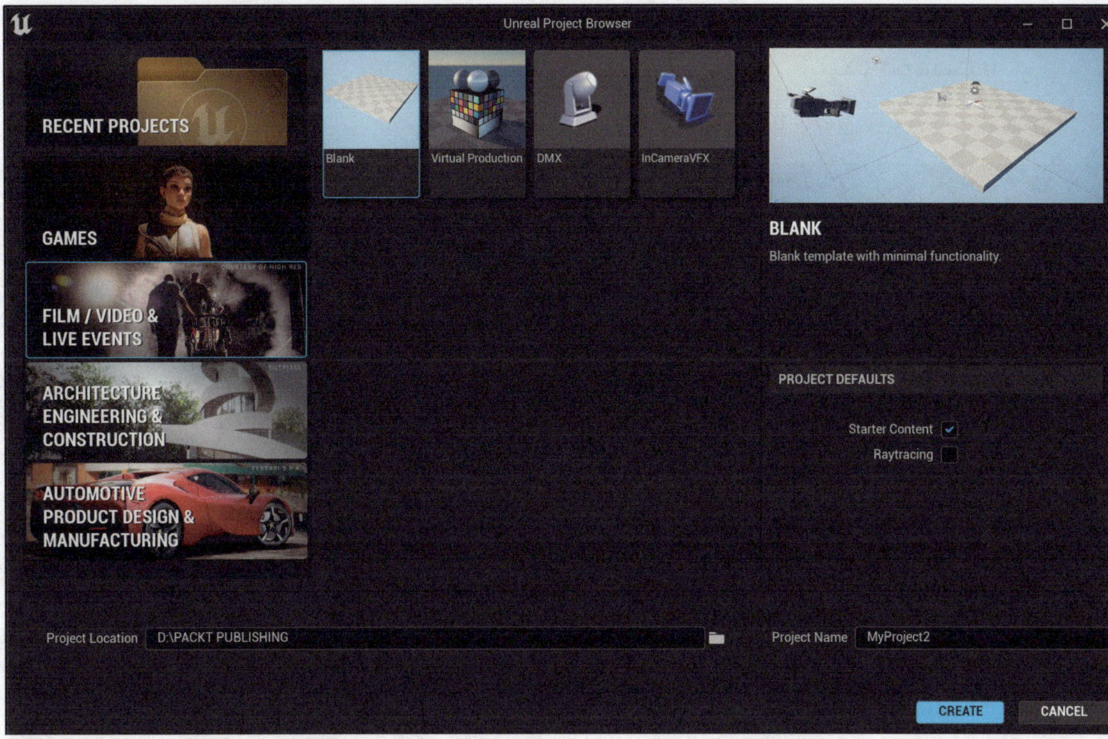

Figure 1.9: Unreal Project Browser

On the left-hand side, you'll see a column listing the following:

- **RECENT PROJECTS**
- **GAMES**
- **FILM / VIDEO & LIVE EVENTS**
- **ARCHITECTURE ENGINEERING & CONSTRUCTION**
- **AUTOMOTIVE PRODUCT DESIGN & MANUFACTURING**

Each one of the listings gives you templates to choose from. Each template will automatically load certain settings and enable various preinstalled plugins required for that nature of work.

Because we are just interested in **FILM / VIDEO & LIVE EVENTS**, when we click on that, we get to choose from a small number of templates related to that type of work:

- **Blank**
- **Virtual Production**

- **DMX**
- **InCameraVFX**

This is what the screen will look like:

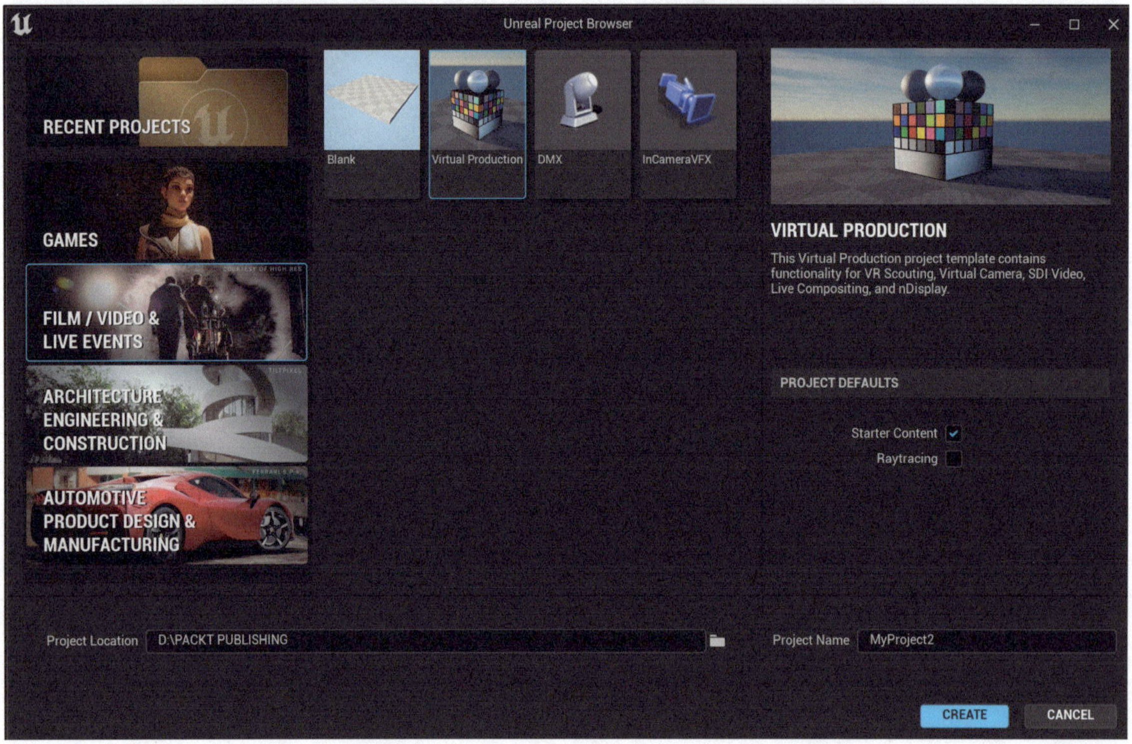

Figure 1.10: Virtual Production template

> **Note**
>
> If you happen to have a lower specification machine that doesn't support raytracing, it's wise to keep **Raytracing** to the default off mode. You can always enable it again in **Project Settings** at a later stage.

From this list, we're just going to focus on the **Virtual Production** subtemplate. Then, we need to choose our new project location and create a project title. For my project, I'm going to create a folder titled `Lost Girl` and it will be in the D drive. The project folder will be `Lost_Girl_SC_01`. You can name your project file whatever you like.

Feel free to save your files to whatever directory you wish but be advised that it is best practice to avoid the C drive where your operating system is stored.

You'll see a splash screen again and you will be prompted that the project is loading. This will take a minute or two depending on your machine's specifications. After this, you may get a number of popups:

- You may also get a dialog box just as earlier warning you that a plugin isn't designed to work in UE5 and asking whether you still want to proceed. Choose **Yes** if that happens again.
- You also may get asked whether you want to update the project. Choose **Yes**. This will just take a second or two to update.
- Finally, it will ask whether you want to manage plugins. You can choose **Yes** and then close down the plugin window if that happens. You can also choose **No** and enable the plugins later as you import your character into the engine, but I do recommend selecting **Yes** at this point.

That's it! We now have the engine up and running.

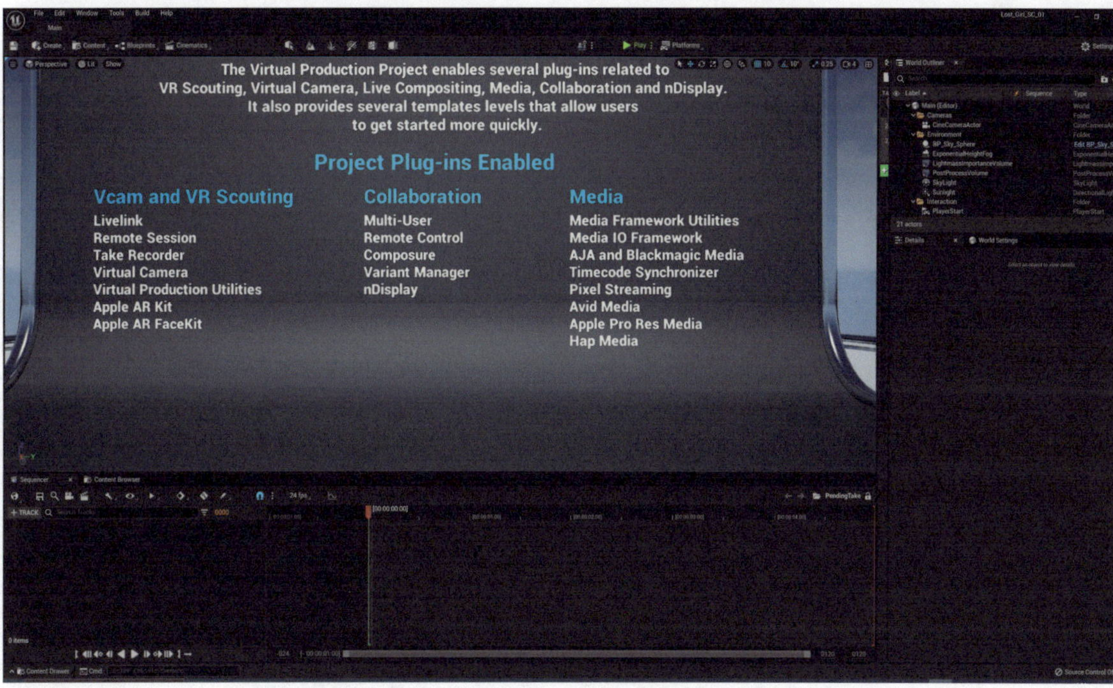

Figure 1.11: The Unreal Engine interface

Next, it's time to install Quixel Bridge.

Installing Quixel Bridge

MetaHuman Creator is an online application from Quixel. To get that up and running, first, we need to go to their website and download the application called Bridge that allows us to launch the MetaHuman Creator online application.

This sounds a little complicated, but the Bridge application works like an asset management tool with your account details. For example, it will fire up your personal MetaHumans projects and allow you to download many other assets, such as Megascans Trees, grass, buildings, and so on while keeping tabs on everything you've created or downloaded in the past.

This can come in incredibly handy because MetaHumans take up a lot of hard drive space, so you get to store your creations in the cloud, which allows you to download them wherever you are. In addition, once installed, Bridge also works as a plugin within Unreal Engine, making asset management even easier.

So, to get started, complete the following steps:

1. First, go to the Quixel website: `www.quixel.com`.
2. Next, click on the **DOWNLOAD BRIDGE** button (we don't even need to log in at this stage):

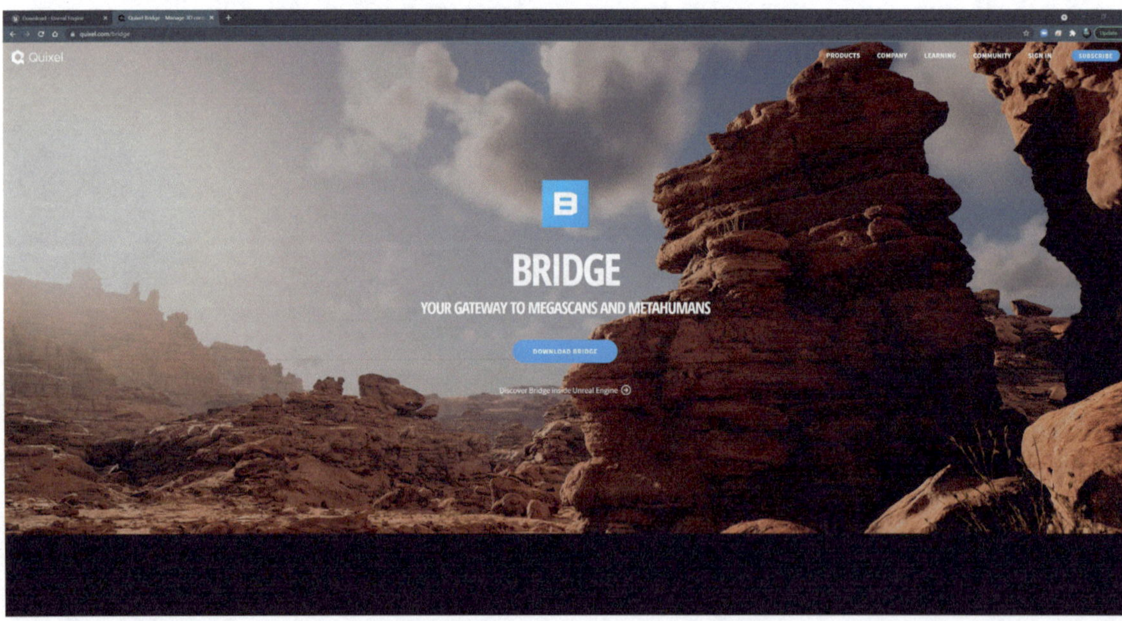

Figure 1.12: Downloading Quixel Bridge

3. Once we have downloaded the installer, `Bridge.exe`, run it by double-clicking the file.

This will install and open Bridge automatically and should pop up as a small window like so:

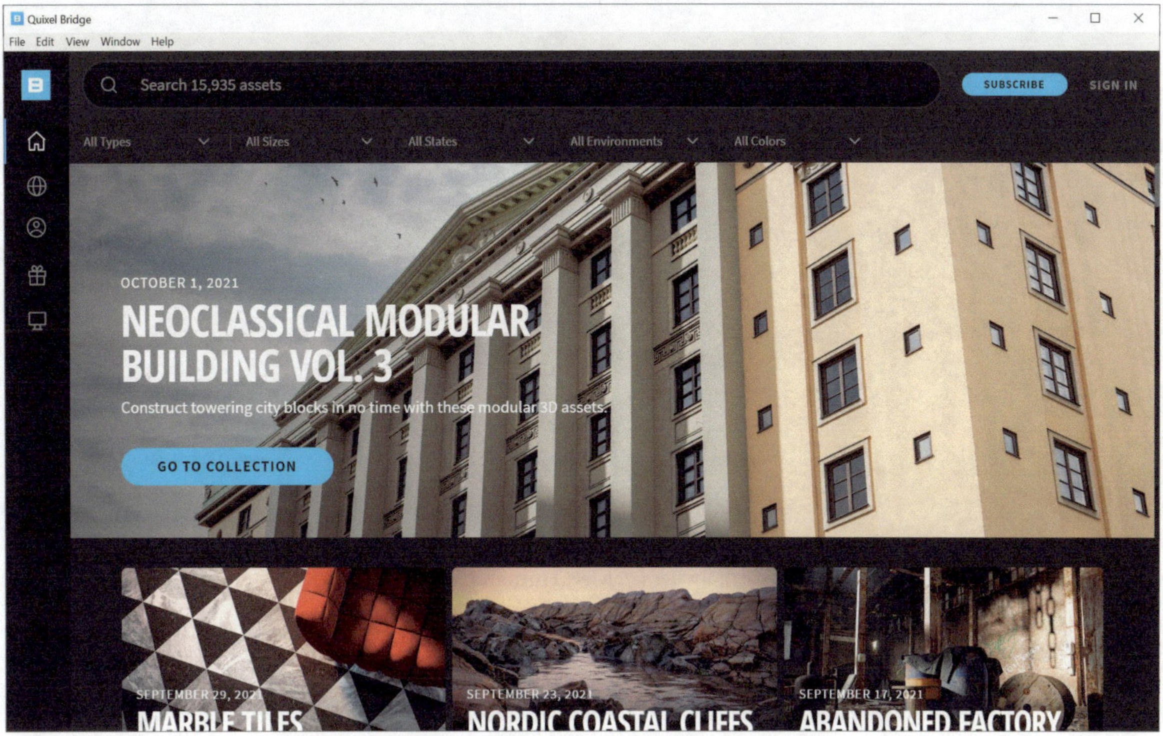

Figure 1.13: Quixel Bridge pop-up application

4. Click on the **SIGN IN** button in the top-right corner of the page.
5. This will lead to another dialog box where we can choose **SIGN IN WITH EPIC GAMES**.

SIGN IN at the top right will change to a person icon, indicating that you have successfully signed in:

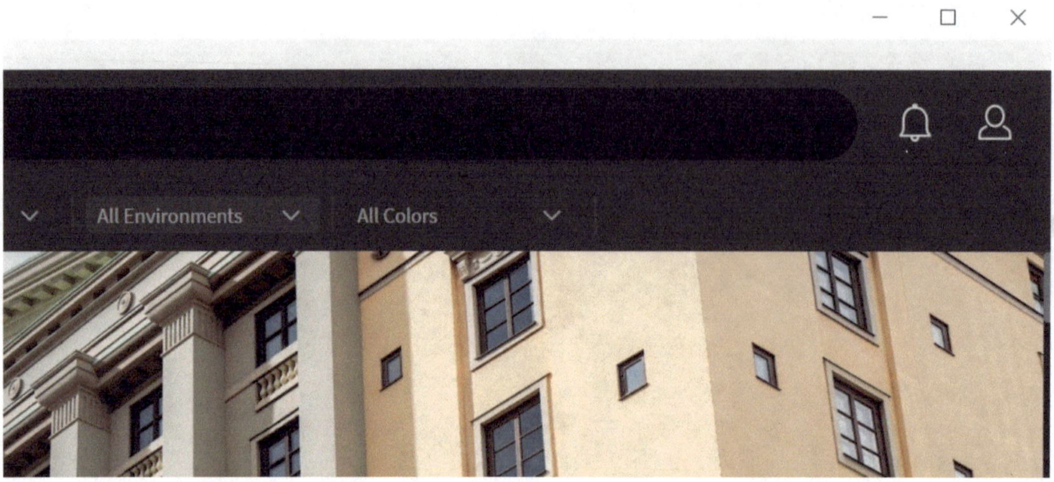

Figure 1.14: Successfully signed in

We're nearly all set up. Now, let's finally set up MetaHuman Creator.

Booting up MetaHuman Creator

Now that you've downloaded Bridge onto your computer and signed in using the same login credentials you used for the Epic Games Launcher, you are now ready to boot up MetaHuman Creator. The difficult part is over, and this is where the fun begins.

It is worth noting at this point that Quixel's Bridge has more features than just MetaHumans. Bridge gives you access to an enormous library of 3D assets, such as Megascans, and 2D assets, such as textures and materials. Unlike most 3D asset libraries, Bridge provides scanned models. In other words, these models are based on data taken from real objects, which is why they look so realistic but come with a hefty file size.

To get straight into MetaHumans, look for the person icon in a circle on the left-hand side of the screen:

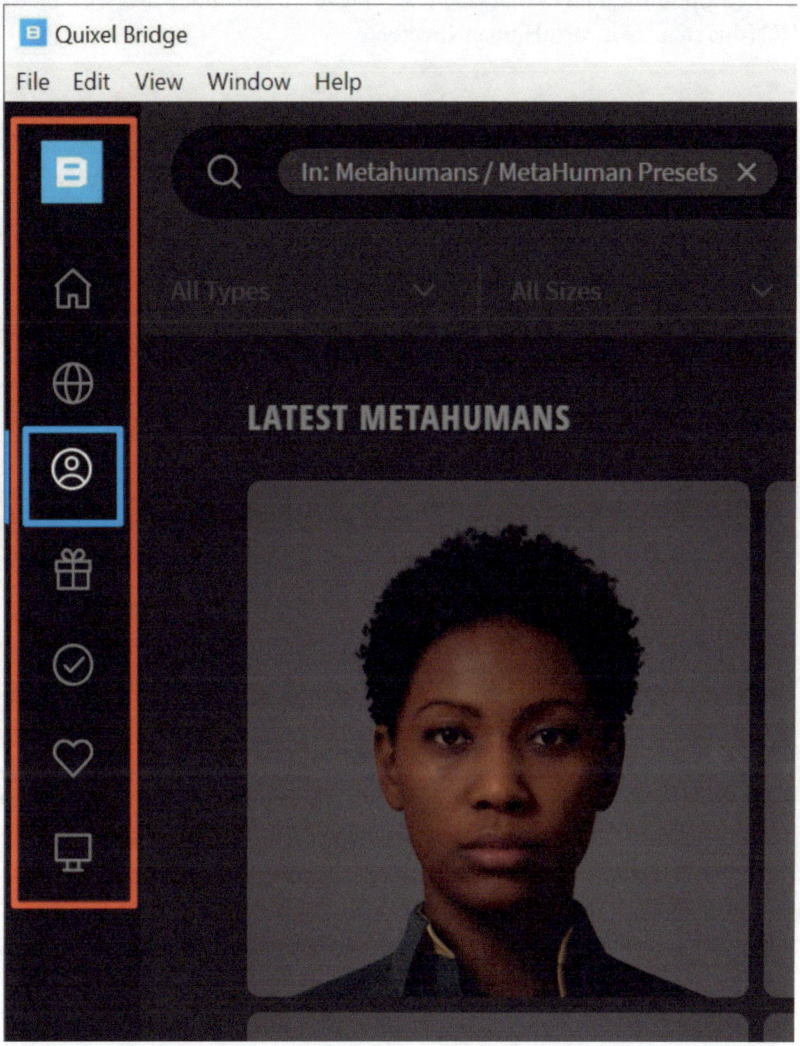

Figure 1.15: The MetaHumans icon

You will see numerous thumbnails of MetaHuman templates. By clicking on any one of these thumbnails, you will see a new option related to that character you've clicked, and you'll see a blue button titled **START MHC** (this stands for MetaHuman Creator):

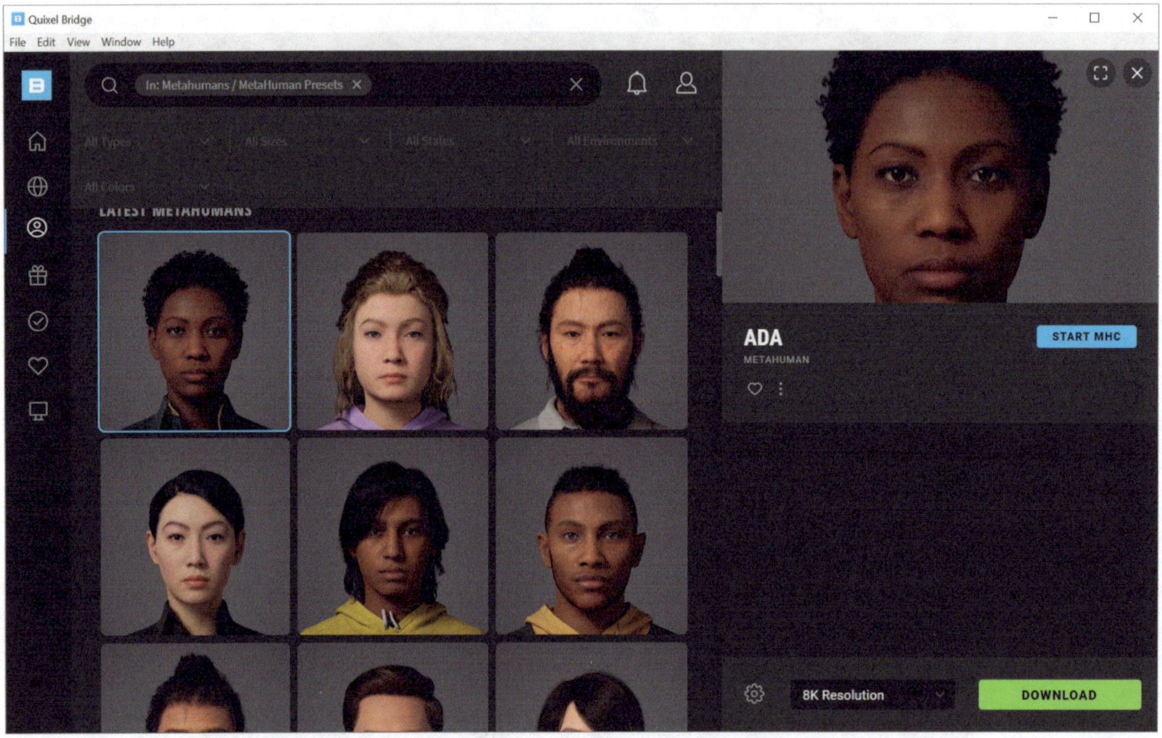

Figure 1.16: Starting MHC

And that's it. Once you click the blue button, you will start your MHC session. This will take a few moments to boot up and you'll get a page looking something like this:

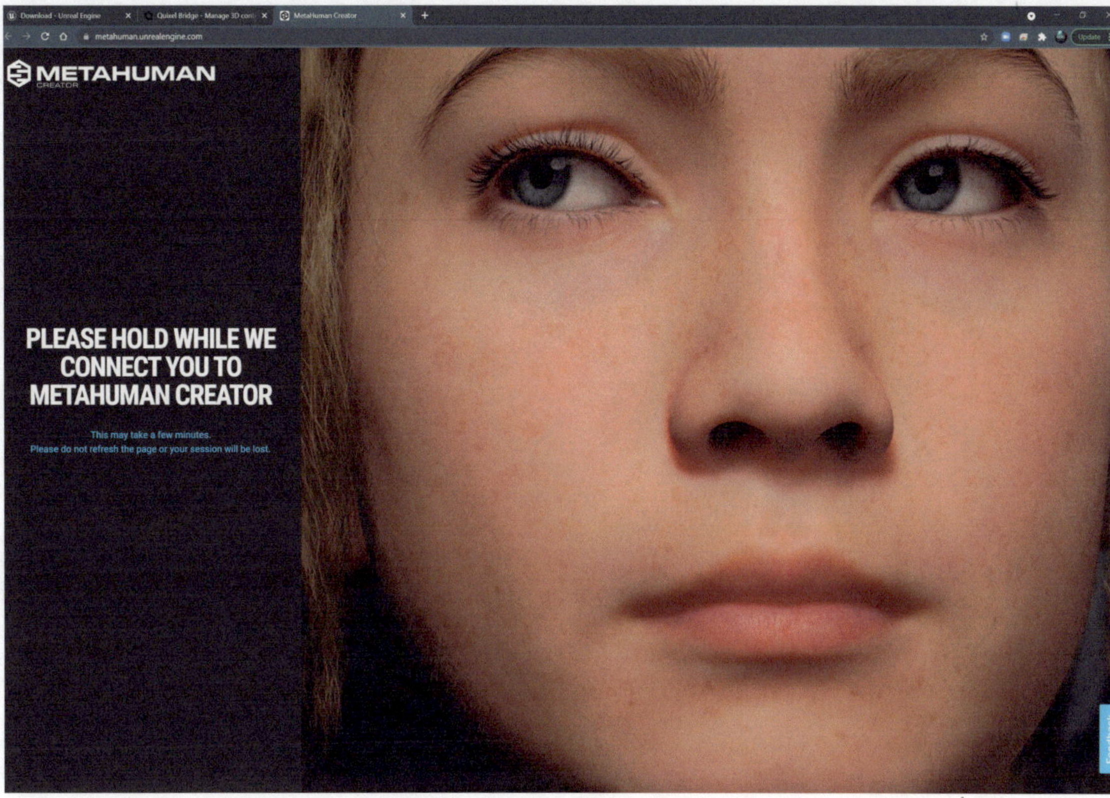

Figure 1.17: Connecting to the MetaHuman Creator online session

As mentioned earlier in this chapter, be sure to have a reliable internet connection to speed up the process of MHC.

Summary

In this chapter, you've learned what Unreal is, what MetaHumans are, and what software applications you need to create MetaHumans.

The next chapter is entirely about the MetaHuman Creator online session. While there are a lot of features, you will find that the application is very intuitive and, in many ways, what you have learned in this chapter is much more complicated than what's to come. In fact, you're going to find the next chapter quite enjoyable!

2

Creating Characters in the MetaHuman Interface

In the previous chapter, you learned how to install the Epic Games Launcher, the UE5 engine, and Bridge to your machine. Additionally, you went through the steps of setting up an Epic Games user account, which you must use again to sign into Quixel Bridge.

This chapter will cover everything you need to know about the **MetaHumans Creator** (MHC) and the online session where all the character designing takes place. We will look at all the editable features of the many MHC templates, including the face, hair, body, blend, move, and sculpt parameters, as well as the best practices of when to use each attribute within the character design phase.

The primary goal of this chapter is to get you accustomed to the interface and the character design potential, but it will also provide notes on how to implement the same design tools for a more acutely focused design process.

In addition to the various tools and preset editors, you will become familiar with learning just how MHC has become the best-in-class of photorealistic character design as we delve into some of the science around skin shaders.

So, we will cover the following topics:

- Starting up Quixel Bridge
- Editing your MetaHuman
- Using the Move and Sculpt tools
- Downloading and exporting your character

Technical requirements

We will be continuing from the previous chapter, so you will need UE5 and Bridge installed, along with a reliable internet connection. A strong internet connection is particularly important here as you will be downloading over 1 GB of data per character.

Starting up Quixel Bridge

When you are ready, go to Quixel Bridge and open up MetaHuman. You can do this easily by simply typing in **Bridge** next to the Windows start icon at the bottom left of the screen and then hitting *Enter*. This will start up Quixel Bridge, as shown in *Figure 2.1*:

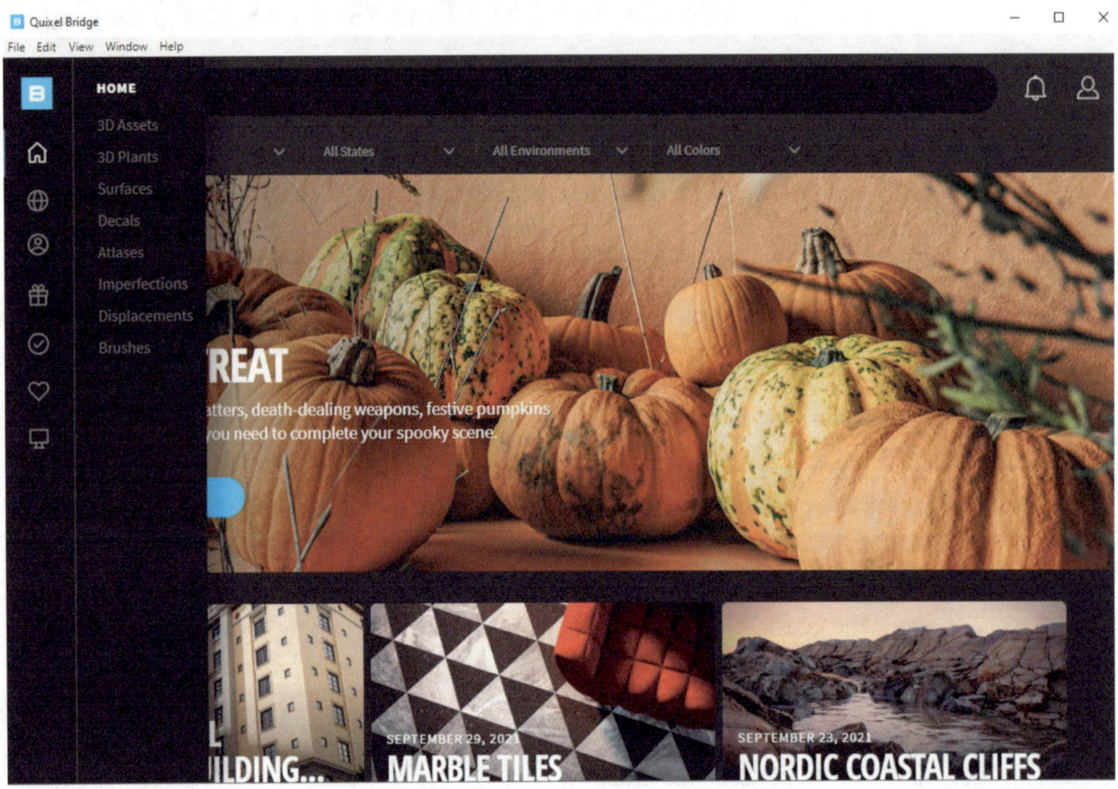

Figure 2.1: Starting up Bridge

Take note of the column on the left-hand side. Clicking on the person icon will bring up the MHC templates, which you need to choose from before you can start your MHC session. This will bring up a few images of male and female MetaHumans with a wide range of ethnicities and age groups.

Clicking on a profile will open a panel on the right, showing you an enlarged image of your selection and the character's name, as shown in *Figure 2.2*:

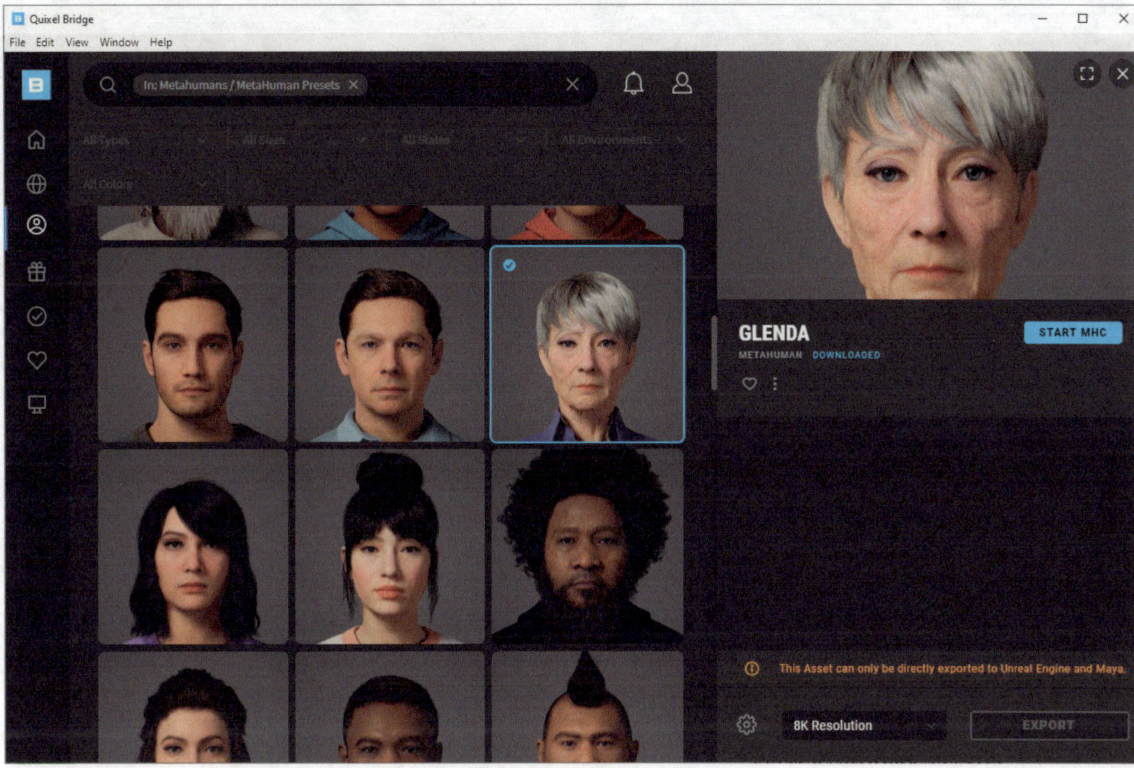

Figure 2.2: Starting the MHC

You'll notice further options at the bottom of the screen, such as **Resolution**, but we will come back to those at the end of this chapter. All you need to do to start your first character creation session is to click **START MHC**.

Once you do this, a web browser will appear, similar to what's shown in *Figure 2.3*:

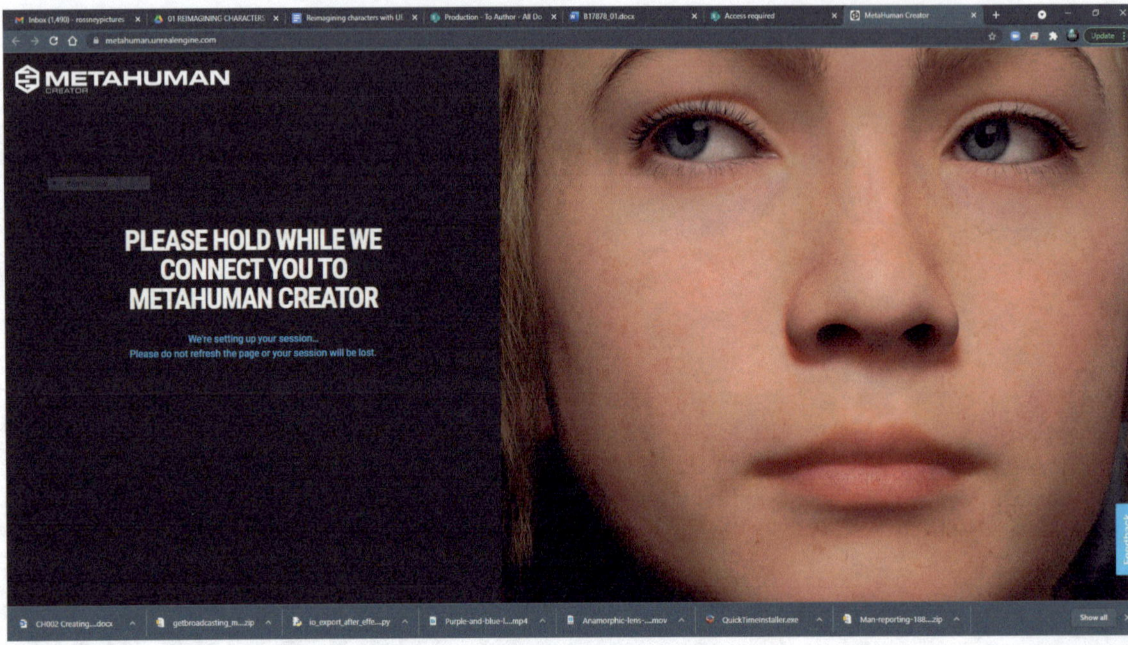

Figure 2.3: Waiting for the MetaHuman Creator connection

At this point, you may need to be patient as the session can take seconds, if not minutes, to boot up. However, now is not the time to run off to the kitchen to make a cup of tea. The reason is that the MHC will also time out if left idle for a few minutes. If you do happen to walk away mid-session and find that the session has closed due to the session being idle, simply refresh your web browser and it will start up again.

Once the session has loaded, you can choose another template if you want. If, however, you have had a previous MHC session, Bridge will automatically save your session under **MY METAHUMANS**.

However, if you're happy with your original selection, click **NEXT**, as shown in *Figure 2.4*:

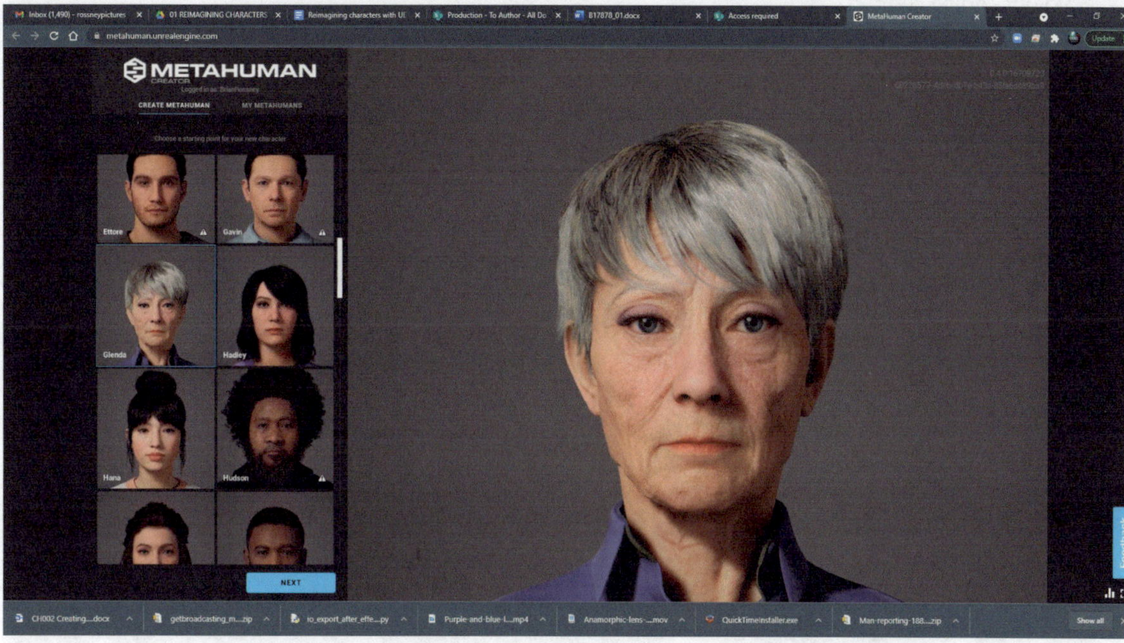

Figure 2.4: Choosing from CREATE METAHUMAN or MY METAHUMANS

> **Note**
>
> It is worth noting that by this time, you will have been given two opportunities to pick a template. If you have a specific character design in mind – for example, an elderly African-American male – it wouldn't make sense to choose a young Caucasian female as a template to start from. That's not to say you couldn't edit one preset to resemble the desired design you are going for. However, while you could potentially edit the ethnicity of your character from one to the next, you will have problems when it comes to gender. This comes down to some templates having limited editing abilities. So, in short, ensure that you choose the age and gender that best matches the design you have in mind (if you have one) when you start your session.

After choosing **NEXT**, your session will begin. By default, you will be greeted by the template character of your choice coming to life:

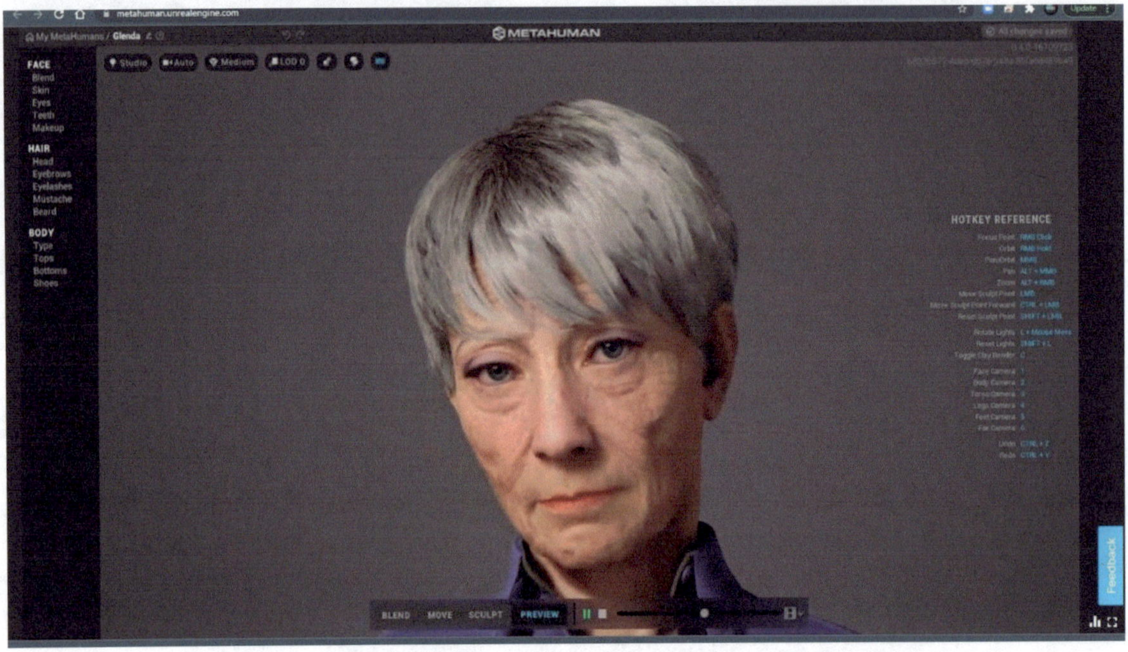

Figure 2.5: Editable parameters

At the bottom of the screen, you will see player controls. By default, it is on **PREVIEW**. Note that while in **PREVIEW** mode, you can't make any edits to your character.

However, this is a great opportunity to see just how realistic MHC is. You will be given three options to choose from when it comes to animation previews. You need to click on the filmstrip icon to see these options, as illustrated in *Figure 2.6*:

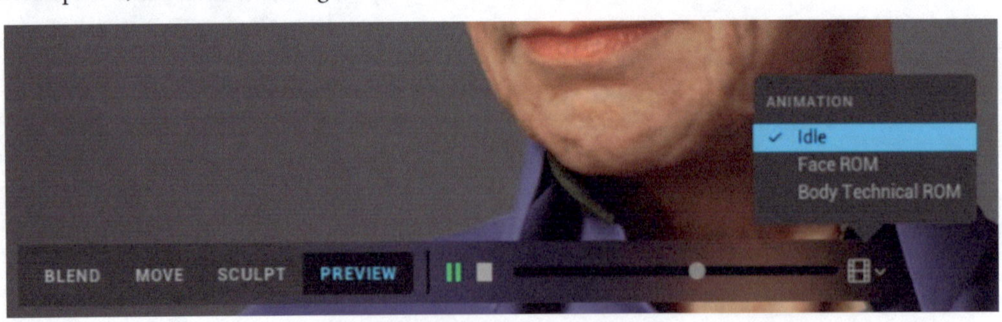

Figure 2.6: Animation previews

The options are as follows:

- **Idle**: Provides a small range of motion, which is suitable for a background character.
- **Face ROM**: Provides a full range of motion for the face, where the animation is extreme enough to effectively show any potential issues that may come up should your project require close-up facial animation.
- **Body Technical ROM**: Provides animation that's extreme enough to show any potential issues where there is a lot of body motion.

> **Note**
>
> The MHC gives a range of motion designed to give you an idea of what your character will look like animated. It is not a definitive debugging tool for all possibilities of what could go right or wrong when you add your own animation.

If you are familiar with 3D character design in the traditional sense, character design must take the full range of motion into account to work effectively. The model or mesh must allow for the desired type of movement. At a very basic level, the animation must not alter the mesh of the character where parts of the character intersect with other parts. For example, a very thin person can walk in a way where their hands can be closer to their sides – effectively, their wrist bones can come very close to their hip bones during a stride – however, this wouldn't be the same for somebody larger, even with the same type of stride and range of motion.

With all that said, the fidelity of MHC characters does a lot of this calibration. So, what would have been very laborious for someone working in Maya, 3ds Max, or Houdini to account for a varying range of motions is done automatically in an MHC session.

We will come back to some of this later in *Chapter 3, Diving into the MetaHuman Blueprint*, when we introduce animation to the MetaHuman character within Unreal, but in short, you can push the attributes of characters as much as you want without finding any unusable oddities within any given range of motion during the MHC session.

While we are in the preview mode, it is worth getting to know some of the hotkeys, which will allow you to preview the range of motion or character in static form at any angle you wish. If you take a look at the **HOTKEY REFERENCE** area shown in *Figure 2.7*, you'll notice a list of keyboard and mouse click combinations that will allow you to navigate freely:

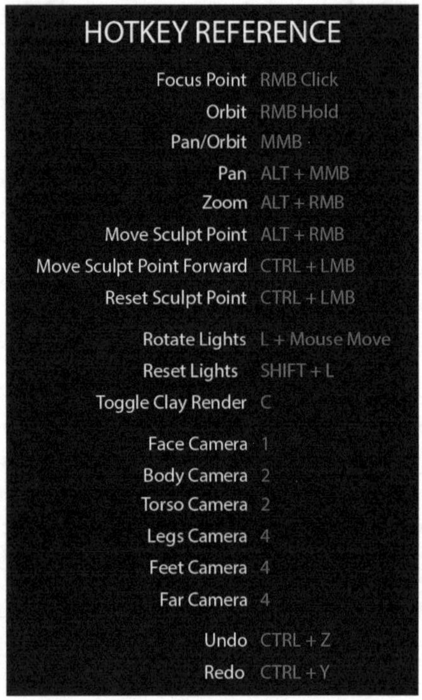

Figure 2.7: HOTKEY REFERENCE

If you are new to 3D applications such as Maya and Unreal, it is certainly worth paying close attention to these as some of the navigation hotkeys are the same. You can have a lot of fun simply navigating around the viewport of the MHC while previewing the animations.

In this section, we launched our MetaHumans session and started to become familiar with the interface where we will be spending most of our time designing the character. In the next section, we will look at the face. This section will be split into several subsections to coincide with how it is broken down in the MHC interface.

Editing your MetaHuman

Now, it's time to edit your MetaHuman. You can find the editable parameters at the top right of the interface, as per *Figure 2.8*:

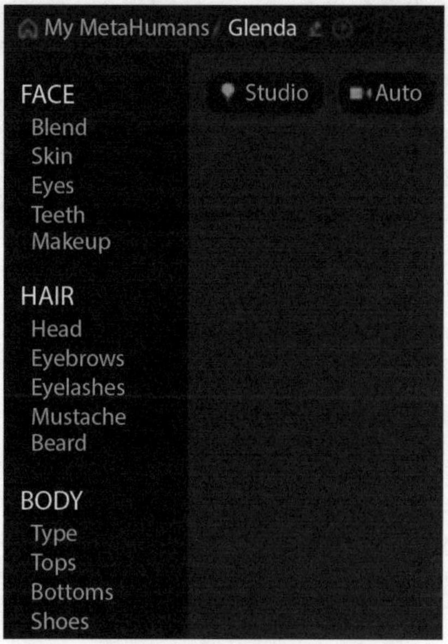

Figure. 2.8: FACE, HAIR, and BODY

We're going to go through all of these options in the upcoming sections. All of these are very powerful editors and, as I write this, I'm confident that Quixel and Epic Games will have added more functionality by the time this book goes to print.

Face

First, we'll take at the editable options for our MetaHuman's face. Under **FACE**, we have the following subcategories:

- **Blend**
- **Skin**
- **Eyes**
- **Teeth**
- **Makeup**

Let's explore these five subcategories now. To get started, ensure you have stopped the animation preview of any range of motion. In *Figure 2.9*, we can see a couple of options to choose from:

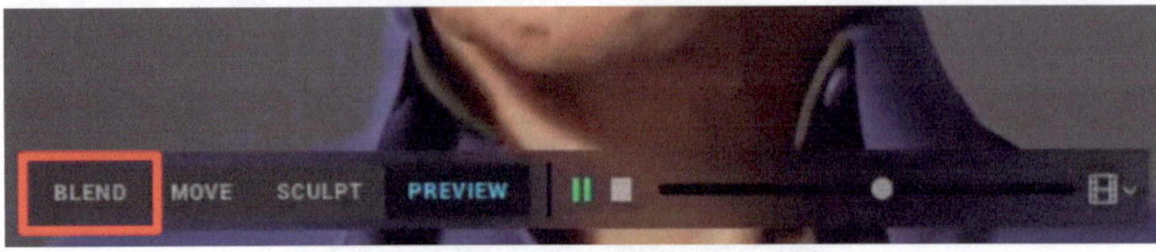

Figure 2.9: Choosing BLEND

We will want to click **BLEND** to continue to the next section.

Blend

First, we will take a look at the **Blend** function. Put simply, **Blend** allows us to blend the facial features of our chosen template with other existing templates. This is a great starting point as it is a very intuitive process. For example, we may have selected a male character from our template, but we would like to make him look a little more feminine or perhaps older. Taking that second example, we can target the eyes and blend just the eyes with that of an older character template.

In *Figure 2.10*, I have dragged three template characters into the circle at the top left. The Glenda character in the main viewport on the right is now set for editing:

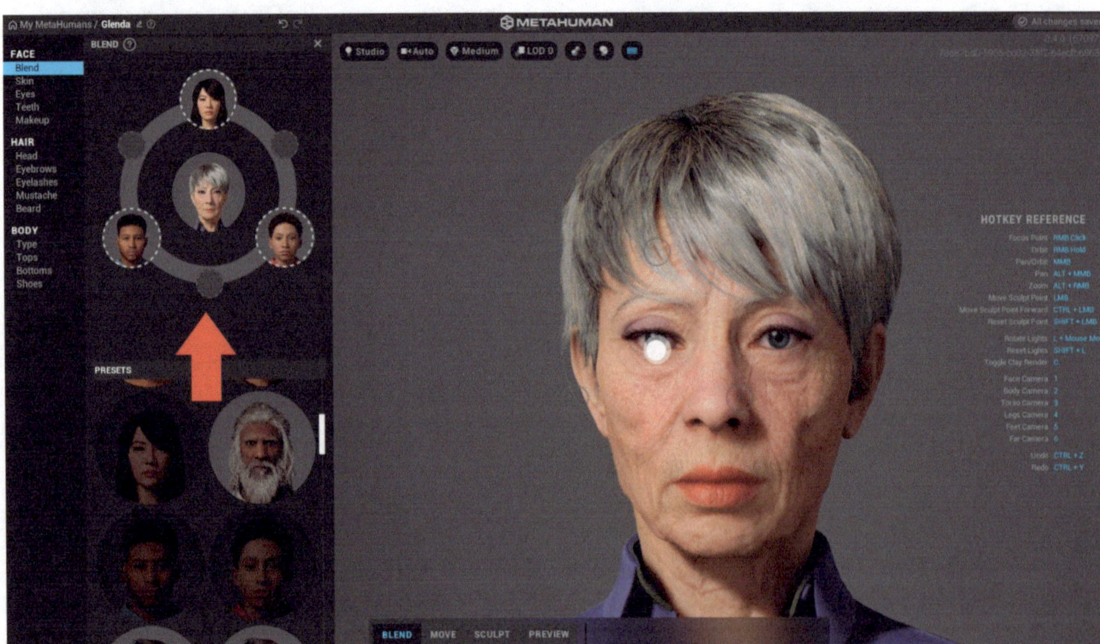

Figure 2.10: Edit points

Take a close look at the many small and very subtle circles around her face. Each circle represents a feature of the face that is editable. By left-clicking a small circle and dragging in the direction of one of the three characters I have added to the left, it will blend that feature into the corresponding feature in the main viewport. I have placed a young lady at the top, so if I click and drag upward, just the eyes will blend into the eyes of the young lady's eyes:

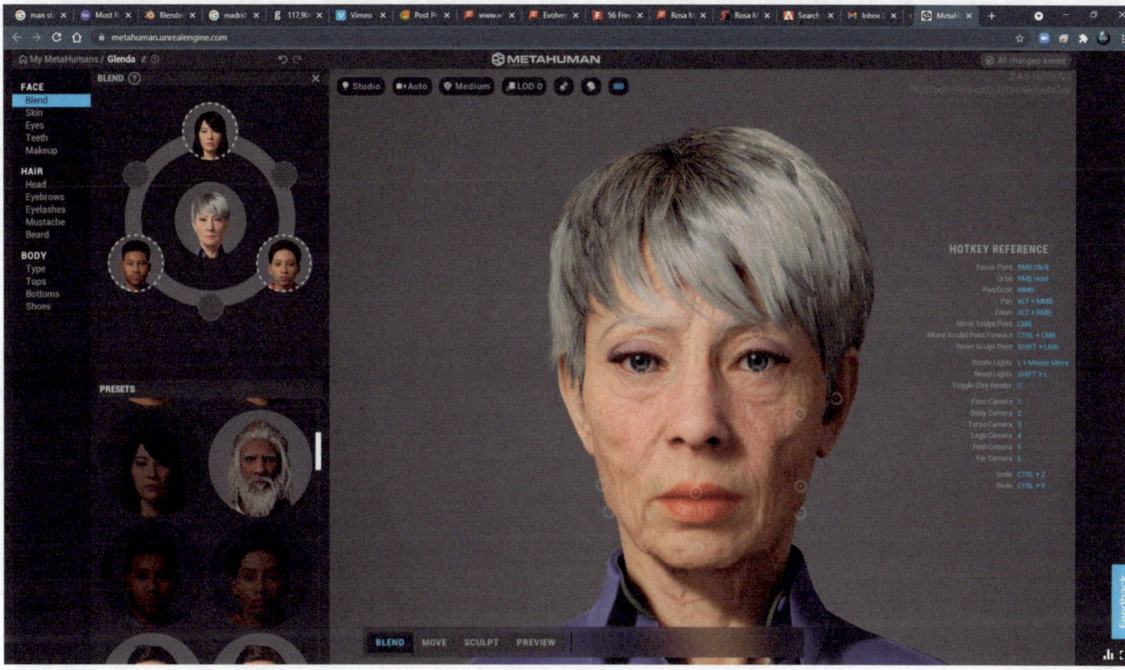

Figure 2.11: Blending the eyes by clicking and dragging

> **Note**
>
> Note that the edit points are very subtle. You must click on a point in the main viewport on the right and drag toward your preferred character in the corresponding circle on the highlighted viewport.

In the example given here, I have loaded up three characters into the **Blend** viewport on the left. You can load up as many as six templates but note that the first three will have a greater influence. The second set of three, denoted by the smaller circles (which I have left empty), is helpful for subtle blending.

Editing a character with blending requires a little planning. It's best practice to choose a character that resembles your desired design as much as possible and then use the **Blend** option to get the template as close to your imagined design.

Skin

While we can do quite a lot with the **Blend** tool, such as changing the shape of facial attributes, it isn't helpful if you want to change a character's skin tone. This is where the **Skin** editor comes in useful, as shown in *Figure 2.12*:

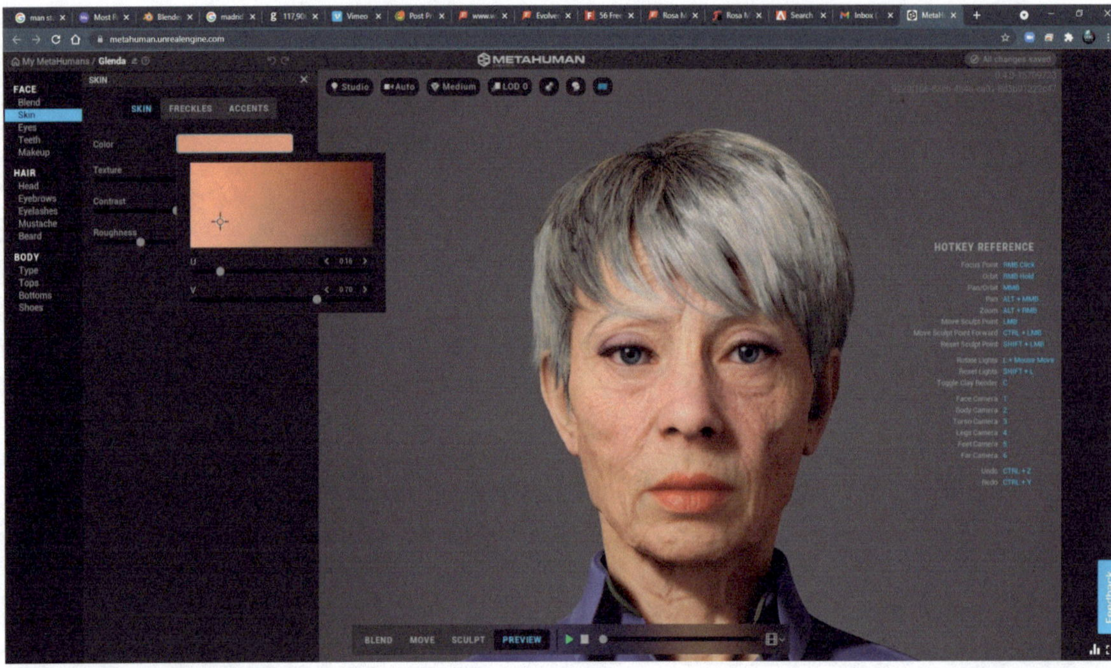

Figure 2.12: Skin

Here are some features that we can edit when it comes to skin:

- **Texture**: A very important feature when it comes to aging or de-aging your character. It introduces fine lines and wrinkles but also broader deformation such as sagging skin.
- **Contrast**: This is another useful feature for aging your character, further deepening those wrinkles and folds.
- **Roughness**: In CGI, the word "roughness" is a common term used to describe how shiny or reflective a surface is. We know that if a surface is rough, light isn't bounced back in as much of a direct way as that of a smooth surface such as a mirror. On skin, a smooth surface could be due to the oiliness of the surface, and this gives us a more realistic effect. Rarely do we get a completely rough surface on the skin without the help of foundation makeup. Another factor that introduces roughness to skin is the micro hair follicles on the surface of the skin, which are barely visible to the human eye but are factored into the final model. (At the time of writing,

there is no direct way to edit roughness in terms of both skin and micro follicles within the MHC, but they are editable once we get into advanced editing within Unreal Engine.)

Figure 2.13 is the Glenda character with **Texture**, **Contrast**, and **Roughness** set to zero. The reduction of texture and contrast makes her look much younger; we can see that contrast had a significant impact on the geometry (shape) of her face:

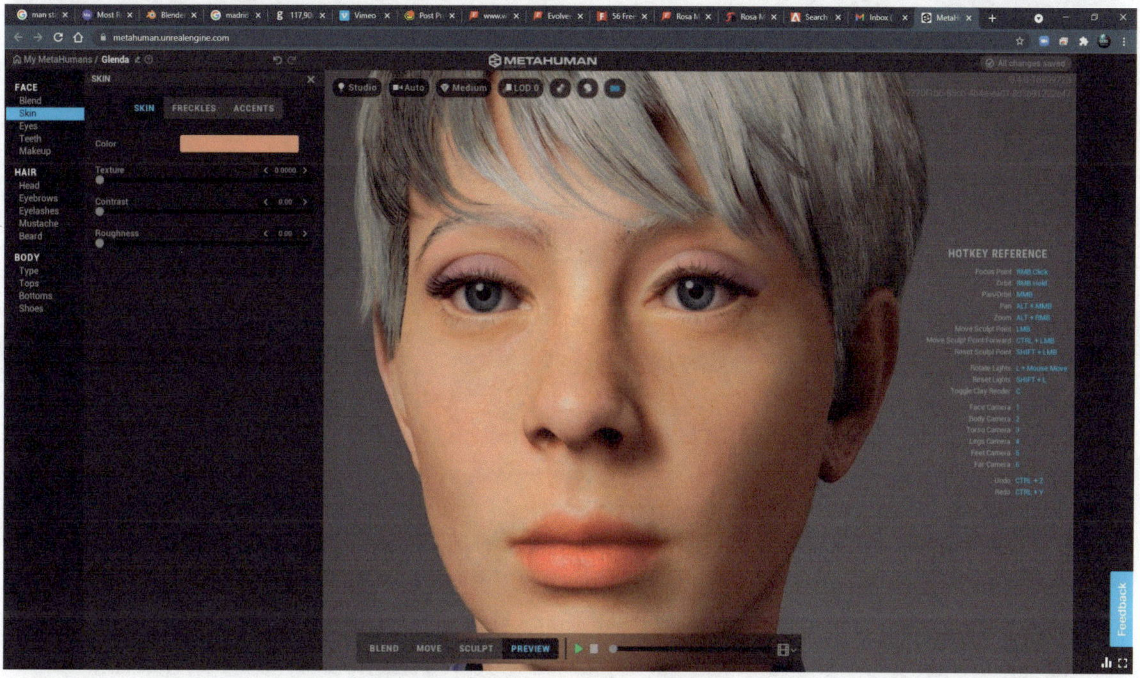

Figure 2.13: Texture, Contrast, and Roughness

However, the reduction of roughness down to zero does give us a slightly unrealistic look, which is probably not what you want. You can play with these settings to make the skin look more realistic.

Freckles

In *Figure 2.14*, you can see that I have re-applied all the texture and contrast that the Glenda template had before and that I have now added freckles:

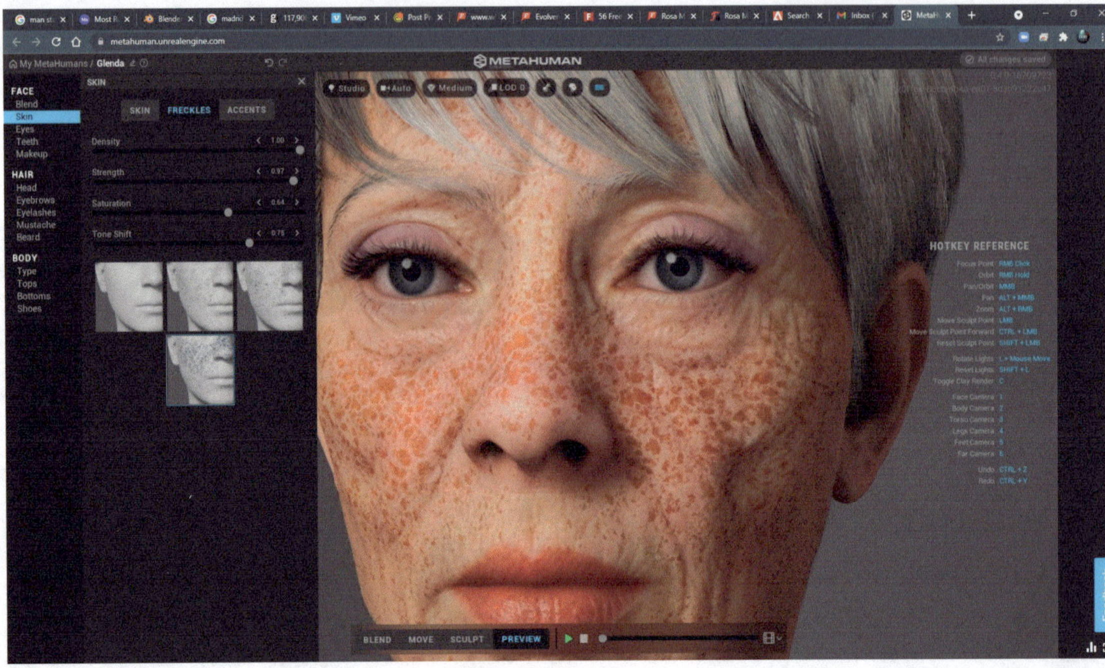

Figure 2.14: Freckles

Note the four gray images – each of these are presets of freckle patterns. The fourth is the most prominent freckle pattern with the highest density. In this example, I have the density up high just for illustration, but subtle use of this tool will give you very realistic results.

Be sure to edit the saturation and strength to your liking. As you add freckles, no matter how extreme or subtle you want them, it is helpful to go back to the **Skin** tab and play around with texture, contrast, and roughness again. One reason is that the addition of freckles will change the overall skin tone of your character and you may want to adjust the tone under the skin adjustment to compensate. By adding saturation to your freckles, the overall saturation of the face will also naturally increase.

While we are on the subject of skin tone, the MHC has four preview features that need to be considered for making more informed decisions on skin tone. Due to the subtle variations prevalent in skin tones, additional features that allow us to see those variations are very welcome. Those features are as follows:

- **Lighting**
- **Camera**
- **Render Quality**
- **LOD**

You can see these options here:

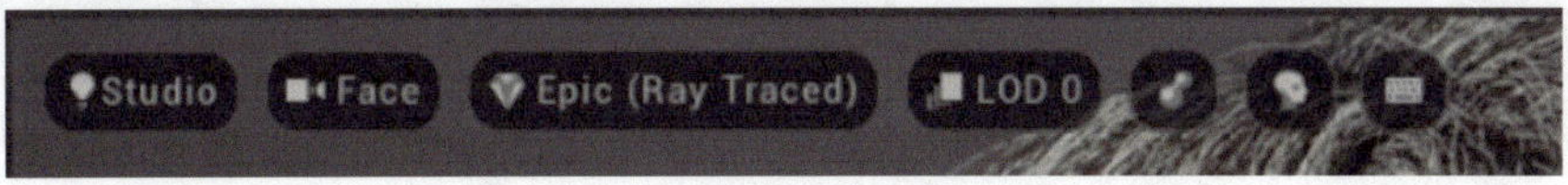

Figure 2.15: Viewing options

Let's take a look at each option now.

Lighting

In most of MHC's lighting setups, **image-based lighting** is used. Put simply, an image-based light is a sphere that has an image on the inside that is used as a light source for the entire scene. This gives us a very realistic lighting result and is also a process used within Unreal. To understand image-based lighting in the real world, take a large piece of paper and hold it close to your computer monitor, and play a video full frame. Make sure all your lights are off and your computer screen is at full brightness. You'll see that the screen is now lighting the piece of paper, with the video influencing both intensity and color. The more reflective the paper, the more obvious the lighting influence is to the eye.

If you click **Studio**, which you can see in *Figure 2.15*, you'll see several lighting setups that will help you design a particular scene you have in mind. There are 13 lighting presets, which you can see in *Figure 2.16*:

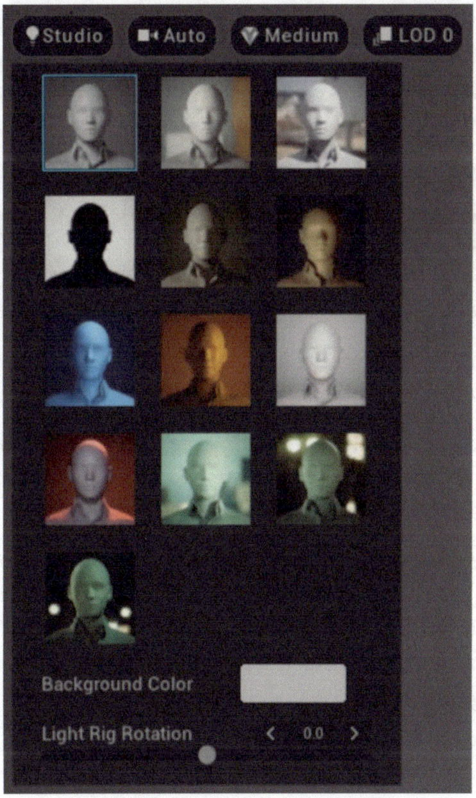

Figure 2.16: Various lighting rigs

Let's go through each option now:

- **Studio** (the default setting): A lighting setup made of a small number of soft lights to mimic soft photography lighting. This is the default lighting rig.
- **Indoor**: This preset consists of lighting that utilizes an image rather than a set of lights (as explained, this is known as image-based lighting). In this case, it is an image of an interior, captured at an angle of 360 degrees, giving us realistic lighting from every angle. This preset allows users to see their characters with the level of contrast typical of when a subject is lit from a window and reflective ambient light.
- **Outdoor**: This is another example of image-based light that allows the user to see the effects of outdoor ambient light but also the harshness of direct sunlight and the resulting shadows cast on the character's skin.
- **Silhouette**: An important yet overlooked feature when it comes to character design is to see the character in a silhouette. It gives us the ability to see the shape of the character quickly without the distraction of color, reflective, and shadow features.
- **Split**: While similar to the **Studio** light preset, **Split** gives us high contrast and is a great way of measuring the translucency of the character's skin due to the intensity of the key light or main light. In this preset, we have a split of high-intensity key light to complete darkness. It is a great way to showcase both realism and extreme lighting and to determine both the realism and style of light falling off from intense light to darkness. The areas between the high-intensity lighting and shadow, particularly on the skin, are known as **roll-offs**, a commonly used term by cinematographers.
- **Fireside**: Similar to **Split**, we get high contrast, but we also get the gradual fall-off and attenuation typical of fire. In addition, we get the tonality typical of fire from orange to deep blue. Most importantly, **Fireside** allows the user to determine the roll-off of intense light and how it falls off into shadow around the face and whether or not detail in the skin is still present with this subtlety compared to the **Split** preset, which would present obvious detail in the skin's surface.
- **Moonlight**: Similar to **Fireside**, we are presented with vibrant tones – in this case, blue moonlight. However, it is a much more ambient light with less intensity from any one angle.
- **Tungsten**: While not completely representing the tonality of a common tungsten lamp, it does allow us to see how the skin tone would respond to a tungsten lamp. A lighting preset like this could determine how much detail in freckles would be lost or gained in a similar scenario.
- **Portrait**: This is a very handy preset as it can double as an indoor and outdoor light to determine how our character's skin behaves. For example, by rotating the scene light using the *Left Mouse + L*, or using the **Light Rig Rotation** slider shown in *Figure 2.16*, we can mimic a window with daylight lighting without the distraction found in the background image that comes with the **Indoor** lighting preset.

- **Red Lantern**: Similar to **Fireside**, we have strong red hues to work with, but we have the advantage of seeing much more intensity without the deep blue background. This allows us to work with a more dramatic lighting setup in mind.
- **GR22 Rooftop**: This is a very effective use of image-based lighting, but one that gives slightly overcast lighting. This is a convenient lighting preset that will work for a lot of daylight scenes because there are areas of high intensity but, for the most part, we get a slightly diffused light. This diffused light comes from direct light being bounced back from buildings and ground surfaces, much like in the real world.
- **Downtown Night**: This is very similar to **GR22 Rooftop**, except it's at night and lit purely by electrical lights from sources such as street lighting and cars.
- **Underpass Night**: This is similar to **Downtown Night** but in closer quarters. It only features fixed lighting, combining multiple tungsten lights of varying hues and intensities.

To take this a step further, the MHC has a background color option. For some of the lighting presets, you can see a strong impact on changing the background color. For example, you may want to see what your character looks like in a generic studio soft light but want to see your character up against a particular color that you had in mind for your scene. In *Figure 2.17*, I have illustrated some lighting rigs with the Glenda character:

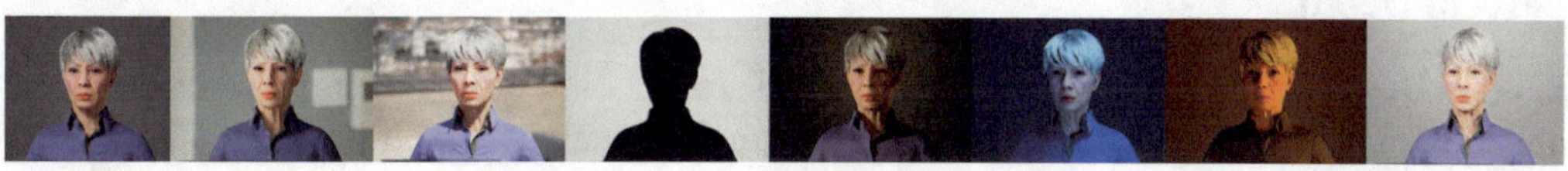

Figure 2.17: Various lighting examples

Camera

As per *Figure 2.15*, the default camera is set to **Face**. However, there are several preset camera angles for which you can use keyboard shortcuts:

- *1*: Face
- *2*: Body
- *3*: Torso
- *4*: Legs
- *5*: Feet
- *6*: Face

Alternatively, you can just as easily navigate with your mouse instead of using any camera presets. If you ever find yourself lost in the scene, a handy shortcut to use is the *1* key to get back to looking at the front of your character's head using the **Face** camera preset.

In addition, we can preview several different render quality presets to emulate the render quality settings that exist in Unreal Engine.

Render Quality

The MHC has three options to choose from when it comes to rendering quality:

- **Medium** (this is the default setting)
- **High (ray traced)**
- **Epic (ray traced)**

If you choose the highest quality with ray traced settings, this won't have any impact on your machine because the processing of the high-quality render is all done in the cloud. However, this feature is a useful indicator of the result you will get when you use the highest settings under a similar lighting setting.

The differences between the render settings are subtle. You may notice the quality under the hair intensify, depending on the quality you use. They are there only to give you an indication of what your character would look like should you provide a similar setting, using the corresponding render quality settings that come with Unreal Engine.

Level of Detail

Level of Detail (**LOD**) is the generation of multiple meshes and texture maps based on one source object. Each mesh and map will have varying amounts of detail.

The purpose of LOD is engine optimization. As one of the design principles of a game engine is real-time rendering, LOD helps this by reducing the number of triangles in a mesh or pixels in a texture map when they're not needed. LOD works on the principle of changing the complexity of a mesh based on camera distance. The further away the camera is from an object, the less detail is required without breaking the illusion of realism.

For example, a close-up shot of a MetaHuman's face would require the best quality possible. In this case, we would need to be looking at the original mesh and texture maps. In general, the original mesh for an MHC is about 35,000 triangles and is made up of texture maps as big as 8,000 pixels in width. It would be a vast waste of resources to be rendering this kind of data if it wasn't necessary.

A good exercise to see how effective LOD is on your character is to go to the viewport and look through the **Face** camera. You can do this by simply pressing *1* on your keyboard. This will give you a close-up of the character. From there, you can choose from all the various LODs, from LOD 0 right down to LOD 7.

At first, you won't notice much of a difference between LOD 0 and LOD 1, but as soon as you get down to LODs 5, 6, and 7, you will notice significant degradation of both the geometry and the texture map quality. You can see this change in *Figure 2.18*:

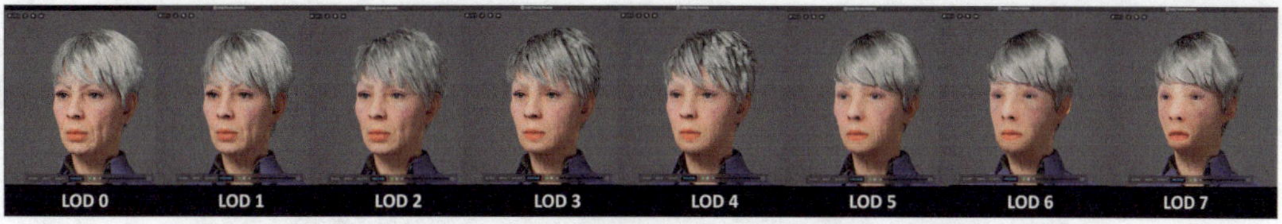

Figure 2.18: LODs from 0 to 7

We can push this illustration further by using the **Far** camera; you can do this by pressing 6 on your keyboard. Unfortunately, this is as far as we can go back with the camera in the MHC. However, by toggling between LODs 6 and 7, we can see a difference. This is because LODs 6 and 7 are designed to be used when the camera is even further back.

In this view, if you toggle between LOD 3 and LOD 4, you won't see much of a difference. Therefore, it would be a clear waste of resources to be displaying LOD 0, which is around 35,000 triangles and 8K texture maps. Without LOD, computers would never be able to handle multiple characters, let alone crowds.

Much of this process is automated for you when it comes to MetaHumans and Unreal Engine, but we will discuss LOD when we bring our character into Unreal, particularly for hair.

We have covered a lot of ground with the skin editor and at this point, I would like to remind you that additional editing of the skin can always be done within Unreal Engine. But for now, in the next section, we will discuss the eyes.

Eyes

The MHC has an incredibly powerful eye-editing tool. What's also very special about it is that some of the eye tools are editable within Unreal. For example, if you wanted to animate the size of the iris, you can do that within Unreal.

Here, we will take a look at the following attributes of the **Eyes** editor:

- **PRESETS**
- **IRIS**
- **SCLERA**

Let's take a look at these now.

Presets

As shown in *Figure 2.19*, the MHC has some great presets to choose from, providing an array of different brown, blue, and green eyes to choose from:

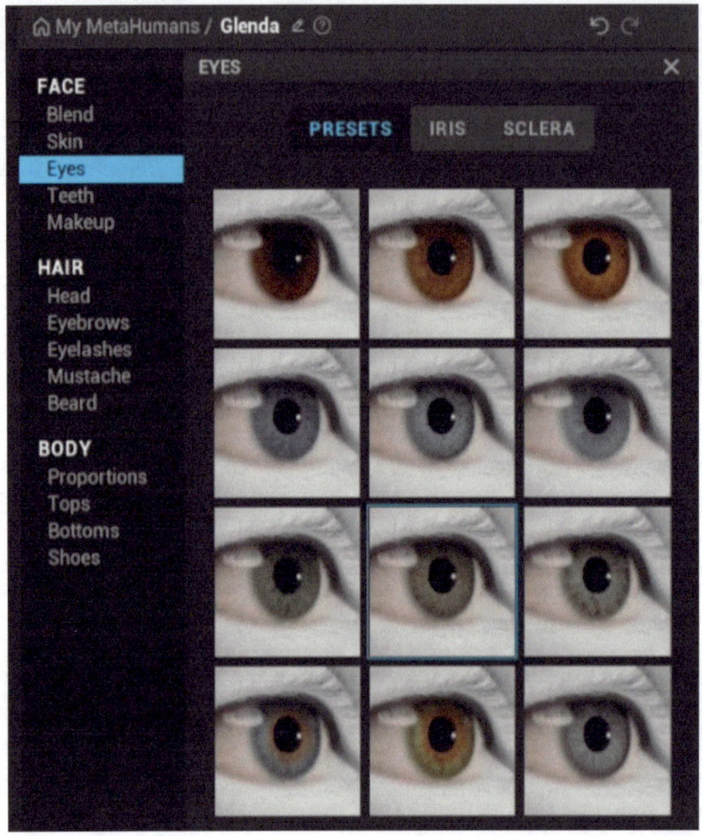

Figure 2.19: Eye presets

For the most part, you can work with the default presets, but you may want to go into specific details (which we will go through in the next section) where you can achieve very specific yet natural looks, from healthy eyes to very unhealthy eyes.

> **Note**
>
> Before you start editing your character's eyes, take advantage of the lighting tools to ensure you have the best lighting available. The eyes have quite a lot of detail, so you'll need to be up and close and at a LOD of 0, thus rendering in the highest quality.

Iris

Let's take a look at the **IRIS** panel next, which you can see in *Figure 2.20*. Without going too far into detail regarding what everything does, the first choice you have is to edit the right, left, or both eyes. **Base Color** allows you to edit the color closest to the iris, while **Detail Color** allows you to edit the outside area of the eye closest to the limbus. You also get to edit the **Color Balance** and **Color Balance Smoothness** options and choose from nine iris patterns:

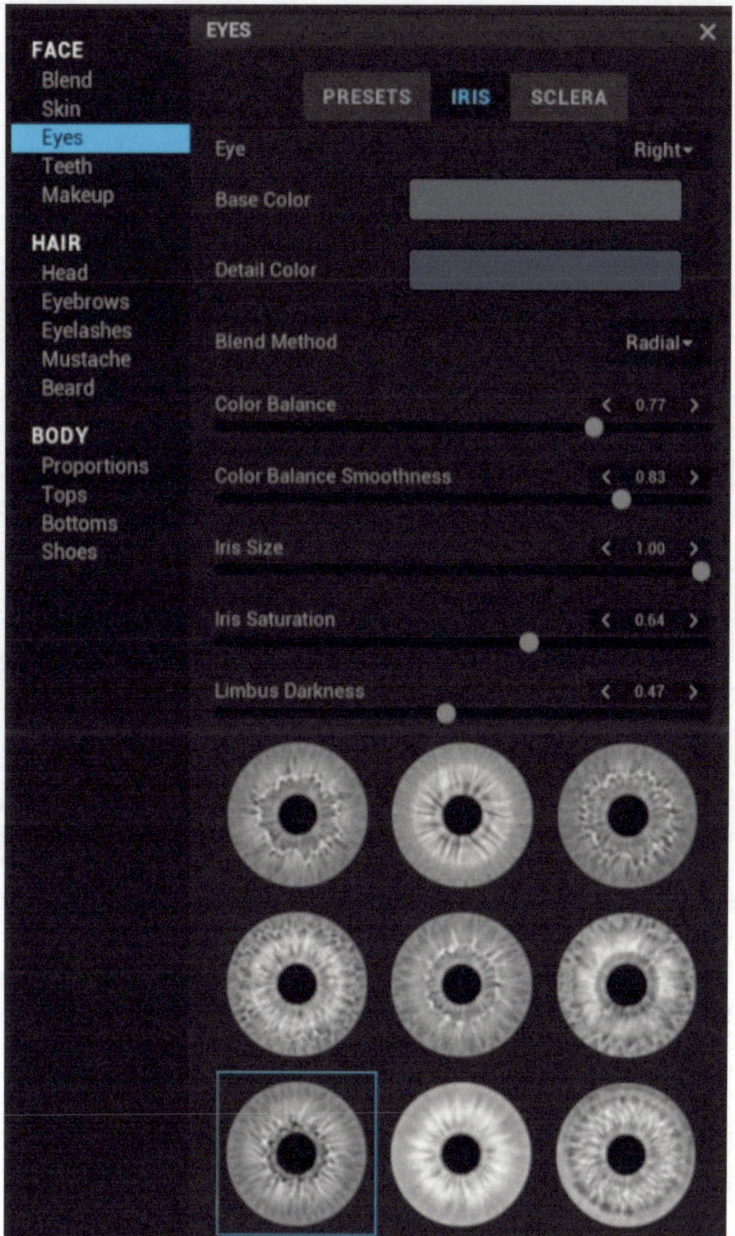

Figure 2.20: IRIS

Just like with skin tones, the **IRIS** editing function is limited to natural looks. However, you can get some pretty wild-looking effects by pushing the limbus darkness and aiming for high saturation in your color editors.

Sclera

While the **IRIS** editor is a great tool, much of the realism comes out of the **SCLERA** tab, as you can see in *Figure 2.21*. Effectively, this involves editing the white of the eye. While you can do a lot with the **Tint** option, which is a balance between blue and yellow, the **Brightness** option in conjunction with **Tint** is very powerful in terms of aging the eye:

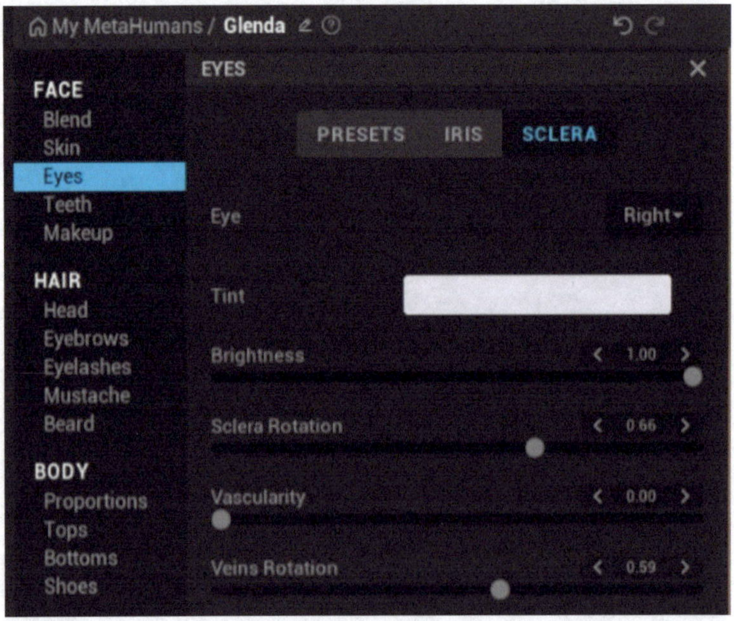

Figure 2.21: SCLERA

The MHC also brings a lot of detail with the **Vascularity** slider. You can see this clearly when you start rotating the veins. These are very powerful tools for extreme close-ups, and it is worth spending some time on them before exporting your MetaHuman. CGI characters commonly lose realism when their eyes are too bright and perfect.

Let's look at an example of combining the **Eyes** editing options. Most of the editing in *Figure 2.22* was done using the **SCLERA** editing tab except for lightening up the limbus in the **IRIS** editing tab and reducing the color in both the base and detail color pickers:

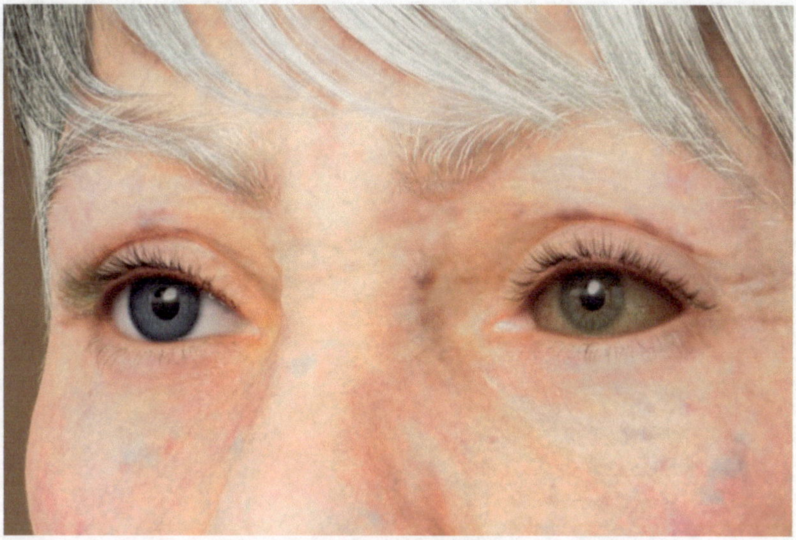

Figure 2.22: Separate eye editing example

My goal here was to simply age the eye. By and large, I went a little too far and poor Glenda should see a doctor at this stage. However, the result of her right eye does look a little more realistic simply because of the added detail and removing the perfect whiteness.

Teeth

Another great yet overlooked tool to add realism to a MetaHuman is the **Teeth** editor. Just like the eyes, the MHC adds a layer of detail and imperfections that make characters more realistic. We can make teeth yellowish from realistic staining and/or realistically crooked. We can even recede the gums. The MHC has quite a lot of editors for teeth and has all you need to achieve a massive variation of looks.

To begin with, it's a good idea to ensure you are in a reasonably well-lit environment, and that you open the jaw of your character to get a better idea of how your changes look when editing the teeth. For the latter, there is a handy **Jaw Open** slider.

Looking at *Figure 2.23*, straight off the bat, we can see that Glenda has great teeth. They are completely uniform, perfectly white, with no signs of plaque or any other issues:

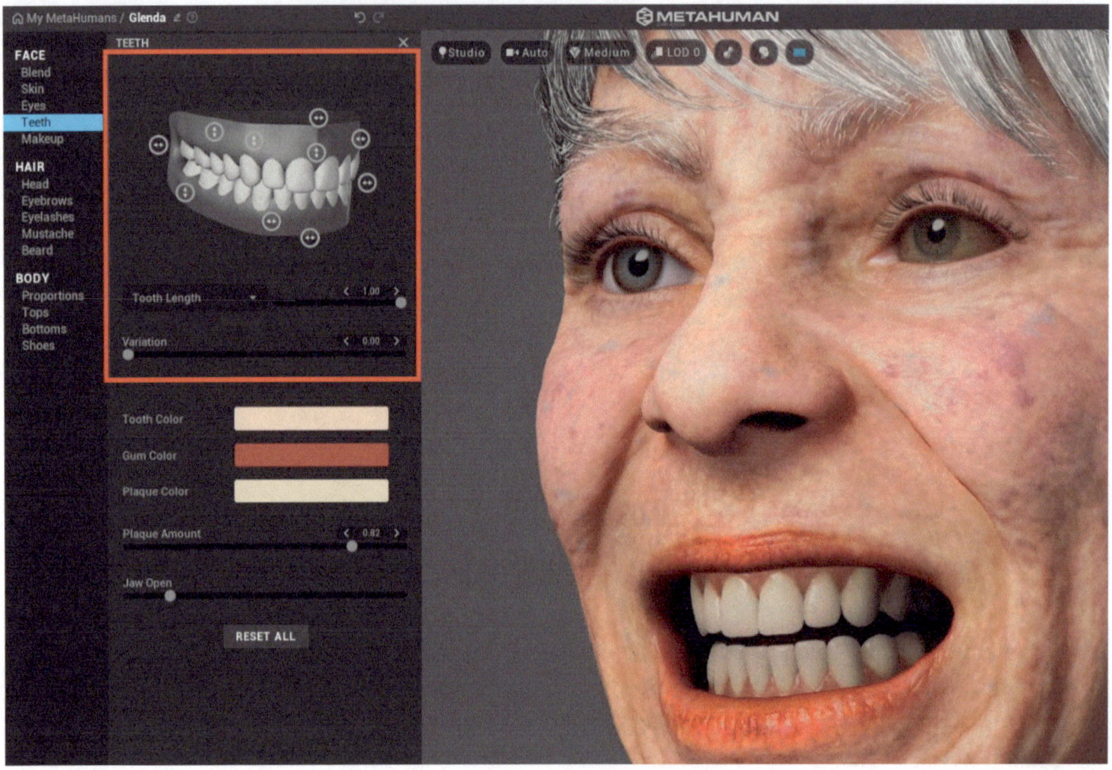

Figure 2.23: Teeth before

There are two ways to go about editing:

- In *Figure 2.23*, the red box indicates the visual way to edit. By holding your mouse on each of the gray circles, you'll see what each slider edits – for example, **Tooth Length**, **Tooth Spacing**, and so on.
- However, another way to do this is using the drop-down list from where it says **Tooth Length**, as shown in *Figure 2.24*:

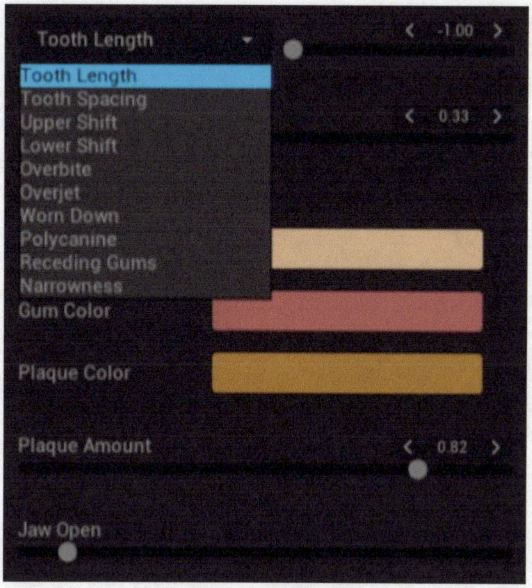

Figure 2.24: Editing teeth

I recommend using the drop-down list for editing as it gives you a slider for the intensity of the edit, plus another slider for variation, all while reminding you of what you are editing, such as **Tooth Length**, **Tooth Spacing**, **Overbite**, and so on. The visual diagram of the teeth has sliders, as shown in the upper left of *Figure 2.25*, but they only allow you to edit the intensity of any given parameter, such as **Overbite**.

Much of the realism can be found by making subtle changes to teeth such as plaque color and adding subtle variations with little intensity to everything in the drop-down menu, again featured in *Figure 2.25*. Working the drop-down menu, sliders, and swatches under the **TEETH** diagram will give you the greatest amount of control:

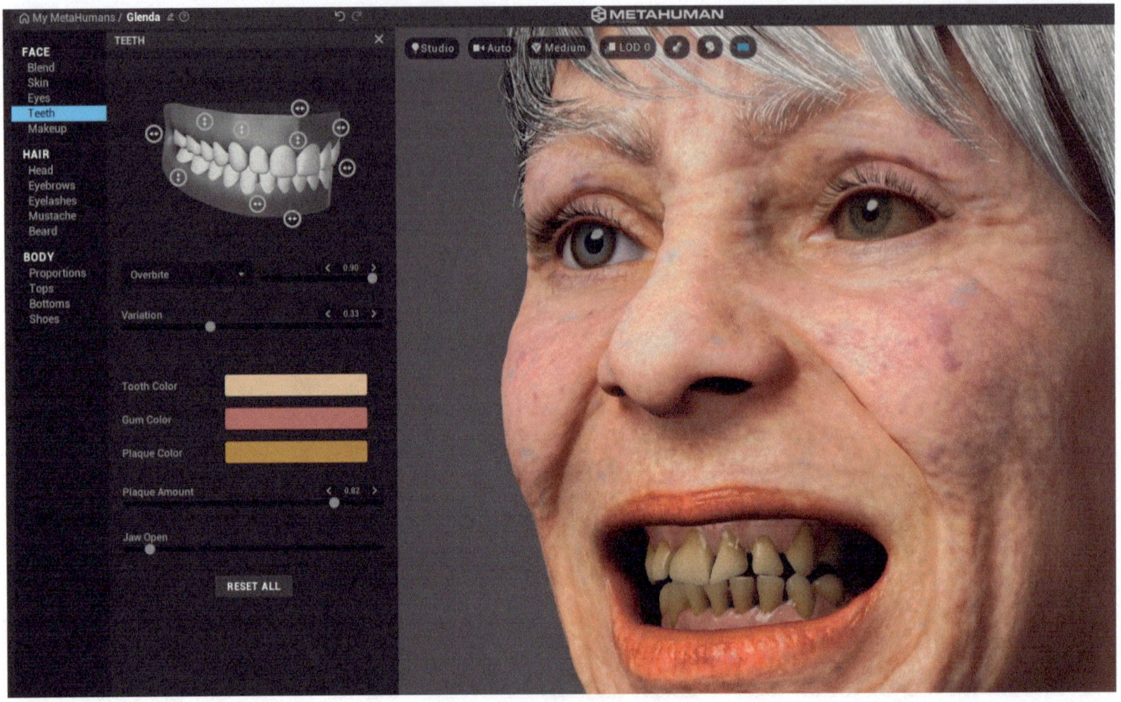

Figure 2.25: The Teeth editor

With that said, if you are making dramatic changes, it is worth previewing the **Face ROM** component as the teeth do have a significant impact on the overall expression of your character. A major consideration would be how much gum or overbite exists. An overbite can give the impression of an undeveloped jaw and a naive expression, while an underbite can give the impression of an over-developed jaw and a stern expression. Of course, a lot of this is subjective but certainly worth consideration.

To wrap up this section on teeth, I would like to emphasize how important teeth editing is to overall character design and that it is frequently overlooked.

We'll now move on and look at a feature that doesn't apply to all character design but is a powerful editing tool within the MHC: makeup, and applying it to characters.

Makeup

The MHC has some very remarkable makeup features that work in tandem with the skin tone of the character. The **Makeup** editor has been divided into four tabs:

- **FOUNDATION**
- **EYES**
- **BLUSH**
- **LIPS**

Let's take a look at each of these now.

Foundation

As mentioned earlier, the **Makeup** editor works in tandem with the skin tone of your character. Earlier, under the **Skin** editor, we were given the option to edit the overall skin tone. This information is factored into the makeup **FOUNDATION** editor to provide the user with a color palette suitable to the skin tone you originally chose for your character. This is to simulate real-world makeup decisions. For example, the makeup selection of a Caucasian would be different from the makeup selection of an African American.

As you can see in *Figure 2.26*, the palette available to us for the foundation is very much limited to the character's skin tone; this is to provide the best result:

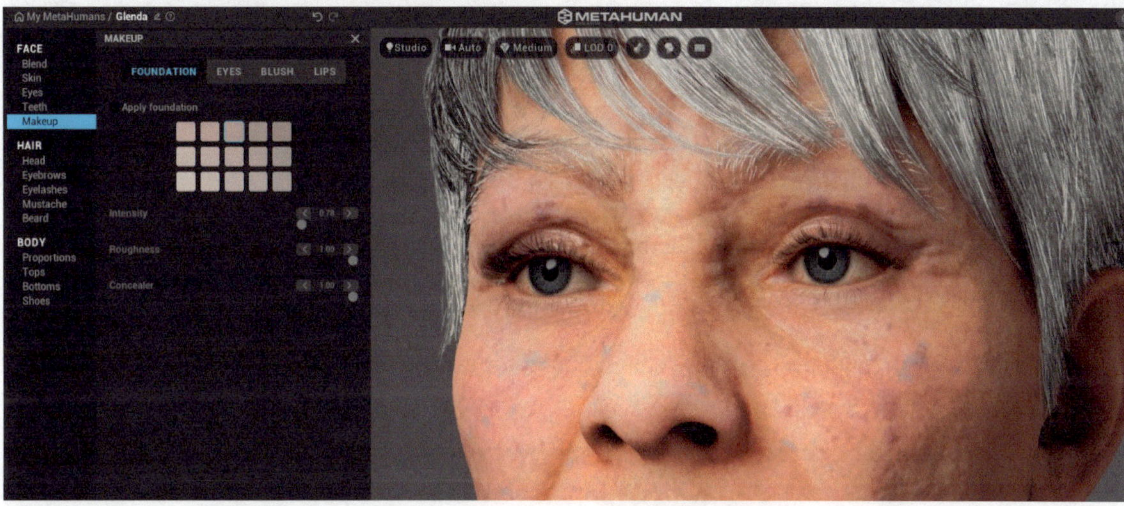

Figure 2.26: With no foundation makeup

Be sure to check **Apply foundation** and select one color from the palette given. After that, you can edit the **Intensity**, **Roughness**, and **Concealer** options. **Intensity** is self-explanatory, but in makeup terms, it can be understood as how thick the application of the foundation is. **Roughness** can be understood as the difference between an oil-based foundation and a powder-based foundation. **Concealer**, however, is the intensity of the application just under the eyes.

Also, if you were to go back and increase the intensity and density of your character's freckles, you would get a better idea of just how intense or thick the application of the foundation makeup you have made was. In *Figure 2.27*, I did exactly that:

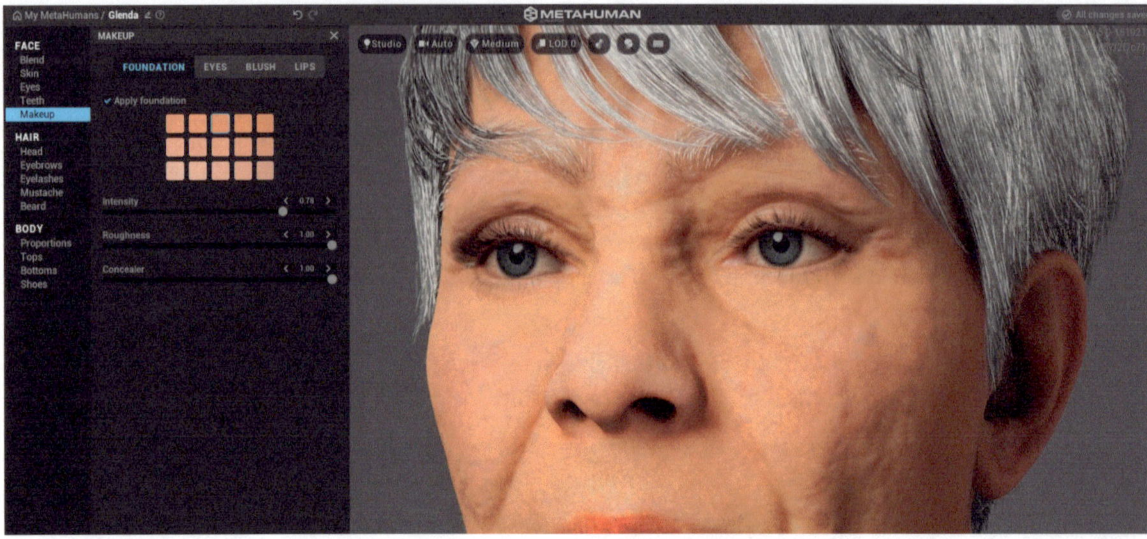

Figure 2.27: Foundation with a new palette

I also made the makeup very rough and dialed the intensity down enough so that we can just about see the freckles come through. Note that the palettes between *Figure 2.26* and *2.27* are very different.

Eyes

Not to be confused with the earlier eye editor, this editor is exclusively for eye makeup. *Figure 2.28* shows an array of presets for eye makeup:

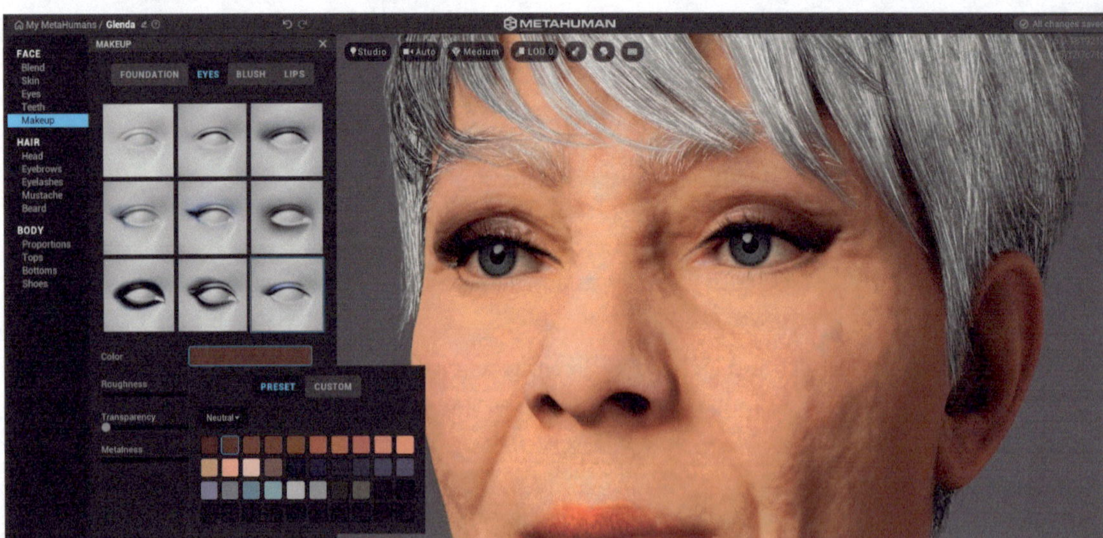

Figure 2.28: Eye makeup

Similar to the eye editor from earlier, we also have a selection of makeup shapes. For example, we could choose from one of the thin liner presets at the top or the dramatic smudge shape at the bottom.

Again, the palette available to us complements the skin tone, which you can see in *Figure 2.29*, but rather than just getting a naturally complementary palette to choose from under presets, you can also choose other options such as **Neutral**, **Deep**, and **Vibrant**; your choice of palette will often depend on your character. You can also create a custom palette:

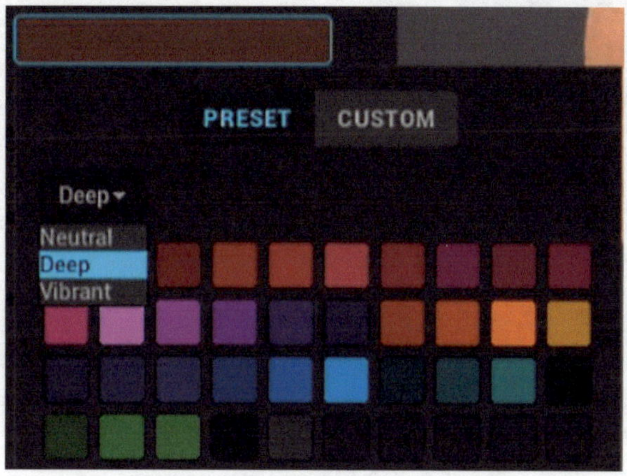

Figure 2.29: Eye makeup palette options

Like the **FOUNDATION** tab, we have sliders that allow us to edit the following:

- **Roughness**: Allows us to edit how reflective the eye makeup is to light. A roughness of 0 is very reflective while a roughness of 1 is non-reflective.
- **Transparency**: This works the same way as intensity did; the less transparent it is, the thicker the eye makeup that's been applied.
- **Metalness**: This is a type of reflectivity and indicates that the more metalness, the more detail we will see in the reflection; a low setting would give us a duller shine. For example, a surface that is highly metallic and has no roughness will appear like a mirror. If it has a low metalness and low roughness, it will be shiny but the reflections will be faint. Finally, if it has low metalness and is very rough, it would be very dull indeed, similar to clay or plaster.

Like many of the previous features, such as foundation, eye makeup gets us some pretty realistic results. We'll see more of this in the next section, where we will look at the cheeks and blush makeup.

Blush

Again, the **BLUSH** palette reflects a palette complementary to the skin tone. Unlike the eye shadow editor, we are only given one palette as blushers tend only to come in complementary tones rather than the vibrant alternatives given under the eye shadow editor:

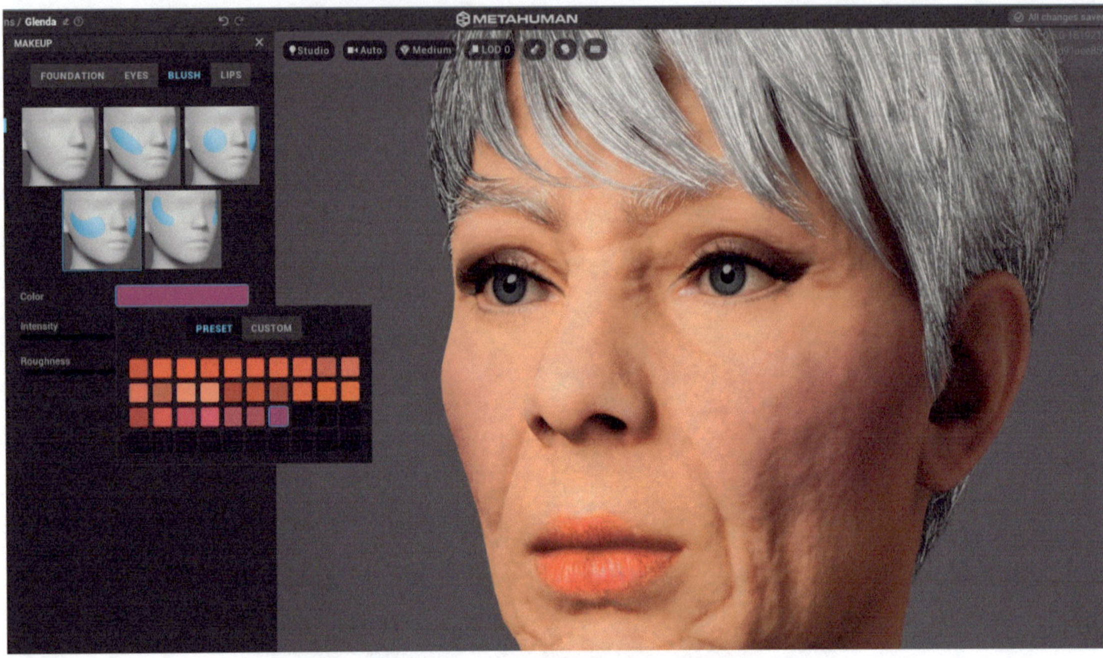

Figure 2.30: Blush palette options

From the top left, we can choose the areas we wish to be affected, which are primarily around the cheeks and temples, as indicated in blue in *Figure 2.30*.

We also get **Intensity** and **Roughness** sliders, which allow us to achieve a further sense of realism. A blusher that has a low roughness will have a shininess different from that of the foundation and different again from the underlying skin tone. All these subtle variations of makeup on the skin add to the realism and are certainly worth playing around with.

Lips

Finally, let's discuss the **LIPS** editor, which you can see in *Figure 2.31*. Like the **BLUSH** selection, there isn't a huge amount of variation, but at least we can play around with **Roughness**, **Transparency**, and **Color**, which is close enough to the variety available in **BLUSH**:

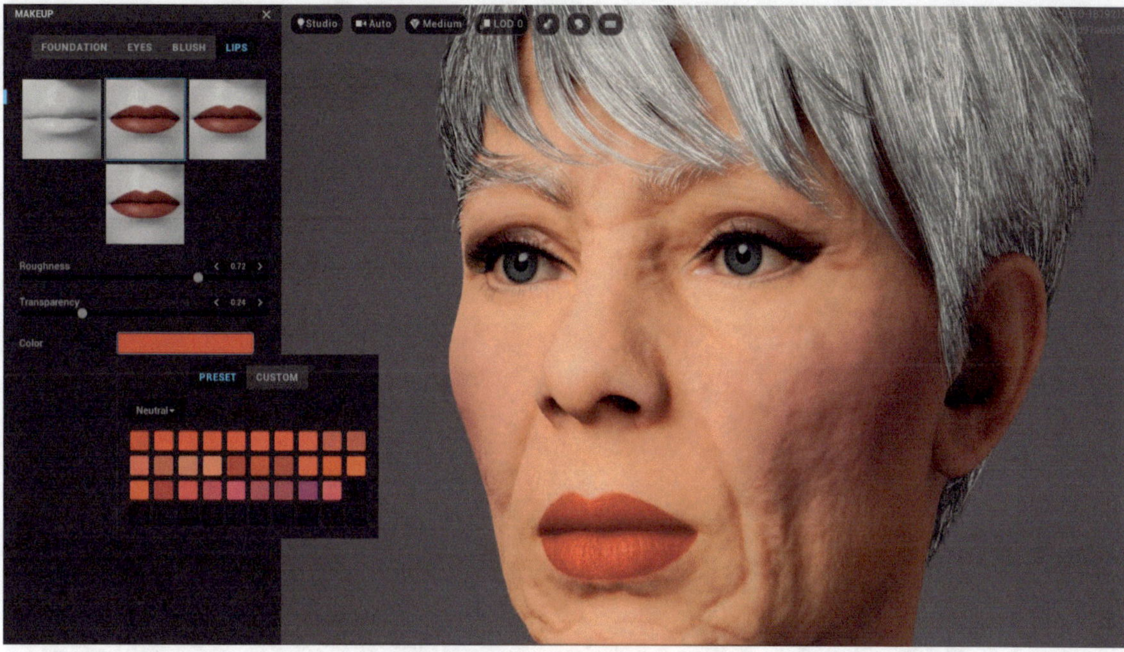

Figure 2.31: Lipstick palette options

The grey thumbnails at the top indicate how the lipstick is painted on: the first indicates no lipstick, while the remaining three options give us very subtle differences in how the lipstick is painted, with some being slightly out of the lip area and some being less liberal.

We do, however, get further options to choose from if we want to go for something a little more vibrant or funky. We can also fine-tune our color selection using the **CUSTOM** button. As before, the **Roughness** slider allows us to make the lipstick shinier and more reflective. At this point, we have played around with roughness a lot; the result of roughness being low will produce an actual response to the light in your scene. In *Figure 2.32*, the white areas of the lips are reflections of a light source:

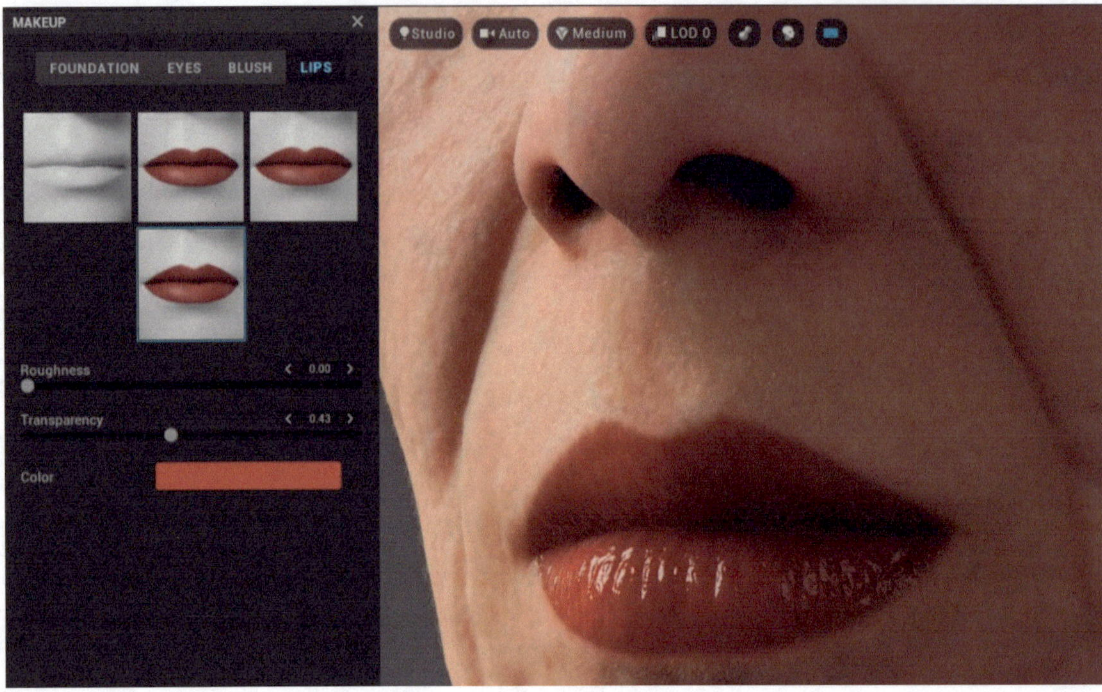

Figure 2.32: Lipstick Roughness set to zero

> **Note**
>
> To see the effect of roughness, try reducing the roughness on the lips to zero, zoom into the lips, and, with the *L* key pressed, left-click your mouse around the main viewport to move the scene lights.

So far in this chapter, we have covered the face in great detail. In the next section, we'll move on to something very different, and you will be introduced to some new concepts as we delve into hair and hair physics.

Hair

Just like the face, the MHC comes with many presets to choose from but also offers some custom modifications. If you load up a long-haired character, you'll notice straight away that the hair moves very realistically; you can expect the very same results within Unreal Engine.

There are two main factors to consider when it comes to hair rendering:

1. **Hair strands** or **Strand Based Grooms**: These use splines for individual hairs, although there is a little bit of cheating to give the illusion of more hair. With strand-based grooms, we get a far more realistic look but the physics of how the hair moves and collides with the body is more accurate.
2. **Hair cards**: These are simple poly shapes with images of multiple hairs. Hair cards are also easier to render and are the default when it comes to displaying lower LODs.

By default, the MHC uses **Strand Based Grooms** for LOD 0 and LOD 1. In other words, they are used for close-ups and mid-shots (head and shoulder shots). When the character is further away from the camera, the complexity of **Strand Based Grooms** is overkill and redundant and so hair cards are used instead. The MHC also offers the option of just using cards should you find that your performance or frame rate is low.

> **Note**
>
> Some of the presets when it comes to LODs are still in development and only offer **Strand Based Grooms**, which, as I mentioned earlier, are available in LOD 0 and LOD 1 only. Because there is no hair card alternative, your character will appear bald at farther distances unless you force a LOD of 0 or 1 within Unreal Engine. You will learn how to do that after we bring our character into the engine.

One more consideration to take on board concerning **Hair LOD** is the rendering quality. You may recall that, in the *Render Quality* section earlier in this chapter, **Epic (Ray Traced)** provides us with much more realistic shadowing within the hair, so it is worth considering that to get the best result from hair. When working with a LOD of LOD 1 or LOD 2, it is very likely you'll need the **Epic (Ray Traced)** setting if you want to achieve photorealism in a close-up shot.

Saying that, depending on your character's distance from the camera, you also may get away with a lower render quality setting, which will allow for a faster rendering time.

In addition to scalp hair, the MHC also provides solutions for eyebrows, eyelashes, mustaches, and beards. We will discuss these elements now. As we go through each of these options, we'll see that there are a lot of similarities in terms of what's available to us for editing. For the most part, it's just color, roughness, and salt and pepper.

Head

The **Head** editor provides us with all the available tools to edit head hair, as shown in *Figure 2.33*. Unlike many other character creation tools, the MHC provides a physics dynamics solution within Unreal. In short, this means that hair will move realistically and interact with objects such as characters' shoulders and respond to factors such as gravity and wind. The shorter the hair, the less obvious the hair dynamics:

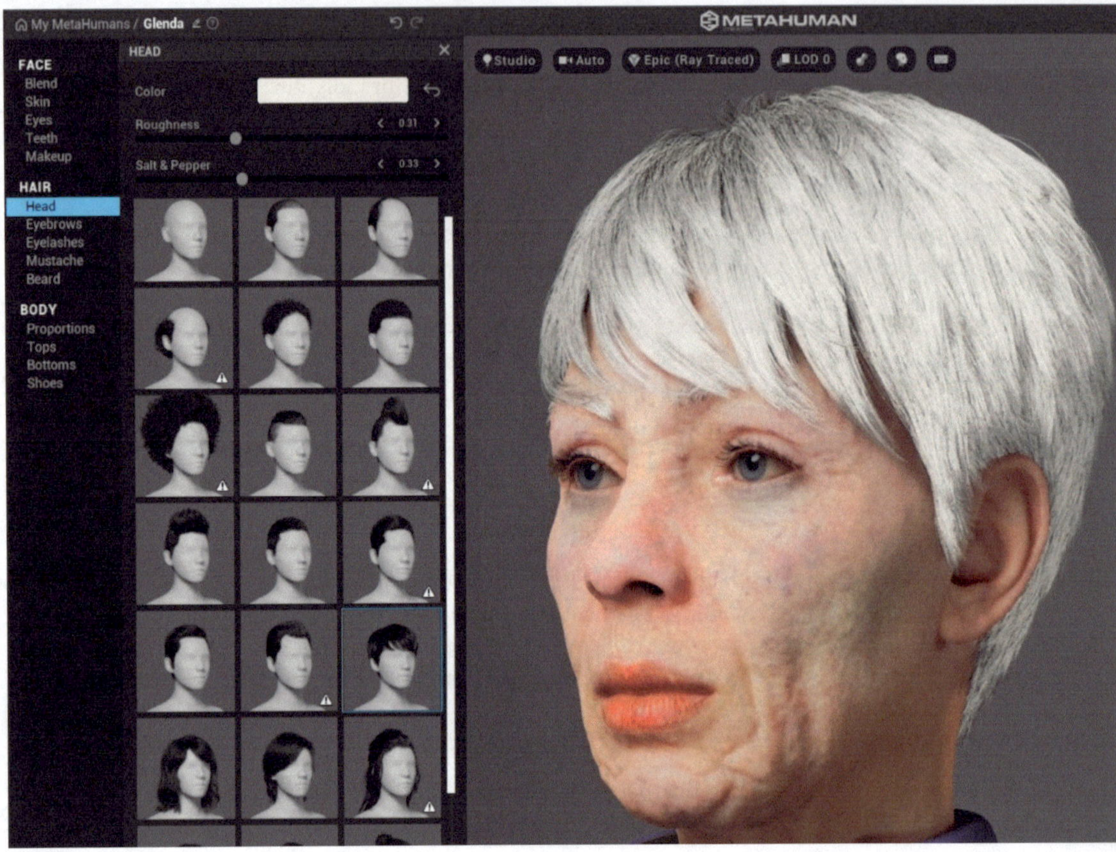

Figure 2.33: Head hair presets

In *Figure 2.33*, you can see that, apart from choosing dozens of presets, there isn't much in terms of editing other than choosing what hairstyle you want from the preset menu.

For the Glenda example, I have retained the gray preset but found that I had to alter the **Color** option before I was able to edit both **Roughness** and **Salt & Pepper**. **Roughness** is perfect for introducing a matte or shiny hair look, while **Salt & Pepper** is for adding or reducing gray hair.

In *Figure 2.34*, you can see just how detailed the hair can be for close-ups. In this example, we can see individual strands of hair:

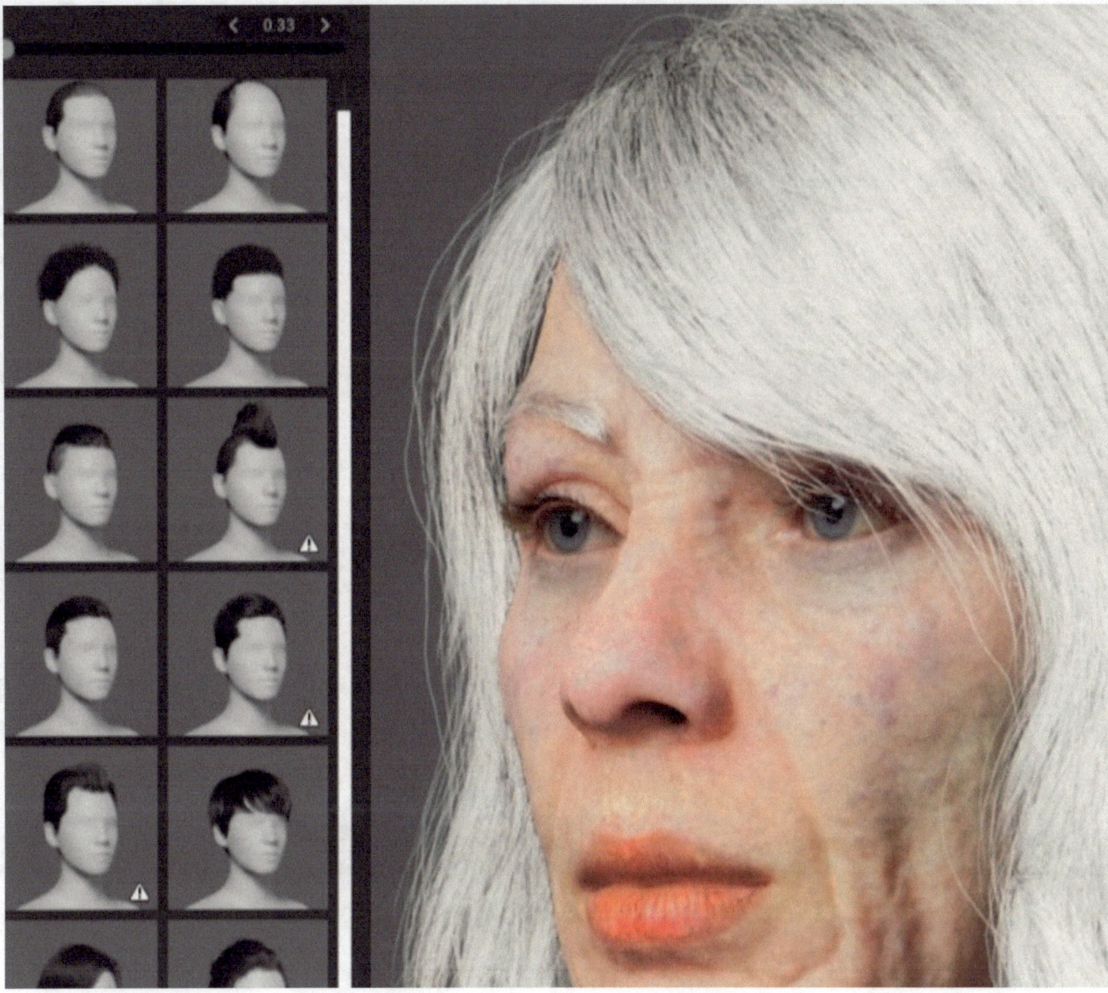

Figure 2.34: Individual hair strands are visible

Like we had for the makeup editor, we can also choose between **PRESET** and **CUSTOM**. You'll see a drop-down menu under **PRESET**, as shown in *Figure 2.35*, allowing us to keep within a **Neutral** palette or **Deep** and **Vibrant** palettes. If you choose **CUSTOM**, you get a much wider color gamut to choose from:

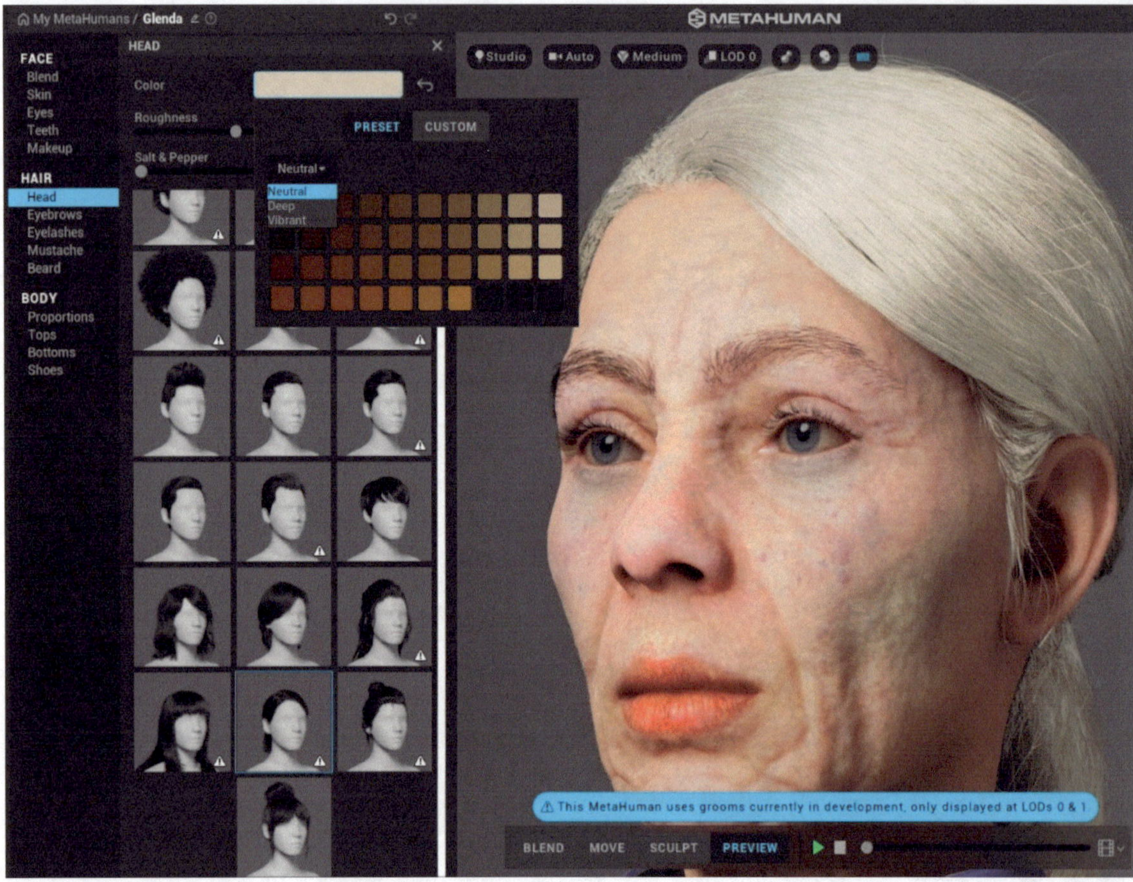

Figure 2.35: Head hair presets

The thumbnails containing the warning icons are presets with limited LODs. You can see these icons on the bottom right of the preset thumbnails in *Figure 2.35*; the warning says that **This MetaHuman uses grooms currently in development, only displayed at LODs 0 & 1**. This means that it can only offer a display of no LOD, which is the maximum strand-based hair rendering, and a LOD value of 1, which is also strand-based. This means that Unreal Engine will try to render the hair at maximum quality, regardless of the camera distance. Inside the engine, it will hide the hair when a LOD value of 2 would normally be engaged. In the instances of characters that don't have a LOD level of 2 or more, Unreal Engine will render no hair. While not being particularly useful with the warnings here, it is good to make a note of these warnings as you will need to force the engine to use no LOD at all when using a character that has limited LODs. Otherwise, your character will appear to go bald if the camera is too distant.

Eyebrows

With the **Eyebrows** panel, as seen in *Figure 2.36*, we have just a small number of presets to choose from (only 11 at the time of writing), with the usual color palette and set of parameters to edit that we saw previously, including **Salt & Pepper**:

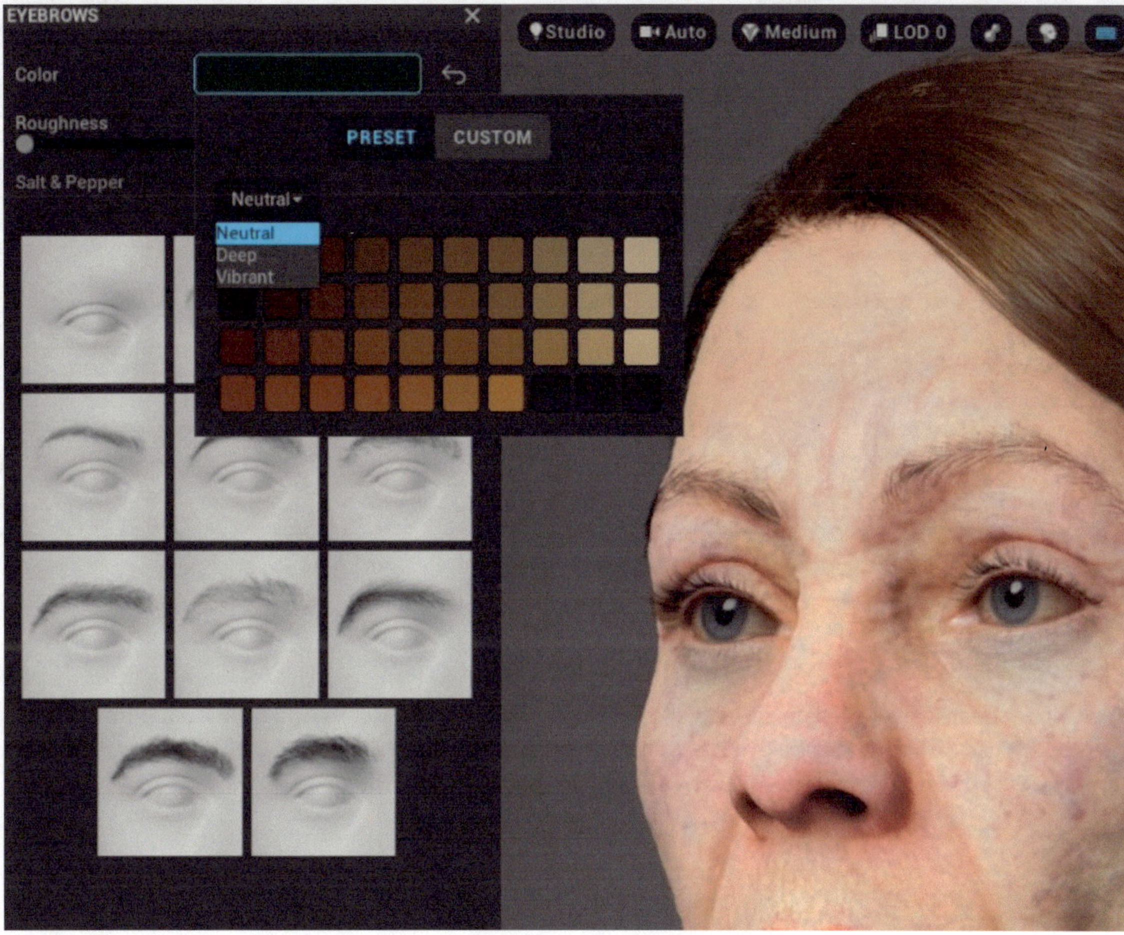

Figure 2.36: Eyebrows

Eyelashes

You'll notice that apart from the presets available to us, the **Eyelash** parameters in *Figure 2.37* are identical to those in the **Eyebrows** panel. However, once within Unreal Engine, we'll get a little more editing control over this parameter:

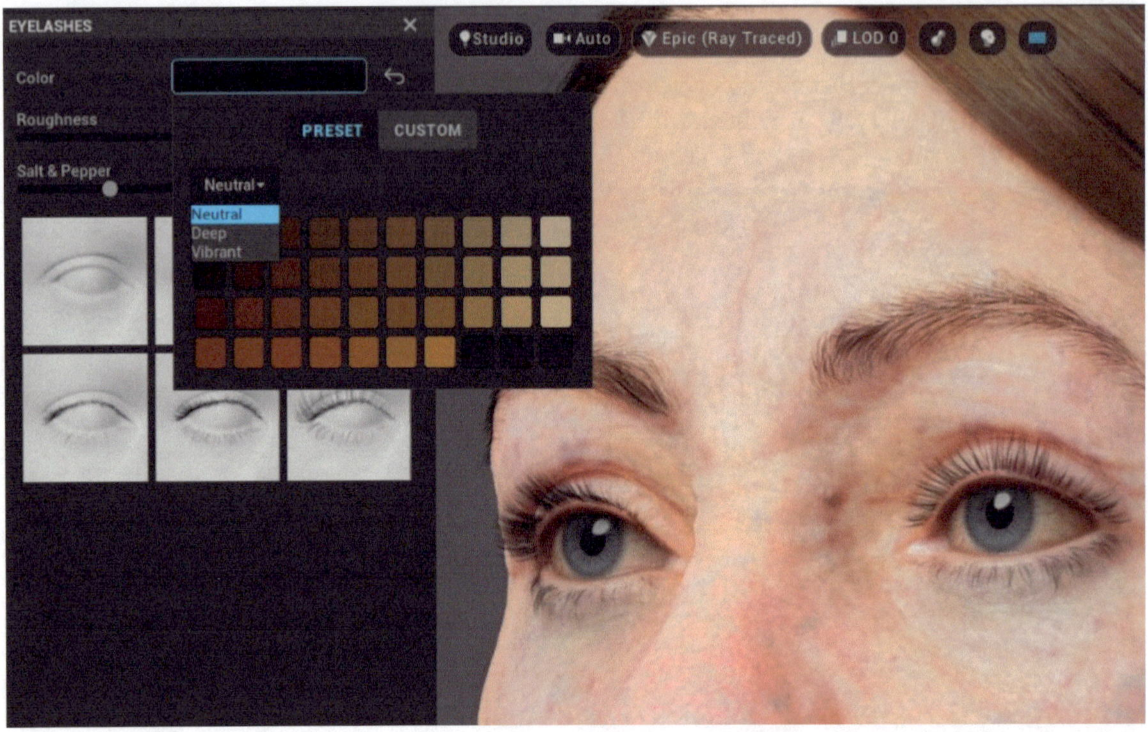

Figure 2.37: Eyelashes

Mustache

There's quite a lot of detail involved in the **Mustache** panel. As you can see in *Figure 2.38*, from what we learned earlier, we can see that it is a spline-based hair solution, which gives us the best detail. Just like the previous two editors, we have the same parameters to edit with:

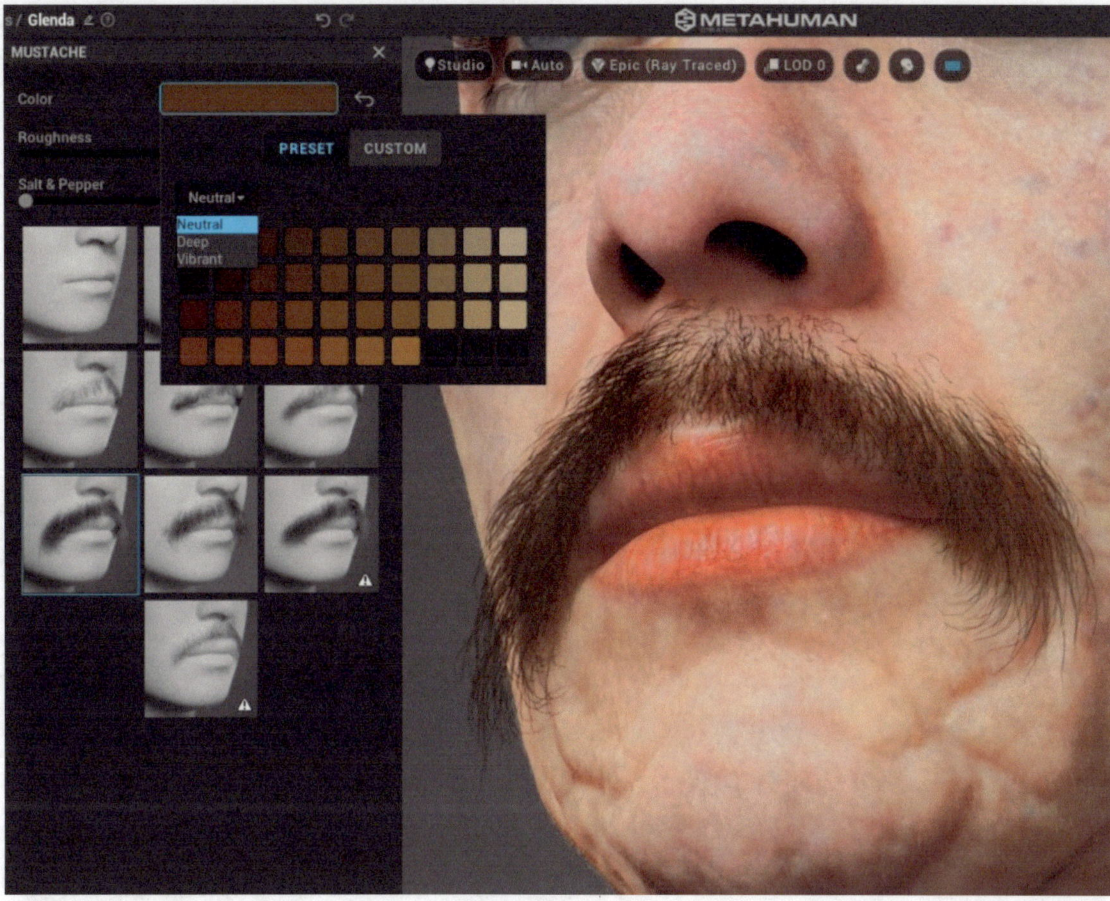

Figure 2.38: Mustache

However, unfortunately, in terms of the pattern of hair growth, we are limited to just choosing a small selection of presets. Similar to the eyelashes, we do have further options to edit once we get the character inside Unreal Engine.

Beard

Finally, we have the last hair-related editor: the beard. Again, we have several great presets to play with, as shown in *Figure 2.39*, and have the usual parameters to edit. Just like the **Scalp Hair** section, the beard will respond well to animation, particularly in terms of collision dynamics such as colliding against the upper chest realistically:

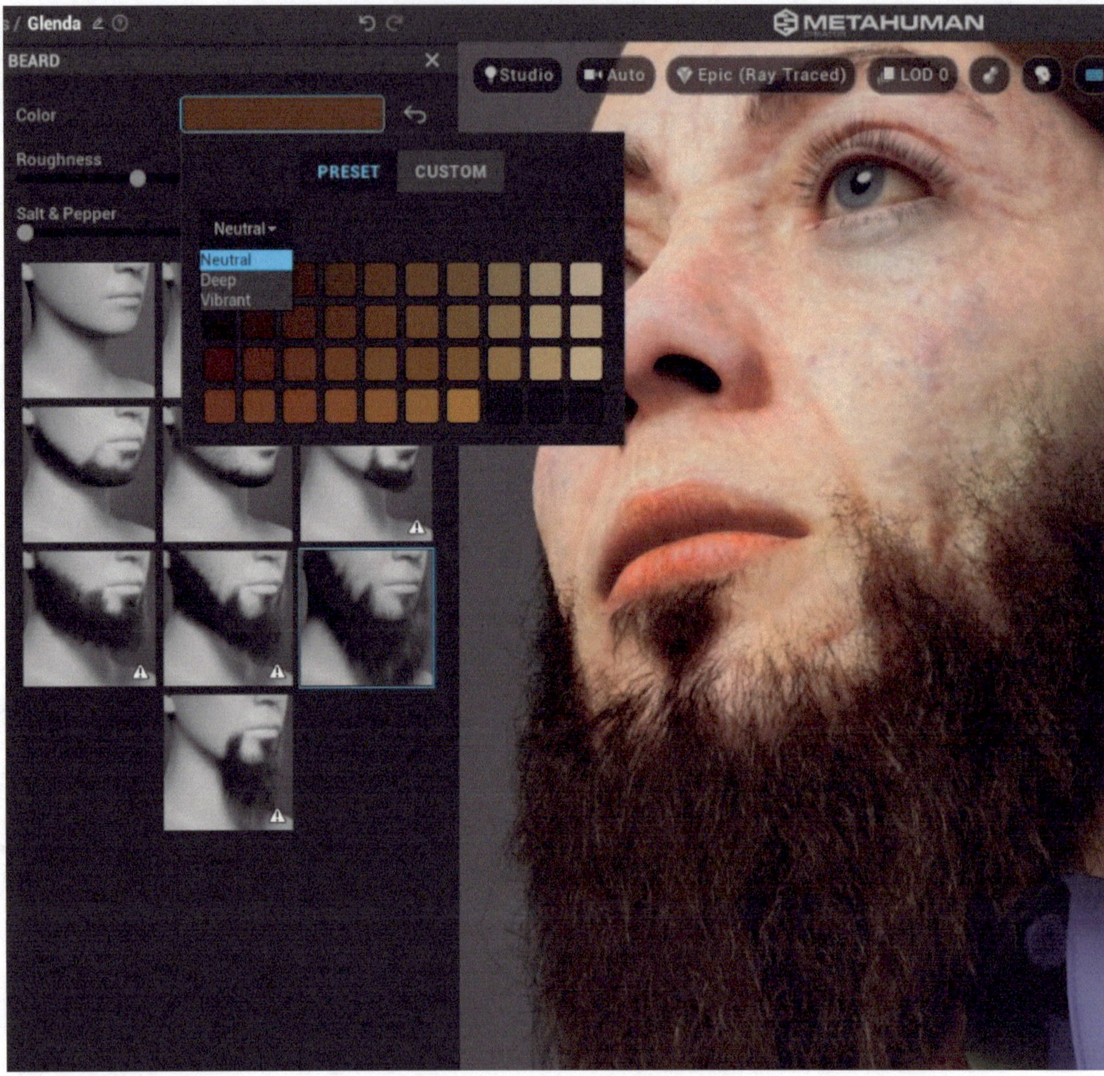

Figure 2.39: Beard

In this section, we covered a lot of the presets that are provided to us concerning editing in the MHC. Some of these concepts are already familiar to us from when we edited the face, such as the color palette's LOD, but we've looked at some new concepts too, such as briefly touching on hair dynamics. It is worth noting that additional editing can be done in Unreal Engine; for example, we can add a separate physics solver to get unique animation results from the eyelashes if we wished. Generally speaking, we don't need to do this.

In the next section, we'll be covering some new ground as we look at the body.

Body

In the **BODY** section, we can edit the proportions of our character, but we also have options to edit clothing and shoes. Let's look at those now.

Proportions

First, we need to take a look at the body proportions and the presets that come shipped with the MHC. We can see these in *Figure 2.40*:

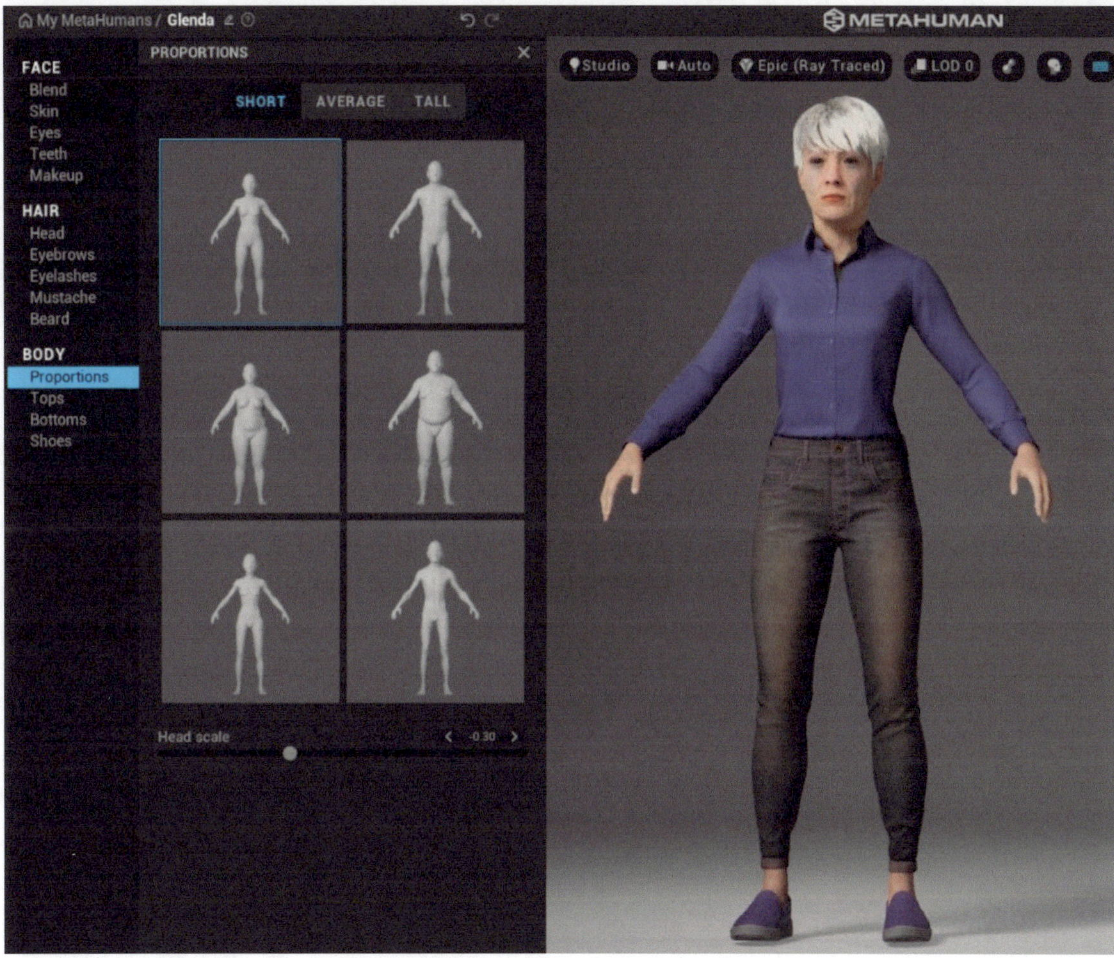

Figure 2.40: Body proportions

There are three proportion categories: **SHORT**, **AVERAGE, AND TALL**. In each category, there are **Male** and **Female** options. Both of these have three main body types: **Mesomorph**, **Endomorph**, and **Ectomorph** (muscular, overweight, and underweight). Unlike the face, we aren't given as much fine-tuning ability (for example, we can't blend between body types).

Compared to other programs dedicated almost exclusively to character creation, such as Character Creator, MHC has limitations. It would be unfair to try to make a side-by-side comparison because the MHC's focus is on realistic humans, whereas programs such as Realusion's Character Creator allow you to make dramatic changes to both physiology and skin type to the extent that you can very easily create a character that is way beyond the realm of a human. So, while the limitations constrain us to create more human characters, it is still a limitation nonetheless. It's also worth noting that MHC is still very much in development, so we'll likely see more features in the future. One example of this is the limitation to only create adults with a very finite set of ratios, such as knee to hip, neck length, foot size, and so on.

With all of that said, currently, in MHC, there are body types per gender, which isn't too bad. If you take a look at *Figure 2.40*, where I have selected the **SHORT** tab within the **Proportions** editor, you'll notice three body types per gender: thin, medium, and large. Because there are three tabs relating to height – **SHORT**, **AVERAGE, AND TALL** – we get nine body types per gender, giving us 18 body types in total. Skin weights and cloth dynamics do come into this but they are outside the scope of this book.

Also, you may be wondering about scale. Rescaling characters is perfectly doable when inside Unreal Engine, without any negative impact on the functionality of the characters.

Tops

Within the **BODY** section of the interface, you'll see from *Figure 2.41* that we also have the option (albeit a limited one) to change the character's clothing:

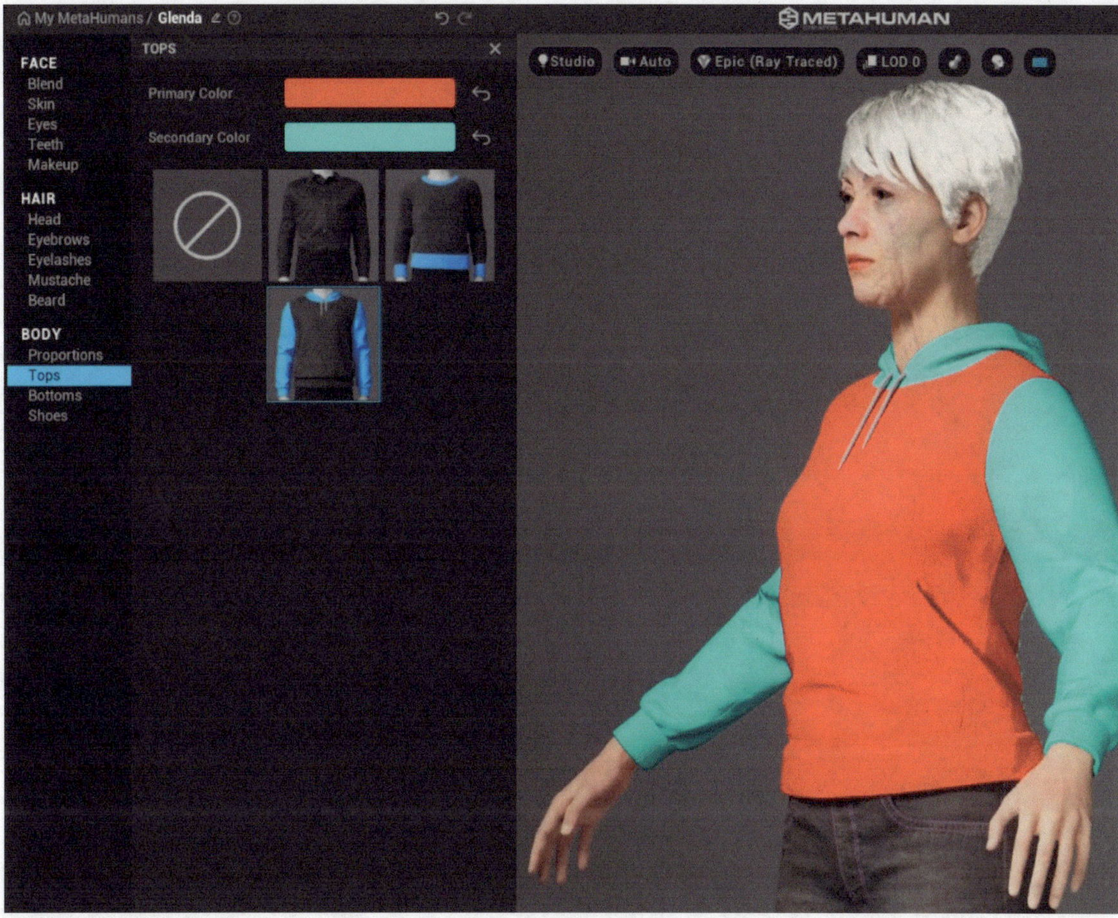

Figure 2.41: Tops

However, a little goes a long way and you can change the color of the various elements of each of the tops here. For example, I've given Glenda a two-toned hoodie.

> **Note**
>
> I can only speculate at this point that Epic and Quixel plan to add more features, but you can imagine how many dials and buttons are required to accommodate the variation of any one person's wardrobe. For now, you can customize your character's clothing, even with accurate cloth dynamics, but it requires the use of third-party software such as Marvelous Designer, Maya, or Blender.

Bottoms

Similar to **Tops**, as you can see in *Figure 2.42*, there are major limitations regarding the **Bottoms** features. As you can see when we compared the two, we only get two extra presets for **Bottoms**, but also like the **Tops** presets, a little goes a long way:

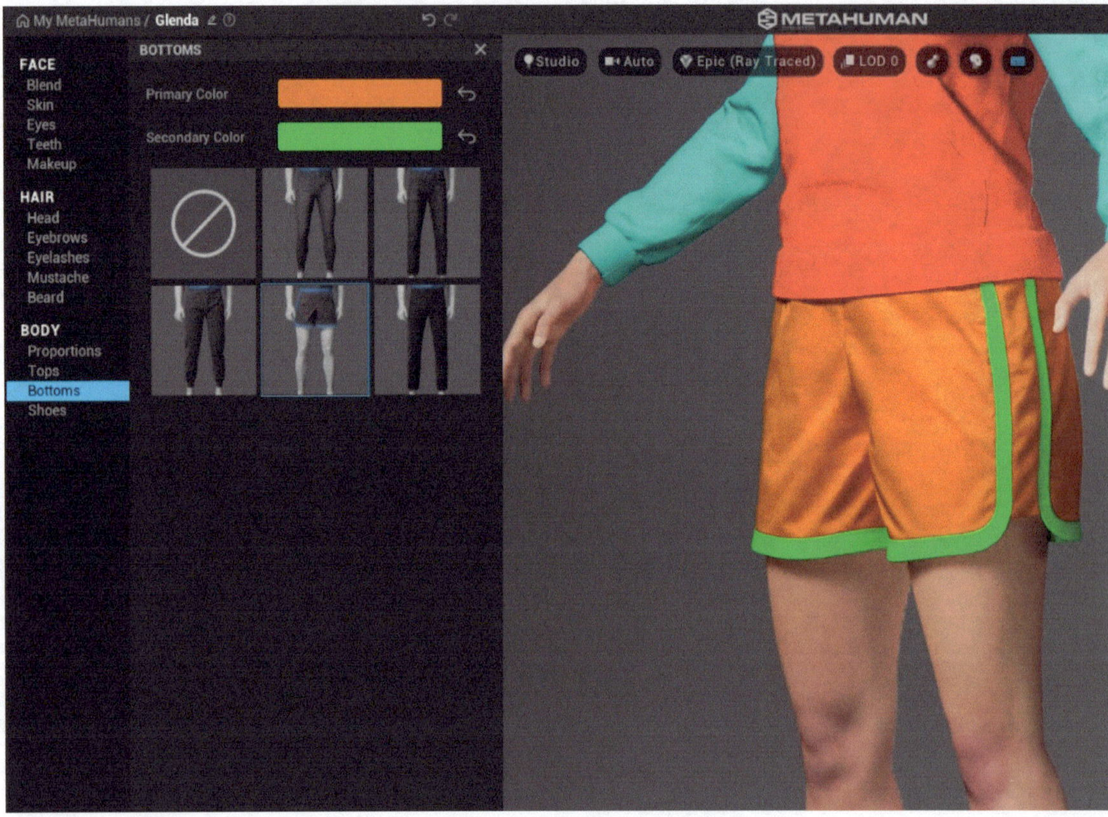

Figure 2.42: Bottoms

Shoes

Similar to **Tops** and **Bottoms**, there are some major limitations when it comes to **Shoes** in MHC; however, the customization in terms of mesh/geometry is much more fluid as it doesn't involve redistributing weight painting concerning cloth simulations. While that sounds complicated, it just means that shoes aren't as complex as a shirt in terms of how the body influences the movement of the clothing. A shoe doesn't change its shape, even when it's not being worn; it is still in the shape of a foot. However, a shirt can be rolled into a ball when not worn.

As a result of this lower level of complexity, it is much more straightforward to model or buy a 3D model of a shoe of your choice and replace it in Unreal. For the time being, we are limited to a small number of shoes where we can edit the primary and secondary colors.

Other than editing the primary and secondary colors, currently, there are no other editing options for shoes in the MHC, as shown in *Figure 2.43*:

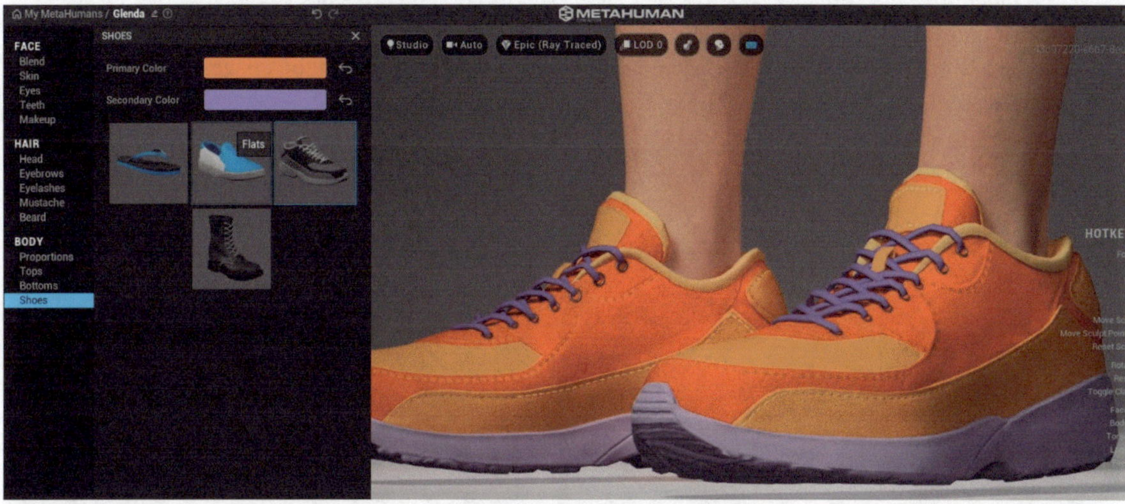

Figure 2.43: Shoes

I'm sure you will agree that the body and clothing editors aren't as detailed as that of the face and skin and other areas covered in this chapter, but you may be surprised to learn that, in this next section, we're going to jump right back into some of the face editors for additional refining.

Using the Move and Sculpt tools

While I could have introduced **Sculpt** and **Move** at the beginning of this chapter, as they relate to the head only, I left them for last for a good reason. Up until now, you have seen that the MHC provides a wealth of options that give very real-world and realistic results. There are also ample opportunities to customize the face using the **Blend** tool. But sometimes, there are occasions when we want to push things a little further and exaggerate certain characteristics. There are also times when we are looking for something less symmetrical that is closer to reality, or when we simply want to hone in on a specific detail.

With the **Sculpt** and **Move** tools, you can add a little more than the preset blending has to offer, but it's harder to get back to where you were should you not get it right. So, **Sculpt** and **Move** should be left until you've exhausted the other areas.

Within the interface, the main visible difference between **Move** and **Sculpt** is the controllers:

- In **Move**, you work with guidelines that indicate the area of the face that you are editing. When moving guidelines, you move clusters of points that influence their surrounding area.
- In **Sculpt**, you work with points on the face and can only sculpt one point at a time.

Both functions work similarly and, to a very large extent, give similar results, so much so that I would say that choosing between the two is a matter of personal preference. In *Figure 2.44*, you can just about make out the points on the left-hand side, whereas the guidelines in the image on the right are much clearer:

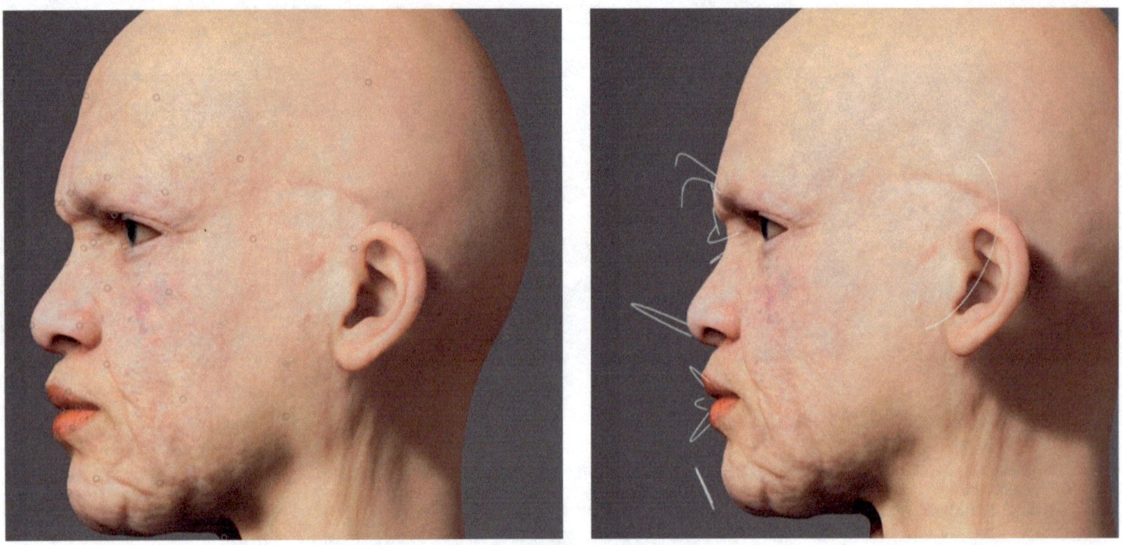

Figure 2.44: Sculpt points and Move guidelines

To see just how **Move** behaves differently to **Sculpt**, look at the front of the face and edit one of the eyebrows. In **Move** mode, when you edit an eyebrow, you will see three points appear as you move the eyebrow, thus indicating that you are moving three points simultaneously in **Move** mode. In **Sculpt** mode, you are just moving one point, with the greatest influence of change occurring at that one point.

Something else to consider is asymmetry. The **Move** guidelines are very helpful indicators to show you just what you can do to create asymmetry in your character. For example, the nose and lips are manipulated by the same guidelines, so it's very difficult to create asymmetry in those areas. On the other hand, the left ear and right ear have their own set of guidelines that you can manipulate.

To disable symmetry, toggle the symmetry buttons, as shown in *Figure 2.45*, to the right of the **PREVIEW** option:

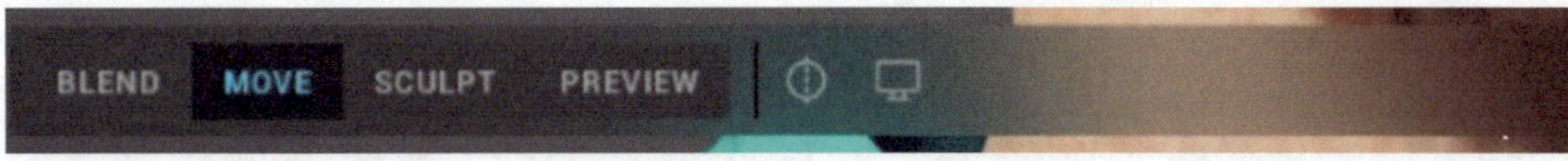

Figure 2.45: Disabling symmetry

I may have gone too far in *Figure 2.46* and poor Glenda has seen better days. However, this is a good example of pushing the asymmetry to the maximum using both the **Sculpt** and **Move** tools with the symmetry option turned off:

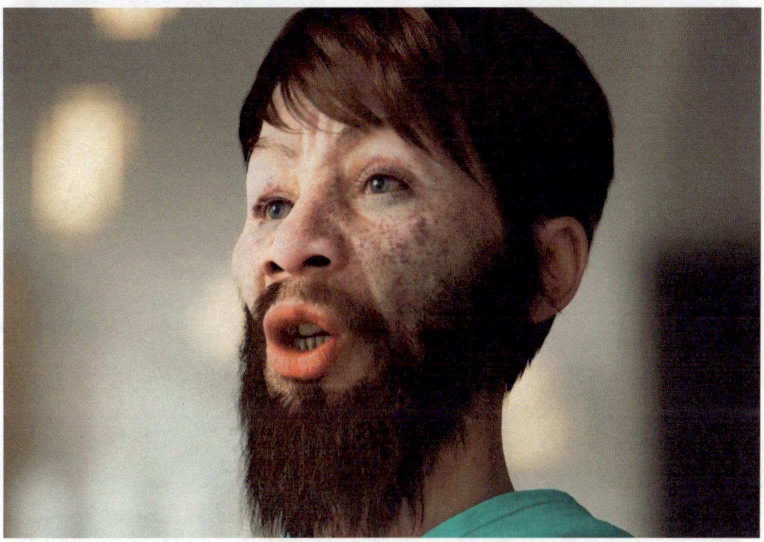

Figure 2.46: Editing beyond realism

> **Note**
>
> Asymmetry is heavily overlooked in the creation of realism when it comes to digital character design. Because humans don't have identical sides of the face, it is very important to introduce some level of asymmetry, no matter how subtle. Historically, CGI characters have suffered from what is known as the **uncanny valley**, and much of this uncanniness is due to the presence of perfect symmetry, which doesn't exist in nature.

We have covered quite a lot of detail in this chapter regarding how we can use the MHC to create a unique character; I urge you to play around with multiple characters before you move on to the next section. In the next section, if you're happy with your character design, you will download and export your character.

Downloading and exporting your character

It's time to download your character and export it from MHC and into Unreal Engine. To do this, you need to open up Bridge and navigate to your character. You may remember this from the moment before you first launched the MHC. However, if you have done some editing, you will notice that the picture of your character in Bridge has also been updated since the last autosave. If you look at *Figure 2.47*, you'll notice that my Glenda character has been updated in Bridge:

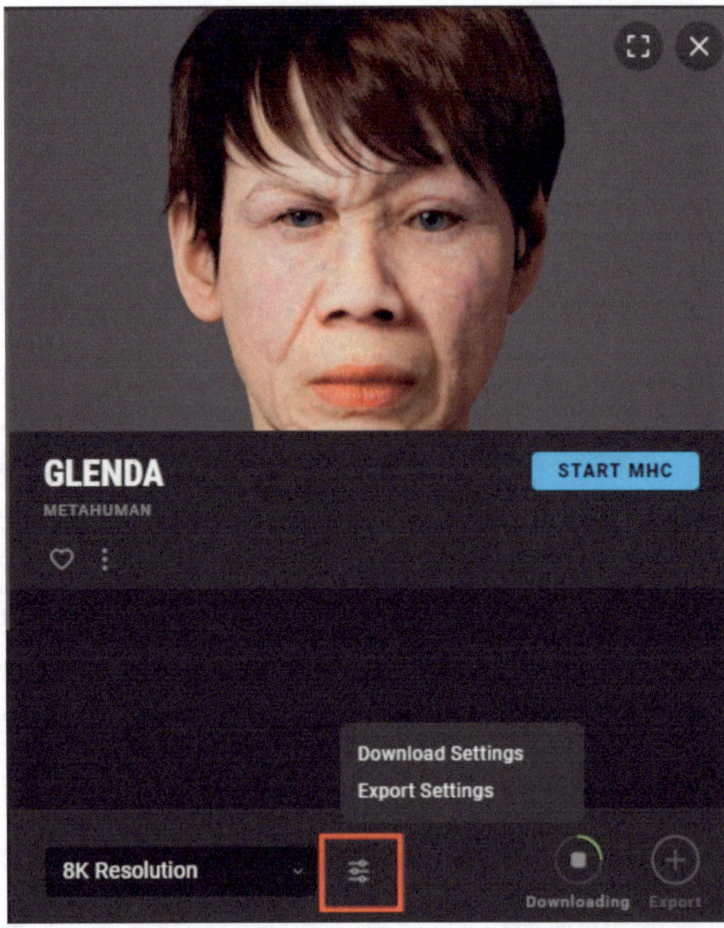

Figure 2.47: Download and Export settings

This is where you can change the **Resolution**, **Download Settings**, and **Export Settings** options, which we will take a look at here.

Resolution

At the bottom left of *Figure 2.47*, you will see a dropdown menu that relates to the resolution of the texture maps for our characters.

The highest available is 8K resolution. This means that the highest texture map is over 8,000 pixels wide. That's a lot of pixels; I strongly recommend starting with 2K or even 1K since characters with 8K texture maps take a long time to generate and download and take a long time to compile when first introduced to the engine.

If your computer screen can display 4,000 pixels across, then the texture map of 8K will be displayed very adequately. In particular, a texture of a face being at 8K is more than enough to display a close-up on a 4K monitor. Also, keep in mind that there are several texture maps for the face that are all blended to give you even extra detail. The combined texture maps for the Glenda character come to 1.6 GB.

> **Note**
>
> You can always swap out your characters at a later stage. So, you can work out your entire production using a lower-resolution proxy of your character and then swap it out for an 8K version when you are at the lighting and rendering phase of your production. This is a very easy process, with the download and export part taking by far the most time.

Download considerations

Whenever you close the MHC or just stop using it, your character is ready to be downloaded at any time from within Bridge. If you have Bridge open, with your character selected, you will see it update from time to time, particularly once you've closed down your MHC session.

To change the download settings, click **Download Settings**, as shown in *Figure 2.48*. You'll see two tabs - **TEXTURES** and **MODELS**.

First, let's look at the **TEXTURES** tab:

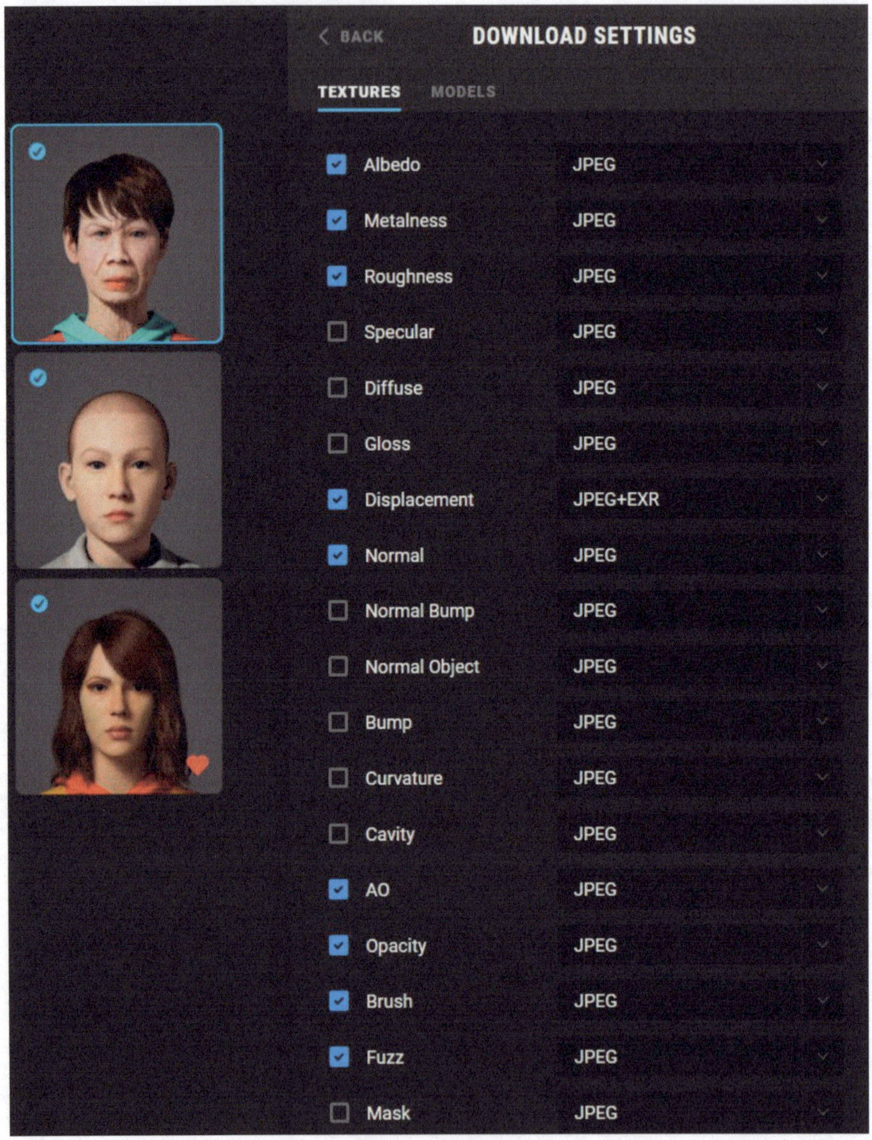

Figure 2.48: Textures settings

TEXTURES has already got just about half of the potential textures ticked by default, which is good enough for most cases. We are given the extra choice of choosing what **Image format** to choose from – that is, **JPEG**, **EXR**, or **JPEG+EXR** I highly recommend that you stick with **JPEG** as EXR files are considerably larger, will add to your download and processing time, and may even cause performance issues in Unreal. In most cases, there isn't enough pixel data to justify the use of the EXR file format.

Now, let's switch to the **MODELS** tab; here, we have different options:

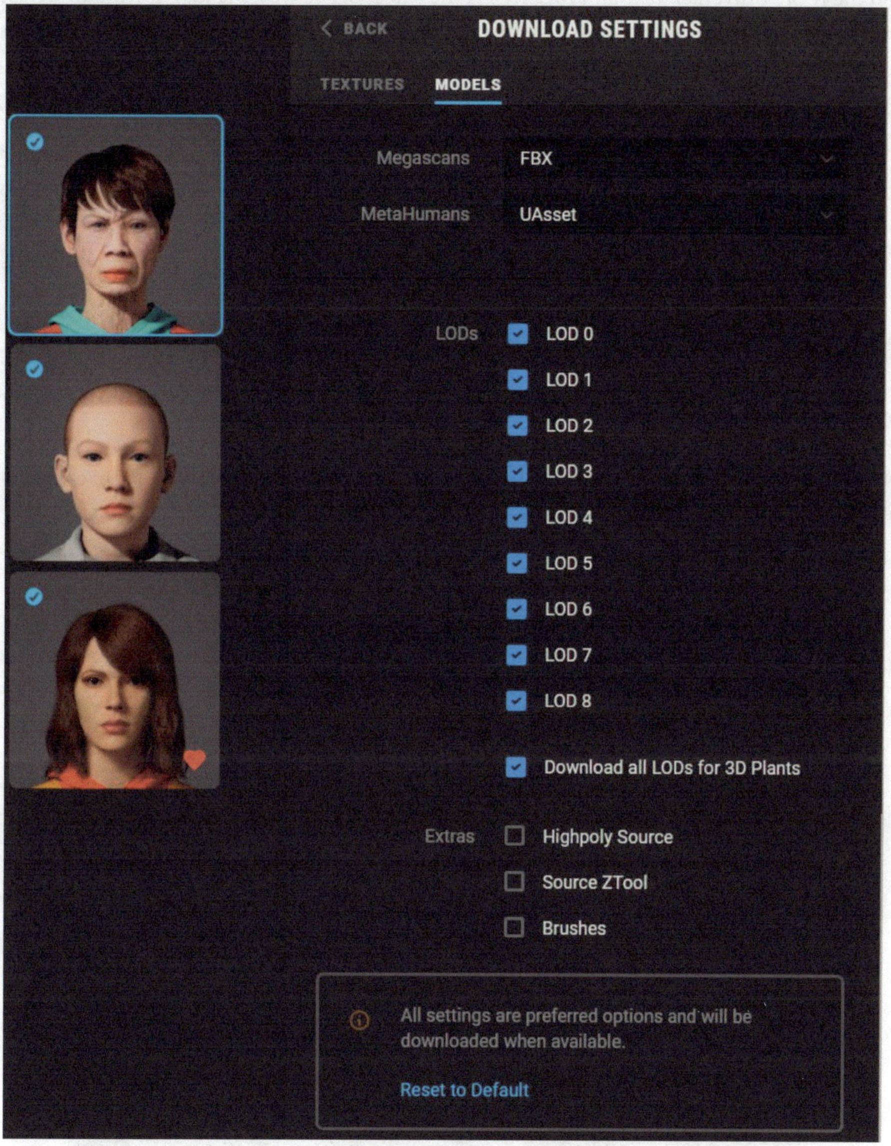

Figure 2.49: Models settings

Because this is Bridge, we have options for **Megascans** and **MetaHumans** when it comes to choosing what format we want our 3D models to be in. We just need to concern ourselves with the **MetaHumans** drop-down list, which gives us two formats to choose from – that is, **UAsset** and **UAsset + Source Asset**.

Choosing **UAsset + Source Asset** will download the character mesh in a format only readable in Unreal and also the more universal format, FBX. This is the safest bet as we can't just download **UAsset** on its own as it will most likely cause the export process to fail. (We can also go to **Export Settings** to give us more options for third-party 3D programs should you only want to work with your MetaHuman in Maya, Houdini, or Blender.)

Once you have reviewed the settings, you can click the **Back** button, and then the green **Download** button that will appear at the bottom of the panel shown in *Figure 2.47*. The download process takes a considerable amount of time because the MHC is baking out the texture maps based on your modifications, generating new meshes, and writing out new Unreal files. It's also compressing and decompressing the files for the download process.

Now, let's look at the **Export Settings** options.

Export considerations

Next, we will look at **Export Settings** (which you can find below **Downloads Settings** in *Figure 2.47*). Here is the window you will see:

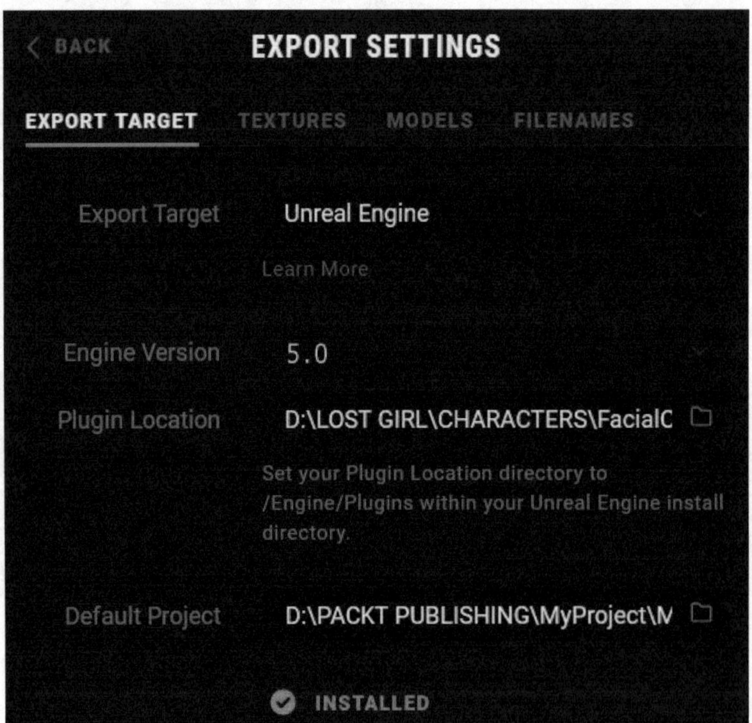

Figure 2.50: Export Settings

To export your character, do the following:

1. Set **Unreal Engine** as your **Export Target**.
2. Set **Engine Version** to the version you have installed, which should be version **5.0**.
3. Set **Plugin Location** to the directory where you installed Unreal (choosing this folder will allow Bridge to install the plugins automatically.)
4. Choose the location of your project folder as the default location under **Default Project**.

> **Note**
> Should you export your character as an Unreal asset only and then later wish to bring your character into Maya, Blender, or another third-party application, you can either download it again from Bridge but change the export settings so that **Export Target** is set to Maya or Blender, *or* export your character as an FBX directly from Unreal using the Level Sequencer.

Once done, you can find the **Export** button in the same panel as shown in *Figure 2.47*.

An alternative and advisable way of bringing your character into the correct project safely is by utilizing the Bridge plugin within your Unreal project. This plugin comes enabled in UE5 by default. It's a mini version of Bridge that is launched exclusively from within Unreal. To use Bridge from Unreal, navigate to the **Content** folder at the bottom of your screen and click on the **+ADD** button. Here, you will see **Add Quixel Content**; click on it. You can see both of these highlighted in *Figure 2.51*:

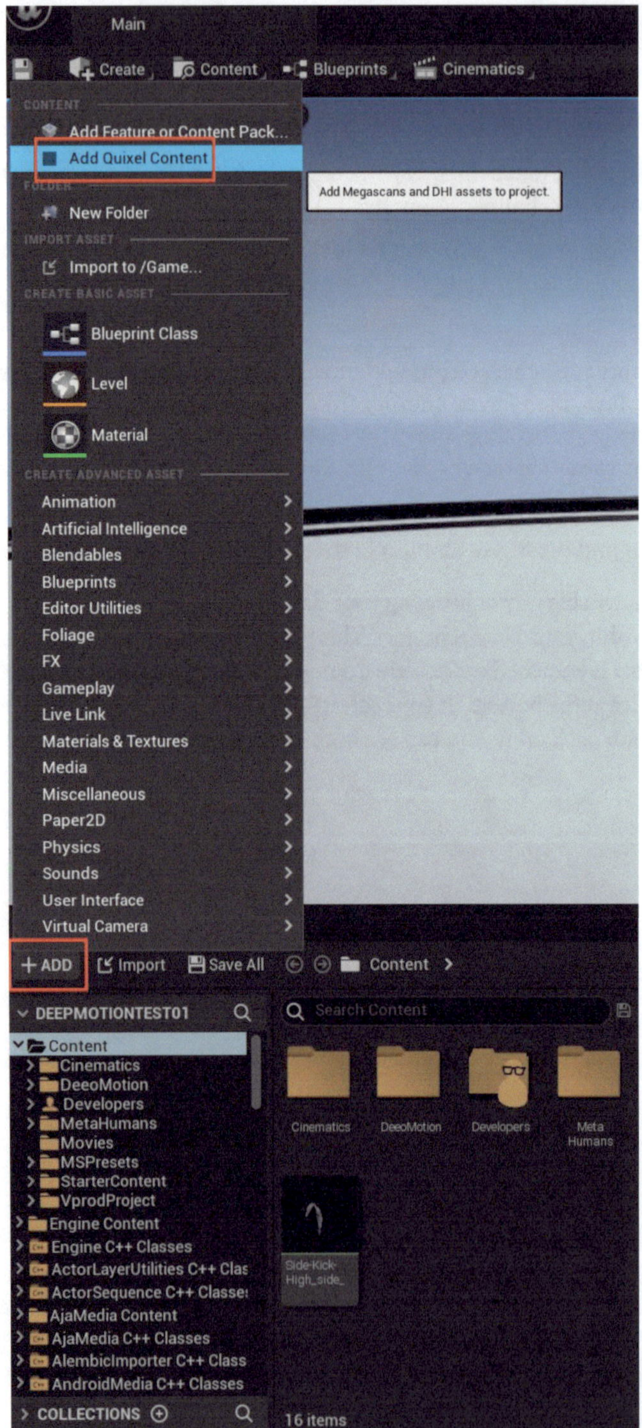

Figure 2.51: Loading Quixel Bridge from within the Content folder in Unreal 5

You may be asked to sign in again at this point. Once signed in using your Epic Games credentials, you'll see your MetaHuman's content and a similar interface where you can download and add the character directly within the open Unreal project.

The advantage of doing it this way is that there is less chance of user error of accidentally exporting your character to the wrong project folder. Also, if your plugins haven't been installed, the Quixel importer that you engaged when clicking **+ADD** will check to see whether the plugins have been installed and will automatically install them for you after prompting you at the bottom right of the screen; we will look at this in more detail in this section.

Processing in the background

UE5 will bring the files that have been downloaded to your machine into Unreal Engine. Simply put, Bridge saves the relative files into a folder called **MetaHumans**, which can be found in the **Content** folder of your Unreal project. If you don't have the MetaHumans plugins installed (such as the Hair Grooms plugin), don't worry – this is where the mini Bridge plugin saves the day by installing them automatically during the export step.

At the bottom of the screen, various notifications regarding all the MetaHumans-related plugins will appear. It may ask you to click **Enable Missing** regarding plugins. Be sure to hit **Enable Missing**, as demonstrated in *Figure 2.52*:

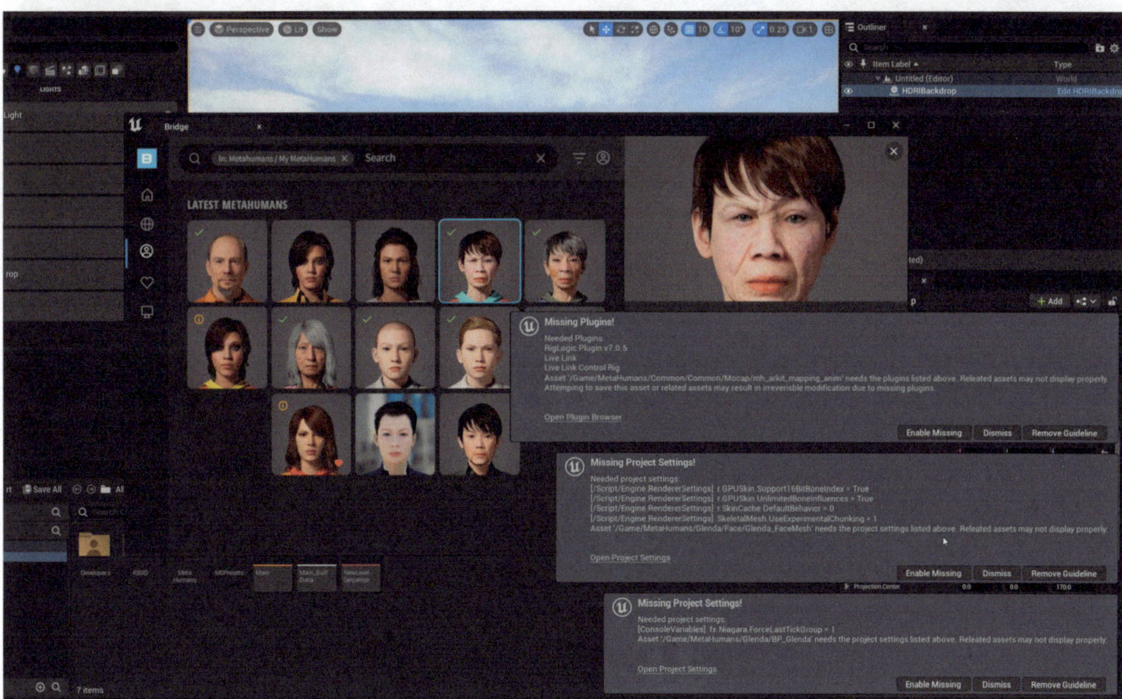

Figure 2.52: Missing plugins and project settings

In addition, UE5 will also compute things such as skin weights and compiling shaders. This will take a couple of minutes and you won't be able to use Unreal Editor while this is happening.

When finished, look for the **MetaHumans** folder that's been created in the **Content Browser** area within your UE5 project, as shown in *Figure 2.53*. All your MetaHuman characters will be imported into this folder; they will be created the first time you go through the export process:

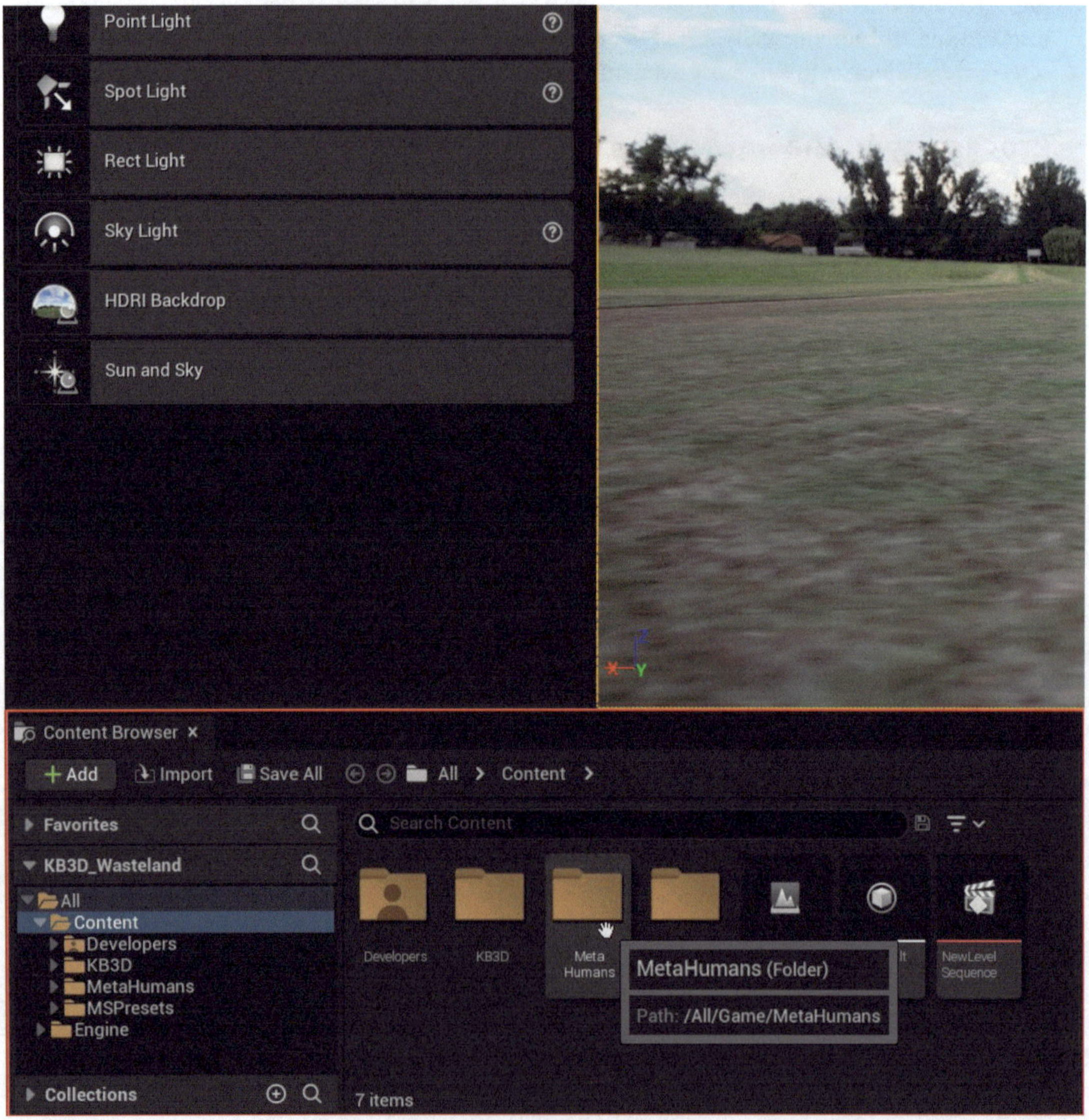

Figure 2.53: The MetaHumans folder

Inside that, you'll see a folder with your character's name on it. Open that and you'll see a little thumbnail of your character. In my case, it's called **BP_Glenda** (BP stands for **Blueprint**).

Figure 2.54 shows that I've brought my character into the viewport. I did this by simply dragging and dropping the Blueprint into the viewport:

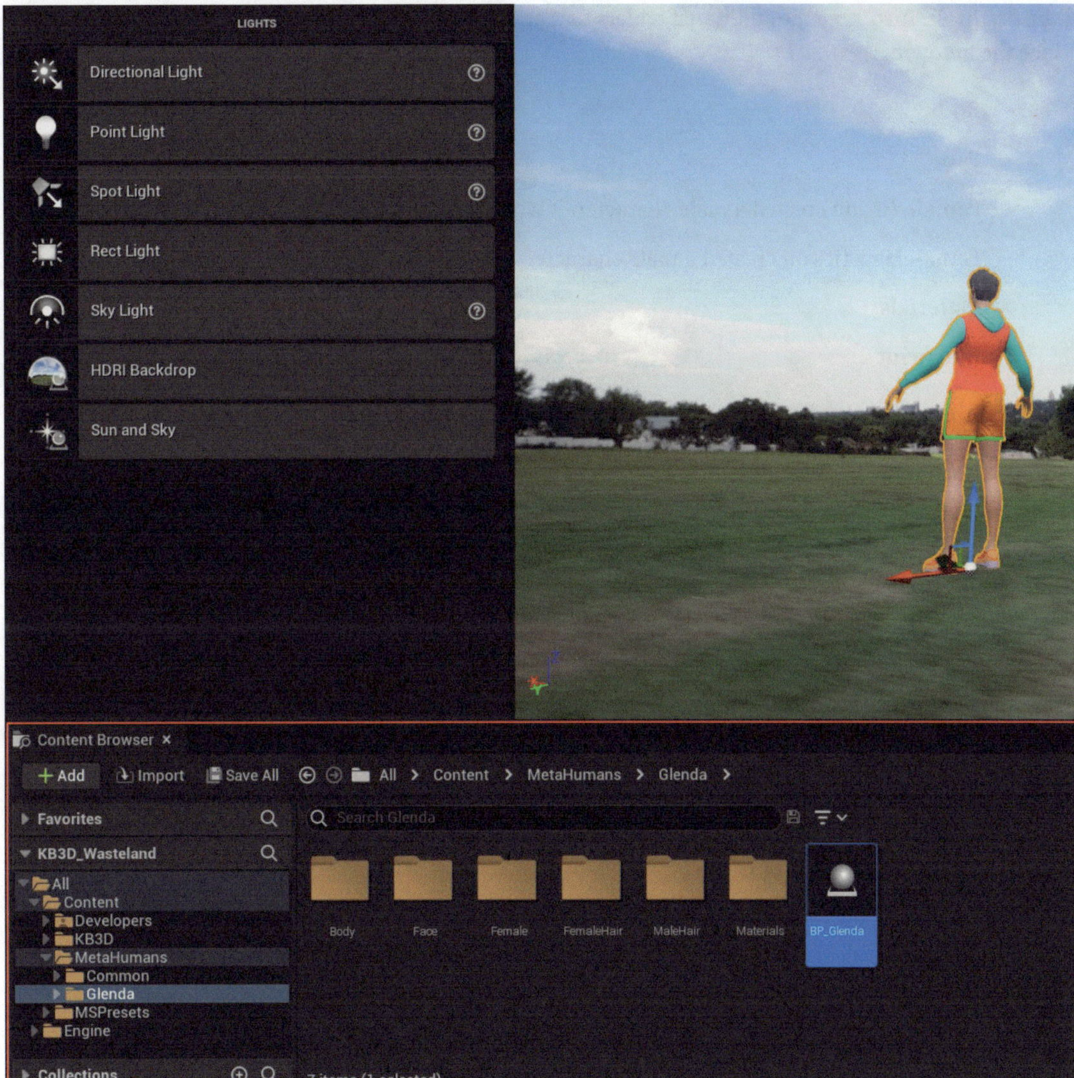

Figure 2.54: Dragging and dropping the Blueprint

> **Note**
>
> You can edit your scene at any time. In *Figure 2.54*, I used a blank template and dragged and dropped the HDRI backdrop into my scene to give me an easy but realistic lighting setup.

Feel free to drag and drop your character Blueprint anywhere in your viewport so that you can start inspecting it. Also, note the additional folders that are created within your character folder. You should see the following:

- **Body**
- **Face**
- **Female** (if you created a male character, it would say **Male**)
- **FemaleHair** (if you created a male character, it would say **MaleHair**)
- **Materials**
- **Blueprint**

You can browse through these folders to find the various texture maps.

In this section, we focused on how to get your custom MetaHuman into Unreal Engine. This is where you're likely to notice just how much data is involved in each character by the download and export time required. We have just begun to look at Unreal Engine and the folder structure behind the characters, but rest assured, you will become much more familiar with them by the end of the next chapter.

Summary

In this chapter, we learned how to get up and running with the MHC, all the various parameters that we can use to customize our characters, and some best practices to aid our design process.

We also learned a little about how textures and shaders work and how they are used to provide specific results. In addition to learning about all the available design tools, we learned a little about optimization with the use of LODs.

While we've gone through many of the editable attributes such as the body, face, eyes, hair, clothing, and all of the presets to choose from, we also looked at the **Move** and **Sculpt** tools, which we can use to fine-tune our characters and introduce asymmetry.

Finally, we learned about the download and export stage and some workarounds to some known problems, such as only the Bridge plugin recognizing the UE5 installation.

We leave this chapter having brought our custom character into the engine, but now, we need to learn how to animate our MetaHuman. To do this, in the next chapter, we will explore the concepts of Blueprints, what they are, and what we need to do with them to bring our characters to life.

Part 2: Exploring Blueprints, Body Motion Capture, and Retargeting

In *Part 2* of this book, we will first look at what Blueprints are in Unreal Engine and how to use them with our MetaHumans. Then, we will look at different methods of body motion capturing and how to retarget motion capture data to our character.

This part includes the following chapters:

- *Chapter 3, Diving into the MetaHuman Blueprint*
- *Chapter 4, Retargeting Animations*
- *Chapter 5, Retargeting Animations with Mixamo*
- *Chapter 6, Adding Motion Capture with DeepMotion*

3 Diving into the MetaHuman Blueprint

In the previous chapter, we exported a MetaHuman character using Quixel Bridge and the Quixel Bridge plugin inside UE5. We brought a number of assets into the engine – while most of the assets were images and meshes, the glue to hold them all together was the Blueprint.

In this chapter, you will be introduced to Blueprints, including what they are and what they are used for. Using Blueprints, you will learn the first steps required to prepare your MetaHuman for animation, repurposing motion capture data from another character that we will import into a project. We will then edit features within the skeletons of both our MetaHuman and the Unreal Engine Mannequin.

So, in this chapter, we will cover the following topics:

- What are Blueprints?
- Opening a Blueprint
- Importing and editing skeletons

Technical requirements

To complete this chapter, you will need the technical requirements detailed in *Chapter 1* and the MetaHuman that we imported into UE5 in *Chapter 2*.

What are Blueprints?

So, what on earth is a Blueprint? If that's what you're thinking, I wouldn't blame you.

Blueprints are effectively a visual representation of templates written in the C++ programming language. Epic Games could have easily just created a console within Unreal to let users write C++ code but because not everyone is familiar with the C++ programming language, they created an easy way for artists to edit the relevant code. In addition, for those familiar with C++, Blueprints are a very handy way of creating tools that are relatively easy for artists to use.

The good news is that you don't really need to spend a huge amount of time using them when working on a MetaHuman character and animating it, but they are an integral part of the process and are being used by the engine in the background. It would be good practice for artists to get to grips with the fundamentals of Blueprints, as they are a fantastic way of reducing repetitive work; however, it must also be said that there are tasks that simply can't be carried out without working with Blueprints.

In terms of functionality with the MetaHumans character, Blueprints essentially hold most of the information relating to the character in one place and we use the Blueprint to make changes to our character. The changes we will make relate to how the character is animated, and by the end of this chapter, you will be familiar with what areas of the Blueprint you will need to edit to animate your characters correctly.

You can look at a Blueprint as if it were a driver. Its function is to drive the mesh of your character using a skeleton. It does this by driving the bones, which in turn drive the skin. Because there is a cloth simulation at work, the skin drives the cloth. Because there is also a hair simulation at work, the skin drives the hair. All of this is driven by the Blueprint.

But where does the Blueprint get the initial instructions? Well, the answer is *you*. You tell the Blueprint what kind of instruction it will use to animate the character, and then you point to various animation modes for the Blueprint to use. There are just a couple of different types of animations that can be applied, listed here:

- **Prerecorded data**: This is simply a file that has motion data, usually one file for the face and another file for the body. We can get these files from plenty of resources. We can also use animation files that come with the third-person game template in UE5 or create our own files by recording our own motion capture data (we call these **Takes**).
- **Live motion capture data**: The Blueprint gives us the option of using live data that is coming from a piece of hardware, such as the following:
    - An iPhone for facial motion capture.
    - Software such as Faceware Studio, utilizing a video camera.
    - Motion capture suits also provide us with live data via third-party software. Live data is information relating to the transformation and/or rotation of bones that is streamed in real-time into the engine.
- **Animation Blueprints**: These are primarily used for game logic, but they can use the same animation file types used in prerecorded data or saved when using live motion capture data that we would use in traditional 3D animation filmmaking.

Blueprints also allow for new data taken in from the user, such as a player in a game, and will engage a relevant animation file depending on what the player does. For example, if the player runs, the Blueprint will execute the `run` animation file, which drives the character to run. That file would usually be in the format of FBX or BVH. The files are referred to as **assets**.

So, let's look at the Blueprint inside the engine.

Opening a Blueprint

Once you've successfully imported a MetaHuman character into UE5, you'll see a few folders and a file starting with the **BP_** prefix, as shown in Figure 3.1. The folder contains all the assets required to display your character.

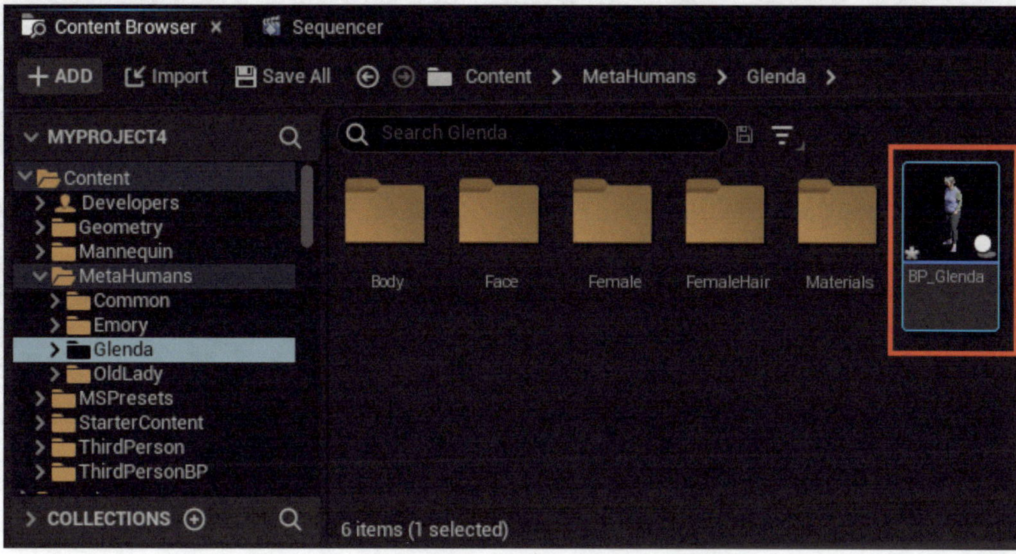

Figure 3.1: The Blueprint inside the Content Browser

When you double-click on the Blueprint, this will open your character's Blueprint. You will see that the screen is made up of six tabs, as shown in *Figure 3.2*:

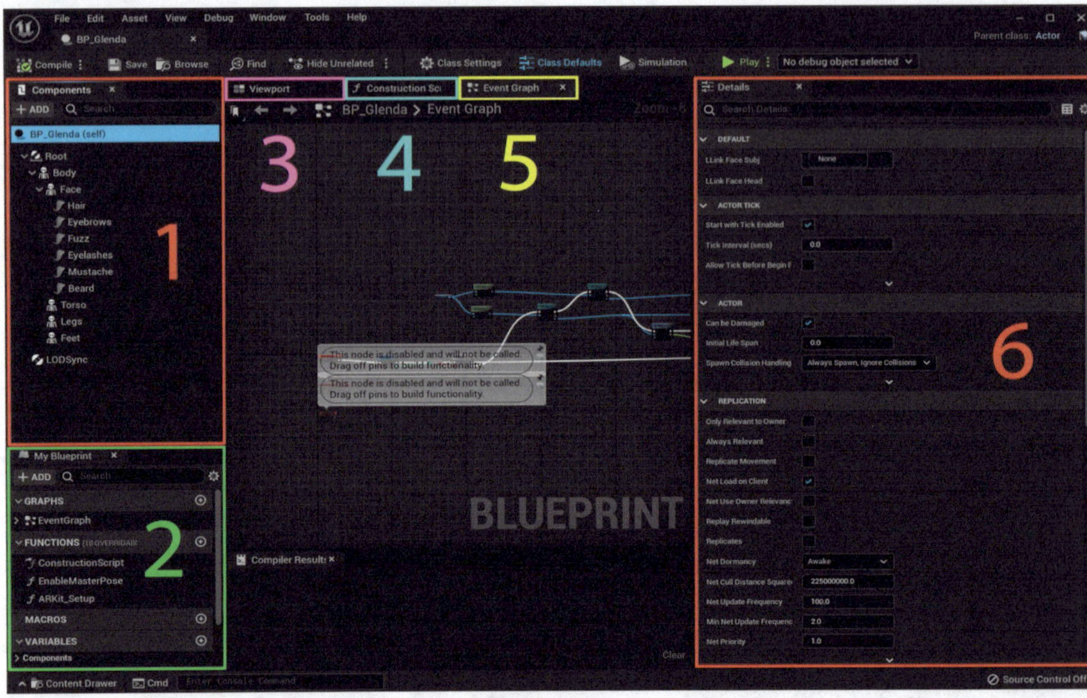

Figure 3.2: The six panels of the character Blueprint

Let's break down the tabs:

1. **Components**: This is where we can select what part of the MetaHuman we wish to edit. We can also add additional components, such as meshes, cameras, and lights to our MetaHuman.
2. **My Blueprint**: Here, we can see what functional elements are associated with our MetaHuman, such as the ARKit setup, which allows for facial motion capture to be directed to our character.
3. **Viewport**: This gives us a view of our character without showing us the rest of the level. This comes in handy if we have brought a character into a busy scene and wish to inspect or edit our character without the distraction of a busy environment.
4. **Construction Script**: A construction script allows the engine to read and write data to the Blueprint regardless of which level we are using. In the game world, this is useful, as the construction script can hold data such as character health. For the purposes of what we are using our MetaHumans for, we won't need to make any changes to this.
5. **Event Graph**: The event graph contains important information relating to events. An event can be a game starting or the result of pressing a particular key on the keyboard. In terms of MetaHumans, the event graph determines what LOD values the character should use. For example, if the camera moves far away from the character, that is an event that triggers the character to display an LOD value greater than 0.

6. **Details**: This is where we do most of our editing. It is context-sensitive, so we will see different information depending on what we have clicked on in the **Components** tab. For instance, the body will give us different parameters to edit other than the face.

As we just mentioned, when it comes to editing our characters, we do so in the **Details** panel by editing various assets. Many of these assets are image files but many editors also allow you to further refine your character. In fact, in some instances, you are given even greater control over many aspects of your character. This additional control can bring even further realism to your character than you could have achieved with the MHC alone.

To see an example of how much extra editing power you have, click on **Face** within the **Components** tab and then double-click on one of the **Eye materials** options contained in the **Details** tab. Depending on which eye you chose, it would be labeled **M_EyeRefractive_Inst_L**.

Once you've opened the material editor for that eye, you can edit certain attributes that weren't available to edit in MHC. For example, you can edit the cloudiness of the eye and ambient occlusion within the iris, which adds a lot of depth to the eye, as demonstrated in *Figure 3.3*:

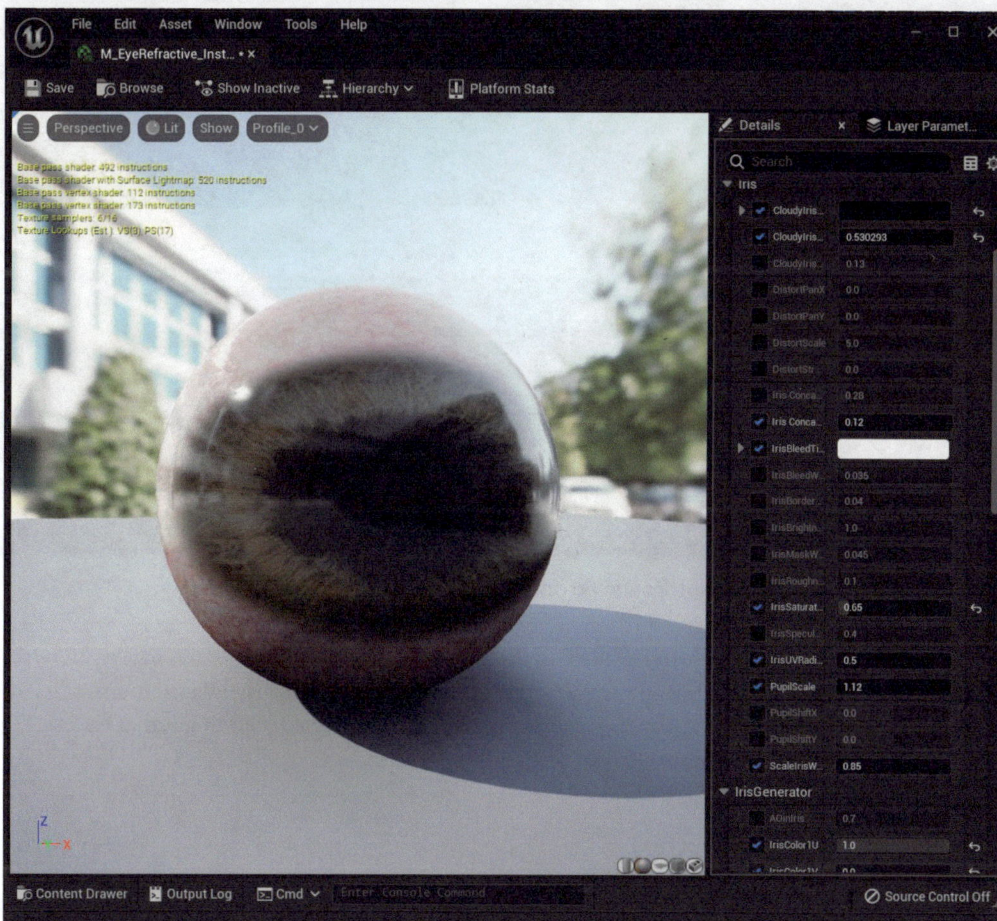

Figure 3.3: Editing the eye material

> **Note**
>
> Adding further edits to your character using parameters exclusively available in Blueprints won't affect your original design in MHC. You will always have a safe backup copy via Bridge.

Just as a reminder, the Blueprint acts like a driver and the character subfolders act like passengers. While you can access all these components directly through the character Blueprint, you can also gain access by diving into the individual subfolders; there may be occasions where you'd prefer to have multiple folders open at a time, so in many cases, it just comes down to personal preference.

Using the folder structure to navigate around the Blueprint

To show you how to navigate using folders, as seen in *Figure 3.4*, I have gone directly into the **Hoodie** folder and double-clicked on the **Hoodie Material** asset to change its color:

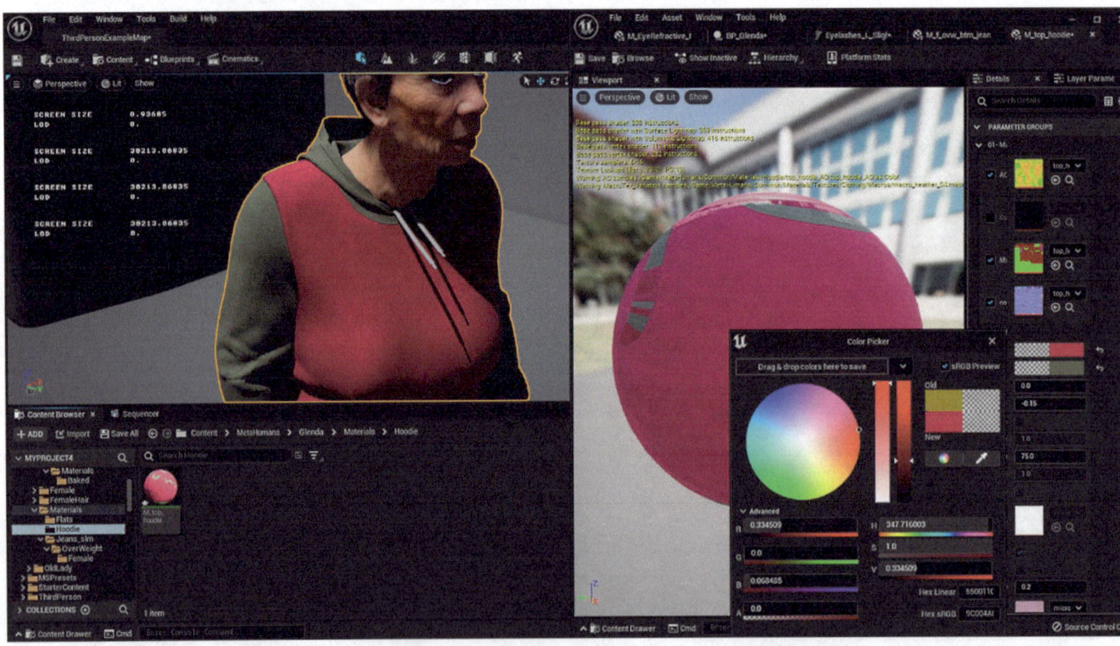

Figure 3.4: Further editing done directly within the folder structure

As you can see, there is even greater control of this particular asset than we would have gotten from just MHC alone; for example, using the color picker tool to change our MetaHuman's hoodie. You may remember from *Chapter 2, Creating Characters in the MetaHuman Interface*, that we used the MHC color tools to make changes.

Navigating around the Blueprint without using folders

In *Figure 3.5*, you can see that the same edit is taking place, but we are using the character Blueprint to edit the same asset. Both methods are equally effective.

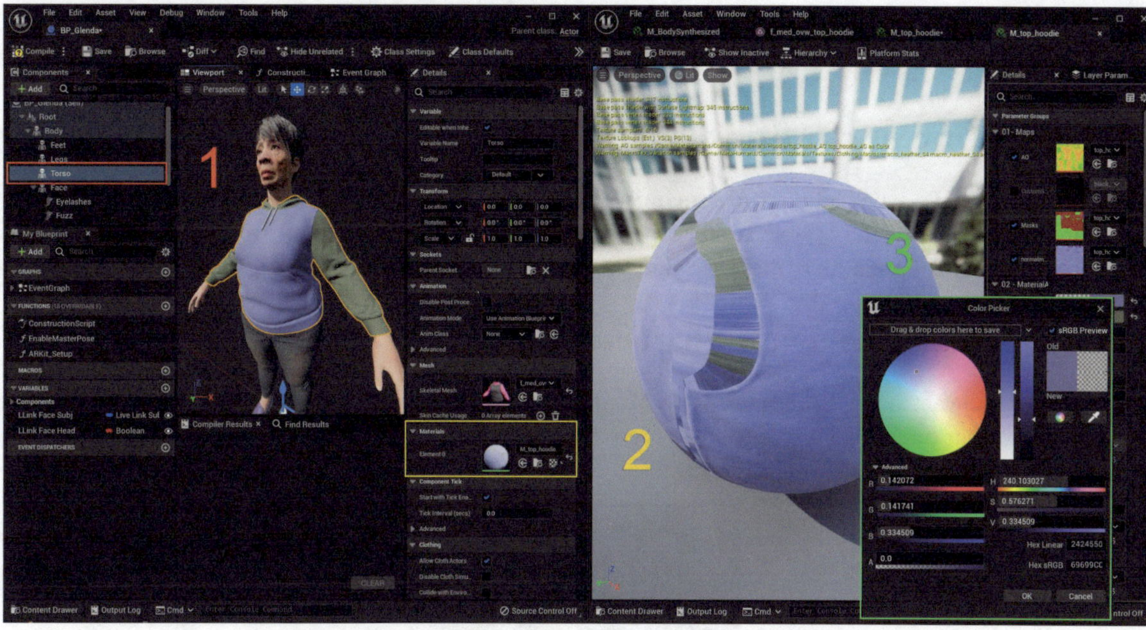

Figure 3.5: Editing a color inside the character Blueprint

You can see in *Figure 3.5* that I followed the following steps:

1. I chose **Torso** from the **Components** tab.
2. I clicked on the **Material** element slot, which in turn opened **Material Editor**.
3. I clicked on the current color, which opened **Color Picker**, allowing me to change the color.

While there are many additional editors within the Blueprints relating to the appearance of the characters, they are mostly for refining materials. For the most part, the results are subtle, but you can completely change color schemes.

As daunting as this all looks, rest assured that you will only really be editing a tiny section of the Blueprint. At the very least, you will just need to choose what kind of animation you want to drive for your character, and for repurposing animation from another character, we only need to edit skeletal details.

It makes sense to get up and running with some body animation first. UE5 comes with several starter packs to help us. One of the starter packs is a third-person game that comes with a **Mannequin** character that is rigged with a skeleton. It also comes with a few animations that we can use to test out our own character.

For the remainder of this chapter, we will look at Blueprints with the view to repurposing the animation from the starter game pack and applying it to our own character in the next chapter.

Importing and editing skeletons

In this section, we will add our **Mannequin** character to our project. Then, to be able to retarget animation from one character to another, the source and target characters both have to have skeletons. We will be looking at both of these skeletons in the following sections.

Adding the Mannequin character

To start, we want to use the skeleton of the **Mannequin** character that comes shipped with Unreal. To add it to your project, all you need to do is go to **Content Browser**, click on the **+ADD** button, and choose **Add Feature or Content Pack...**:

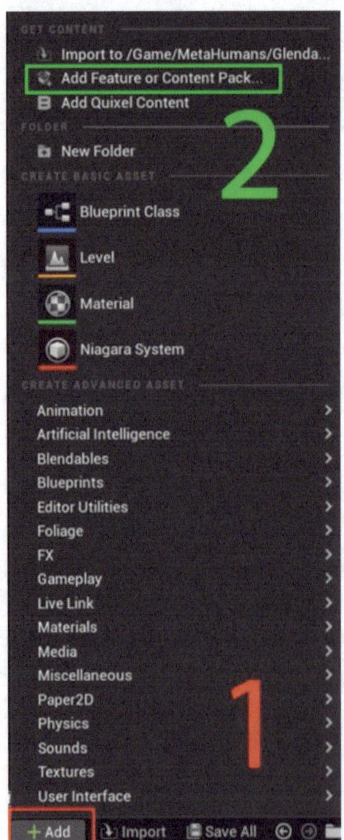

Figure 3.6: Adding a content pack

Once you've clicked on **Add Feature or Content Pack...**, you'll see a pop-up window where you can choose **Third Person** from the **Blueprint** feature tab:

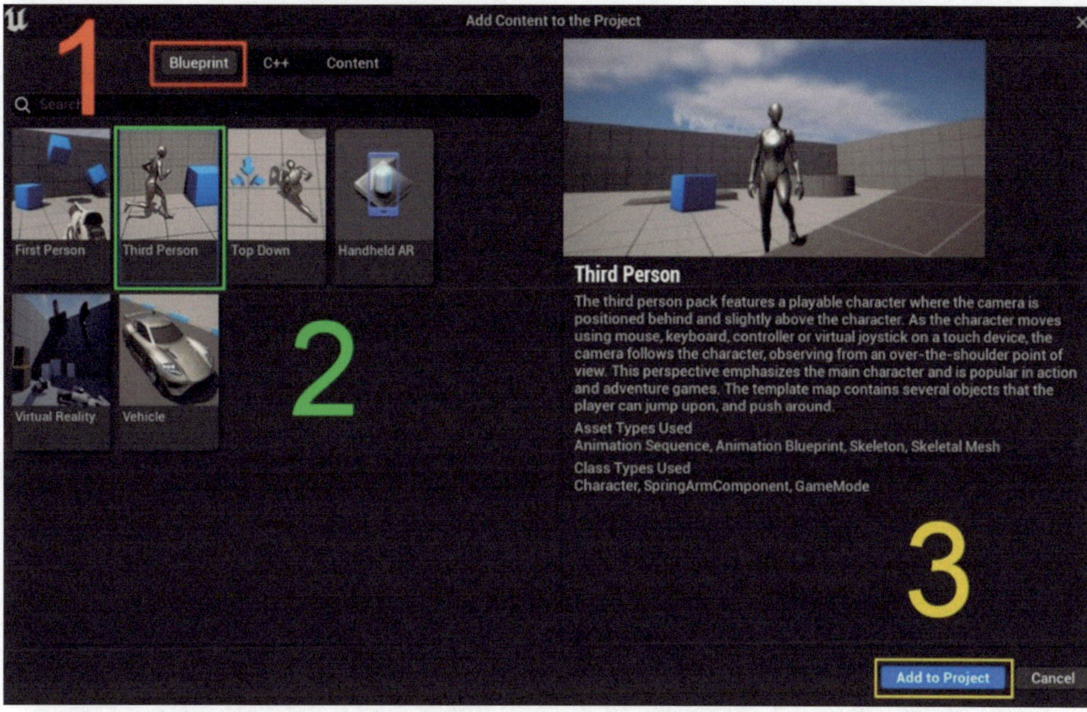

Figure 3.7: Add Content to the Project

The reason we choose **Third Person** is that it has a full character, including a mannequin, in the project, which we can repurpose. Then, click on **Add to Project**. This will load the project into your Content Browser.

You'll notice that there are now two new folders in your Content Browser: **Mannequin** and **Third PersonBP**.

What we want to do at this stage is edit the **Mannequin** skeleton so that the structure, naming convention, and animation method are the same as for our MetaHuman. That way, we can repurpose the animation from **Mannequin** and apply it to our MetaHuman.

As mentioned earlier, there are two ways we can go about editing. We could go through **Mannequin**'s folder structure and search for the skeleton Blueprints, but we will play it safe and look for the main character Blueprint and navigate our way to the skeleton Blueprint from there.

Moving forward, here are the steps we need to take:

1. Edit the **Mannequin** skeleton's retargeting options.
2. Edit the MetaHuman skeleton's retargeting options.

So, let's get started.

Editing the Mannequin skeleton's retargeting options

In this section, we are going to tell the skeleton of Unreal Engine's **Mannequin** character and our MetaHuman character that we are only interested in their rotational data.

Once we've added the **Third Person** content pack into the project, we'll see a new folder called **ThirdPersonBP**, so that's a good start. You can see that in *Figure 3.8*:

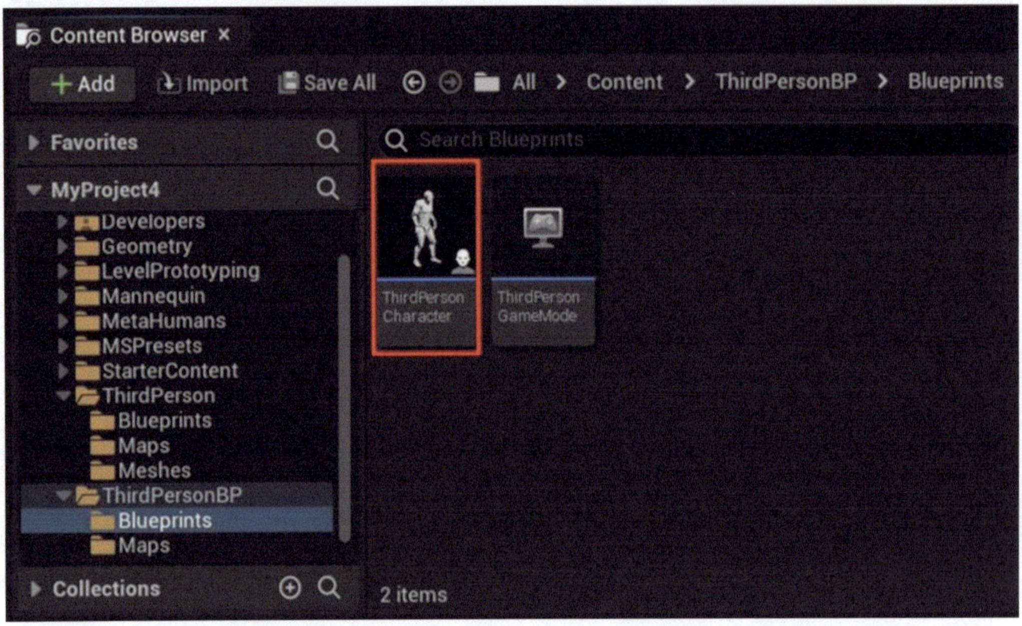

Figure 3.8: The ThirdPerson Character Blueprint

In the **ThirdPersonBP** folder is another folder labeled **Blueprints,** and within that is **ThirdPersonCharacter**, which we need to edit. Double-click the Blueprint to open it.

In the **Components** tab, when clicking on **Mesh (CharacterMesh0)** as per *Figure 3.9*, you'll notice the **Details** panel on the right change. Under **Mesh**, you'll see **Skeletal Mesh.** Double-click on the little thumbnail for **SK_Mannequinn:**

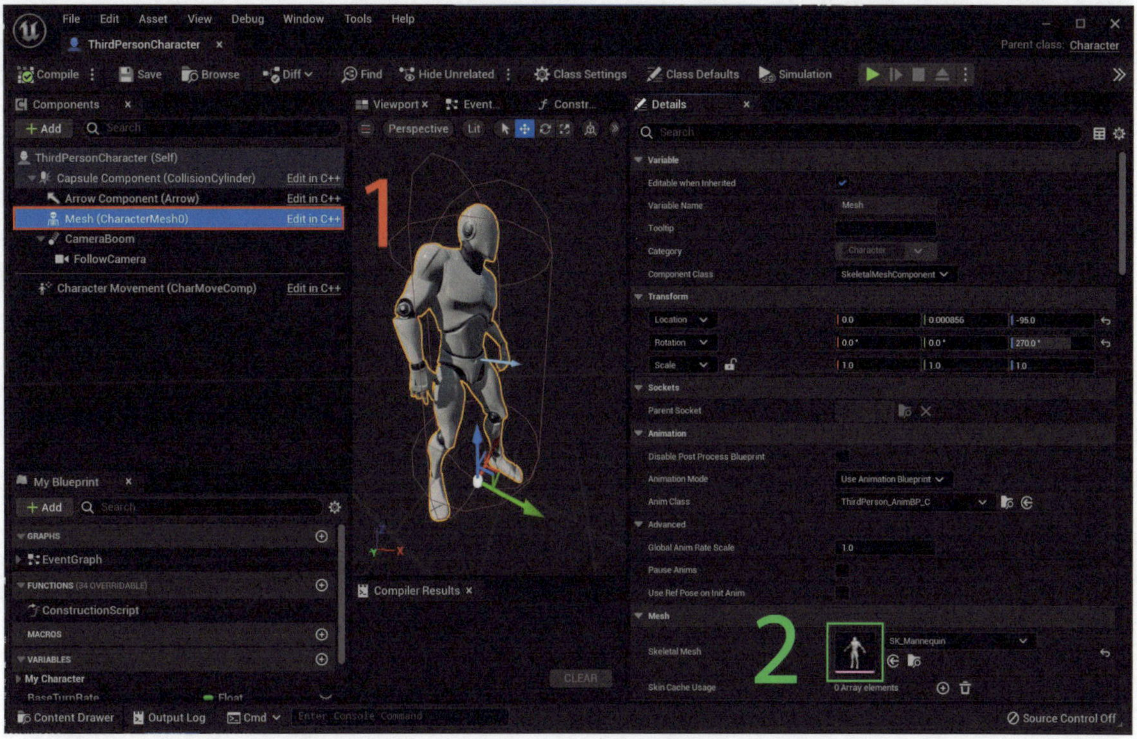

Figure 3.9: Accessing the Skeletal Mesh editor tab

This will open an additional tab in the Blueprint that will contain two more tabs, as well as a viewport showing **Mannequin** and its skeleton, as shown in *Figure 3.10*:

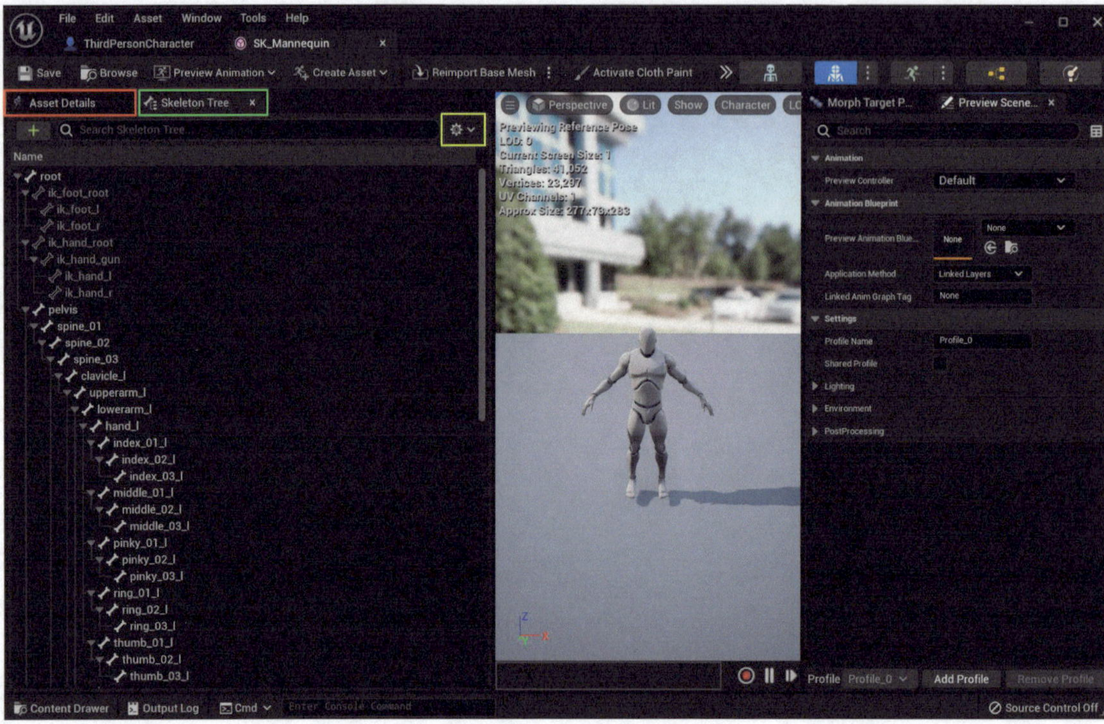

Figure 3.10: Inside SK_Mannequinn

The two tabs are as follows:

- **Asset Details**: Provides us with a lot of options should we want to edit the character for which we are repurposing animation. However, we are only interested in this character's rig and the animations that are associated with it.
- **Skeleton Tree**: Where we want to do most of our editing. This shows us the relationship that each bone has with the others. Every bone is connected to **root**. If the **root** part moves or rotates, the rest of the bones in the hierarchy will move. Bones lowest in the hierarchy will have the least influence.

In *Figure 3.10*, in the **Skeleton Tree** tab, you can see that every bone is named, from **root** down to **thumb**. What we want to do is make sure that the retargeting option is set to the skeleton, but don't worry, we don't need to meticulously check through each bone. We can do this in four mouse clicks:

1. Click on the cog.
2. Select **Show Retargeting Options**.

3. Right-click on **pelvis**.
4. Then, left-click on **Recursively Set Translation Retargeting Skeleton**.

Let me walk you through those steps in more detail. So, click on the cog highlighted in *Figure 3.11*:

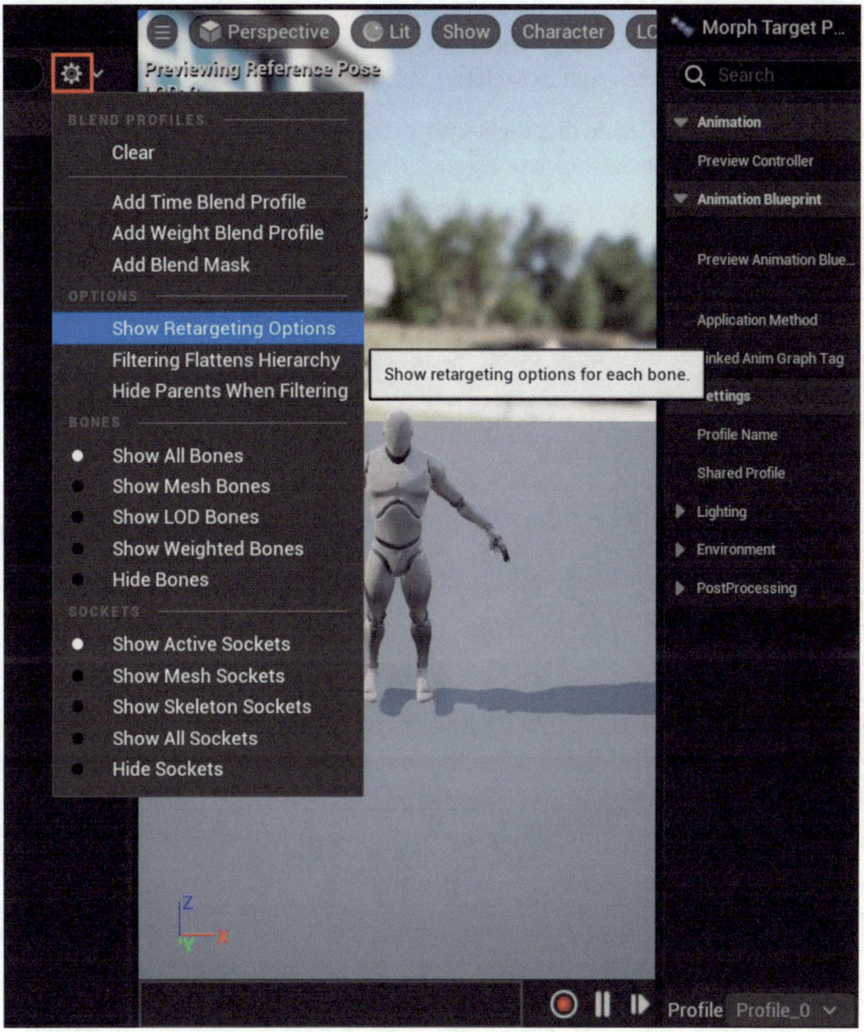

Figure 3.11: Show Retargeting Options

Under **OPTIONS**, click **Show Retargeting Options**. All we are doing is making sure that the hierarchy of the skeleton is being used effectively to drive the animation of each bone. Because all the bones are connected in a hierarchy, moving one bone can have a chain reaction effect on the whole body naturally. This is known as **Inverse Kinematics** (**IK**). In some animation data, every bone has animation, so the natural hierarchy of the skeleton isn't very important. For IK animation, not all animation, such as rotation and transformation, for every bone is carried through; therefore, relying on an IK solution is important.

We are going to take advantage of the skeletal hierarchy in the next step because that is how the MetaHuman characters are designed. Because there is a bone hierarchy within this skeletal system, we can quickly change the nature of the bones' translation by utilizing a handy retargeting option. In this case, we want to set **Translation** to **Skeleton**, starting with the **pelvis** bone.

Fortunately, there is a fast way to do this. Right-click **pelvis** and choose the **Recursively Set Translation Retargeting Skeleton** option, as shown in *Figure 3.12*:

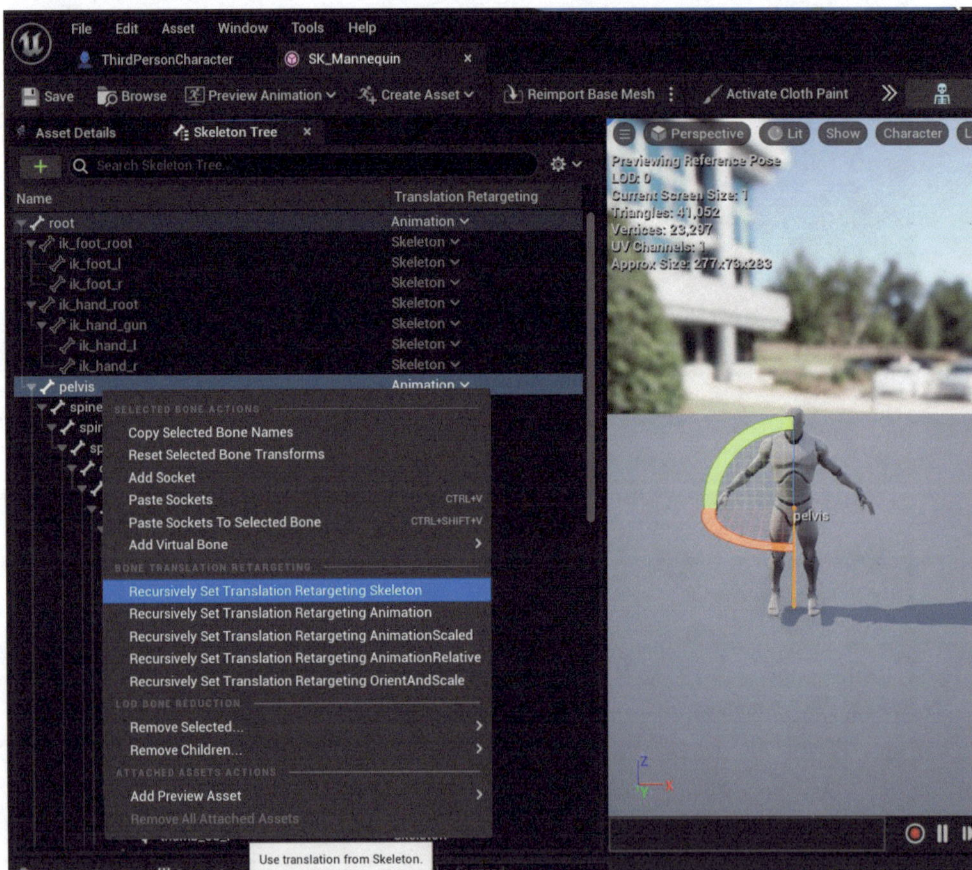

Figure 3.12: Recursively Set Translation Retargeting to Skeleton

You've now set all of the bones from **pelvis** to **skeleton** in one click.

> **Note**
>
> Be sure to hit **Save** in the **Blueprint** tab when you have edited the retargeting options.

In addition to making sure our characters are both using skeletal animation, by doing things this way, we are only retargeting the **rotational data**. Put simply, *this will allow us to retarget the rotation animation of each bone from this character and not the transformation data*. If we copied over the transformation data from the original skeleton to the new skeleton, such as a MetaHumans skeleton, the bones would move disproportionately.

These issues are most notable when the new character has significant proportional differences from the original. For example, if the original skeleton was tall, then its bones would have very different transform data from that of a small character. Its bones would be longer than its smaller counterpart. While the rotation data would be fine, the transform data of the tall character would stretch the small character, as it would try to make the bones occupy the same locations in 3D space despite the rotational values being relatively correct.

In *Figure 3.13*, you can see the correct data transformation. That is to say that the three characters all share the same pose without any drastic stretching or deforming of the meshes. Had the transformational data been carried from character **A** to character **B**, character **B** would be stretched to the same height and character **C** would be squashed to the same height as character **A**.

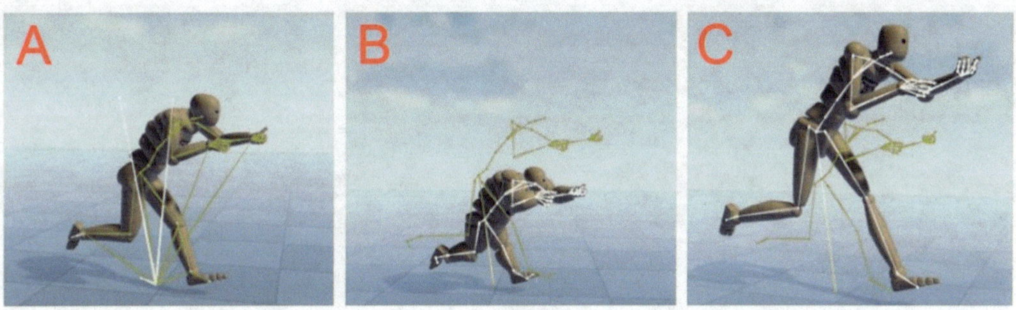

Figure 3.13: Correct translation of motion data

If you find that you have successfully managed to get through all these steps and have animated your MetaHuman, chances are you haven't followed these steps correctly. A common mistake is forgetting to save changes within the Blueprint.

The next step is to edit the retargeting options for the new skeleton, which is our MetaHumans character.

Editing the MetaHuman skeleton's retargeting options

To start editing the MetaHuman skeleton's retargeting options, in your character's Blueprint, click on **Body** in the **Components** tab. Then, in the **Details** tab, double-click the thumbnail next to **Skeletal Mesh** under the **Mesh** section. Don't worry if you don't have an accurate thumbnail of your MetaHuman in the same way you did with **Mannequin**.

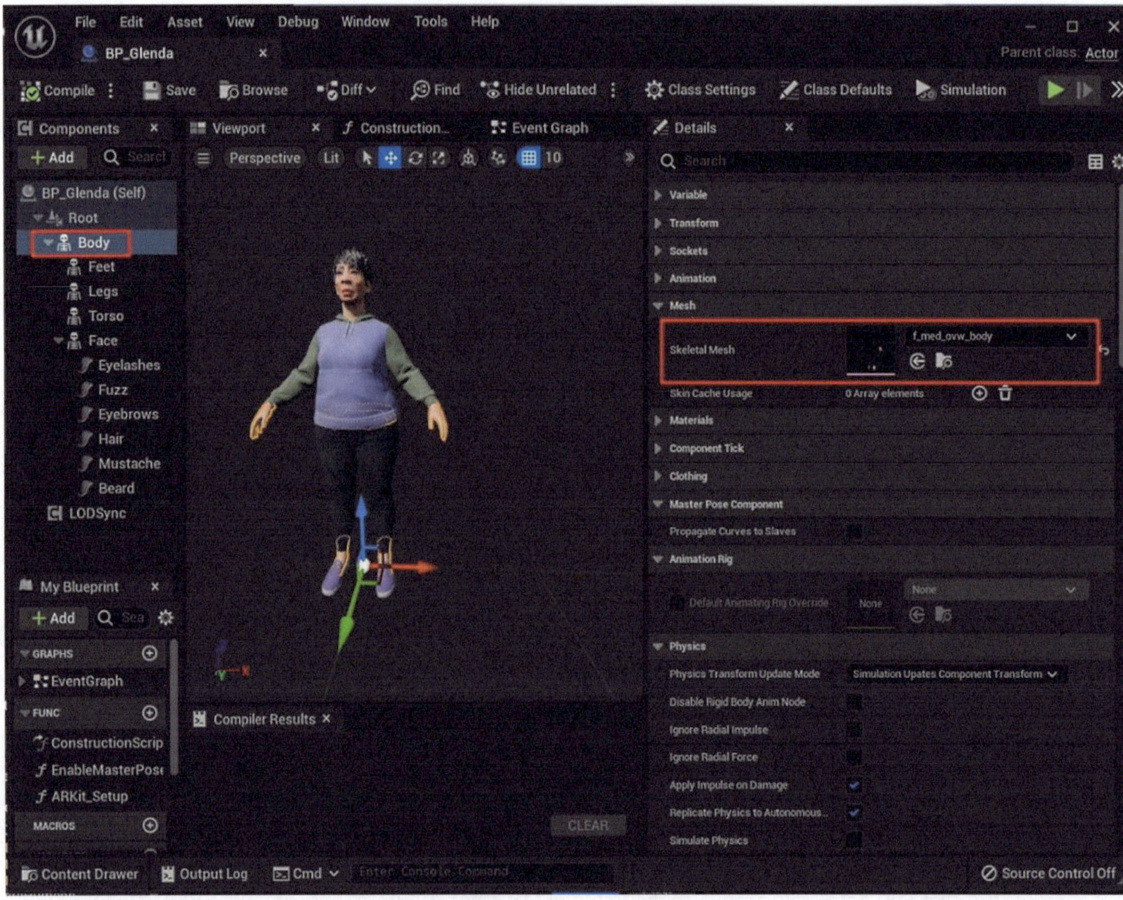

Figure 3.14: Editing the MetaHuman's retargeting options

Once you double-click on the thumbnail, you'll be greeted with the screen shown in *Figure 3.15* (it's an identical tab to the one you saw earlier in *Figure 3.12* when you edited the **Mannequin** skeleton). You just need to follow the exact same steps as we did in the previous section. So, click on the cog and select **Show Retargeting Options**. Then right-click on **pelvis**, and select **Recursively Set Translation Retargeting to Skeleton**:

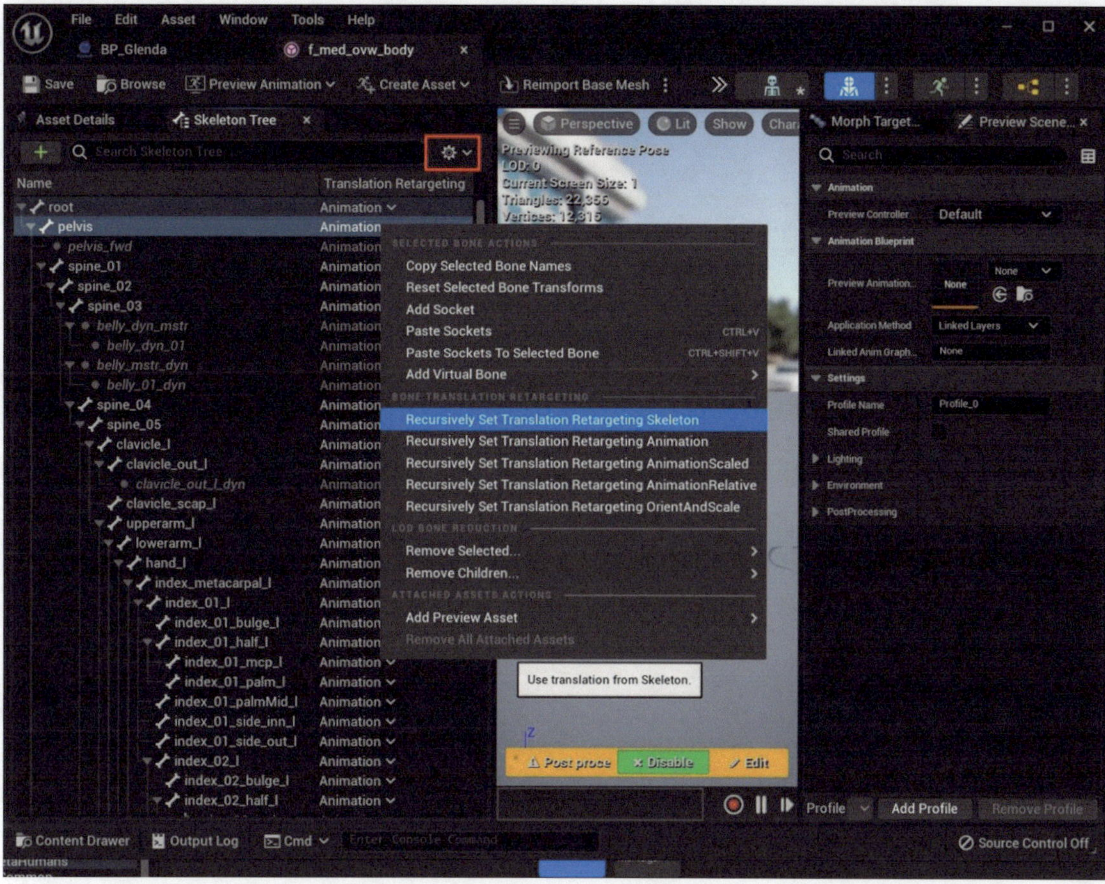

Figure 3.15: Recursively Set Translation Retargeting Skeleton in the MetaHuman Blueprint

After this, save the Blueprint. Now, we have edited both the Mannequin and MetaHuman skeletons, retargeting their options so the two can work together.

Summary

We've covered a lot of ground in this chapter. We've covered some key concepts regarding Blueprints in Unreal, what they are, and what they can be used for. We've done some basic editing of both Unreal's Mannequin character and our own MetaHuman character so that they can effectively speak to each other by setting the translation targeting to **Skeleton** for both. We've also briefly discussed IK and how that solution works with our characters.

In the next chapter, we will jump back into Blueprints to retarget the animation from one character to the next and explore ways to fix any minor yet common problems. We will create IK Rigs for both the Mannequin character and our MetaHuman and use an IK Retargeter to export the animation data onto our character.

4
Retargeting Animations

In the previous chapter, we were introduced to Blueprints and conducted some basic editing to the MetaHuman Blueprint and the Mannequin character Blueprint so that they shared some common settings.

In this chapter, you will be introduced to a new set of tools that we can use to retarget the animation files that come with the Mannequin onto our MetaHuman character: the IK Rig tool and the IK Retargeter tool.

So, in this chapter, we will cover the following topics:

- What is an IK Rig?
- Creating an IK Rig
- Creating the IK chains
- Creating an IK Retargeter
- Importing more animation data

Technical requirements

To complete this chapter, you will need the technical requirements detailed in *Chapter 1*, and the MetaHuman plus the Unreal Engine Mannequin that we imported into UE5 in *Chapter 2*.

What is an IK Rig?

Well, to answer that question, we actually have to ask two questions:

- What is a rig?
- What is IK?

Let's answer them now.

What is a rig?

In 3D animation production, a **rig** is a simplified means of controlling a character's movement, tailored for use by animators. Instead of the animator manipulating the character's bones, a rig provides handles that the animator can quickly identify and select. Many 3D software applications come with rigs that are designed for people and animals. In animation studios, rigs are designed at varying levels of complexity depending on how complex the animation is. Ultimately, the purpose of a rig is to simplify the process of animation. In this chapter, we will take advantage of these simplified rigs for the purpose of applying animation data to them.

The MetaHuman comes with a built-in rig for character animation called an IK Rig. In fact, it comes with an IK Control Rig that allows animators to take full control of all the animation of a MetaHuman character. As you can see in *Figure 4.1*, a rig is a simplified way of manipulating bones:

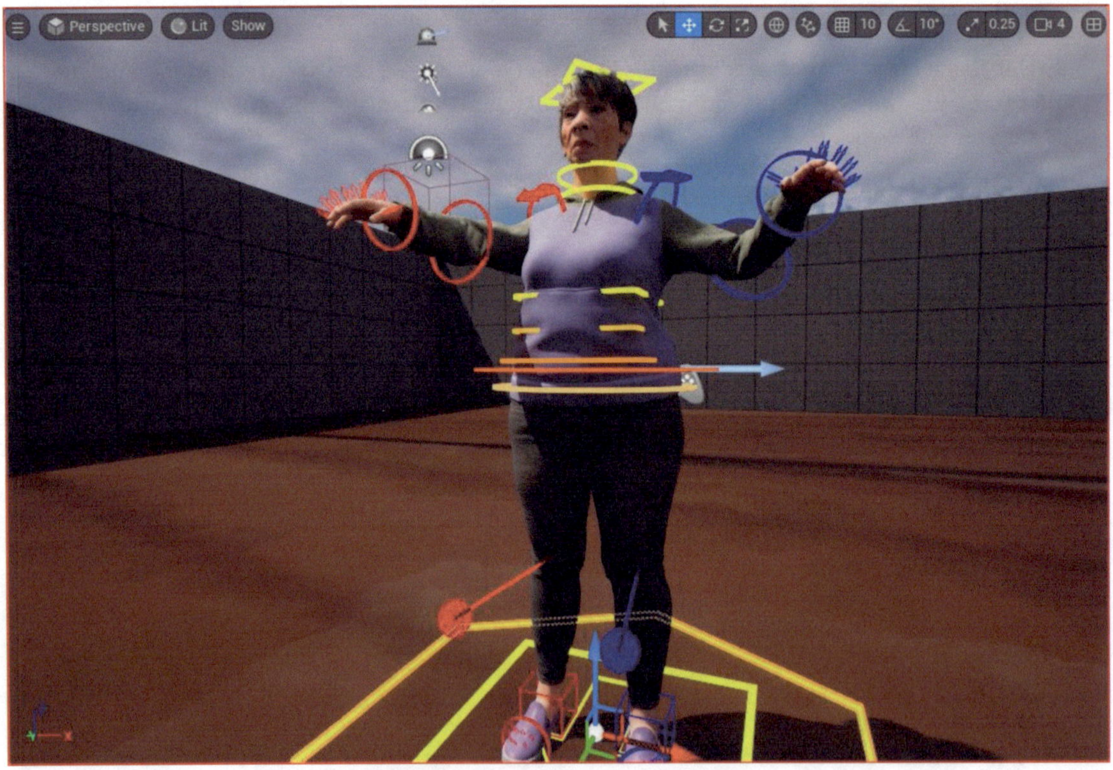

Figure 4.1: MetaHuman IK Control Rig

So, now that we understand what a rig is, let's look at what IK means.

What is IK?

To answer this question, we need to understand that in character animation, we use bones. These bones have a distinctive relationship with one another in terms of how they move; if we want to phrase this in a slightly more technical way, these bones have a distinctive relationship in terms of how their kinetic relationship is defined. These bones exist within a hierarchy of bones, and how they move depends on whether the hierarchy has **Forward Kinematics** (**FK**) or **Inverse Kinematics** (**IK**).

When it comes to human bones, very few can move on all axes and no human bones have the freedom to move 360 degrees on any axis. However, unlike real human bones, computer-generated bones are very simple in their shape and can be displayed as simple lines, cylinders, spheres, pyramids, or capsules. Regardless of their shape, they all contain one or two pivot points that determine the point of rotation for the bone. In addition to the point of rotation, it is also possible for us to define what axis the bones rotate on and what axis they don't. Let's look at *Figure 4.2*, which demonstrates how bones are visualized in UE5. By selecting any bone, we are presented with a gizmo that allows us to edit the rotation of each bone; however, using this for animating is cumbersome, as it is difficult to make a selection or see what we are doing.

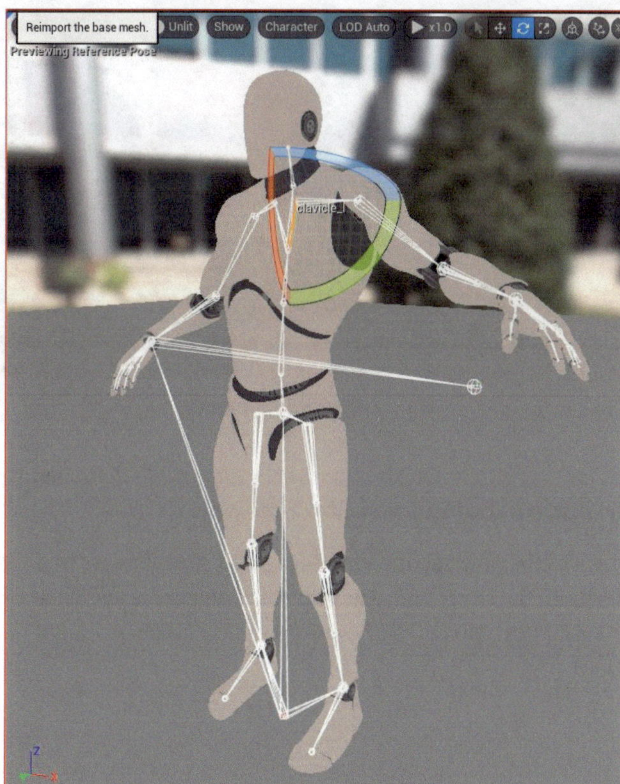

Figure 4.2: A Mannequin bone system in Unreal

Let's think about our shoulder joints as an example. We know that we can swing our arms around in a particular direction, but we soon meet resistance when we try to move in other directions. That resistance in terms of joints is known as a **constraint**.

Now, see *Figure 4.3* for an illustration of a shoulder joint as it appears on a MetaHuman; you can see that we don't have to worry about rotational constraint:

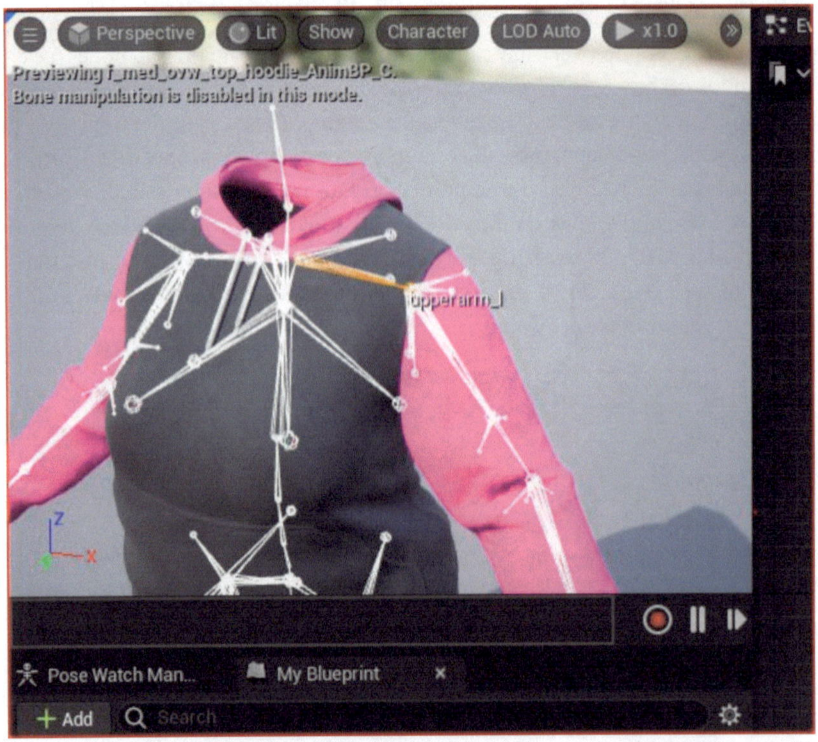

Figure 4.3: Shoulder joint

You'll also note that it isn't very clear which bone is selected, which demonstrates that working with bones directly isn't very practical when it comes to animation.

Regardless, let's get back to the point about what FK and IK actually are. In order to understand FK, first, we need to understand the simple relationship between parent and child (we use this analogy a lot in 3D graphics and robotics). *A child will go wherever the parent goes, but the parent doesn't have to go where the child goes.*

FK

Let's apply the parent-child relationship concept to joints, exploring FK by taking the example of the shoulder. Moving or rotating the hand joint has no effect on the shoulder joint. In fact, we would have to rotate the shoulder joint first, followed by the elbow joint, to affect the position of the hand to get the desired result. In other words, to define the position and rotation of the hand (the end effector), we must calculate the position and rotation of the shoulder and elbow first.

In *Figure 4.4*, I have demonstrated that by rotating **Joint 01** (as seen on the left), I can then rotate **Joint 02** (as seen on the right):

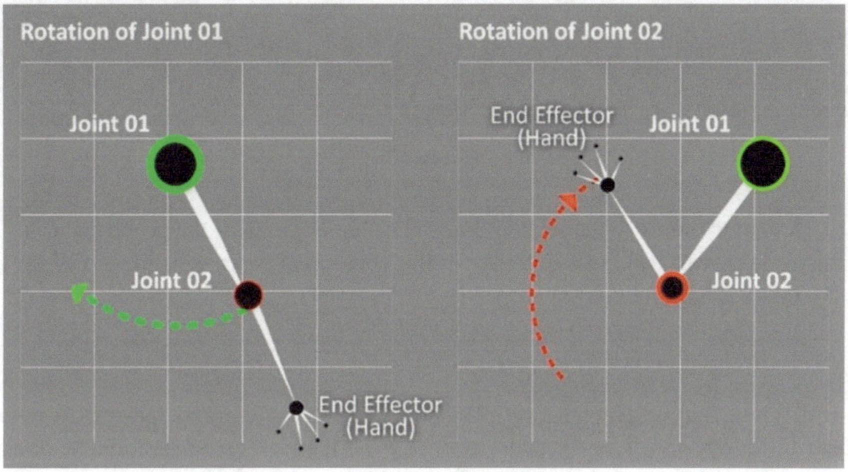

Figure 4.4: FK

Here, we are working out the position of the hand by applying rotations to **Joint 01** (the parent) and **Joint 02** (the child). This is called FK because we are solving the problem of motion by calculating the rotation of the parent first, so we solve this problem in the direction of *parent to child*.

IK

IK gets its name because it solves the problem of motion by calculating the rotation of the child first instead. Taking the example of the shoulder again, the IK solution can determine the rotation of the shoulder joint when the user or artist is affecting the position of the hand end effector (the child in the hierarchy). Therefore, it's the opposite of FK, solving the problem of motion in the *child-to-parent* direction.

In *Figure 4.5*, I have demonstrated that I only need to move the hand, which, in turn, automatically works out the rotation of **Joint 01** plus the rotation and subsequent position of **Joint 02**:

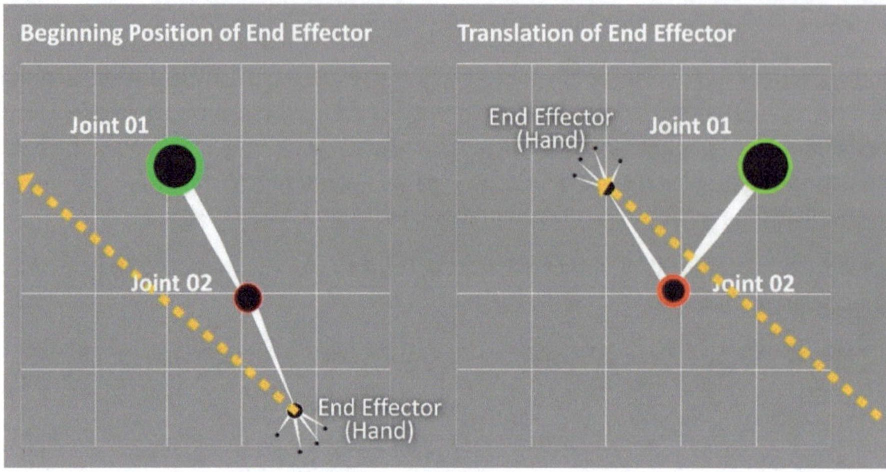

Figure 4.5: IK

In essence, IK is much more dynamic than FK and works out a lot of the problems for us. With IK, we can effectively move a hand of a character as if it were a real person's hand, and all the rest of the bones will follow realistically.

> **Note**
>
> It is worth noting that switching between IK and FK solutions is common practice in animation. The use of IK is often used for the majority of work, as it adds a certain amount of automation to the workflow, whereas FK is put to use for subtle changes and fine-tuning.

You'll be very pleased to know that you don't require a full understanding of FK or IK to work with MetaHumans, particularly when it comes to working with motion capture data, but an understanding does demystify some of the jargon that you are presented with regularly in the process.

In the next section, let's get started with creating our own IK Rigs.

Creating an IK Rig

You may be asking, why do we need to create an IK Rig if MetaHumans already have one? Considering that our goal is to retarget an animation designed for one character (as the source) and apply it to our MetaHuman character (as the target), we need to make sure that the rigs have the correct naming conventions. For example, we need to ensure the left arm of the source matches the left arm of the target; some rigs will refer to **shoulder** as **clavicle**, so we need to ensure the naming convention is the same for both rigs.

So, we are effectively going to create a new IK Rig that translates information from the source and to the target. This will become much more visually apparent as we progress with the chapter and deal with IK chains. The reason we are doing this is that the naming conventions for the source rig could be different from the target rig, so the IK Rig we are going to create for each is effectively just a simple set of instructions to make the translation easier. It also adds the extra benefit of keeping us from editing the original IK Rig of the character.

So, let's create an IK rig for our source:

1. If you remember from the last chapter, we acquired a character from **Third Person Template**. So, inside the **Blueprint** folder, then inside the **Third Person Template** folder, right-click anywhere within that folder and choose **Animation**.
2. You'll see a list of **Animation** tools to choose from. Choose **IK Rig** from the list, as you can see in *Figure 4.6*:

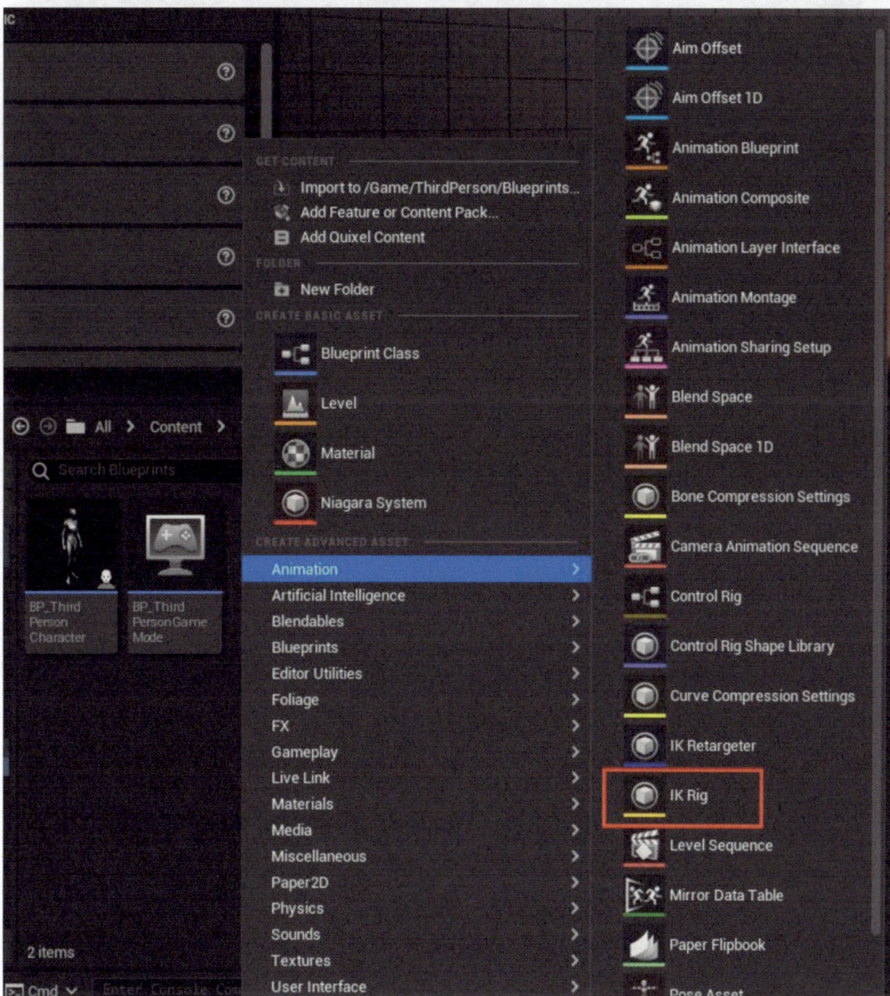

Figure 4.6: Choosing IK Rig from the Animation list

3. Once you have selected **IK Rig**, it will ask you to pick a **Skeletal Mesh** option. At this point, we want to pick the skeleton related to our source character. For this, we want to choose **SK_Mannequin**, which you can see in *Figure 4.7*:

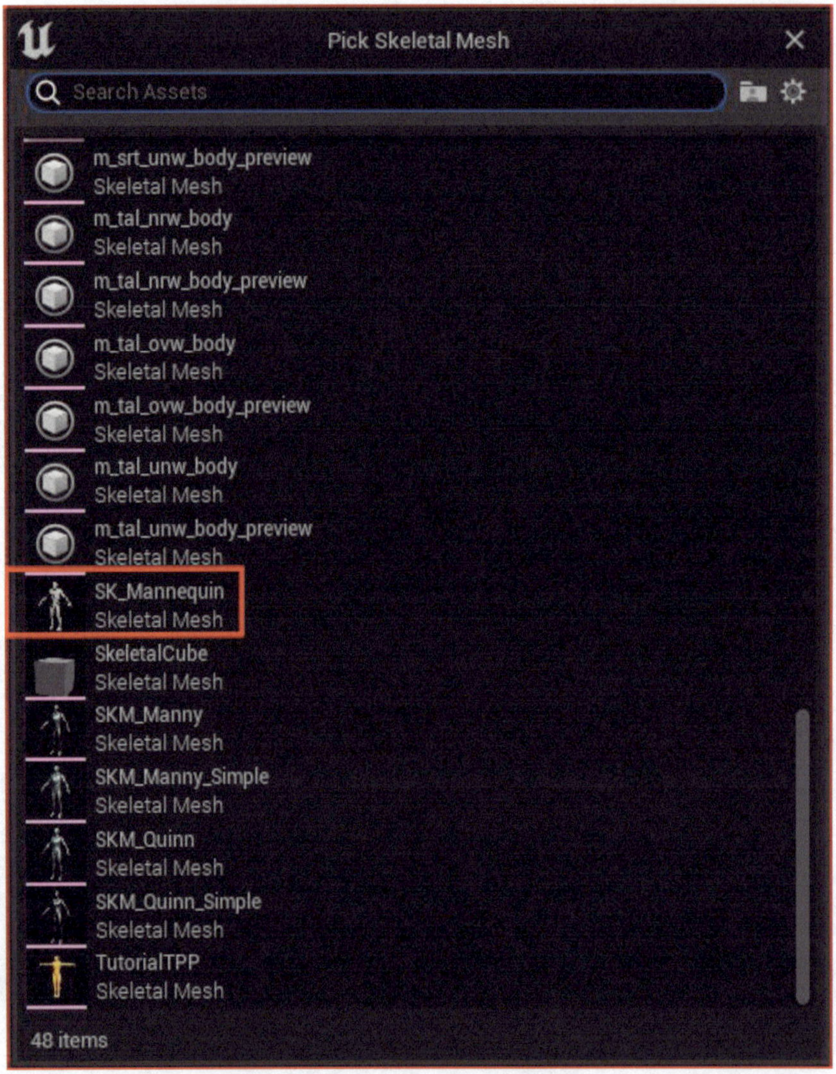

Figure 4.7: Choosing the source skeletal mesh

Once you've done that, it will create the IK Rig inside the same Blueprint folder you've been working from, as demonstrated in *Figure 4.8*. Make a note that I have clearly labeled this IK Rig **SOURCE_Mannequin**; this will help us when looking for it later and is also just good practice.

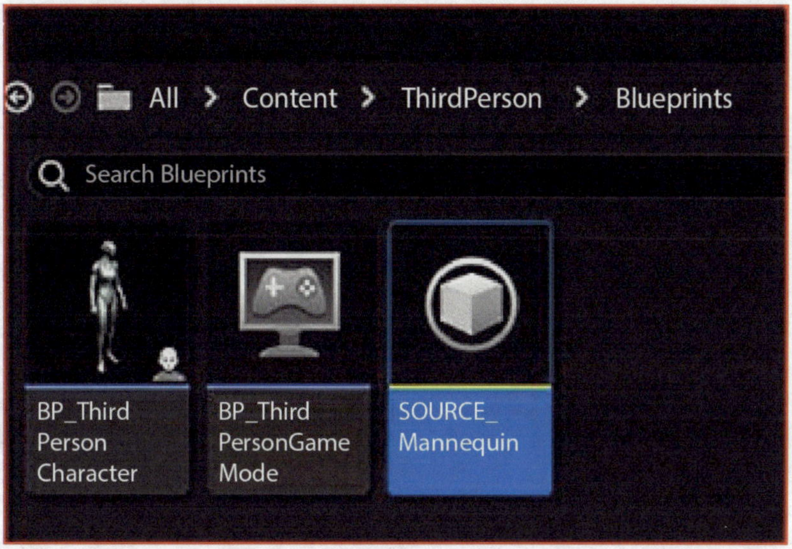

Figure 4.8: IK Rig inside the source folder

With the source IK Rig created, our next step is to create the target IK Rig.

4. For this, we need to go to our MetaHuman's folder and repeat the same steps that we just completed. So, right-click anywhere within the folder, choose **Animation**, and select **IK Rig** again:

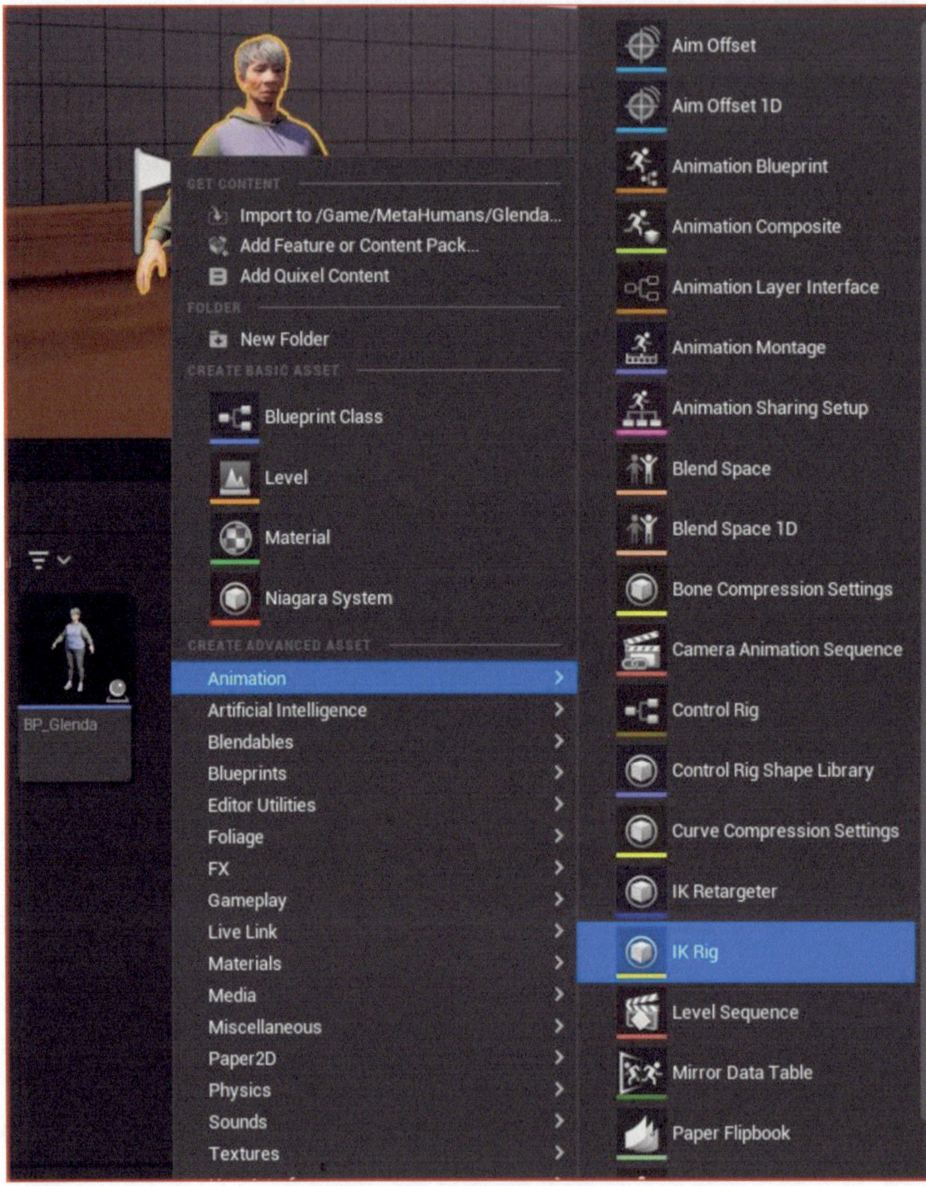

Figure 4.9: Creating a target IK Rig

5. Now, we need to choose a skeletal mesh for our target. In this case, I'm choosing the **f_med_ovw_body** mesh, which corresponds to Glenda being a female character of medium height and overweight (where **f** stands for **female**, **med** stands for **medium**, and **ovw** stands for **overweight**). It's important to choose the correct one, as not doing so will cause issues later.

> **Note**
>
> As another example, you may have a character that is male, short, and underweight; in this case, the correct character mesh would be **m_srt_unw_body.**

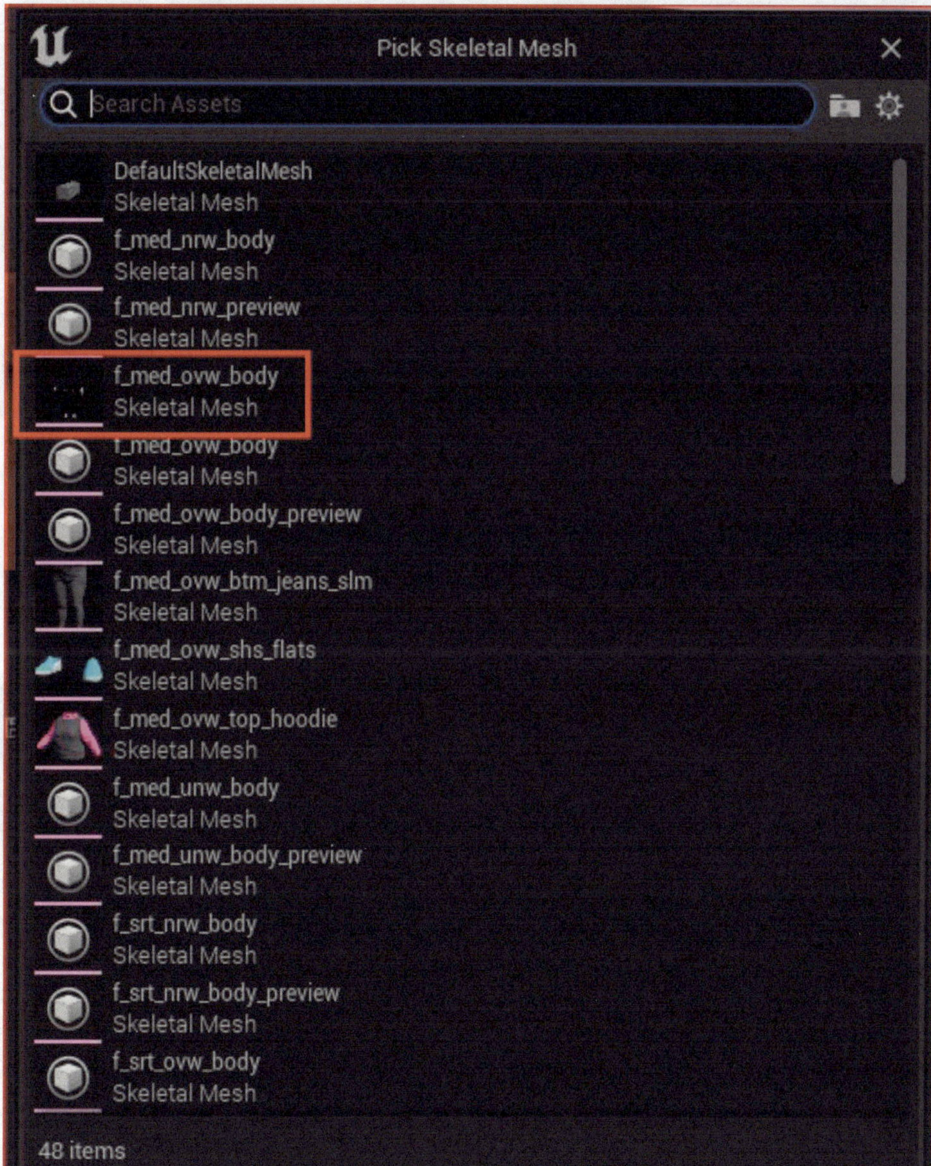

Figure 4.10: Picking the correct skeletal mesh for the target IK Rig

As before, once we've selected the skeletal mesh, we now have a new IK Rig in our character folder (mine is called Glenda). Take note again that I took the time to label this **TARGET**, as seen in *Figure 4.11*:

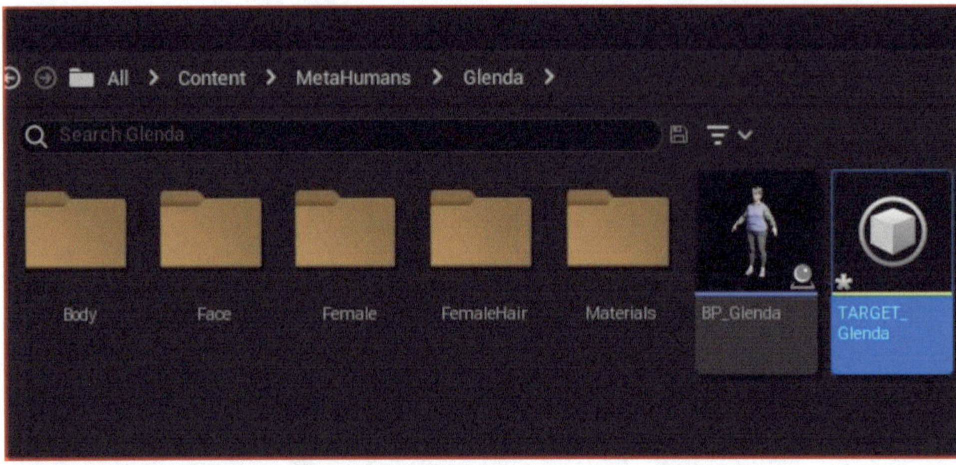

Figure 4.11: Target Rig created inside the character folder

Now, we will open both IK Rigs, and from here on, we will try to keep both rigs side by side. In *Figure 4.12*, I have arranged the two IK Rig windows, the source and target, respectively, so that the interfaces are as close as possible. I highly recommend that you do the same, as it will help you reduce the chances of making mistakes, but it also gives you a visual representation of exactly what is happening.

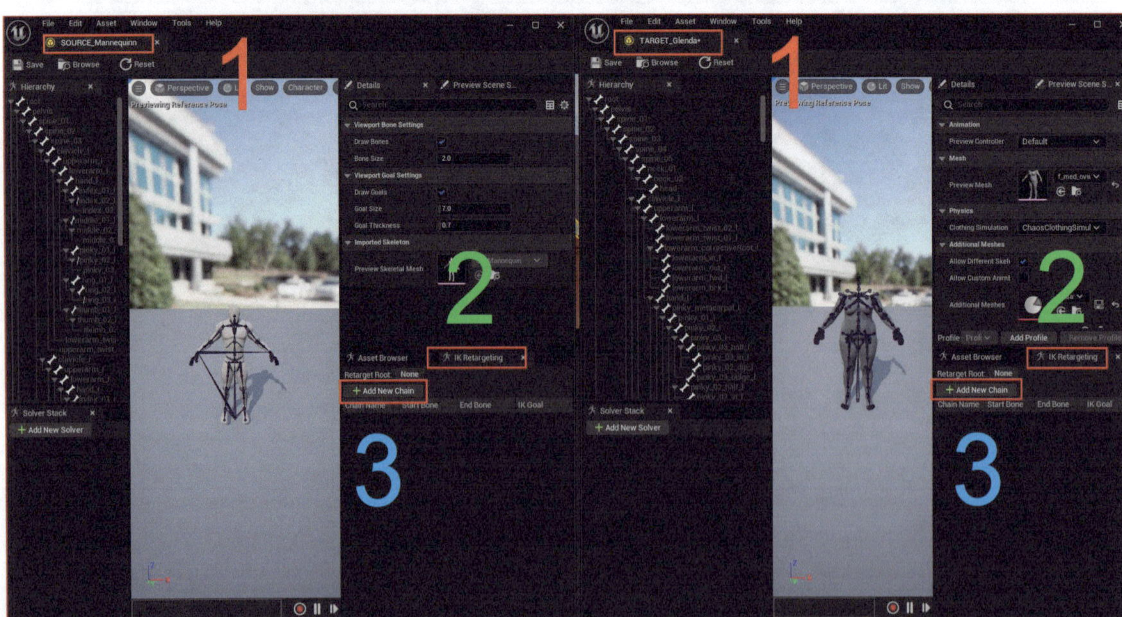

Figure 4.12: A side-by-side comparison of both the source and target IK Rigs

Splitting the screen is good practice, as it allows us to easily visualize how the source and target correspond to each other in relation to our changes. I have labeled key parts of the interface that you need to pay attention to:

1. We have positioned the source IK Rig interface on the left-hand side of the screen and the target IK Rig interface on the right-hand side of the screen. This arrangement works as a visual aid to help us make comparisons quickly.
2. The **IK Retargeting** tab is active. We need to ensure this tab is selected for both the source and target, as that is where we will be doing most of our editing.
3. We have the option to click the **+Add New Chain** button because we will be simply adding IK chains and labeling them appropriately in both interfaces.

Under the IK Rig name in each IK Rig, on the left in each window, you'll see that the skeletal hierarchy is written out as a list. You'll also notice that the lists aren't identical. For example, the source IK Rig has a skeleton with three spines, whereas the target IK Rig, which is more complex, has five spines.

You'll also notice that both skeletons have a root at the very top of each of their hierarchies. For 3D characters, it is quite common for skeletons to have a root at the top of the hierarchy but in many cases, 3D characters use the pelvis as the top of the hierarchy. For Unreal and MetaHumans, we take the pelvis as the top of the hierarchy, so we'll need to do a little editing.

To do this, see the following:

1. Select **pelvis**, right-click on it, and locate the **Set Retargeted Root** option, as seen in *Figure 4.13*. Resting your cursor over this option, you'll notice a prompt saying **Set the Root Bone used for Retargeting. Usually 'Pelvis'.**:

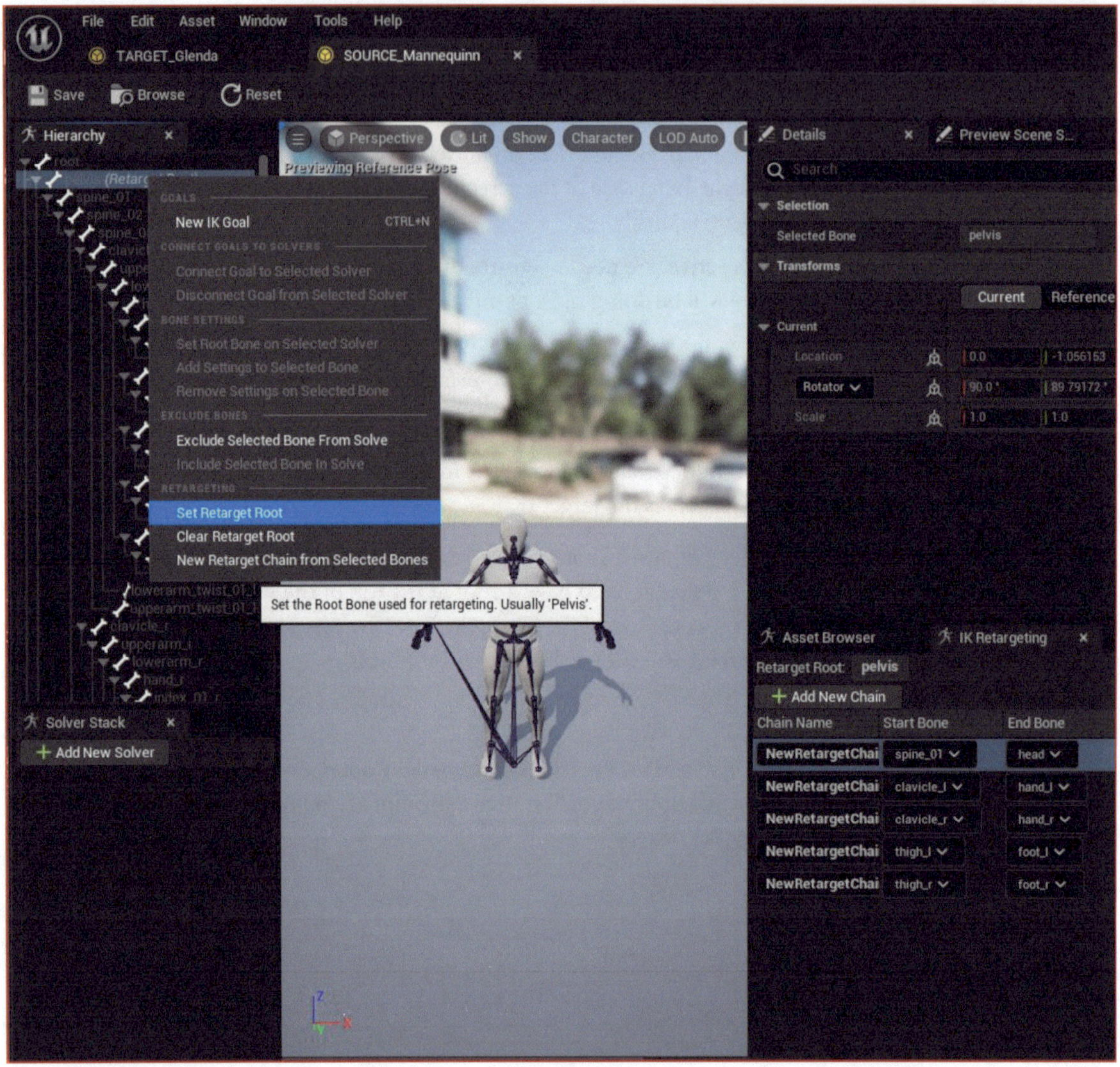

Figure 4.13: Setting the root on the source skeleton

From this, you'll gather that, in most cases, the pelvis is set as the root, so in this case, I have selected **pelvis** as the root by clicking **Set Retarget Root**.

2. Next, you'll need to do the same for the target. In my case, it's **TARGET_Glenda**. Again, as prompted by Engine, we are told that the **root** bone is usually the pelvis, so we'll set the target to root to **pelvis** in both the source and target IK Rigs, as seen in *Figure 4.14*:

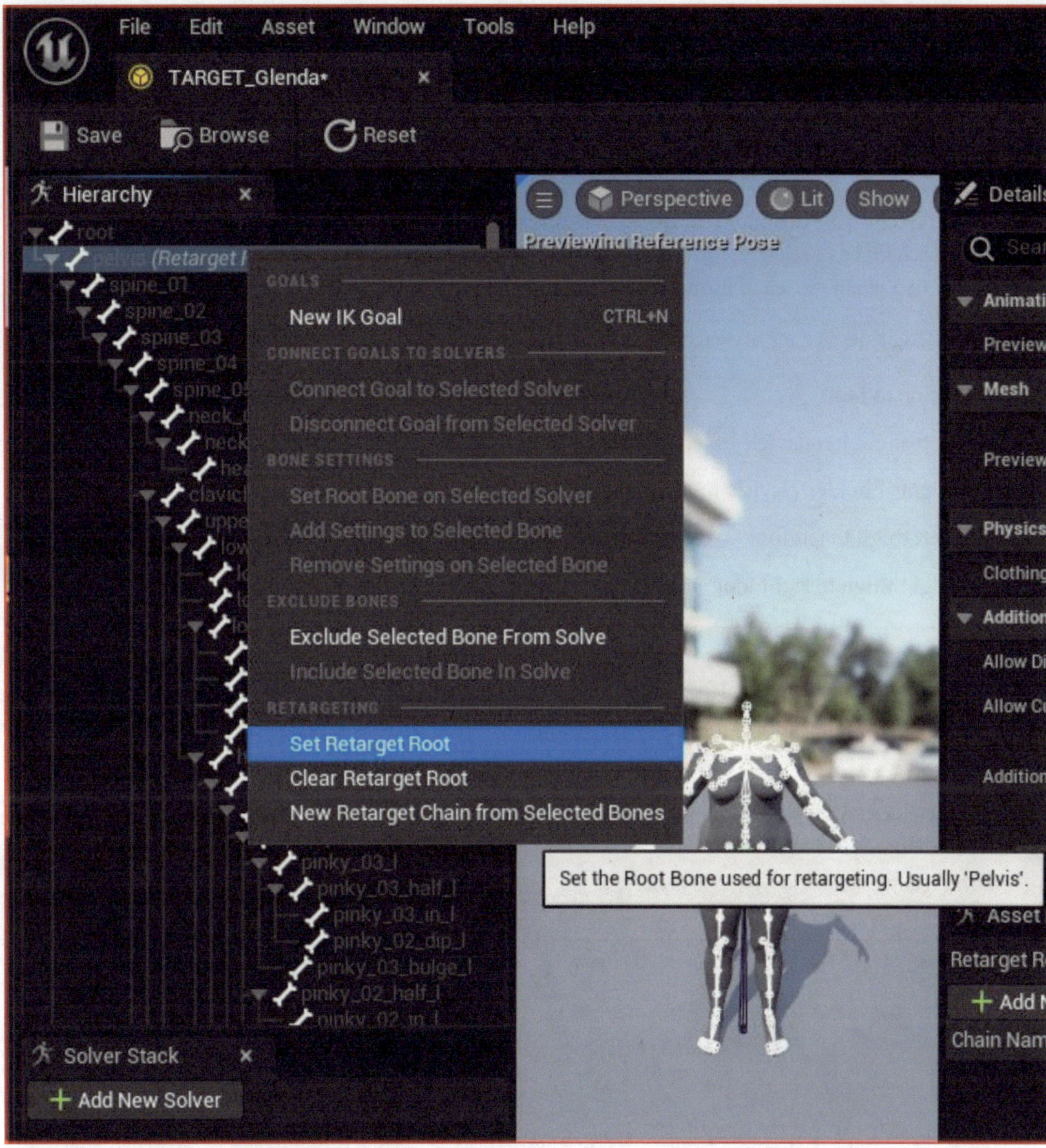

Figure 4.14: Choosing the pelvis as the root in the target IK Rig

> **Note**
>
> Some character rigs use a separate bone as **root** rather than the pelvis, so any issues with animation usually have to do with **root** being changed to either **pelvis** or **root**.

At this point, you've created two IK Rigs, one for the source and one for the target, and applied some very minor editing to both. Now, we'll need to make sure that each limb in both the source and target corresponds to each other effectively. To do that, we need to take a look at IK chains.

Creating the IK chains

What are IK chains? Put simply, an IK chain is like any other chain, such as a bicycle chain, where each link in the chain has a relationship with the next. This applies to limbs in a body where each bone makes up a link in a chain. So, each limb, such as the shoulder down to the hand, makes up one IK chain.

All an IK Rig does is simplify each rig into the following five IK chains:

- Spine to head
- Left shoulder/clavicle to left hand
- Right shoulder/clavicle to right hand
- Left thigh to left foot
- Right thigh to right foot

> **Note**
> Ensure that you create each chain in the order that I have written them here and that the order applies to both the source and target skeletons.

To do this, let's take a closer look at the **IK Retargeting** tab. In *Figure 4.15*, knowing that I just need five IK chains, I clicked on the **+Add New Chain** button five times:

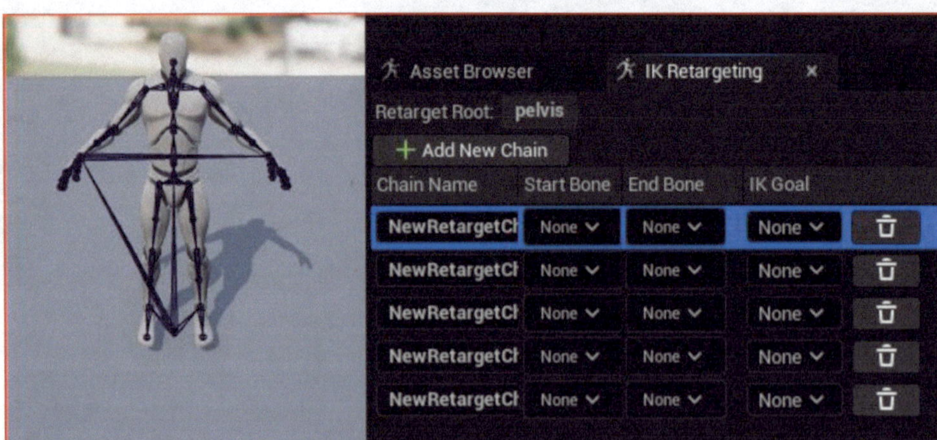

Figure 4.15: IK Retargeting tab for the source

By default, the start and end bones for each chain are set to **None**. To change this, click on **None**, and type `Spine`. This will activate a search through all the available bones; from the results, we can see that this skeleton has three available bones titled **spine**. Select **spine_01**.

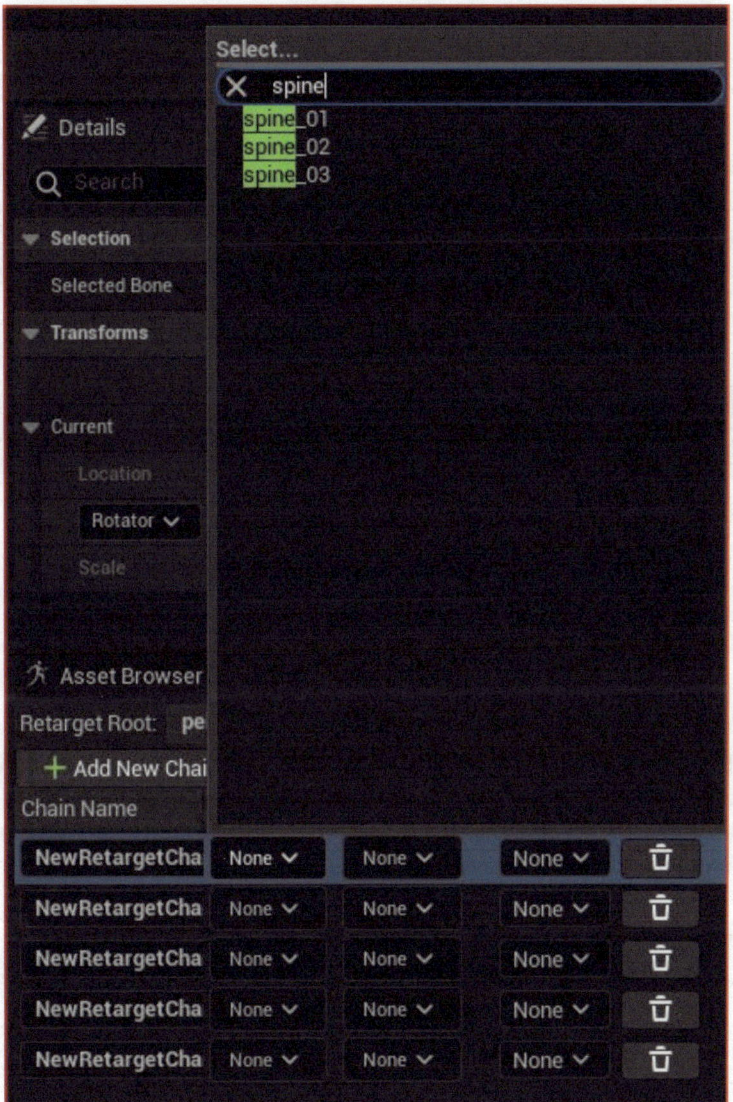

Figure 4.16: Selecting the spine

Selecting **spine_01** will make it the given **Start Bone**. Do the same for **End Bone** but this time, type `Head` to complete the chain.

With both IK Rigs displayed side by side, we get a visual guide for our first IK chain because when we select an IK chain, it turns bright green. To select a chain, click anywhere beside any one of the fields (that could be between the **Start Bone** and the **End Bone** fields or even just next to the trash can icon). You can see from *Figure 4.17* that I have highlighted the first IK chain by clicking next to the **End Bone** field on each. This, in turn, highlights the chain in both viewports, which works as a great visual aid.

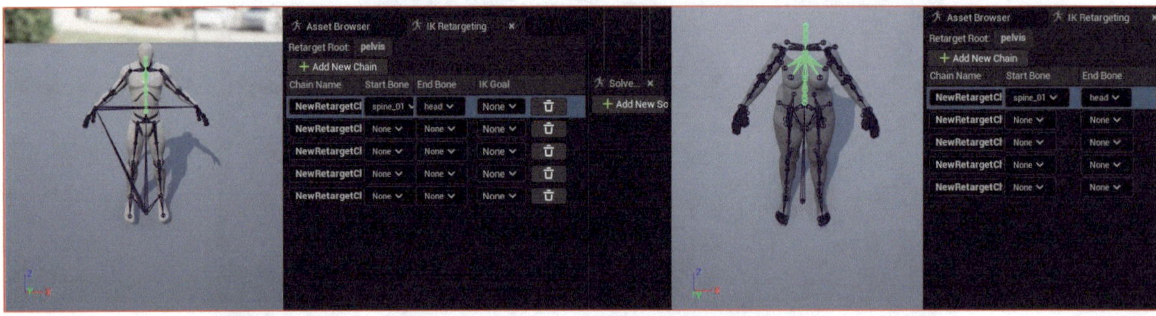

Figure 4.17: Visualizing the first IK chain

Now, we have an IK solution for both skeletons even though the skeletons are different.

Referring back to the list at the start of the section, let's continue with the second IK chain. For the source IK Rig, choose **Clavicle Left** for **Start Bone** and **Hand Left** for **End Bone**. Then, do exactly the same for the target IK Rig.

By following the table and the previous instructions, you will be able to create the third, fourth, and fifth IK chains yourself, so that your source and target IK Rigs look similar to *Figure 4.18*. As you can see, I have selected the last IK chain, which is **Left Leg**. You can see in both Rigs that **Start Bone** is **thigh_l** and **End Bone** is **foot_l** and they are selected, and that this is represented in both viewports, with the relevant chain in each character highlighted in green:

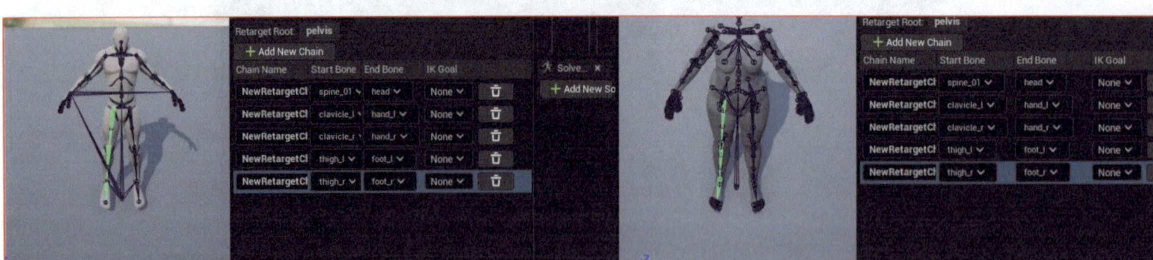

Figure 4.18: Side-by-side visualization of IK chains from both the source and target Rigs

This precise matching between the source and target Rig is vital for the animation to be translated correctly. With that done, in the next section, we are going to create an IK Retargeter.

Creating an IK Retargeter

With the hard work out of the way, now it is time to create a tool that can make these two IK Rigs talk to each other. This is effectively what an IK Retargeter does, translating the animation from the IK chains of one character onto another. In this example, I have gone back to my **Glenda** folder to create the Retargeter. So, let's go through the following steps:

1. Just like when we were creating the IK Rig, right-click anywhere in your character's **Blueprint** folder, choose **Animation**, and select **IK Retargeter**, just like in *Figure 4.19*:

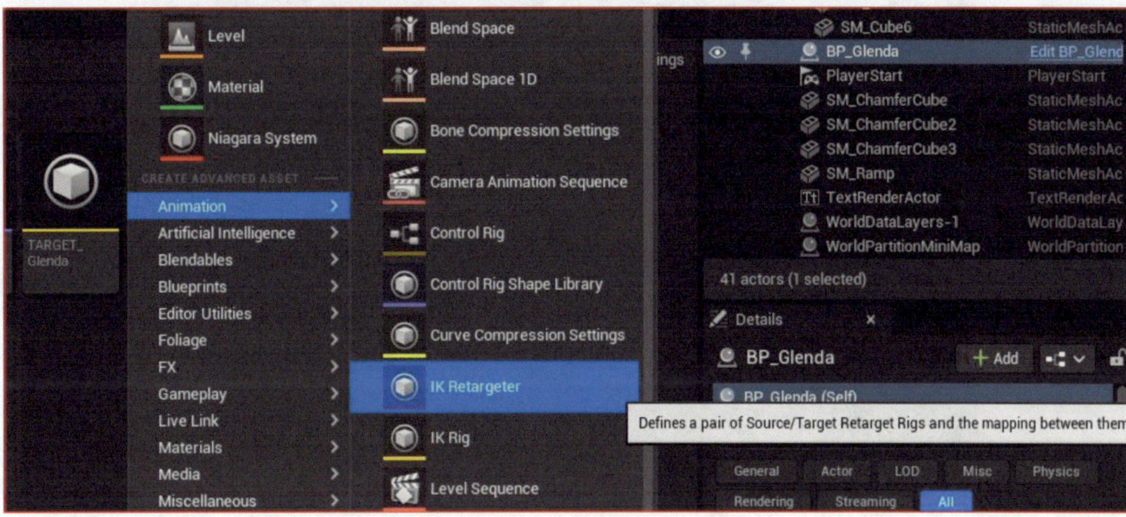

Figure 4.19: Creating the IK Retargeter

2. When creating the IK Retargeter, you are prompted to pick the IK Rig from which you want to copy the animation. To make things easier for ourselves, we already labeled the IK Rig **SOURCE_Mannequin** earlier so that we could easily identify it as a source. You can see this available in the list in *Figure 4.20*:

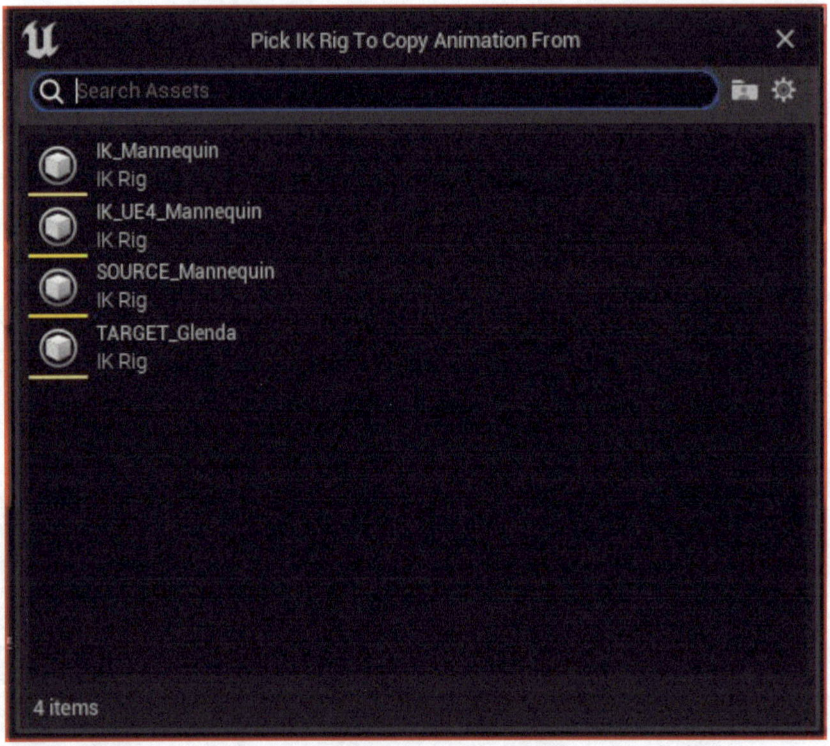

Figure 4.20: Picking the source IK Rig

3. Once picked, we will see another dialog box that shows us the source skeleton. Find the **Target IKRig Asset** option, which I have highlighted in red in *Figure 4.21* (we will come to the option highlighted in green in a moment):

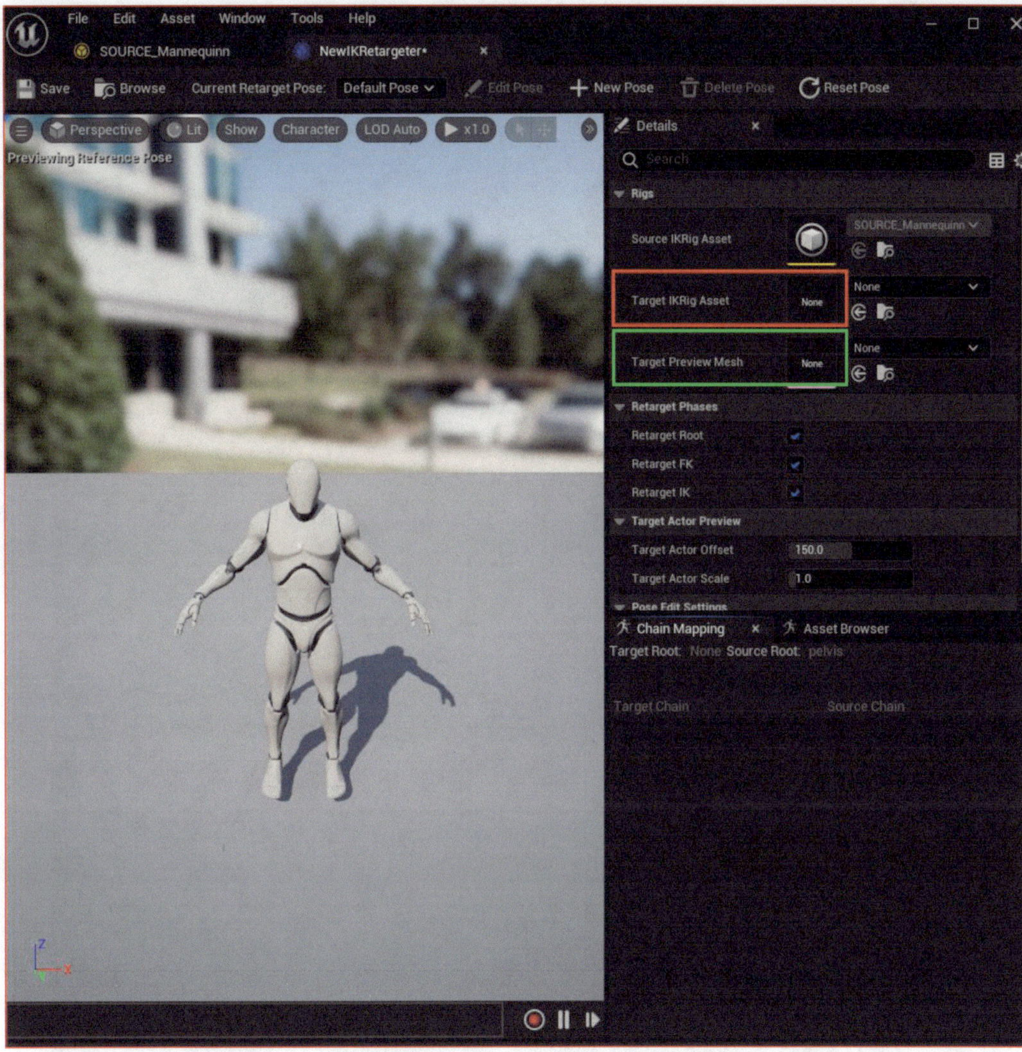

Figure 4.21: The IK Retargeter dialog box

The drop-down list beside it will show any available IK Rigs. The target IK Rig I want is aptly labeled **TARGET_Glenda**:

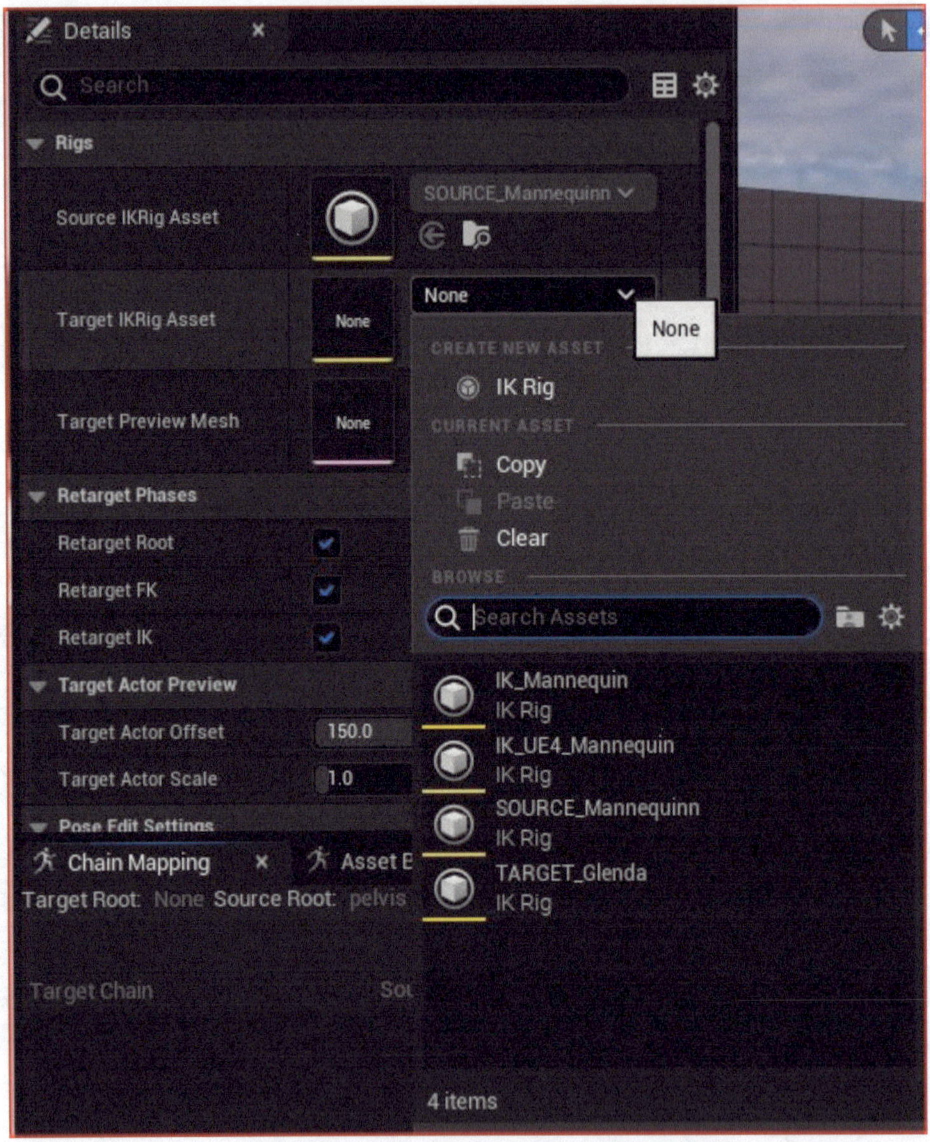

Figure 4.22: Selecting the target IK Rig within the IK Retargeter

When selecting **Target IKRig Asset**, you should see a MetaHuman mesh appear next to **Mannequin**. If you don't see it, return to *Figure 4.21*, where I have highlighted the **Target Preview Mesh** selection box in green.

4. Now, in *Figure 4.23*, you can see how the IK Retargeter gives you a viewport with both the **Mannequin** character and the MetaHuman character next to one another. In addition, note that you have two tabs at the bottom of the screen: **Chain Mapping** and **AssetBrowser**. Make sure you're looking at the **Chain Mapping** tab and click on the **Auto-Map Chains** button.

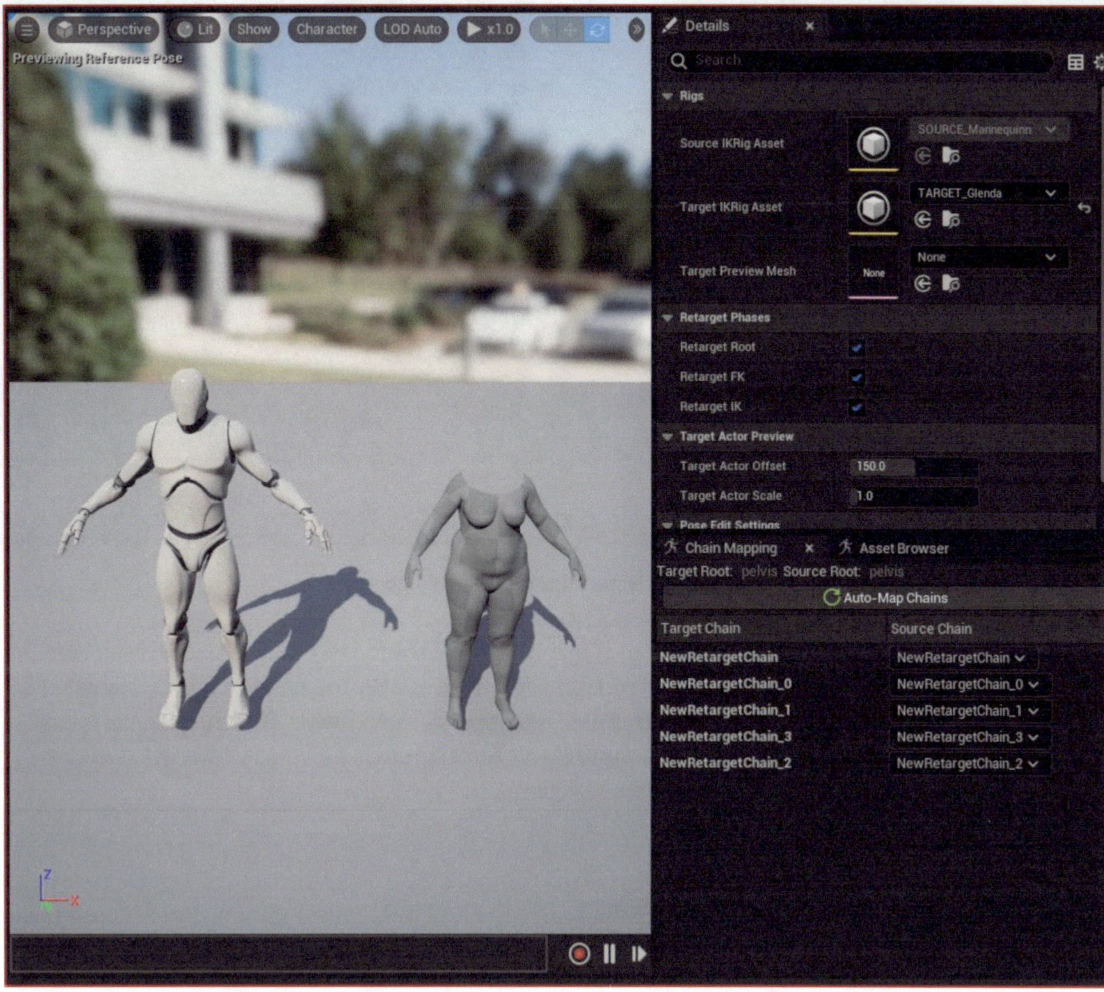

Figure 4.23: Chain Mapping and Auto-Map options in the IK Retargeter

5. Next, switch over to the **AssetBrowser** tab, where you will see the available animations. In my case, I have just one animation available titled **Jog_Fwd** (you may have more). Click on one and the viewport will update with the animation applied to your MetaHuman.

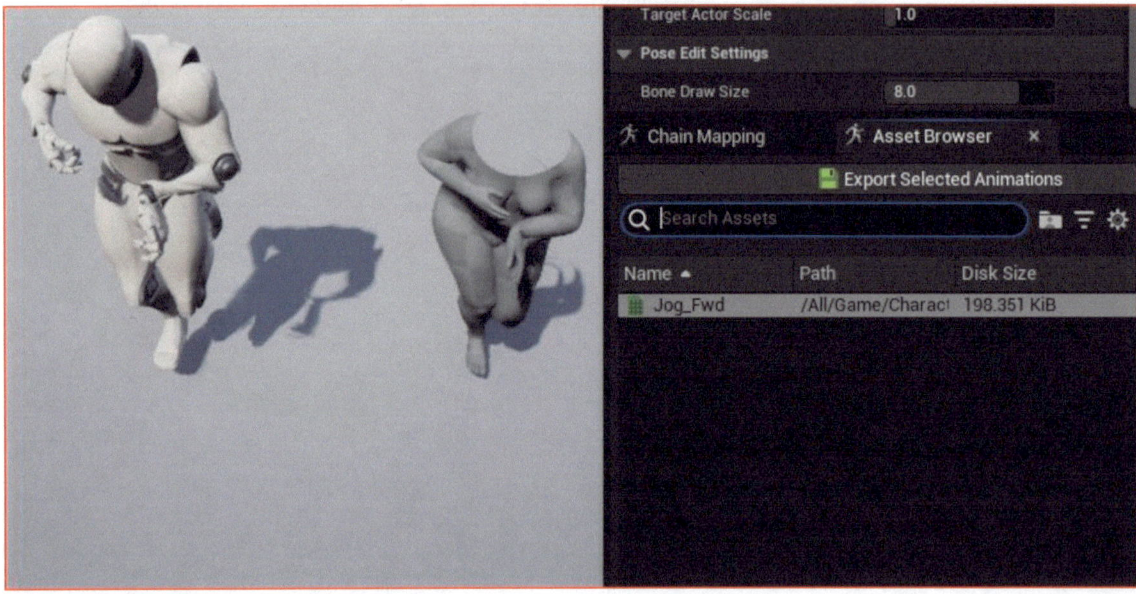

Figure 4.24: Exporting selected animations

6. You can now export that animation so that it is retargeted to your MetaHuman. If you have more than one animation available, you can select them as well. To export, select the animation and click on **Export Selected Animations**. Here, you will see a dialog box asking you to select an export path. I suggest that you choose your **MetaHumans** folder to which to export the retargeted animations, as I have done in *Figure 4.25*:

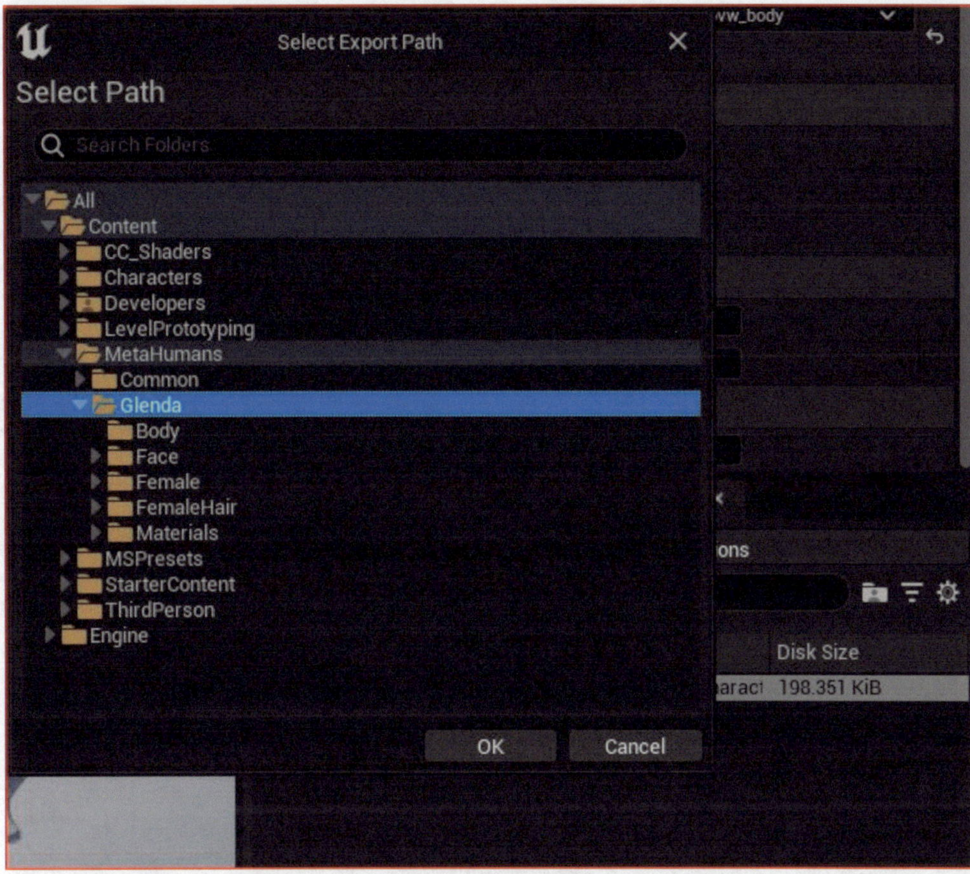

Figure 4.25: Choosing a directory in which to save your retargeted animations

> **Note**
>
> When choosing the folder and pressing **OK**, the IK Retarger will create a new file using the animation name. In my case, it was **Jog_Fwd**. The file created will have the **Retargeted** suffix, which is a convenient way of differentiating the original animation from the retargeted animation files.

At this stage, you have seen your animation on your MetaHuman, but only in the IK Retargeter viewport. To get the animation in the scene, one way of doing this is to open up your character Blueprint (in my case, it is **BP_Glenda**).

7. With the Blueprint open, you can now choose the retargeted animation in the **Animation** section under the **Anim to Play** drop-down menu, or you can just drag and drop your retargeted animation into the box beside it as per *Figure 4.26*:

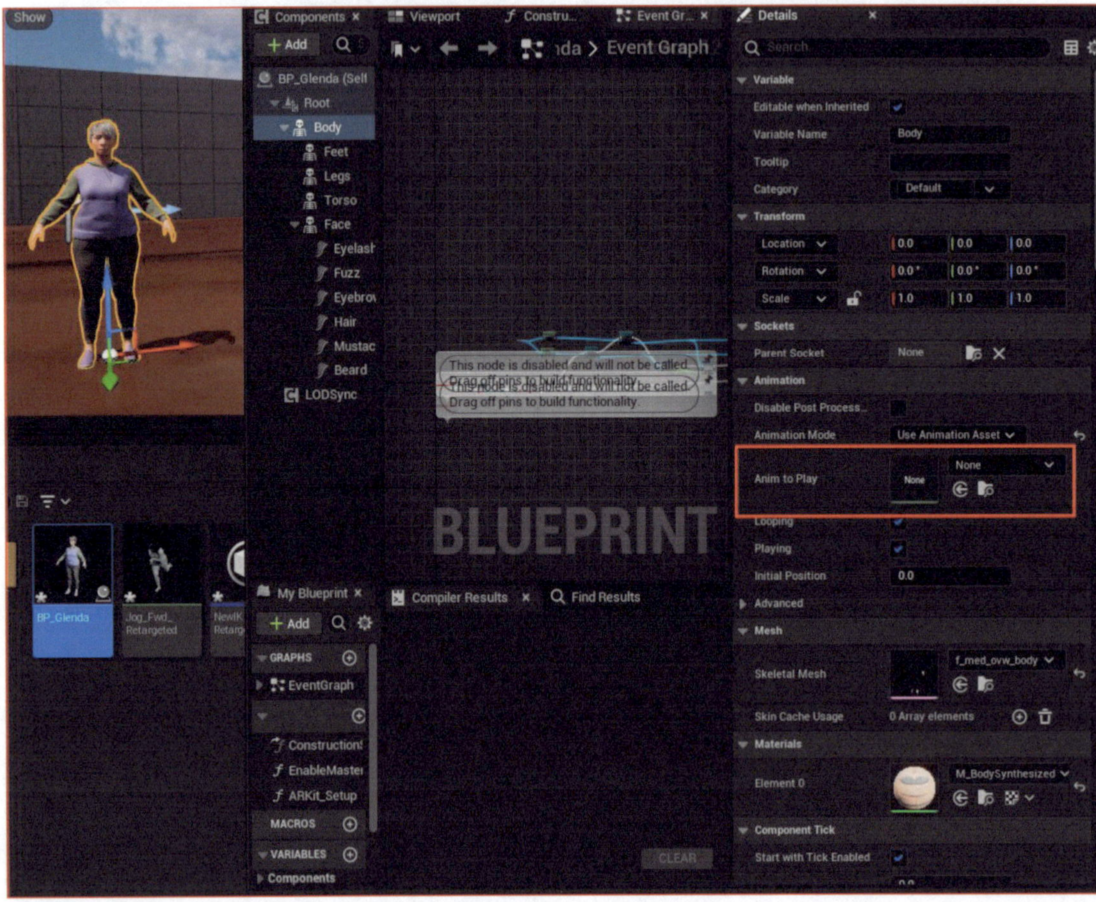

Figure 4.26: Applying the retargeted animation to the character Blueprint

8. Similar to *Figure 4.24*, we can run a search to find the animation, and with the **Retargeted** suffix, we can confirm that we have selected the correct animation as per *Figure 4.27*:

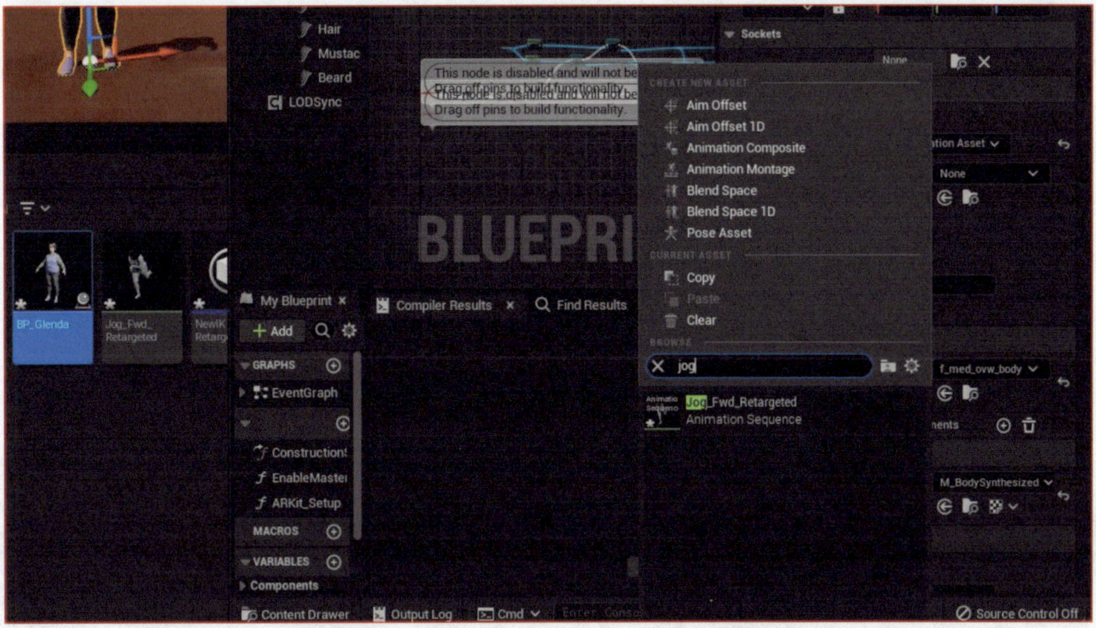

Figure 4.27: Using the search function to find the retargeted animation

9. If you haven't done so already, drag and drop your **BP_Glenda** file from your **MetaHumans** folder into Unreal Engine's main viewport. Then, hit **Play** to simulate a game and see your animation play in the viewport.

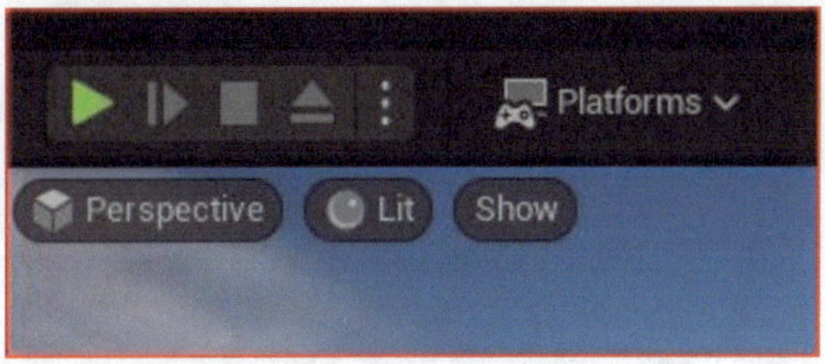

Figure 4.28: Hitting play

We've gone through the steps to creating an IK Retargeter to make a source IK Rig talk to a target IK Rig, but we focused on just one animation. Let's take a look at what to do when we have additional animation.

Importing more animation data

To see more animations at work, you can go to the Unreal Engine Marketplace and search for the Animation Starter Pack. This is a free animation pack that works with Unreal Engine version 5.0 and you can add it to your project if your project is still open.

So, why don't we see how easy it is to retarget animation without the need to open the IK Retargeter using the Animation Starter Pack?

1. With your project open, enter Epic Games and go to **Marketplace**.
2. Under **UE5**, choose **Animations**. Then, under **Filters**, choose **Max Price** as **Free**.

   This should bring up the Animation Starter Pack, and by clicking on it, you will see a page as per *Figure 4.29*:

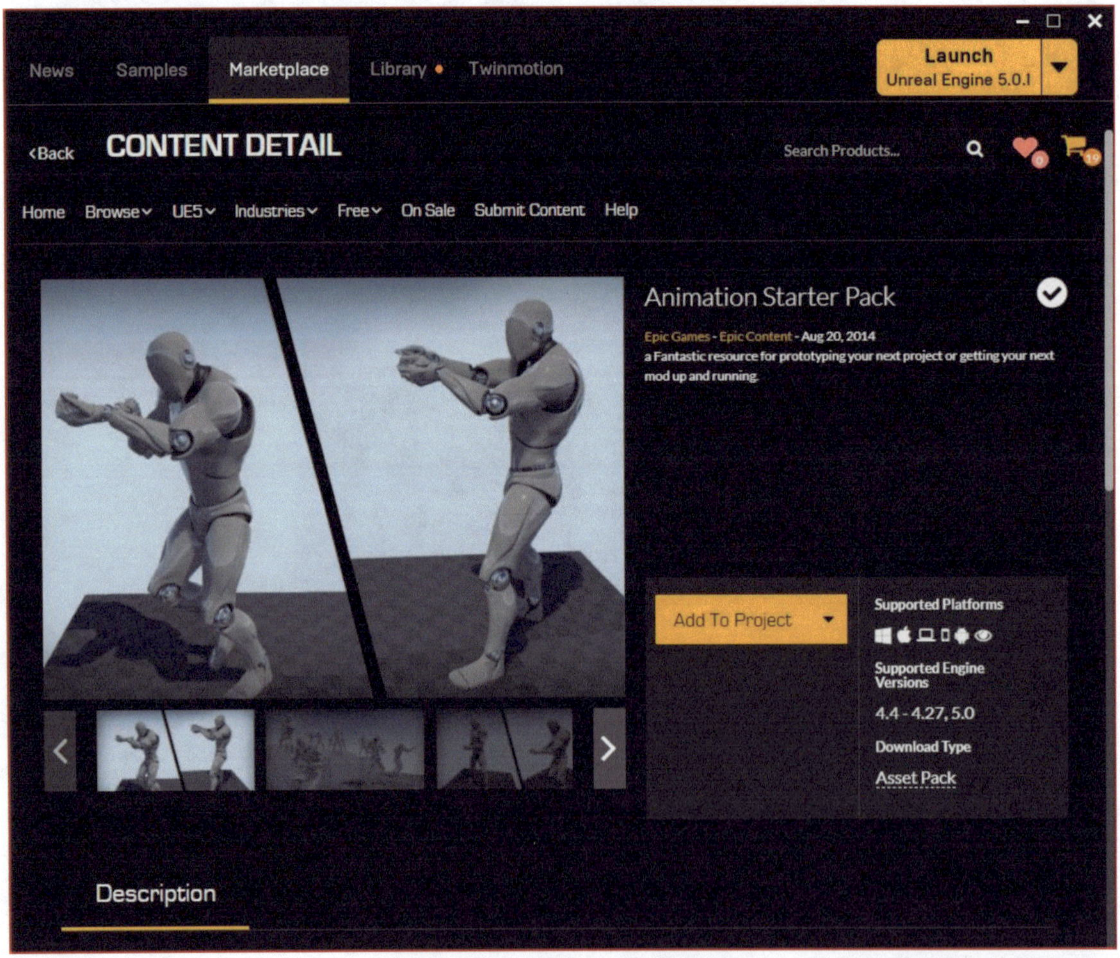

Figure 4.29: Animation Starter Pack

3. Click **Add To Project** to add the pack directly to your open project.

   By doing this, an **AnimationStarterPack** folder will appear in your Project Content folder.

4. Navigate there and right-click on one of the animation files, as per *Figure 4.30*. Select **Retarget Animation Assets** and you'll see that your only option is to choose **Duplicate and Retarget Animation Assets**:

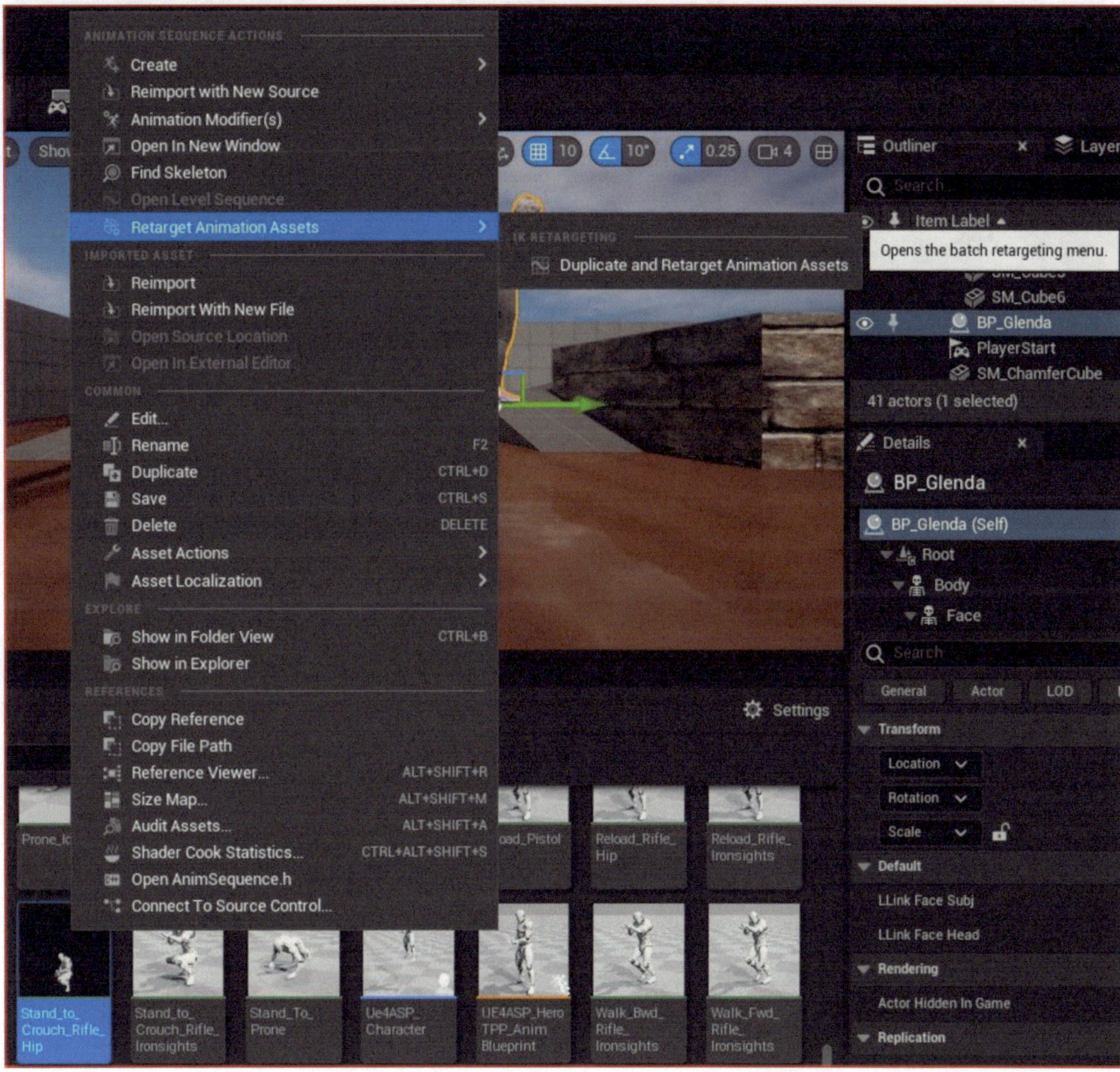

Figure 4.30: Right-click to retarget animation asset

Once selected, you will be brought to the dialog box illustrated in *Figure 4.31*:

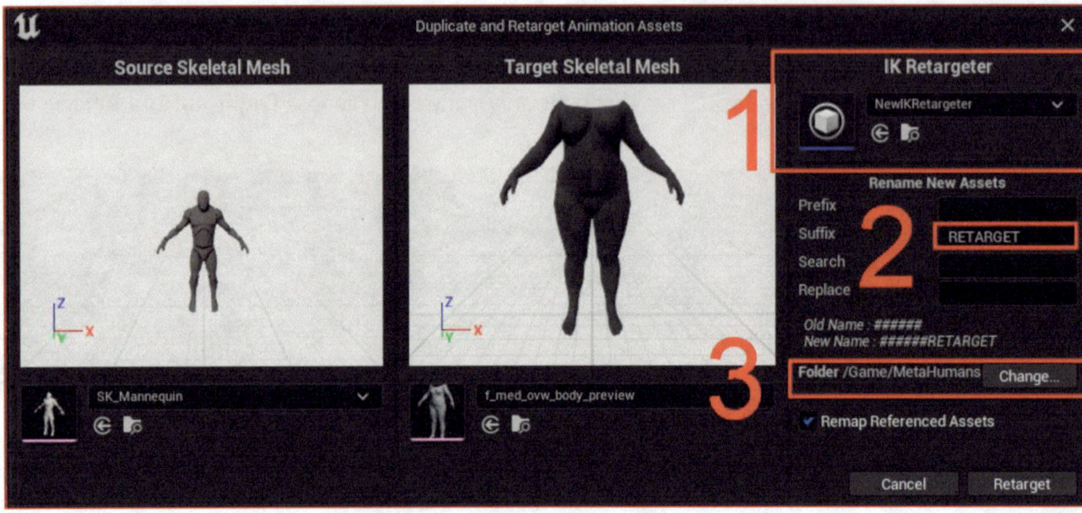

Figure 4.31: Duplicate and Retarget Animation Assets dialog box

There are three points to note regarding this figure:

- Under **IK Retargeter**, I chose **NewIK Retargeter**. Once you've selected the correct IK Retargeter, both viewports will instantly update; in my case, it will show **SK_Mannequin** as the source and **f_med_ovw_body_preview** as the target.
- I changed the **Suffix** option to **RETARGET**. This is just good housekeeping so that you can find it easily at a later stage.
- Choose what directory you want to save your new asset into and click on **Retarget**.

> **Note**
>
> While only for previewing, take note of the drop-down lists under each viewport in *Figure 4.31*. Here, you can preview the associated mesh of both the source and target skeletons.

Now, we've managed to import a new animation and added it to our character without having to use the IK Retargeter again.

Summary

In this chapter, we learned a little about IK and FK, and explored both the IK Rig and the IK Retargeter tools.

More importantly, we uncovered the principles of IK chains, visual aids, such as the highlight function for comparing the source and target IK chains, and the procedures that allow us to create effective and accurate IK chains that the IK Retargeter can use.

We also retargeted an animation effectively and applied it to our scene using the IK Retargeter and applied an alternative method of retargeting the animation assets.

In the next chapter, we will look at Mixamo so that we can use an extensive library of body animations and apply them to our MetaHuman characters. We will also look at using the IK Retargeter to retarget multiple animations in one go.

5

Retargeting Animations with Mixamo

In the previous chapter, we were introduced to the idea of retargeting animations, as well as discussing IK Rigs, IK chains, and IK Retargeters.

In this chapter, we are going to go further afield and take animation from a third-party supplier, **Mixamo**, a very large online library full of motion capture files that you can preview on a web browser. You will learn how to use external resources such as Mixamo in order to give much more variety to your animations; this is important, as repurposing the same animations repeatedly makes for poor productions. We will also remain focused on working with body motion only in this chapter.

So, in this chapter, we will cover the following topics:

- Introducing Mixamo
- Preparing and uploading the MetaHuman to Mixamo
- Orienting your character in Mixamo
- Exploring animation in Mixamo
- Downloading the Mixamo animation
- Importing the Mixamo animation into Unreal

Technical requirements

To complete this chapter, you will need the technical requirements detailed in *Chapter 1*, and the MetaHuman and the Unreal Engine Mannequin that we imported into UE5 in *Chapter 2*. Both of these will need to be saved in the same project in UE, and you will need to have UE running for this chapter.

You will also need a stable internet connection, as we will be uploading a MetaHuman mesh and downloading numerous animation assets. We will effectively be repeating steps taken in *Chapter 4*, but instead, we will be retargeting motion capture from a third-party source.

Introducing Mixamo

For a lot of artists planning on using MetaHumans in Unreal, Mixamo could easily be all they need in terms of body animation. Mixamo is an online library of thousands of **motion capture (mocap)** files created over a number of years by motion capture performers. In addition to housing this extensive library of mocap files, Mixamo also has many premade characters. Mixamo allows you to upload your own characters, where it will run an automated process of applying a Mixamo Rig with skin weights. This automated process removes the need for a lot of tedious work that would normally be done in programs such as Maya or 3ds Max, which is beyond the scope of this book.

Many of the animations within Mixamo allow you to further refine the mocap animation and solve problems during the online session to avoid further editing in Unreal. As you already have experience using an online character creator such as the MHC, you will find Mixamo much less complicated to use and a very fast and efficient way of adding animation to your characters quickly.

The first thing you need to do is go over to `www.mixamo.com`. This is where you'll see the landing page for Mixamo as per *Figure 5.1*:

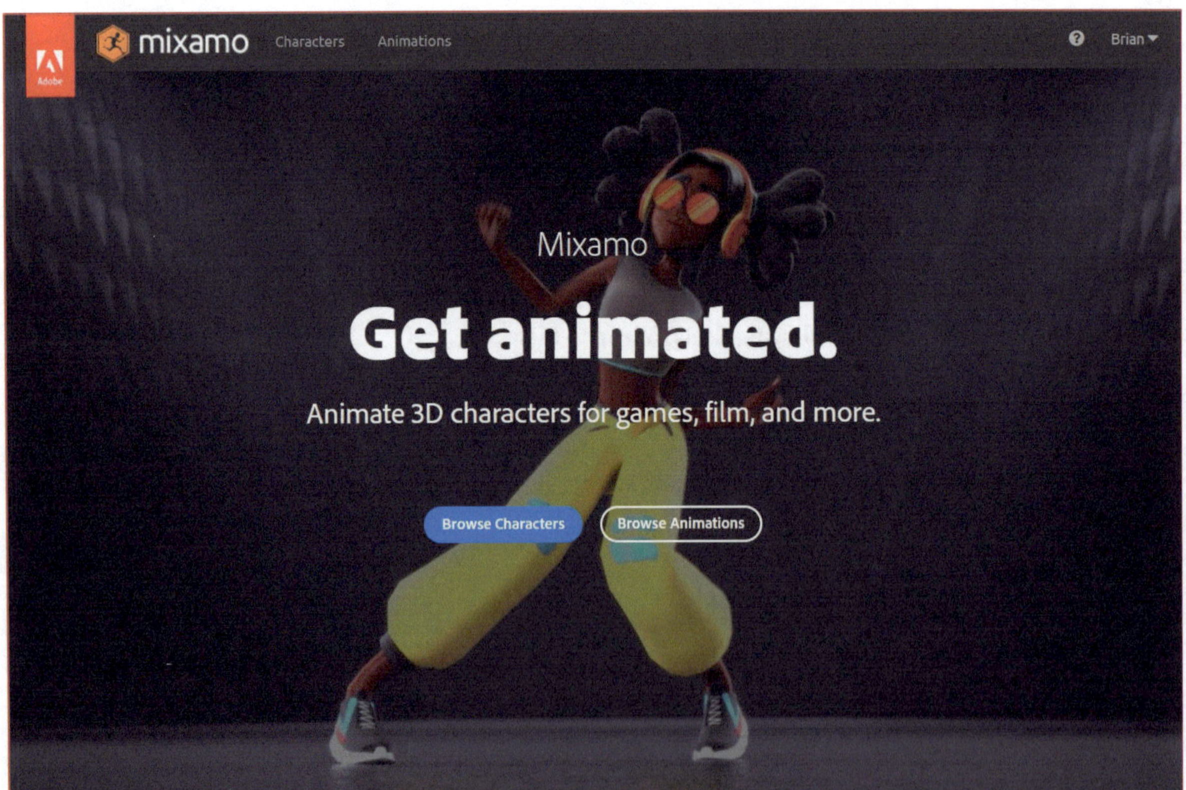

Figure 5.1: Mixamo home screen

In the top-left corner, you will see an Adobe logo. Adobe, the maker of Photoshop and After Effects (to name but a few), acquired Mixamo but has kept it running, as it is a tremendous tool for character designers and animators.

You will also notice in the top-right corner that I have already signed in. Before you sign in, you need to create a Mixamo account. If you have an Adobe account, you can use that. If not, using an email and creating a password will suffice.

Once you've logged in, you'll be taken to the main Mixamo interface:

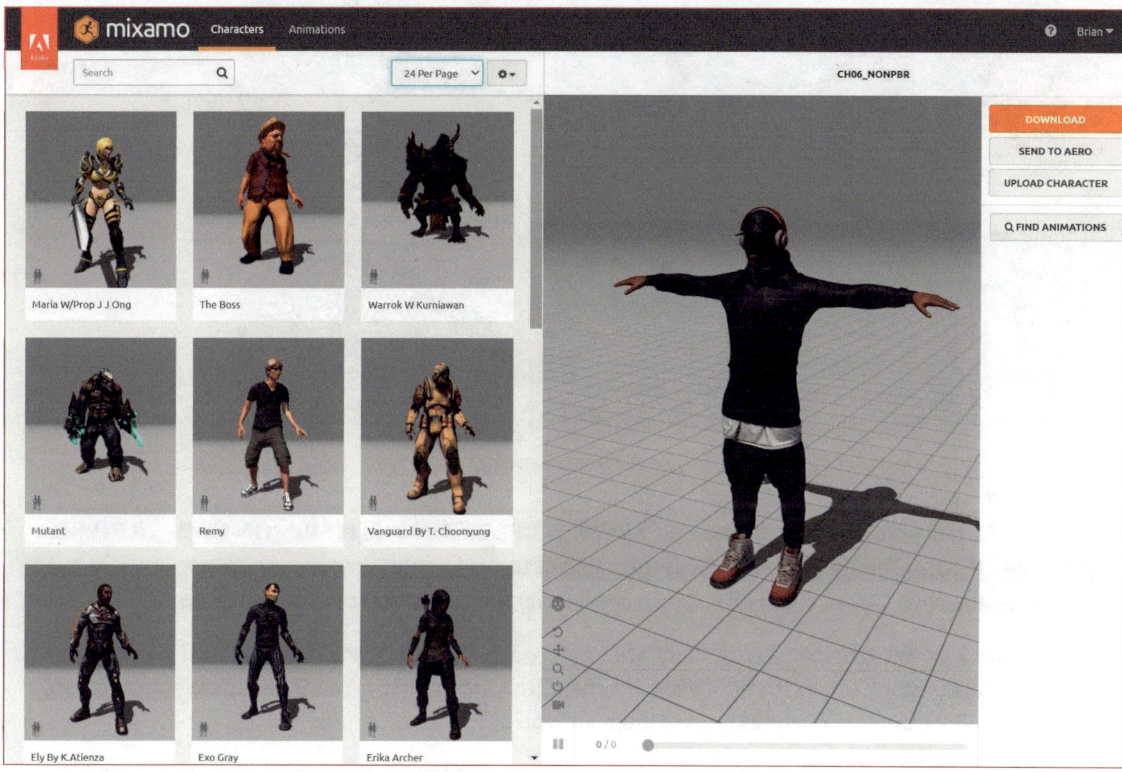

Figure 5.2: The Mixamo interface

In *Figure 5.2*, you'll see that the interface is made of two tabs: **Characters** and **Animations**. These two tabs will display thumbnails of the relative assets and a viewport for you to preview them. In this book, we are only concerned with animations and so you should select **Animations** (however, it is worth noting that regardless of which tab we are in, we can always upload our own characters).

Once the **Animations** tab is selected, we are greeted with an almost identical interface with the exception that our thumbnails on the left now feature animation assets rather than character assets. In most cases, the thumbnail characters are in the Mixamo Mannequin style.

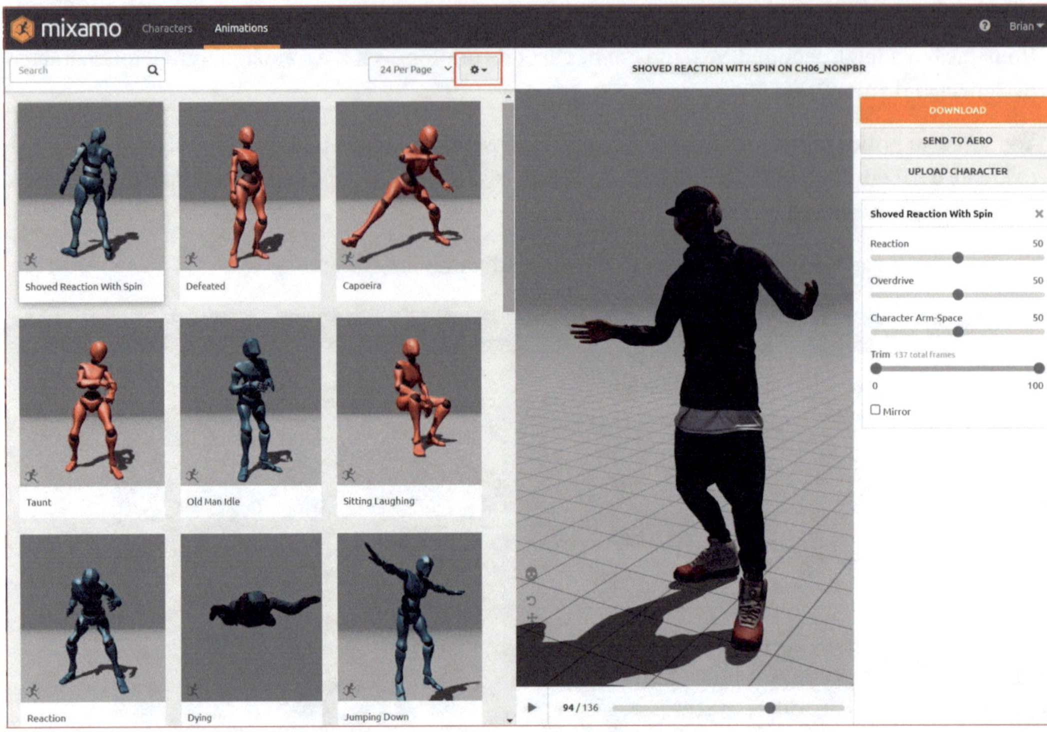

Figure 5.3: The Animations tab

Above the viewport, you can see the name: **SHOVED REACTION WITH SPIN ON CH06_NONPBR**. **SHOVED REACTION WITH SPIN** is the name of the animation that corresponds to the selected thumbnail, while **CH06_NONPBR** relates specifically to the character in the viewport.

If you click on the cog icon as highlighted in *Figure 5.3*, options to see previews of the animation thumbnails or static image thumbnails will appear (the first option is more taxing on your internet connection; however, it's helpful to have them animated).

Before we download any animations, we first need to upload our MetaHuman character mesh into Mixamo to increase the chances of compatibility. To do that, we must prepare our MetaHuman first.

Preparing and uploading the MetaHuman to Mixamo

To prepare our MetaHuman for Mixamo, first, we must make sure that we are exporting our MetaHuman character with the correct body type. You may remember from *Chapter 4*, *Retargeting Animations*, that when we were retargeting our character directly from the animation asset, we had an option to preview the mesh of the MetaHuman. This is an important step because we need to use the preview mesh to tell Mixamo how much of an influence the bones will have. In addition, the step also gives us a visual idea of exactly how the motion capture animation we choose works with our mesh of choice.

My character had a particular description, being female, of medium height, and overweight; this was notated by **F_Med_Ovw_Preview**. We need to ensure that the exact mesh is what we are using to export from Unreal. So, to start preparing our MetaHuman, see the following:

1. First, we need to find the right mesh. To do this, go to your character's folder and then navigate to the **Body** folder. In my case, I need to go to the **Glenda** folder, then the **Female** folder, then the **medium** folder, then **Overweight**, and then finally, the **Body** folder.
2. Next, drag the character into your scene. You'll notice that your character isn't being displayed correctly. In fact, it will most likely only display a portion of your whole character. That is because a MetaHuman is made of the following meshes:
    - A head mesh
    - Clothing meshes
    - A full nude body mesh
3. Now, very importantly, in the **Details** panel, under **Mesh**, you'll see a drop-down menu allowing you to choose which mesh you want to be displayed for your character.

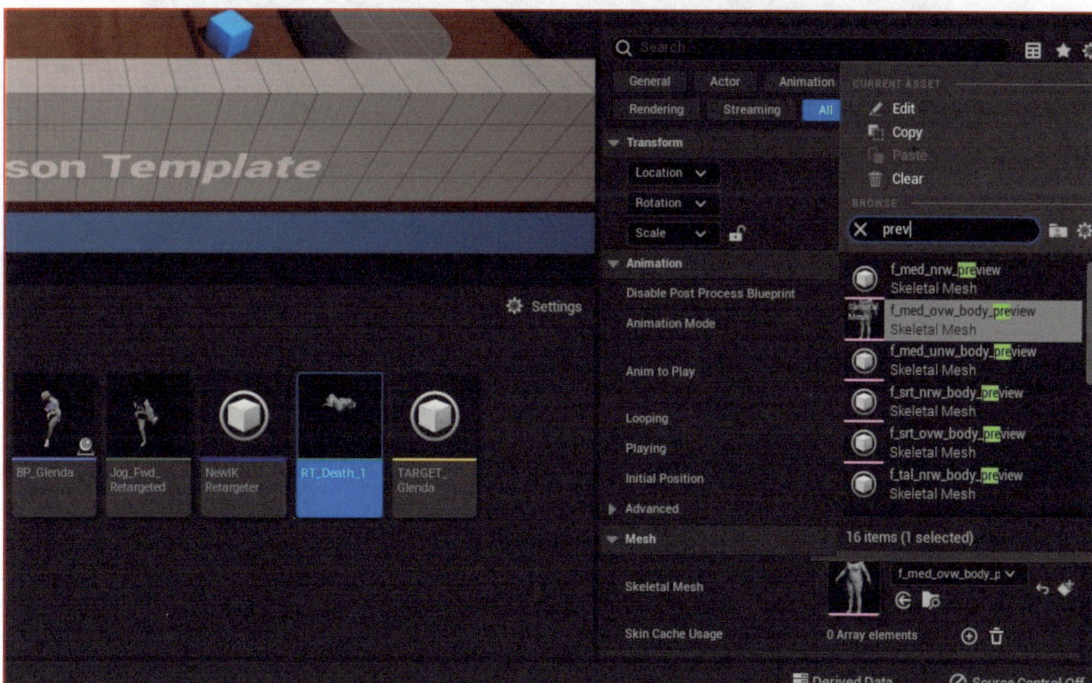

Figure 5.4: Using search to find the preview mesh

If you type in `preview` in the search bar, you will see a list of all the **preview** meshes available. It is important to select the correct one, as we are about to export that mesh for use in Mixamo. We're only interested in the body when it comes to Mixamo because Mixamo doesn't give us any facial animation data; for that reason, in my case, I will select **f_med_ovw_body_preview**.

When you select the mesh, you'll see the mesh in the viewport change to that of a headless nude body. Despite not having a head, this is all we need for Mixamo, as we are only interested in body motion and that is all that Mixamo can offer us anyway.

4. Before exporting this mesh, we need to ensure that the mesh is at the origin of the scene, or in other words, at the very center of the scene. By dragging the mesh from the content panel to the scene, we are merely placing it into the scene based on the mouse cursor position, which generally gives us a random result – but we can quickly fix that.

   Back in the **Details** panel, just above where we chose the preview mesh, there's a **Transform** section. Next to **Location**, you will want to set each of the *x*, *y*, and *z* coordinates to **0.0**, and voila, your character will now be centered in the scene and ready to export.

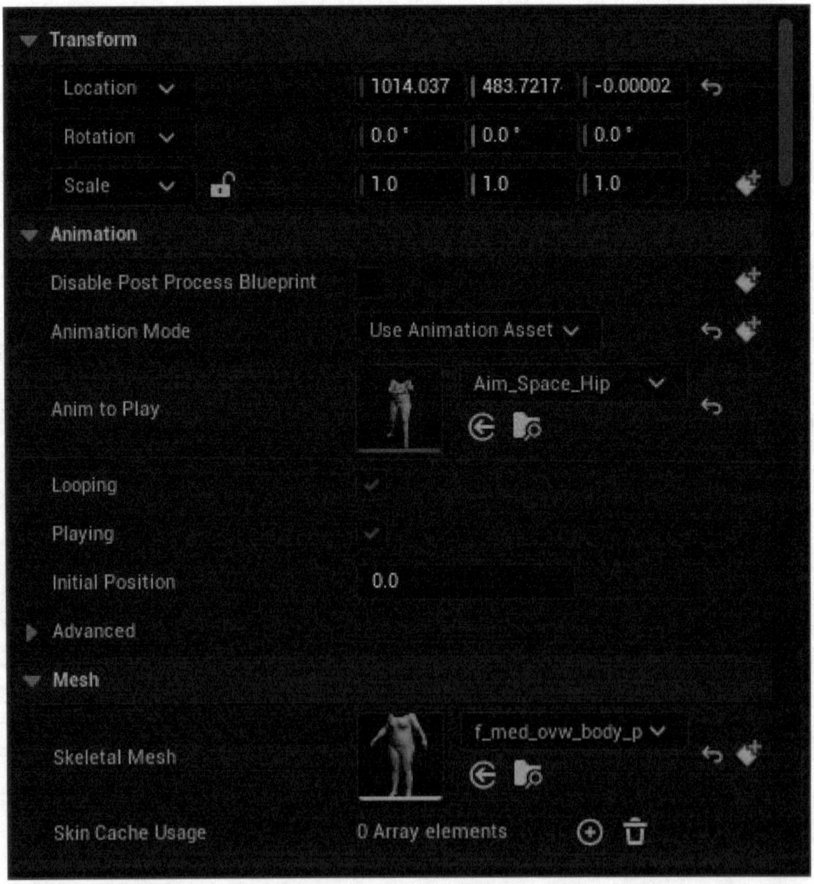

Figure 5.5: Setting the Location value in Transform to the origin

5. Before exporting the mesh, be sure to have the preview mesh from your scene selected, then simply go to **File**, and click **Export Selected…**:

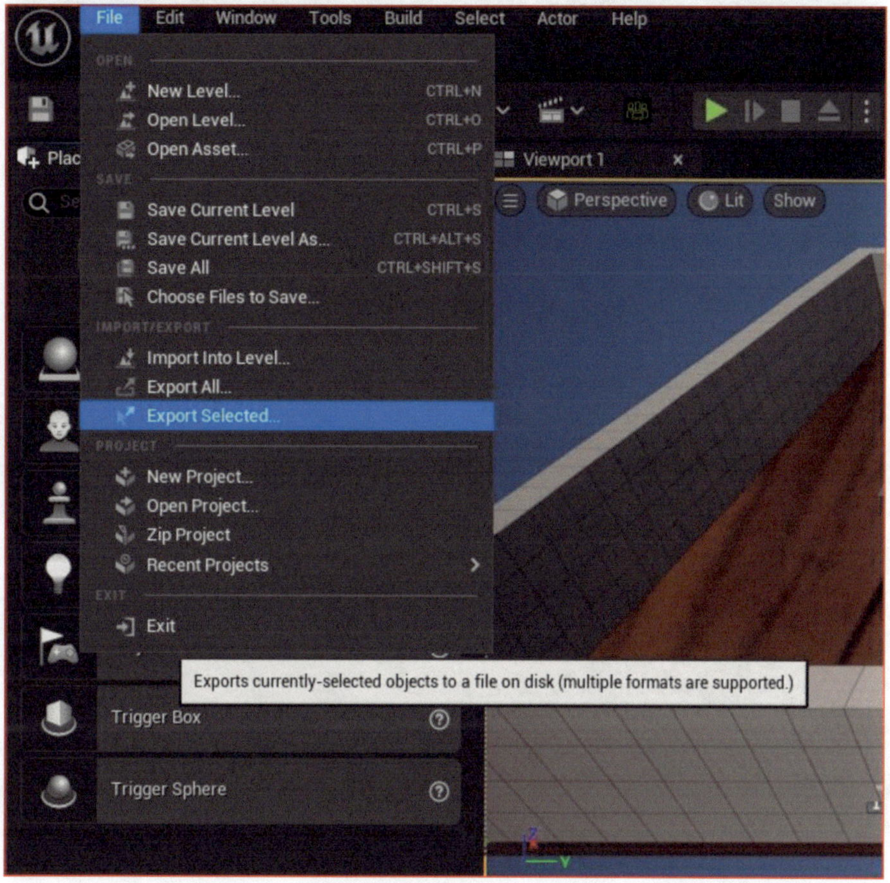

Figure 5.6: Export Selected…

> **Note**
>
> We need to have the preview mesh in the scene in order to export it as an FBX file. We can't export the asset from within the content panel.

6. Next, choose **FBX** as your file type and give it a name that you'll remember (such as **GlendaToMixamo**).
7. Ensure you don't have **Map Skeleton Motion to Root** ticked. Keep all the settings as their default settings and click **Export**, as seen in *Figure 5.7*:

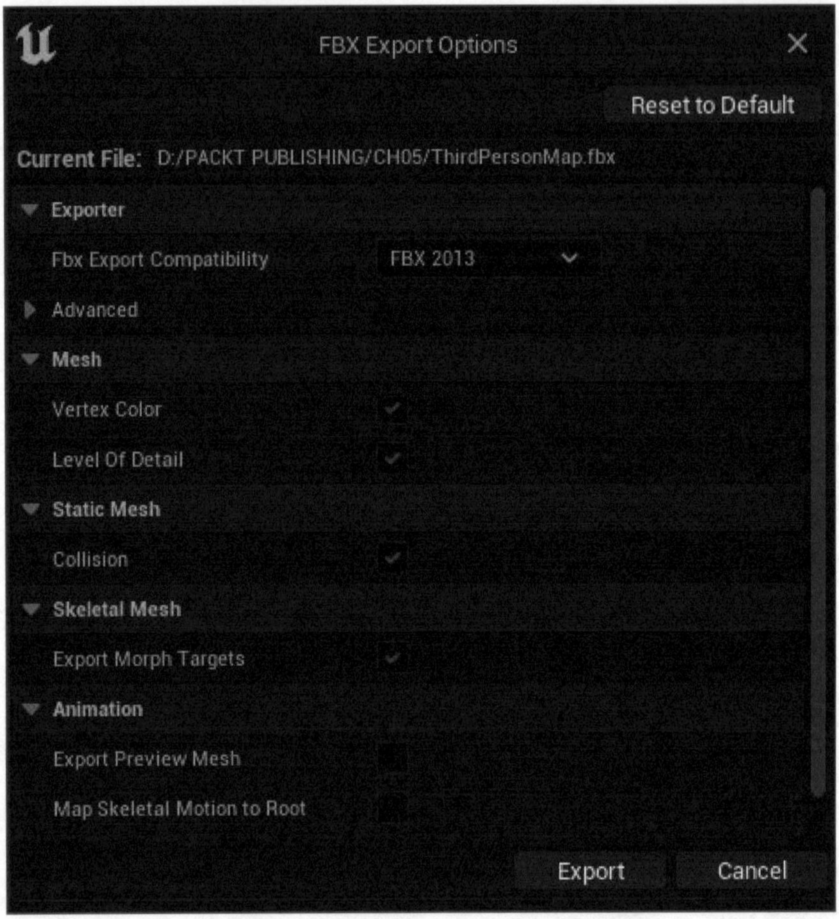

Figure 5.7: Map Skeletal Motion to Root unticked

Next, we will upload our character into Mixamo to apply animation to it.

8. Regardless of whether you are in the **Character** or **Animation** mode in Mixamo, you will always have the opportunity to click on the **Upload Character** button; this will open the following interface:

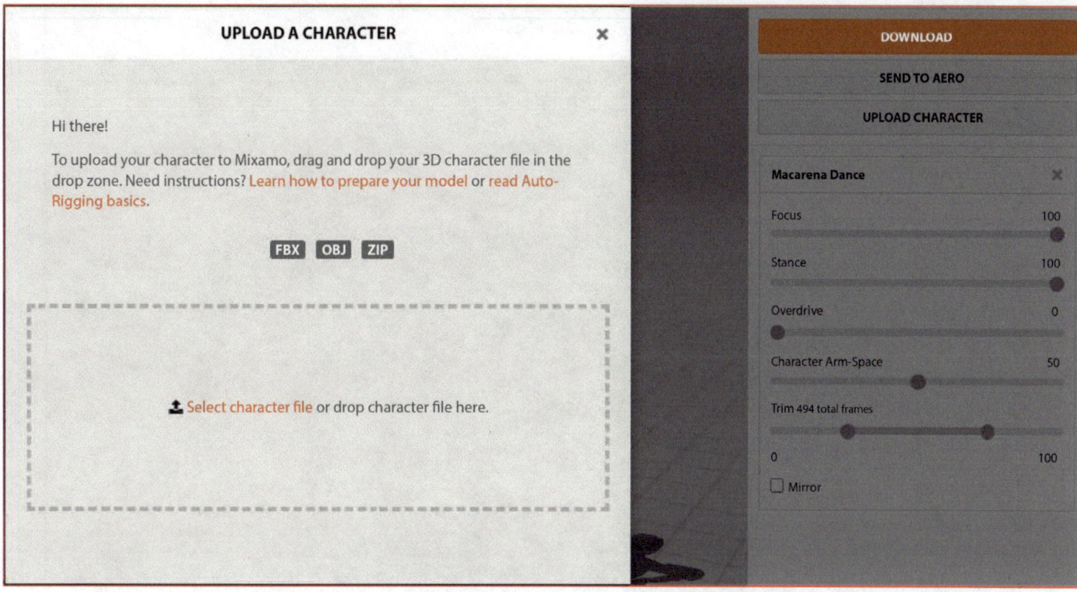

Figure 5.8: Uploading your MetaHuman preview mesh to Mixamo

9. You have the choice of either dragging and dropping your mesh into the rectangle or clicking on **Select character file**. Either way, when uploading your file, be prepared to wait a while, as it can take a few minutes to process – in which case, you'll see the following message on the screen:

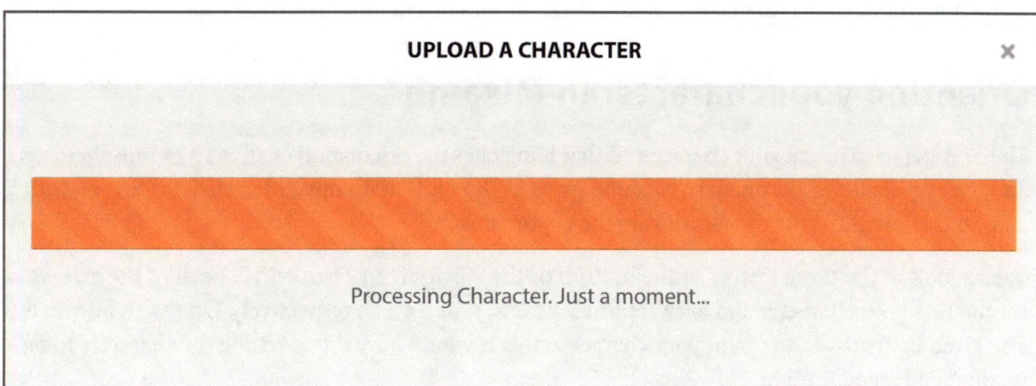

Figure 5.9: Mixamo processing the mesh

When Mixamo has finished processing your mesh, you should be greeted with the interface shown in *Figure 5.10*:

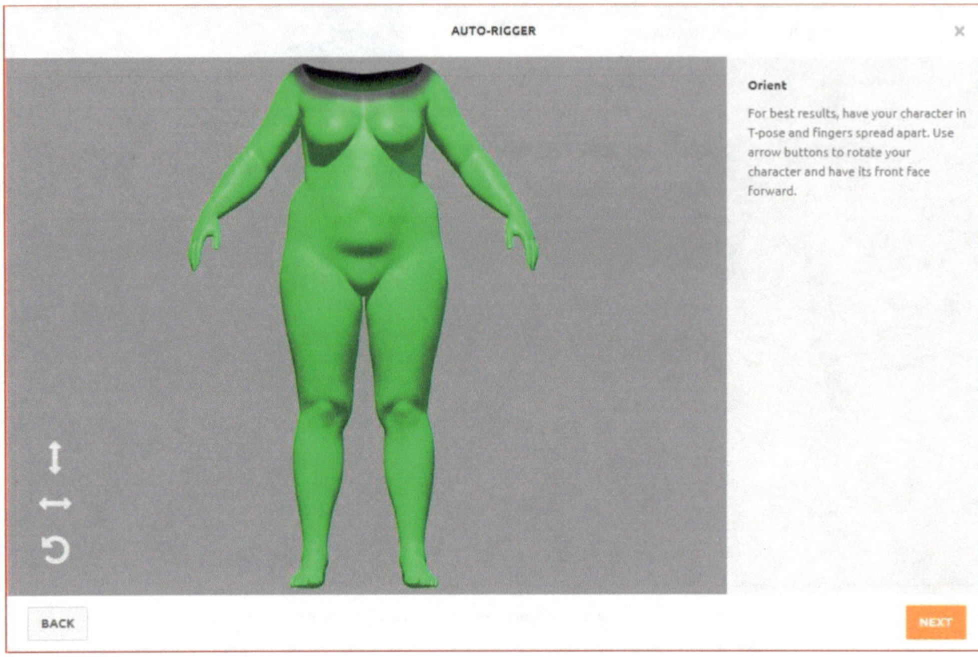

Figure 5.10: Mixamo has finished the processing phase

Now that we have our character mesh inside Mixamo, we are on our way to applying animation to it, but before that, we need to make a few adjustments and orient our character first.

Orienting your character in Mixamo

The next step is to orient your character so that it matches the orientation of all the Mixamo characters and their animations. Fortunately, Mixamo gives us the tools to do this rather than leaving us with a laborious trial-and-error process during the export stage.

Take a look at the three arrows at the bottom of the viewport in *Figure 5.10*. Each of the arrows is for rotating your character and each represents the *x*, *y*, and *z* axis respectively. On the right, you are also given instructions to orient your character; this is what I have done, setting the character to face forward and stand upright.

Now, you may have noticed from the on-screen instructions that Mixamo has asked for the character to be placed in a **T-pose** position for best results: a T-pose is where the character is in the shape of a T – that is to say, that their arms are straight out to either side, rotated at 90 degrees. In my case, and in the case of all MetaHumans, the default pose is **A-pose**, which is where the character's arms are not fully extended and only rotated at approximately 45 degrees. However, Mixamo does a really good job at interpolating between the two and successfully aligns the Mixamo character rig to our preview mesh.

> **Note**
>
> We will be looking at modifying the MetaHuman from **A-pose** to **T-pose** in *Chapter 6, Adding Motion Capture with DeepMotion*.

Despite Mixamo taking care of most of the work, we still need to give Mixamo's auto-rigger a bit of a nudge. When you click the **NEXT** button, seen at the bottom-right corner of *Figure 5.10*, you will be brought to the following page:

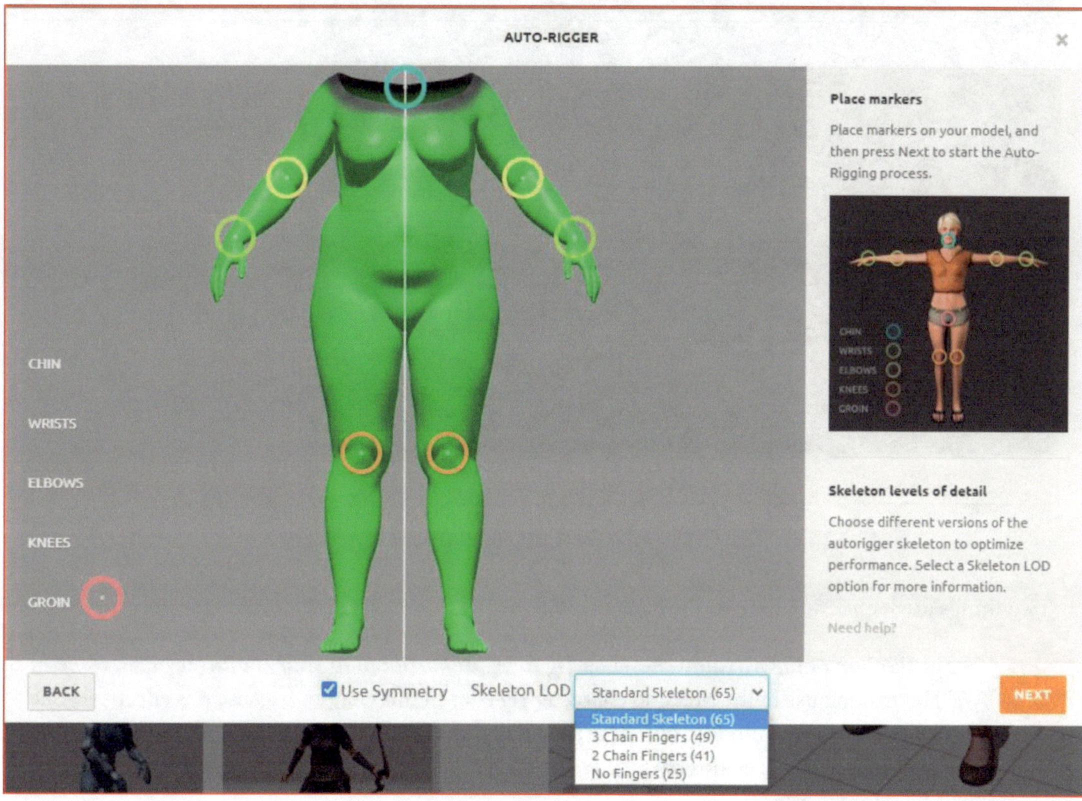

Figure 5.11: Auto-rigger marker placement

Effectively, this is a calibration tool where we get to ensure the proportions of the Mixamo character rig match that of our MetaHuman's preview mesh. We get to make those fine-tuned adjustments by simply dragging the markers from the left of the screen to their associated body parts. With **Use Symmetry** left on, you'll do this much faster and more accurately. Also keep **Skeleton LOD** as the default setting, **Standard Skeleton (65)**, which has the highest number of bones; this makes a noticeable difference when it comes to finger articulation.

Once you're happy with the placement of the markers, select **NEXT,** where you will see the character being processed; this can take a couple of minutes and you will see your character spinning while this happens.

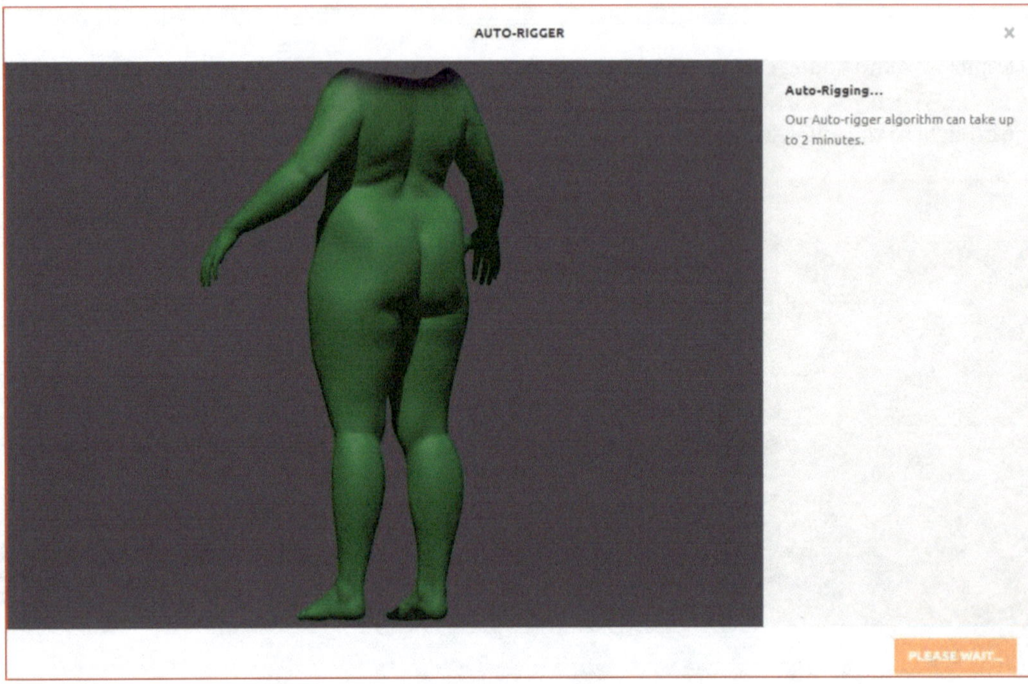

Figure 5.12: Auto-rigging processing

Two things are happening here in the background:

- *The generation of the Mixamo character rig to be proportional to your character preview mesh*: We'll be making use of the Mixamo character rig later in this chapter because it is effectively like Unreal's own Mannequin Rig, but there are small differences. However, with the IK Retargeting work covered in the previous chapter, we'll tackle the differences between the Mixamo Rig and the MetaHuman Rig.
- *The adjustment of skin weighting regarding the rig aligning with the proportions of the mesh*: Fortunately, we don't have to know anything about skin weighting to progress further through this book, as Mixamo does this automatically. However, for those of you who have any experience manually rigging characters, you'll be all too aware of the somewhat painful process of painting weight influences.

All this means is that we are telling each part of the mesh how much it is influenced by each bone; for example, a foot bone would have no skin weight influence over the mesh of the arm, but a foot bone could have a small degree of influence over the mesh covering the lower leg.

> **Note**
>
> For more seasoned 3D artists, there are methods to adjust the skin weights in third-party applications such as Maya, Blender, or Houdini.

When the auto-rigging process is complete, you should see your rig moving using a default temporary animation supplied by Mixamo, as shown in *Figure 5.13*:

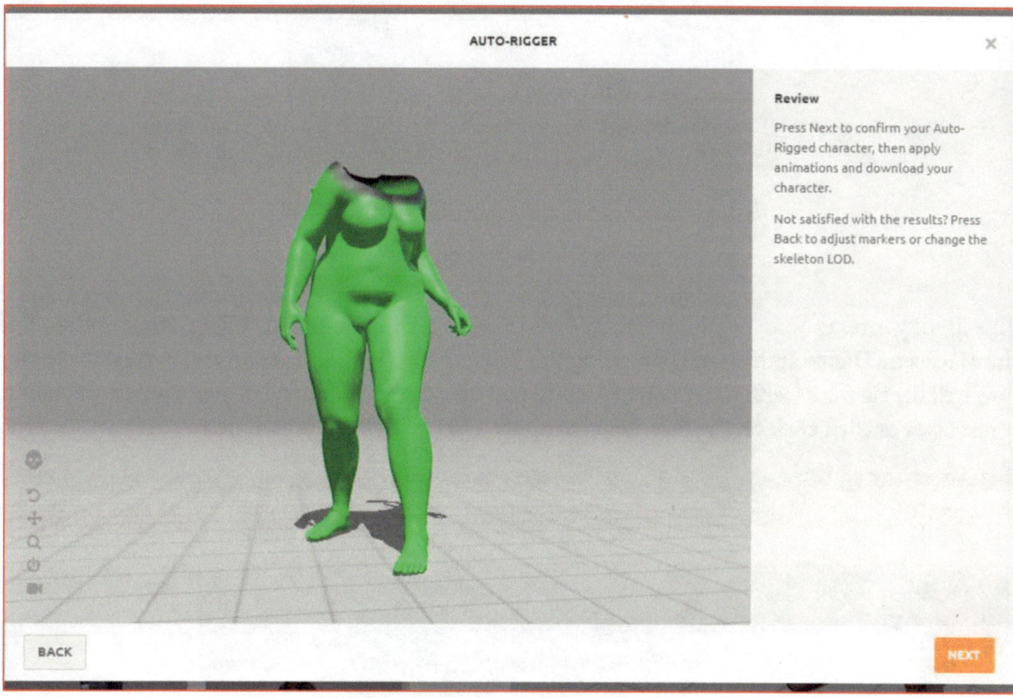

Figure 5.13: Auto rigging completed

You'll also notice that while most of the body is green, the top of the mesh is gray and black. This means that the gray and black area of the mesh isn't being influenced by the Mixamo Rig as much as the rest of the mesh. This is good because we want our MetaHuman Rig to influence the head and we are only interested in Mixamo for body animation.

When you are happy with the rigging, click **NEXT**, and we can now get ready to apply animation from the huge Mixamo motion capture library.

Exploring animation in Mixamo

In the Mixamo motion capture library, you'll see that all the animations are separated into different genres, just like in *Figure 5.14*:

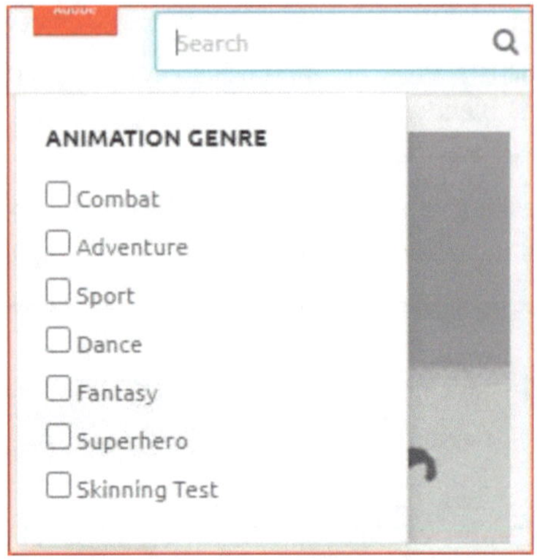

Figure 5.14: Animation genres

This list of genres is quite helpful but there's also a handy search function. Using either option, find the **Macarena Dance** animation (I am using this because it's a long animation and is great for testing how well the rig works with my character). Once you can see the thumbnail of your chosen animation, it just takes one left click on the thumbnail to apply it to your MetaHuman mesh.

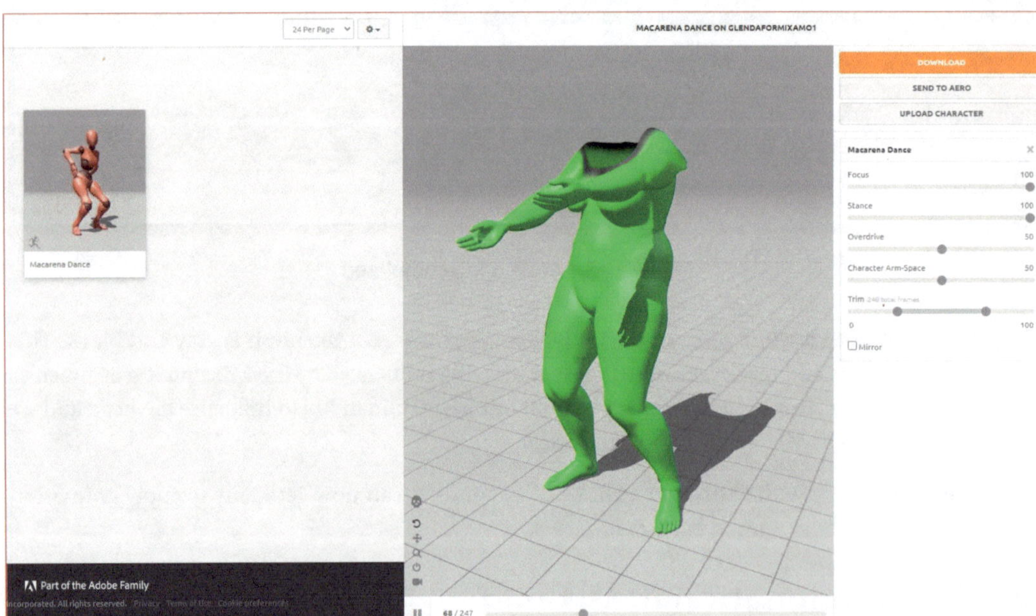

Figure 5.15: Completed rig with articulated fingers

Take note of the sliders on the right-hand side, which you can manipulate to your liking. The parameters are not the same from one animation to the next. For example, in relation to the Macarena dance, **Focus** is the first parameter; however, this parameter isn't available for most Mixamo animations.

When you play the animation with **Focus** at the minimum value versus the maximum value, you'll see a slight difference. Most likely, you are just blending between two separate motion capture performances. The minimal value, in this case, is where the dancer is not focused very well on their dancing, or in other words, they are dancing badly with poor rhythm and timing. The maximum value is another take where they are dancing very well and on time with a good rhythm. Often, each motion capture file will have one or more bespoke parameters depending on the nature of the performance.

The three most useful parameters in all animations that you will find yourself editing are as follows:

- **Character Arm-Space**: This determines the distance between the character's arms and its torso. When reviewing how your mesh performs within the Mixamo viewport, you may see moments where the mesh intersects with itself, such as an arm going through a waist. Of course, you'll need to widen the arm space to accommodate that. For the Macarena dance, the mocap session may have been performed by a lean dancer rather than an overweight Glenda, so this intersection is likely to occur. With that said, there could be instances where the mocap performer and model are similar, but you still need to create a wider arm space to accommodate heavy clothing or armor, so it is worth being mindful of this when making these adjustments.
- **Trim**: This refers to how much of the animation clip we want to trim. You are simply editing out a portion of the original animation if you use the default setting. As a rule of thumb, it's better to have more frames of animation than to not have enough.
- **Overdrive**: This will affect the speed. Overdrive simply means faster, so if you want to speed up, set the animation slider to a higher value in the **Overdrive** settings.

Go ahead and play with these settings until you're happy with how it looks. When you are done, click **DOWNLOAD**. In the next section, we will explore some of the settings that you will see.

Downloading the Mixamo animation

Continuing from the last section, when you click **DOWNLOAD**, Mixamo will take you to the following dialog box illustrated in *Figure 5.16*:

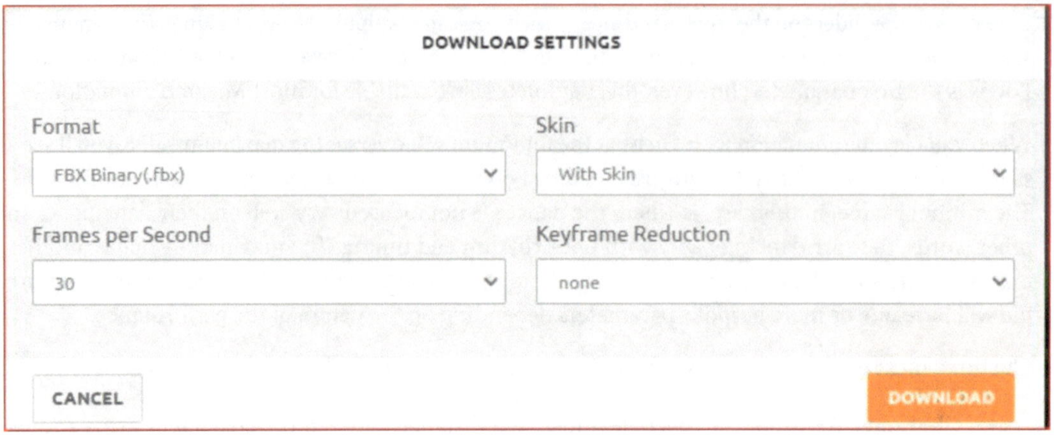

Figure 5.16: DOWNLOAD SETTINGS

Let's look at each of these options:

- **Format**: **FBX** is the same format you used when you exported from Unreal Engine; for the Unreal Mixamo pipeline, I strongly suggest you work with this preset. In the **Format** drop-down list, you will see other formats. Mostly, they consist of alternative and older versions of FBX. Another available format is **DAE**, however it is not compatible with Unreal.
- **Skin**: The default setting is **With Skin**; this means that when you download the file, it will contain your original mesh along with the Mixamo Rig and the animation all within the FBX file format. If you have multiple animations for your character, you only need to include the skin on the first animation you download. Choosing **Without Skin** will contain the animation data only.

> **Note**
>
> The first time that you download your animation, keep all of the default settings. However, once you've downloaded the first animation with **Skin** intact, you don't need the skin for any subsequent animation downloads for the same character.

- **Frames per Second**: The options are **24**, **30**, and **60** fps. Higher frame rates are good if you wish to edit the timing of your animation within Unreal Engine, particularly if you want to slow it down. Most motion capture is captured at a higher frame rate, allowing for retiming of the motion. It is better to have that higher frame rate than to attempt to interpolate slow motion in Unreal synthetically in an advanced workflow. A lower frame rate would be good if you are taking in really long animations and running them on a substandard machine.
- **Keyframe Reduction**: This is best left alone. The data size of these files and Unreal's ability to read them don't require keyframe reduction or optimization. Without keyframe reduction, Mixamo bakes a keyframe for each joint rotation on every frame. With keyframe reduction, Mixamo adds a little math in order to reduce the data size and this can reduce the quality of the animation. It's best for Unreal Engine to get that data to work. If there is any keyframe reduction required in Unreal, there are plenty of tools within Unreal to give you better and controllable results.

After clicking **DOWNLOAD**, Mixamo will ask you where you want to download your new FBX file; choose somewhere you will remember, ideally somewhere inside your project folder, as this will allow you to skip the following step.

If you save it directly to somewhere within your project **Content** folder and you have Unreal running, you will get a prompt as per *Figure 5.18* (which you will see in a moment) to allow the import to take place.

However, let's assume it's saved somewhere else so we can now take a look at manually importing your animation in the next step.

Importing the Mixamo animation into Unreal

If you've downloaded your FBX to some arbitrary location, you will need to import it into Unreal from the same location. To do that, first, create a new folder inside your Unreal Project and call it **MIXAMO_ANIMATIONS**. Double-click the folder so that you are inside it and then right-click to see the following menu:

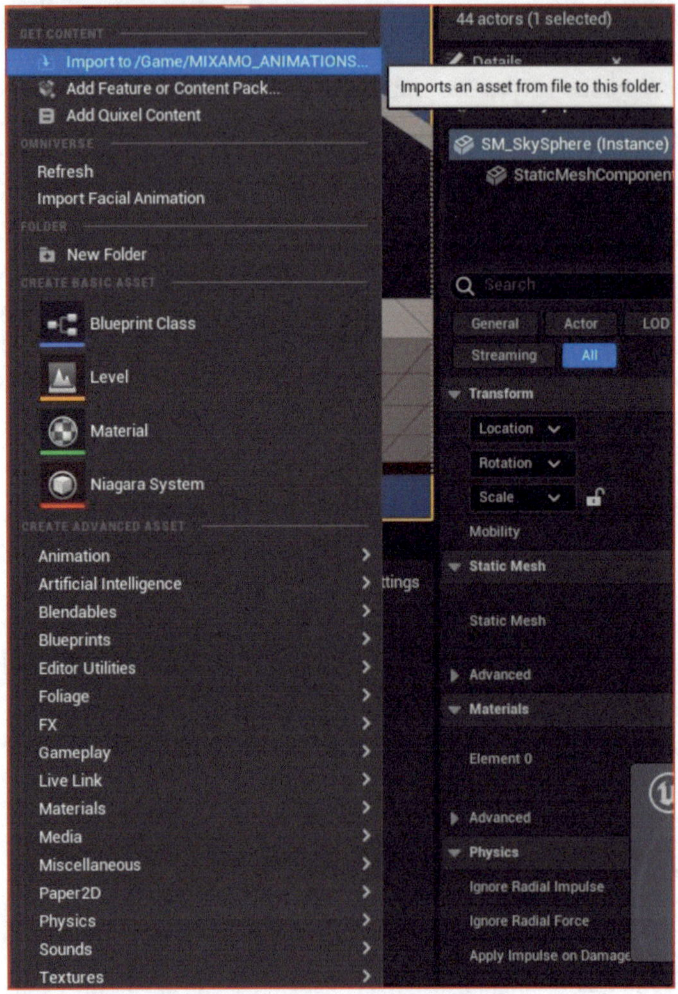

Figure 5.17: Importing FBX animation

To import the animation and the Mixamo Rig, choose **Import to**, along with the folder you are about to import the asset into. You can see from the highlighted text in *Figure 5.17* that I am importing the asset into **Game/MIXAMO_ANIMATIONS**.

Once selected, it will bring up **FBX Import Options**, as shown in *Figure 5.18*:

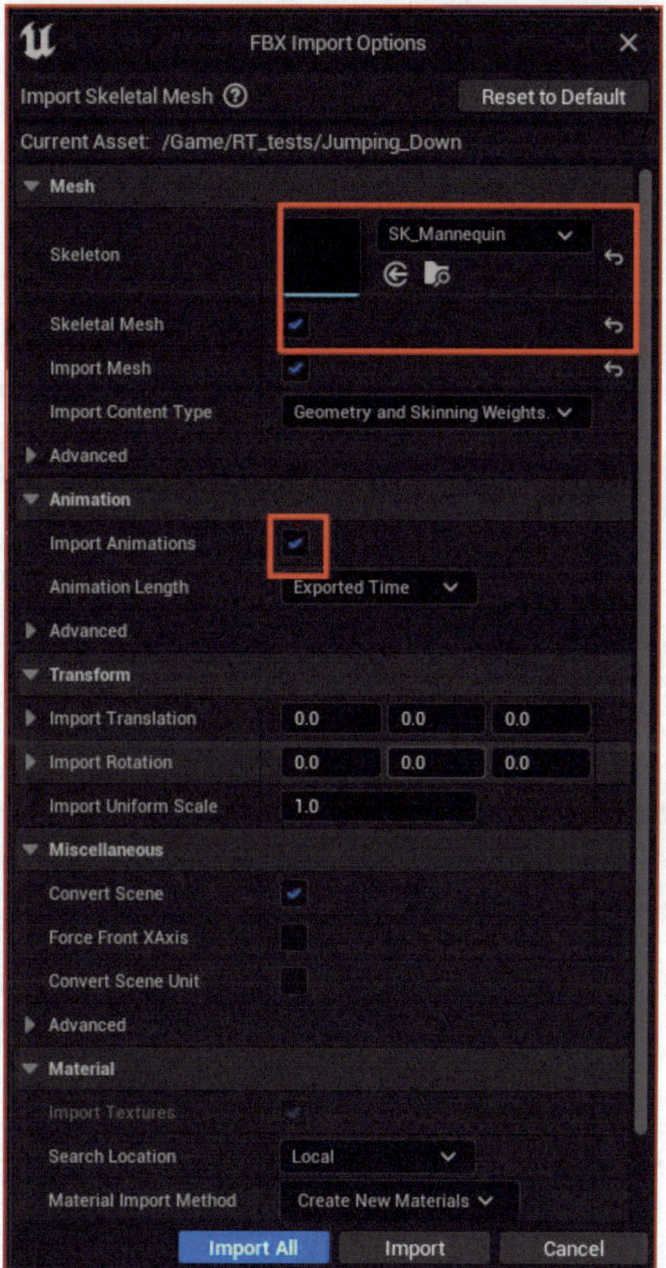

Figure 5.18: FBX Import Options

In *Figure 5.18*, you can see that there is a wealth of options to edit. Ultimately, the **FBX Import Options** dialog box allows us to import the Mixamo Rig, the Mixamo animation, the geometry of our MetaHuman character, and the skin weights associated with it. Importing all these components into Engine is essential for us to retarget the animation onto our MetaHuman character correctly.

However, if you've followed all the previous steps mentioned in this chapter, you'll find there's very little to do here. The default settings will be enough, with the exception of the following two:

- **Mesh Skeleton**: You need to choose what skeleton you want to use the Mixamo Rig on. Unfortunately, we can't use the MetaHuman skeleton with the Mixamo Rig directly, as it's far too complex; instead, we will use the next best thing, **SK_Mannequin**, which will be available once you click on the drop-down list, as shown in *Figure 5.18*.
- **Import Animations**: It may seem a little obvious, but yes, we need to make sure that this **Import Animations** box is checked so that we can import the animation that has been embedded within the FBX file.

> **Note**
>
> If you have already gone through this process of downloading the Mixamo Rig, skin weights, and animation, you will see that your Mixamo Rig is now an option to choose from **FBX Import Options** instead of **SK_Mannequin**.

Once you have ensured you've selected the correct **Mesh Skeleton** and checked **Import Animations**, click on **Import All**. This will take a few minutes to load into your project. Once imported, you will find that you now have newly imported assets, looking similar to *Figure 5.19*:

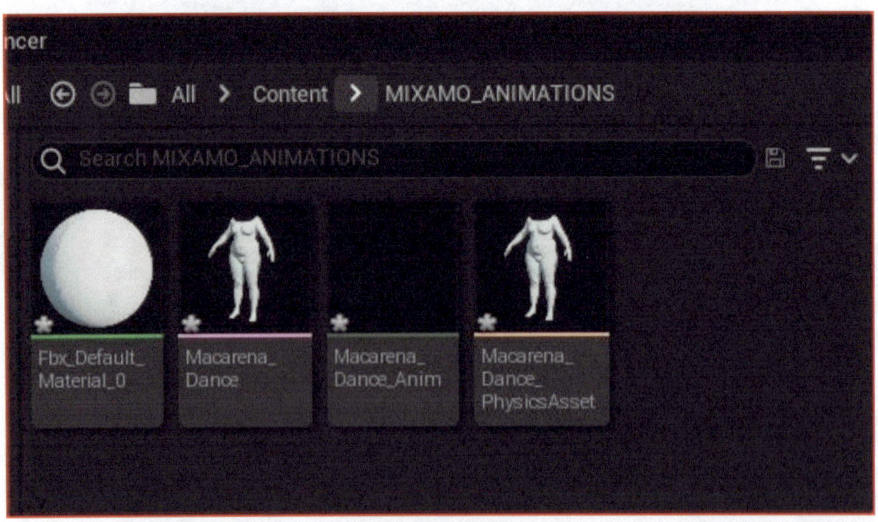

Figure 5.19: Imported assets

At this point, we've just successfully brought in the Mixamo animation, along with a rig that has all the skin weights enabled to properly manipulate the MetaHuman body mesh. From *Figure 5.19*, you can see those assets; from left to right, we have the following:

- **Fbx_Default_Material_0**: This is the default material as exported from Mixamo. As we're only interested in animation from Mixamo, we can ignore this.
- **Macarena_Dance**: This is the Mixamo Rig that has the skin weights that we need.
- **Macarena_Dance_Anim**: This is the actual keyframe data of each of the joints.
- **Macarena_Dance_PhysicsAsset**: This was created automatically by Unreal during the import process, containing physics simulations that are beyond the scope of this book.

> **Note**
>
> To learn more about **PhysicsAsset** in UE, you can review the following link: `https://docs.unrealengine.com/5.0/en-US/physics-asset-editor-in-unreal-engine/`

Currently, we have a Mixamo Rig but no skeleton, and because of this, we can't apply the Mixamo animation to our MetaHuman Blueprint. So, just like in *Chapter 4*, we need to use two IK Rigs so that we can repurpose the Unreal **SK_Mannequinn** and retarget animation from it to the MetaHuman. While it may be familiar to you, I've outlined the process again for our new Mixamo assets:

1. In the new **Mixamo_Animations** folder, create a new IK Rig and call it **Source_RigMixamo**. Then, create another IK Rig and call it **Target_RigMeta**.

   As a reminder on how to do this, look at *Figure 5.20*; you can see that when you right-click anywhere within the **Content** tab, you can choose **Animation** and then select **IK Rig** from the list:

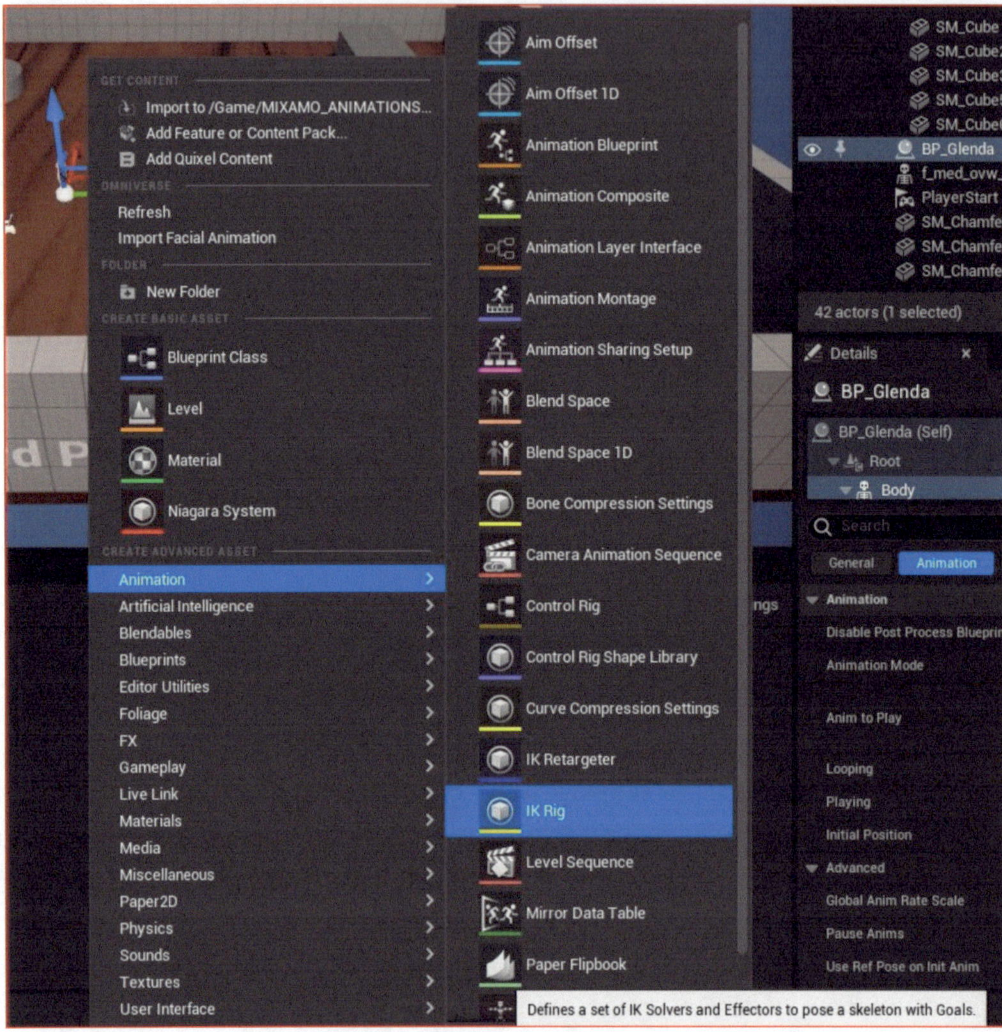

Figure 5.20: Creating an IK Rig

2. With both IK Rigs created, the next step is to create five IK chains for each and ensure that the following chain order is completed:

    - The spine to the head
    - The left clavicle to the left hand
    - The right clavicle to the right hand
    - The left thigh to the left foot
    - The right thigh to the right foot

3. Using the IK Rigs, we need to use **SK_Mannequin** as the skeleton for the source and leave the **Glenda_Med_Ovw** skeleton as the target.

   Just like in the previous chapter, I recommend opening up both the source and target IK Rigs and putting them side by side, as shown in *Figure 5.21*. This way, you can ensure that you are getting them to match as much as possible in terms of the IK chains and the order in which the IK chains are created.

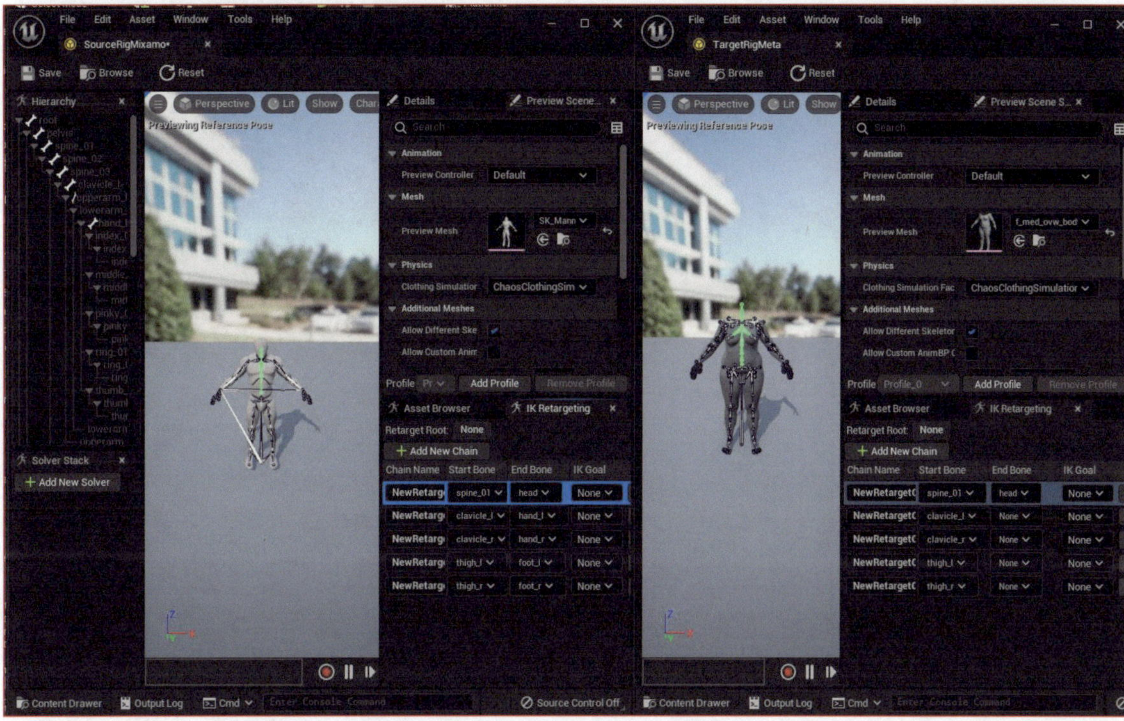

Figure 5.21: IK Rigs side by side

4. Next, you now need to create an IK Retargeter. To do this, right-click in the **Mixamo_Animations** folder, then under **Animations**, choose **IK Retargeter**. This creates a new IK Retargeter, which you can rename to something such as **Mixamo_MetaRetargeter**.

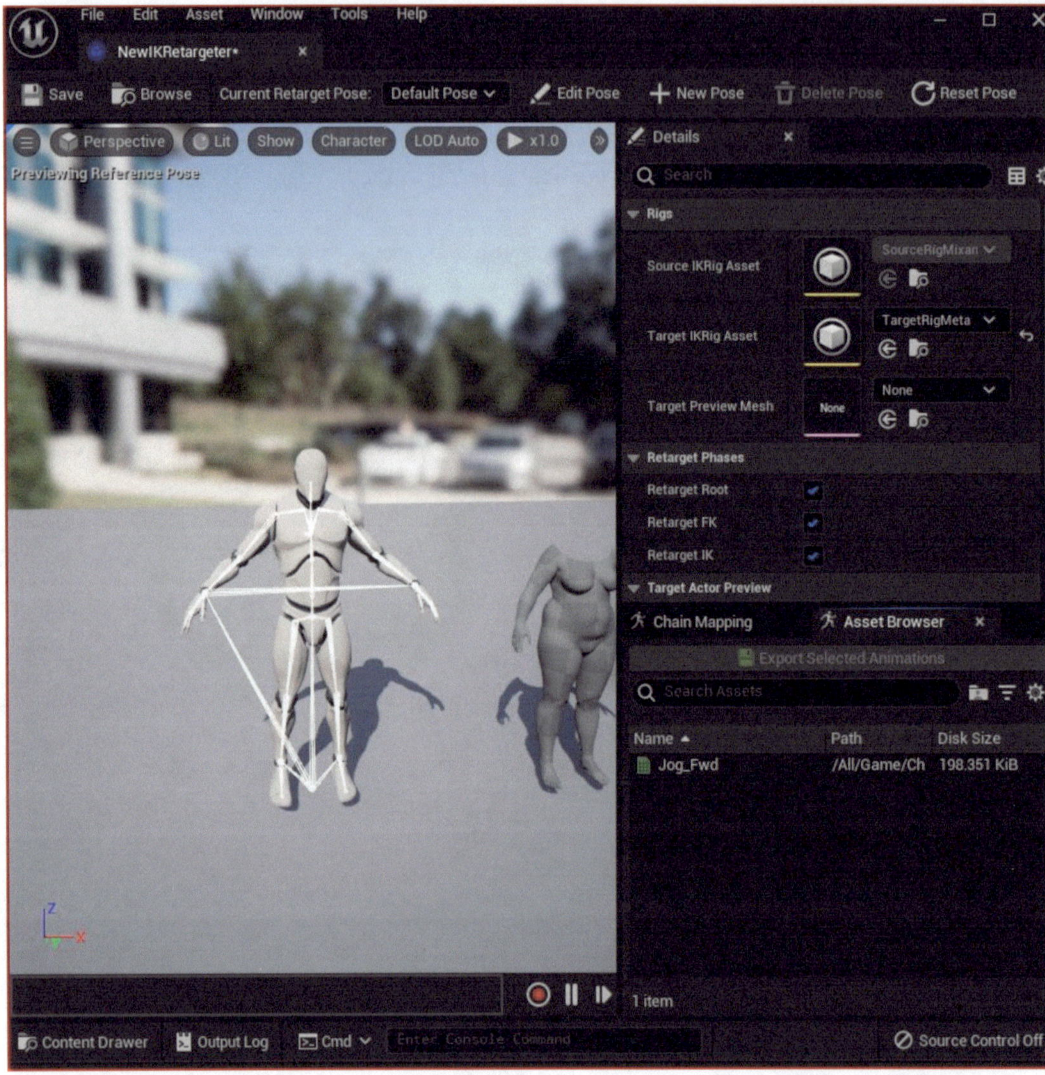

Figure 5.22: The IK Retargeter

5. Once you've done that, open the IK Retargeter and you will see that at the top right, the source is ghosted out. This is because you already chose the source while you were creating the IK Retargeter. However, it is still waiting for you to input what the target is. Be sure to choose the new IK Rig you made for your target.
6. Next, click on **Asset Browser**, as shown in *Figure 5.23*. You'll notice that **Export Selected Animations** is green (if you hadn't chosen a target, it would have remained ghosted). Click **Export Selected Animations** now.

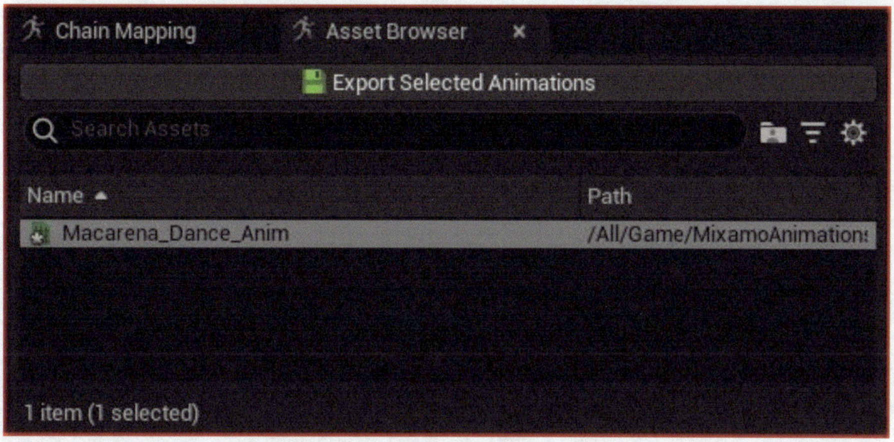

Figure 5.23: Export Selected Animations

Once clicked, Unreal will write a new animation file; here, you will need to pick the destination, as shown in *Figure 5.24*. I recommend placing this new animation in the **Mixamo_Animations** folder. Don't worry, you'll be able to distinguish it from the original un-retargeted animation, as it also amends the animation name with the **Retargeted** suffix to make it easier for you to find it.

7. Next, click **OK**, and you've just retargeted a Mixamo animation, ready to use on your MetaHuman character.

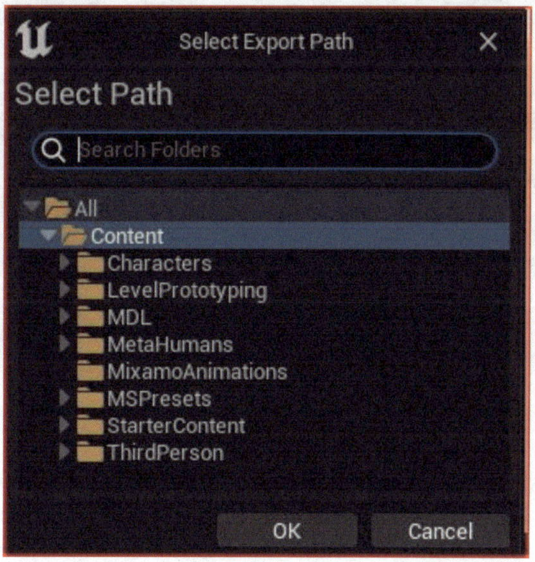

Figure 5.24: Select Export Path

8. To test it out, ensure you have your character Blueprint in your scene. You can do this by simply dragging the character Blueprint from the **Content** folder and into the viewport. Then, with your character selected, click on **Body** in the **Details** panel.

   Ensure you have selected **Use Animation Asset** as the **Animation Mode** setting, as shown in *Figure 5.25*. The animation asset it is referring to is any animation compatible with your MetaHuman Blueprint in the scene.

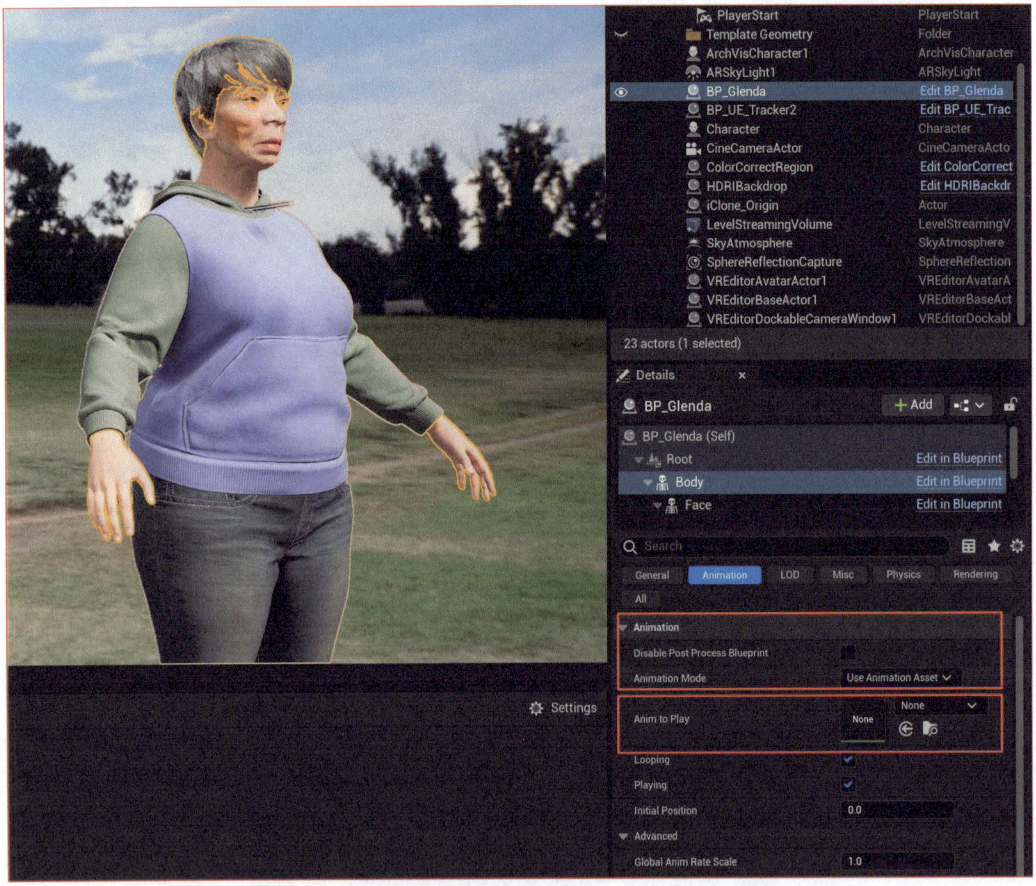

Figure 5.25: Setting Animation Mode as an animation asset

9. Look for **Anim to Play**. Next to it, you'll see a drop-down list. Use this to search for `Retargeted`. This will call up the only retargeted animation asset, which is the one you just created; in my case, it is called **MacerenaDance_anim_Retargeted** (remember, the name **MacarenaDance** was assigned to the file name by Maximo, and the **Retargeted** suffix was assigned by the IK Retargeter).
10. Once the asset is selected, click **Play** above your main 3D viewport and you'll see your animation come to life.

Now, you have successfully imported your animation into Unreal Engine, retargeted the animation using source and target IK Rigs, and used the IK Retargeter tool. You were also able to preview your animation inside the scene.

If you plan to bring in a lot of animations over a period of time, the IK Retargeter will become a frequently used asset.

Working with subsequent animations

For any subsequent animation downloads from Mixamo, you should download **Without Skin** (this option is available when downloading your animation in Mixamo, as per *Figure 5.16*). Then, when importing the new animations into Unreal, you can now choose the skeleton that was created when you created the source IK Rig (in my case, it's called **MaceranaDance_Skeleton**). The headless thumbnail of the Glenda preview mesh dancing the Macarena is also visible, like so:

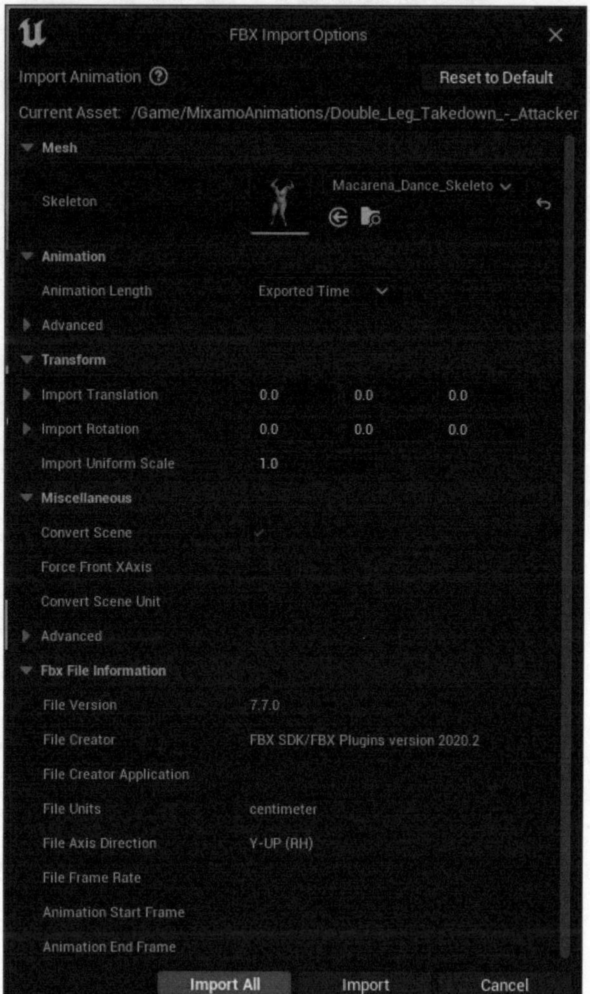

Figure 5.26: FBX Import Options for subsequent animation-only files

It would be good practice to download a batch of animations from Mixamo without skin. Then, you can drag and drop all of them directly from an external folder into your **Content** folder or import them using the **File Import** option and selecting multiple files rather than just one.

When importing multiple animation FBX files, you will get the dialog box shown in *Figure 5.26*. By clicking on **Import All**, the same setting will be applied to all of the animations you are importing. So, if you have 100 animations, you will apply this skeleton to all 100 assets in one single click.

In my case, I have downloaded five soccer animations and imported them into my **Mixamo_Animations** folder that I previously created in my Unreal project. To batch-retarget all these animations, I only need to open up the IK Retargeter.

Opening up the IK Retargeter that I created earlier, I can now see these animations and their skeletons ready to be retargeted to my MetaHuman character:

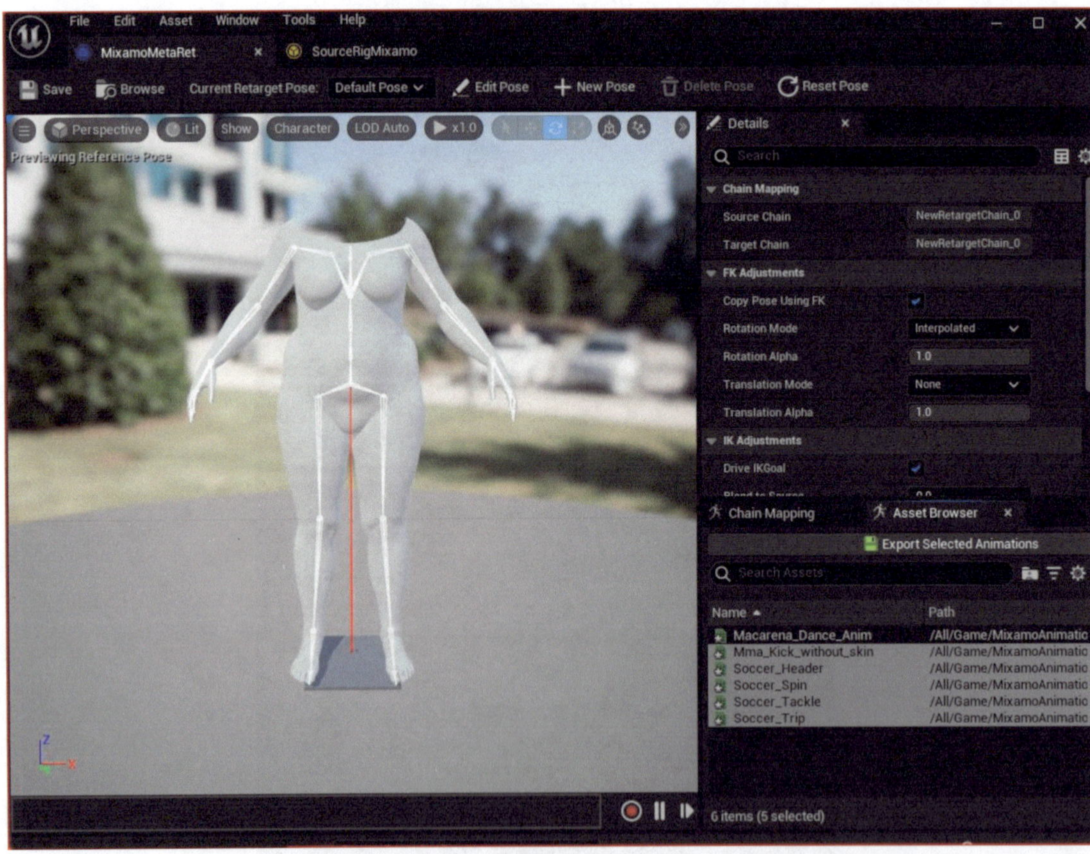

Figure 5.27: IK Retargeter with multiple animations available for retargeting

Because my new animations have been set to use the Mixamo skeleton upon import, they automatically become available in the IK Retarget list. You can see that list at the bottom of *Figure 5.27*. I have brought in five soccer animations and selected them all.

Using the **Export Selected Animations** button, I can now batch-convert multiple animations with just one click.

When exporting these animations, the IK Retargeter retains the animation name and automatically adds the **Retargeted** suffix to each animation asset. As before, you can go to your character Blueprint, and under **Anim to Play**, you can search for your new animations. In *Figure 5.28*, you can see that I searched for **soccer** and found that my new and retargeted animations were ready to apply to my character Blueprint already in the scene:

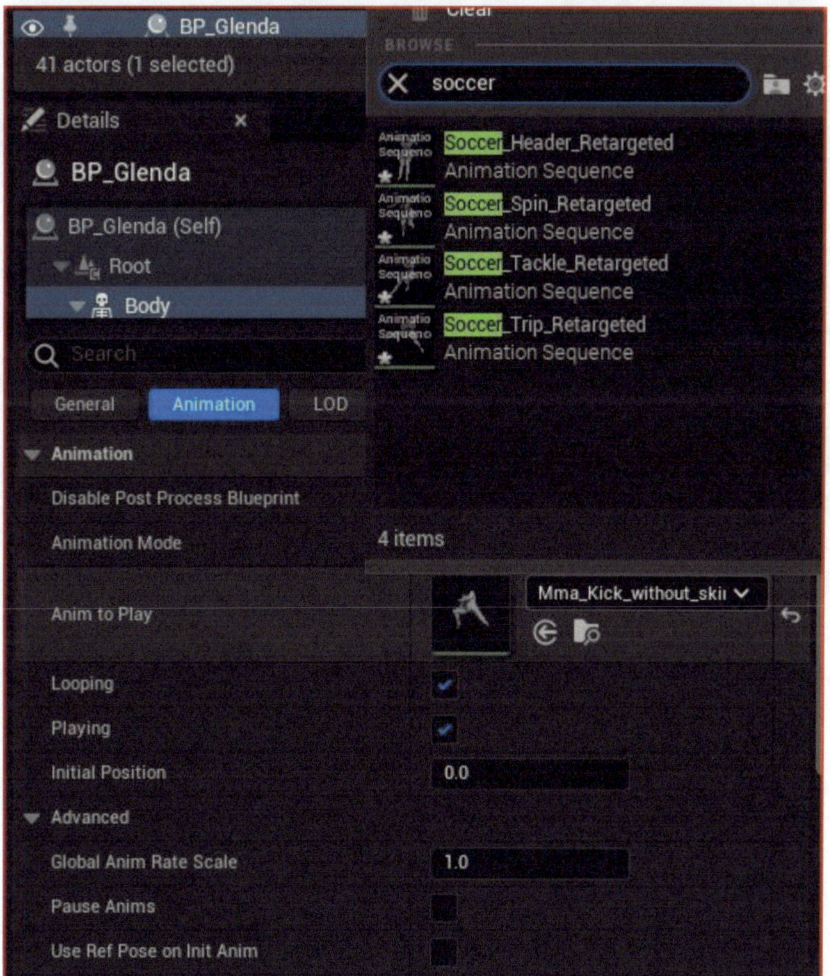

Figure 5.28: Retargeted animation available under Anim to Play

Because of the work done in the previous section, in this section, you were able to batch-import multiple animations and batch-retarget them using the IK Retargeter tool. This is a very efficient approach to creating an entire motion library dedicated to your MetaHuman character.

Summary

In this chapter, we learned about the fantastic and free resource, Mixamo, to bring hundreds of animations into your project. We learned how to best configure our character meshes to get the most out of Mixamo and we also got a little revision time on IK Rigs and the IK Retargeter.

As well as that, we learned about the importance of character proportions, a little about skin weighting, and their connection to character proportions and animation rigs.

Most importantly, we learned about the very powerful automation tools that allow us to batch-import and batch-retarget animation files acquired from Mixamo.

In the next chapter, we will learn about DeepMotion, another online resource that allows us to create our own custom animations using just a video camera.

6

Adding Motion Capture with DeepMotion

In the previous chapter, we were introduced to the motion capture library of Mixamo and how to make the Mixamo animations work inside Unreal.

In this chapter, we are going to build on that knowledge and create our very own animation using another third-party online tool called **DeepMotion**, which includes a tool called **Animate 3D** that analyzes video of human performances and, in return, creates a motion capture file. We will learn how to use a video camera effectively to record a performance, then use DeepMotion's Animate 3D feature to create your very own bespoke motion capture file, and then use it to animate your MetaHuman character in Unreal.

As much as stock motion libraries such as Mixamo are great, you will need to have your own bespoke animation to give you creative freedom. Even if a solution such as DeepMotion's Animate 3D may not be as good as the results that you would get from expensive motion capture suits, it will be much better than the compromises you will make using library stock motion.

So, in this chapter, we will cover the following topics:

- Introducing DeepMotion
- Preparing our video footage
- Uploading our video clip to DeepMotion
- Exploring DeepMotion's Animation Settings
- Downloading the DeepMotion Motion Capture File
- Importing the DeepMotion Motion Animation into Unreal
- Retargeting the DeepMotion Motion Capture
- Fixing position misalignment issues

Technical requirements

In terms of computer power, you will need the technical requirements detailed in *Chapter 1*, and the MetaHuman character plus the Unreal Engine Mannequin that we imported into UE5 in *Chapter 2*. Both of these will need to be saved in the same project in UE, and you will need to have UE running for this chapter.

You will also need a stable internet connection, as we will be uploading a MetaHuman preview mesh and a video file, and downloading numerous animation assets. You will need a video camera – a webcam, smartphone, or a professional video or digital cinecamera will all do, but note that there aren't benefits for video with greater resolution than HD.

Introducing DeepMotion

Until recently, bespoke motion capture solutions required expensive equipment and expensive software; think about movies like *Avatar*, *The Lord of the Rings*, or *Pirates of the Caribbean*, where performers have to wear motion capture suits with either reflective balls or checker markers with infrared sensors. This technology was only viable for large studios that could make such an investment, and as a result, independent studios and freelance artists had to make do with just motion capture libraries, such as Mixamo, as we have already discussed.

Recently, this has changed as more and more affordable solutions have become available to artists. In my research for this book, I worked with a number of motion capture tools specifically with cost in mind. Because **motion capture** (**mocap**) suits and infrared sensors and all that fancy gear are just too expensive for most of us, I looked at DeepMotion's Animate 3D.

DeepMotion's Animation 3D is an example of a **markerless mocap solution**. This involves a process where a video of human performance is captured with a video camera with no special suit or markers required. The video file is analyzed by software that recognizes and tracks each body part. With machine learning aiding this process, the solution is able to utilize libraries or motion data to avoid errors. In addition, **inverse kinematics** is also utilized to further refine the process. This technology is constantly improving, and with machine learning being a key feature, the rate of progress is very fast indeed.

In the case of DeepMotion, the online tool allows us to upload a video of our performance and processes the motion capture for us to use in Unreal (or any other compatible platform). Though this process includes machine learning, fortunately for us, DeepMotion takes care of all that.

In the next section, we will dive into the nuts and bolts of how to record videos effectively.

Preparing our video footage

Before we go over to DeepMotion, there are some key factors we need to know with regard to recording our performances on video. Let's look at them now:

- *Camera quality and position*: DeepMotion is capable of working with low-end cameras such as webcams or old smartphones, all the way up to high-end cinema cameras, so long as the picture is sharp and steady and has a reasonably high frame rate. Many lower-end cameras have a minimum frame rate of 30 fps, but you will get a better result on fast-moving actors if you use a higher frame rate.

  Also, ideally, the camera should be stationary because the software works out the performer's motion based on a fixed floor position. The ideal position of the camera is about 2 meters from the performer.

- *High-contrast filming*: As this markerless mocap solution is tracking pixels rather than sensors, we need to make it as easy as possible for the software to differentiate the background from the performer. This is why we need to have a high contrast between the two. If you plan to shoot against a dark background, such as a curtain, be sure to have your performer wear bright colors, and vice versa. Also, loose clothing can cause problems as, often, the clothing will be tracked; for example, if the performer is wearing very baggy sleeves, it's difficult for the tracker to tell the difference between an arm and a sleeve.

- *Keep head to toes in shot at all times*: Although DeepMotion can do a good job at working out the motion of a character just from video of the waist up, as a rule of thumb, it is better to get more data than you need, so ensure that you capture head to toe shots of your performer as much as you can. Capturing the performer's whole body is also important as, even if your performer's feet or head go out of shot for a second, it can cause poor results throughout the rest of the motion-capturing process.

  With that said, if your intention is to capture the full body performance, then video capturing the full body is a must.

- *Calibration time*: Make sure that you have your performer in shot for a few seconds before and after the performance, preferably in a T-shaped pose and facing the camera. This gives DeepMotion time to align its skeleton to the performer's body before, rather than during, the performance.

- *Occlusion*: It is rare in video footage that we find performers not covering one part of their body with another. Typically, they have their arms in front of their body, but because DeepMotion can determine the skeleton's spine position, in such a scenario, that type of occlusion isn't a problem.

  However, when the body goes in front of a limb, there can be issues. Taking hands as an example, if and when they go behind the body or the head, DeepMotion has to guess where the hands should be because it has no pixels to tell it where the hands are. It will either try to guess or apply no animation at all to those problem areas.

Also, occlusion can occur by objects that are between the performer and the camera, which can cause issues. For example, a tree branch or lamppost might momentarily get in the way but could inadvertently cause a lot more errors than expected.

Therefore, shooting with anything in the foreground obscuring your performers is not recommended.

- *Performance speed*: DeepMotion isn't very good at detecting very fast motion in a clip. For example, for someone tap dancing or boxing, the software has a hard time keeping up with the rapid foot movement and, instead, gives a very poor result. A good rule of thumb is that if you see any motion blur in the video clip, it's not likely to give you a good result. Be sure to play the clip in slow motion to properly analyze it.
- *File size*: If you work with professional video file formats, there is no benefit other than the ability to shoot at higher frame rates. Compressed or lossy video file formats such as MP4 will do the job, and keeping the file size down to around 200 MB is best. Larger file sizes take longer to upload and longer to get analyzed. While MOV files are accepted, I recommend you use MP4 files instead.

In this section, we have covered all the major factors that need to be considered when it comes to recording a video of your performer. Given the nature of video and how every scenario will be different, there will be a certain amount of trial and error, so don't be disheartened if you don't get great results at first. You can always refer back to this section to troubleshoot any issues you may be having.

Alternatively, if you don't want to shoot anything yourself, you could go to a stock library and download a clip that matches the criteria mentioned earlier. For the purpose of this book, I have taken clips from `motionarray.com`.

In the next section, you will upload your clip to DeepMotion, assuming that you have shot something.

Uploading our video to DeepMotion

In this section, we will head over to the DeepMotion site, register, and upload our footage.

The first thing you need to do is go over to `https://www.deepmotion.com/`. From the landing page, click on the **SIGN UP** button and you'll see the form shown in *Figure 6.1*. Fill this out to create a Freemium account (and note the features on the right):

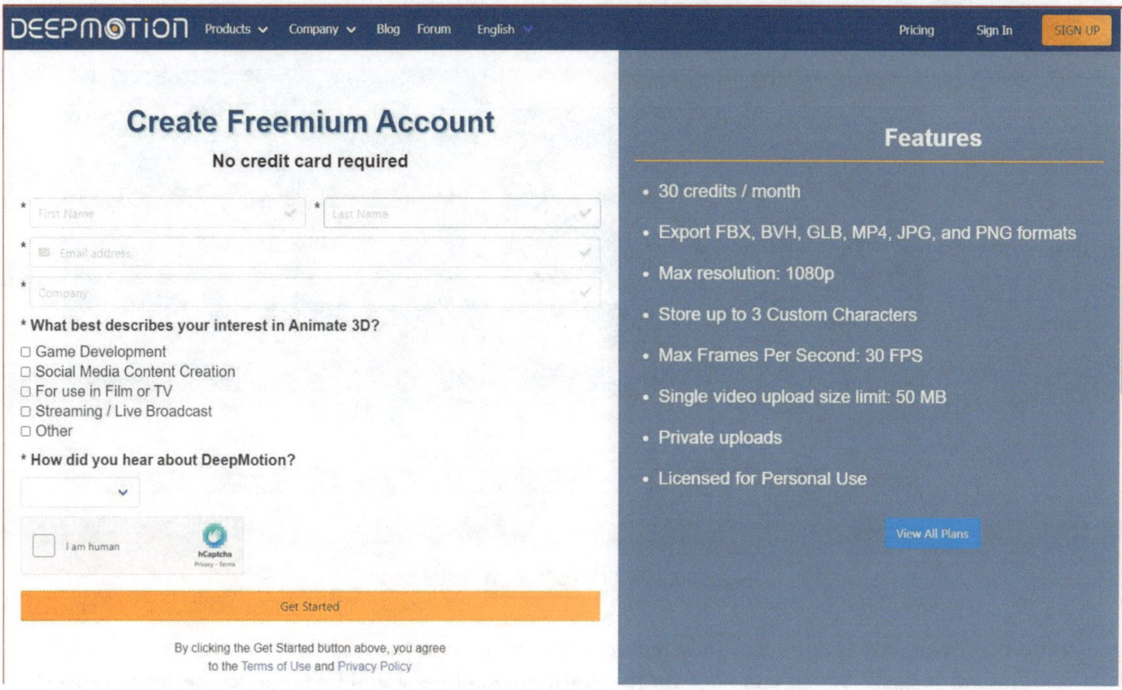

Figure 6.1: Signing up with DeepMotion

> **Note**
>
> DeepMotion's Freemium account will allow you to upload clips no more than 10 seconds long, no bigger in resolution than 1,080 pixels, and with a frame rate of no more than 30 fps. With the free user price plan, you get a maximum of 30 seconds of animation per month. Effectively, this is a trial service and you will have to pay for more usage, but there are various paid plans that have more features, such as allowing you to upload clips with higher frame rates.

Once you have filled in your details, click the **Get Started** button. This will either send a link to your email address or take you directly to the DeepMotion Portal page, as shown in *Figure 6.2*:

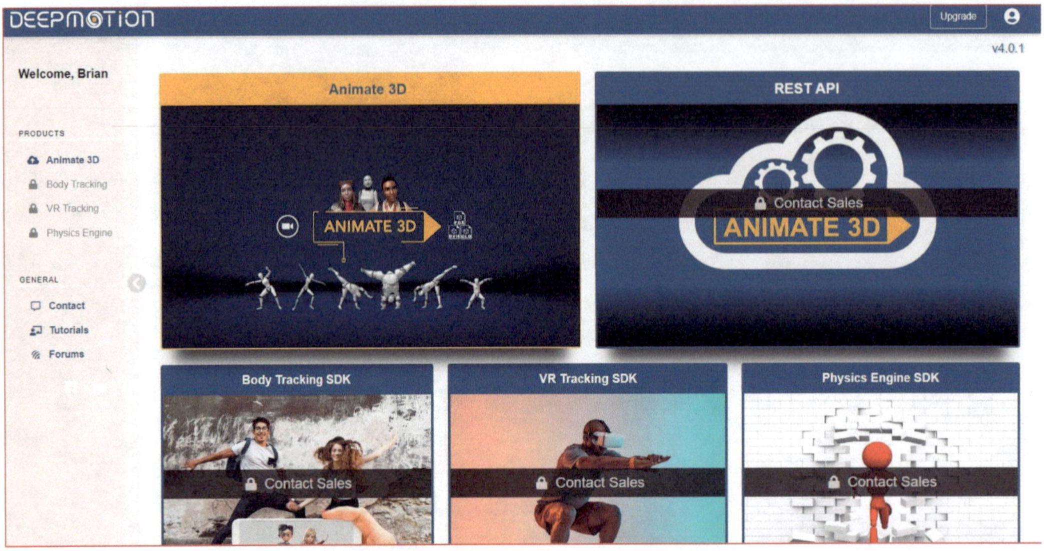

Figure 6.2: The DeepMotion Portal page

With the Freemium account, the only feature available to us is the **Animate 3D** feature (the other features are locked). When you click on the **Animate 3D** box, you'll be taken to the Animate 3D welcome page, as per *Figure 6.3*:

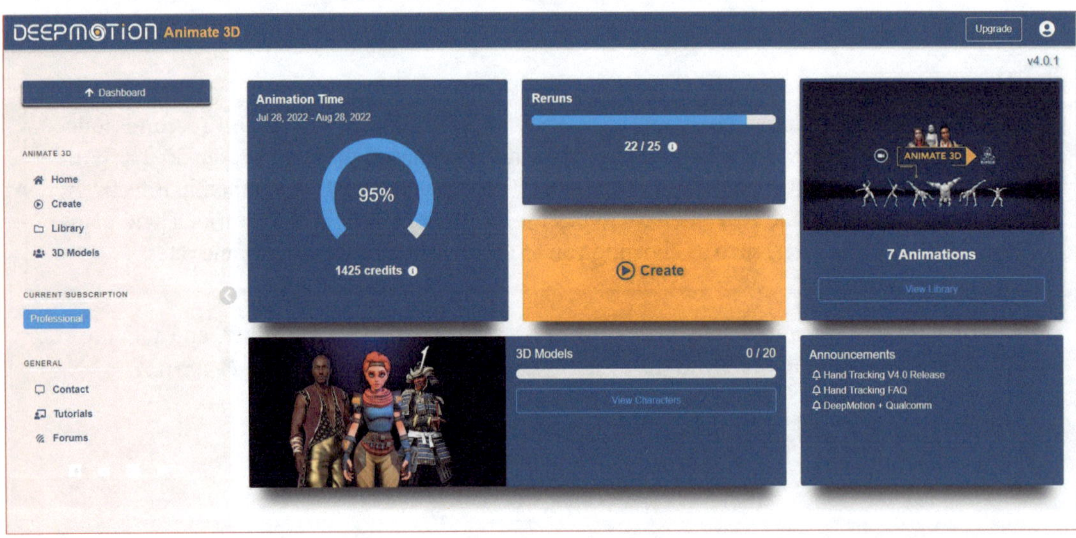

Figure 6.3: The Animate 3D welcome page

Here, you'll see how many credits you have: 1 credit is equal to 1 second of animation. The next box is titled **Reruns**, and this shows how many attempts you have to refine the capture process. Reruns allow you to make changes to your settings without using up any of your animation credits.

Now, click on the big yellow **Create** button and you'll be greeted with the dashboard where you can place your footage, as shown in *Figure 6.4*:

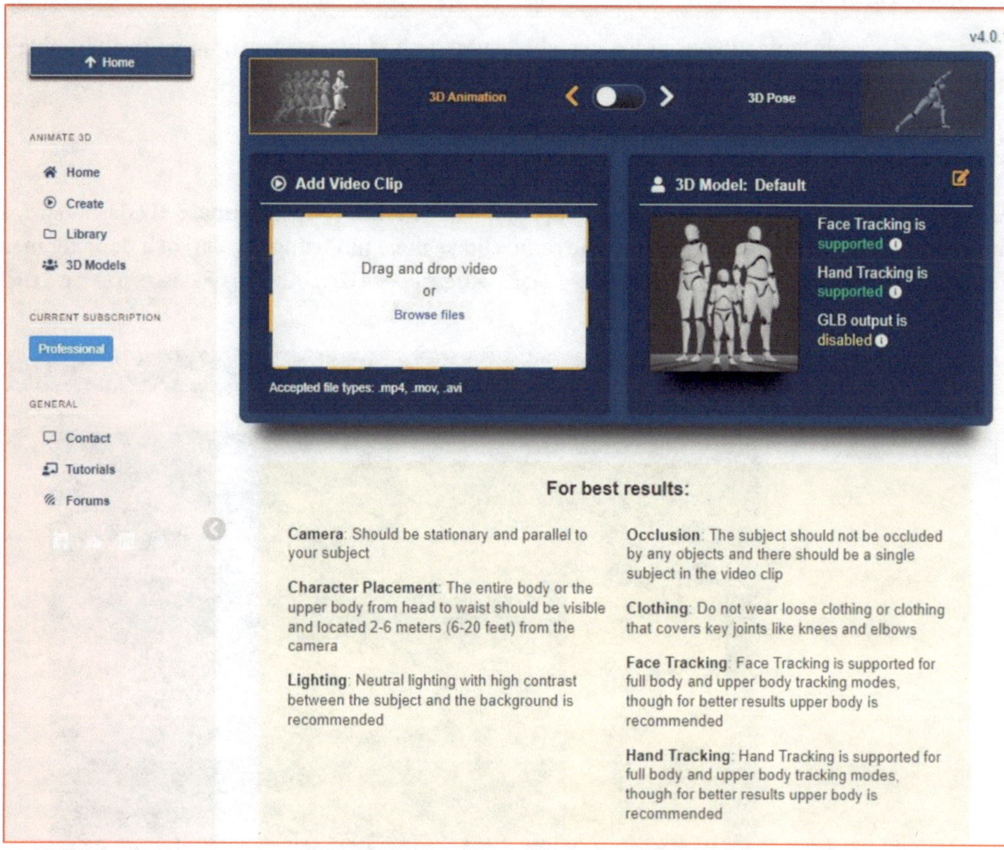

Figure 6.4: The Animate 3D dashboard

At the top of *Figure 6.4*, you can see two thumbnails: **3D Animation** and **3D Pose**. Make sure to switch to **3D Animation**.

Underneath, you have the option to either drag and drop your folder into DeepMotion or navigate through your folders to upload the file. They also provide a list of accepted file types: MP4, MOV, and AVI. If you have any other format, you will need to convert your files using an encoder such as Adobe Media Encoder, VLC Player, or QuickTime Pro.

> **Note**
>
> Unless there is any notable difference in quality from an original MOV file compared to an MP4 conversion, use MP4 as it will reduce the uploading and processing time.

Finally, you'll see a reminder of how to get the best results for your videos (which I expanded upon earlier in the chapter), and I advise you to take a look at that to make sure you get the most out of your limited credit.

Once you are ready, upload your video via whichever method you prefer; now, you will be able to view the video setting.

Exploring DeepMotion's animation settings

As soon as you have uploaded your video clip, you will be taken to the **Animate 3D** dashboard, as shown in *Figure 6.5*. If you want to use the same clip as me, I am using the clip of a dancing man, found here: `https://motionarray.com/stock-video/happy-man-dancing-vertical-814129/`.

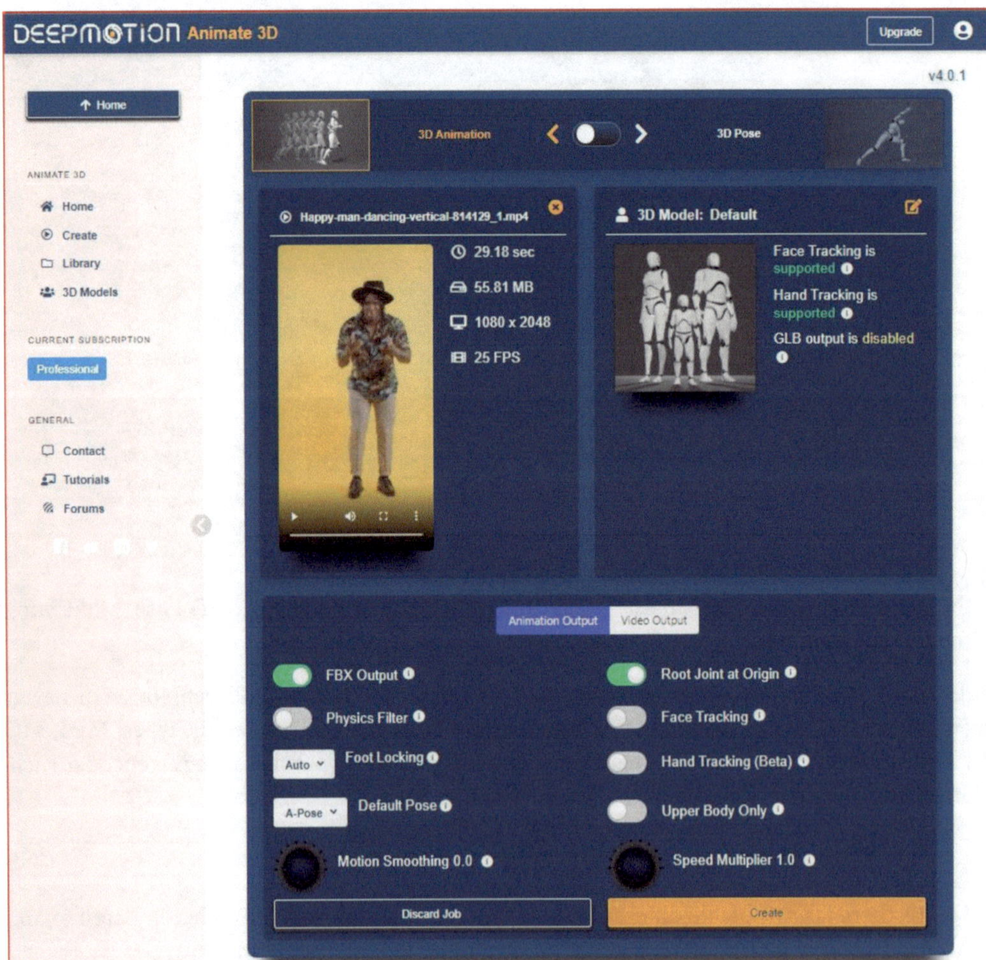

Figure 6.5: Animate 3D dashboard

In *Figure 6.5* you can see a thumbnail of the video clip, along with the clip's filename, `Happy-man-dancing-vertical-814129_1.mp4`.The attributes of the clip are present on the right-hand side of the thumbnail, as follows:

- **Duration**: This allows you to keep an eye on how long the clip is. A clip that is longer than is permitted based on your pricing plan will give you an error; in this case, you will need to upload a shorter clip.
- **File Size**: If the file size is too big for your account setting, you will get an error. You will need to run the file through a compressor (such as Adobe Encoder) to reduce the file size, and then reupload it. If you get an error during the upload process, it is likely that you have breached the limit of one or more of these attributes based on your account setting.
- **Resolution**: Each account setting has a maximum resolution. You will get an error if the resolution is too big, and you will need to reduce the resolution using a converter. For example, a clip that is 4,096 x 3,112 will be too large for the Freemium account, so you will need to scale it down to 1,920 x 1,080 (using Adobe Encoder or similar).
- **Frame Rate**: If you have a Freemium account, using a higher frame rate, such as 200 fps, will produce an error. Typically, a webcam will produce a video with a frame rate of around 25 fps, so using a webcam can reduce the chance of this error.

In the bottom half of the interface shown in *Figure 6.5*, you'll see two options: **Animation Output** and **Video Output**. For the purposes of this book, we are ignoring **Video Output**, so make sure that **Animation Output** is selected instead.

There are 10 features to use, but not all of them are either available or relevant based on your type of account and the complexity of the motion capture you want to achieve. The **Animation Output** parameters are as follows:

- **FBX Output**: This is the file type that you wish to use for your animation. Because we only want to use FBX animations in Unreal later, make sure the output is set to FBX. (We are only given other options if we want to create static poses, which are not relevant to this book.)
- **Physics Filter**: This enforces joint limits and attempts to remove collisions, such as hands drifting through the torso. If there are not any notable issues with the footage, I recommend you first attempt to process the animation with **Physics Filter** disabled, as it may produce a somewhat artificial result. Also, remember to take advantage of the **Rerun** option to experiment with **Physics Filter** if you don't get a good result the first time.
- **Foot Locking**: This addresses a common problem in motion capture, which is to do with when a foot leaves the ground and then is returned. For motion capture with suits, this is less of an issue, but with video motion capture, it can be difficult to ascertain when a foot is in contact with the ground or not. **Foot Locking** comes with four options:

    - **Auto**: This is the most common mode to use as it will automatically switch between locking the foot position to the ground or letting it move. For a character that is walking or dancing, this is the most likely mode to use because the character will inevitably be lifting and resting their feet on the ground intermittently.

> **Note**
> Only the **Auto** setting is available in the Freemium account.

    - **Never**: In animations that involve swimming or continual falling, we know the character's feet will never connect with the ground, so we use this mode to avoid an error.
    - **Always**: Best used for situations when the character's feet never leave the ground. It might seem a little obvious but when given the choice between **Auto** and **Always**, it is best to use Always when we know the character's feet don't leave the ground as the **Auto** mode could cause errors in this instance.
    - **Grounding**: Effectively, this keeps the feet at ground level but doesn't necessarily lock them to a fixed position. **Auto** works in a similar way but isn't as effective in fast movement; if your character is moving their feet in a sliding motion, **Grounding** mode is the best choice.

- **Default Pose**: This refers to a skeleton calibration pose when saving the animation file. Ideally, the calibration pose of the source animation should match the calibration pose of the target character. In this dropdown, we have four options:
    - **A-Pose**: One of the most common calibrations poses used and the same pose in which MetaHumans appear in the UE5 engine. This pose sets the arms at a 45-degree angle.
    - **I-Pose**: This is an unlikely pose to use but one where the arms are straight down.
    - **T-Pose**: Another standard pose and the default pose of an Unreal Engine Mannequin. The arms are straight out in this pose at a 90-degree angle from the body, thus providing a T shape.
    - **Sitting**: Another unlikely pose, where the arms are similar to an **A-Pose** but the character is sitting down.
- **Motion Smoothing**: This option uses AI to determine how the character should move by looking at the trajectory of each joint, and then removes any jitter or noise from the animation, which comes from constant recalibration. While useful to get rid of unwanted jitter, it can introduce some artificial-looking movement; you can dial up and down the intensity of the smoothing to get the results you want.

> **Note**
>
> This feature is not available in the Freemium accounts.

- **Root Joint at Origin**: This is a particularly useful feature for Unreal Engine artists as it creates a bone at the origin, which is on the ground between both feet. This bone is linked to the hip to correspond to the root position of a character. It is recommended that you turn this feature on for motion capture intended for use with UE, so we'll make sure to do that here.
- **Face Tracking**: At the time of writing, this tool is not a practical solution for the level of facial capture complexity that we will attain within the chapters of this book. Despite using ARKit technology, which is the underlying facial animation control technology for MetaHumans, the accuracy with DeepMotion is nowhere near as advanced as other solutions. We will look at much more accurate face tracking using both iPhone and webcam solutions in *Chapters 8* and *9*.
- **Hand Tracking**: This feature simply tracks hand movement but at a more advanced level, attempting to even track fingers. At the time of writing, this feature is only in beta. For Freemium users, it's worth considering the extra cost to use this feature; unless you are seeing significant errors in the hand movement, such as hands moving in strange ways or penetrating other body parts, I suggest you leave this to the default setting (which is off).
- **Speed Multiplier**: This is an advanced feature for Premium users and is a great way of adding more accuracy to the motion capture by using videos with higher frame rates (in other words, slow motion). **Speed Multiplier** allows for a range of multiplication of 0-8. If your character moves at half speed (slow motion), adjusting the multiplier to **2.0** will give you the result of regular motion but with more accuracy. For the Professional and Studio plans, footage shot at up to 120 fps can be used. That footage would be very slow motion, which in turn captures a lot of very detailed and subtle motion. 120 fps is roughly 5 times slower than real-time, so you would use a Speed Multiplier of roughly 5 to get a real-time motion capture result and benefit from the increased accuracy.

Now, once you have gone through all of those **Animation Output** settings, you can click the **Create** button (this is at the bottom of *Figure 6.5*). Once clicked, you'll see a confirmation dialog box, as per *Figure 6.6*:

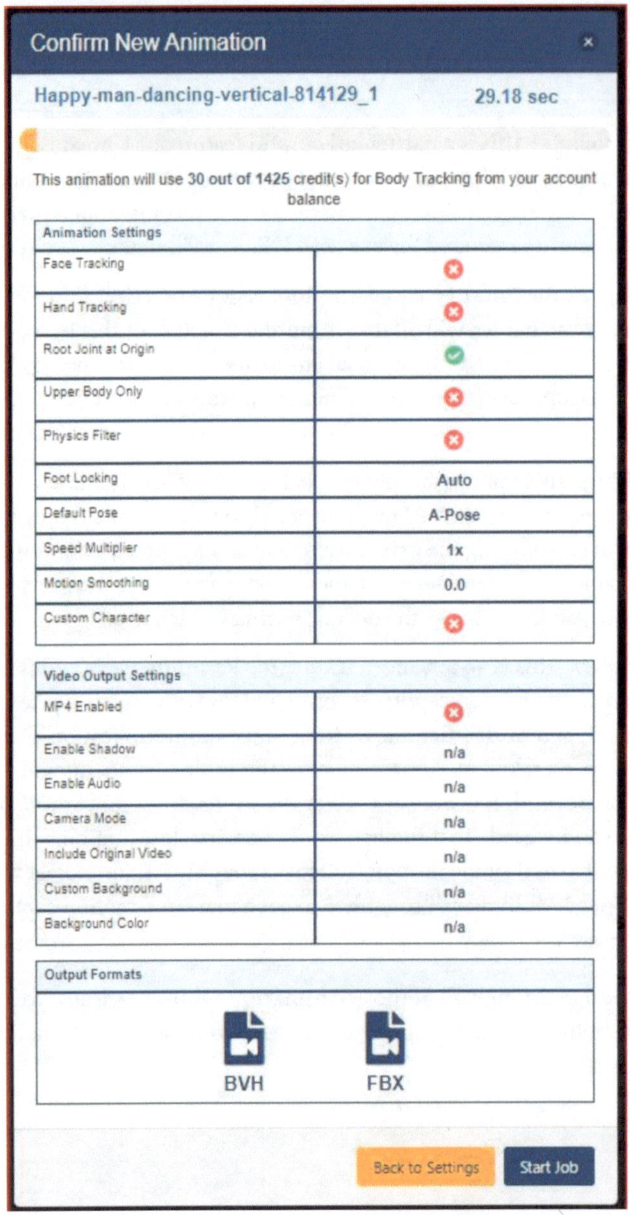

Figure 6.6: Confirm New Animation dialog box

You'll see from the settings that I have enabled **Root Joint at Origin**, set **Foot Locking** to **Auto**, and then set **Default Pose** as **A-Pose**. Everything else was left to the default settings. I'm not interested in downloading any additional video, which is why the **MPF Enabled** option is disabled and everything else is marked **n/a**.

It is also worth noting at this point that we have the ability to rerun this process if we're not happy with the outcome. With that said, it's time to run it for the first time, so click on the **Start Job** button. You will be taken to the **Starting job** interface, as shown in *Figure 6.7*:

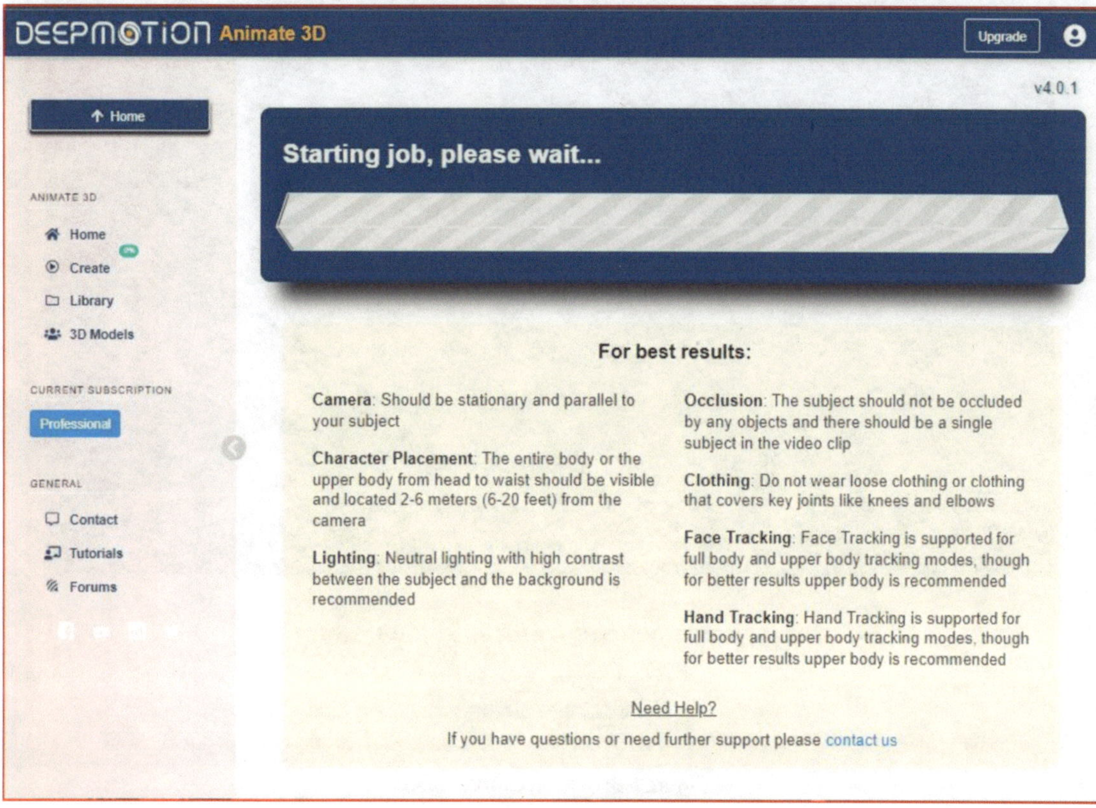

Figure 6.7: Starting job

The processing time varies depending on the file size and file length of your video clip. Also, if your video contains a lot of motion, expect a slower processing time.

Once processed, it's time to see the results. In *Figure 6.8*, you can see the results of the clip I chose; of course, it's impossible to see the results from this one single image, however, I was impressed with the results (after all, this motion capture is acquired from a single camera instead of an expensive motion capture suit and sensor array):

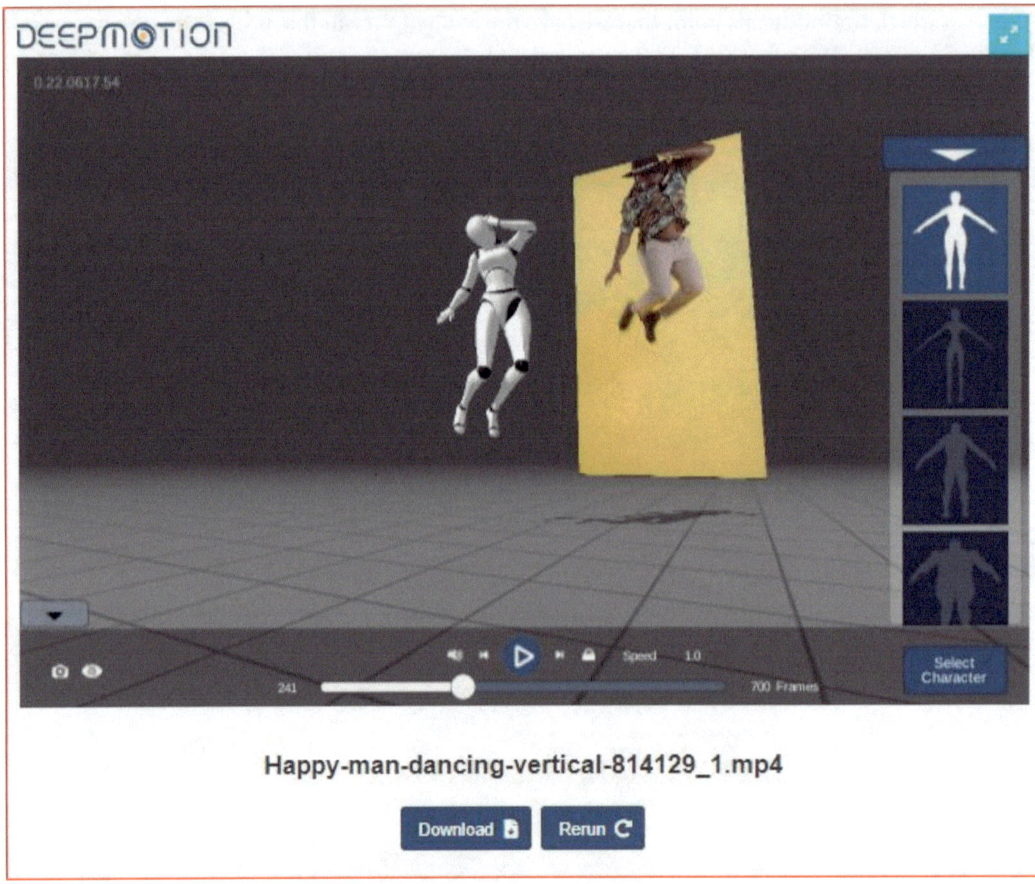

Figure 6.8: Motion capture result

From this screen, you will see an interactive 3D viewport where you can see the result from any angle and play the animation at various speeds.

On the right-hand side of the screen, you'll see a short list of four-character types; similar to the MetaHuman preview mesh, we can preview various body types such as thin, large, male, and female, and choose them for downloading along with our animation. For the best results, select a body type that is the closest to your MetaHuman character. In my case, as Glenda is a little overweight, it would be better for me to choose the overweight character. Doing this would increase the arm distance from the body, which would help with any collisions between an arm and the torso (you might remember that feature called **Arm Spacing** in Mixamo; this works similarly to that).

Also note that you have two options at the bottom of the interface of *Figure 6.8*:

- **Download**: This allows us to download an FBX file with a skeleton mesh of our choosing. At this point, we can choose another mesh other than the preview mesh.

- **Rerun**: This is where we get another chance to refine the quality of the animation. For example, we may be happy with the overall animation, but it is a little jittery; this would be a good opportunity to apply a little **Motion Smoothing**. As another example, we may be unhappy with the feet not locking to the ground as much as they should; perhaps the **Auto** setting just wasn't responsive to the fast movement, so we could go back and switch **Auto** to **Grounding** instead.

Needless to say, but I'll say it anyway, **Rerun** is a very valid tool and it is unlikely that you will get the desired result the first time without having to tweak it. It is better to try and get as close as you can to the desired result using many reruns, rather than try to fix it in the Unreal Engine. By gaining enough experience with reruns, you'll become more efficient at predicting which features should be used over practice and time.

In *Figure 6.9*, you can see the **Rerun Animation** dialog box:

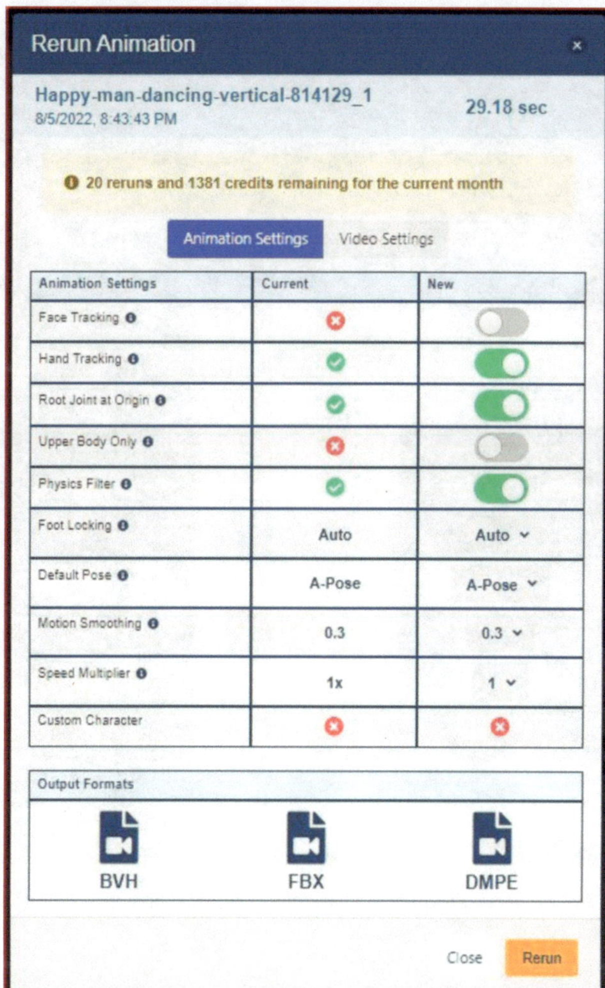

Figure 6.9: Rerun Animation dialog box

The only difference between this **Rerun Animation** box and the **Confirm New Animation** box from *Figure 6.6* is that it shows you the **Current** settings that gave you your last result and the **New** settings that you are about to contribute to your next job. This allows you to make a comparative study and, therefore, a more informed decision for the rerun.

Now, when you have gone through all of the settings and rerun your job until you are finally happy with the results, it is time to download your animation.

Downloading the DeepMotion motion capture file

To download the DeepMotion motion capture file, instead of clicking the **Rerun** option, simply click the **Download** button instead. This will bring up the **Download Animations** dialog box, as shown in *Figure 6.10*:

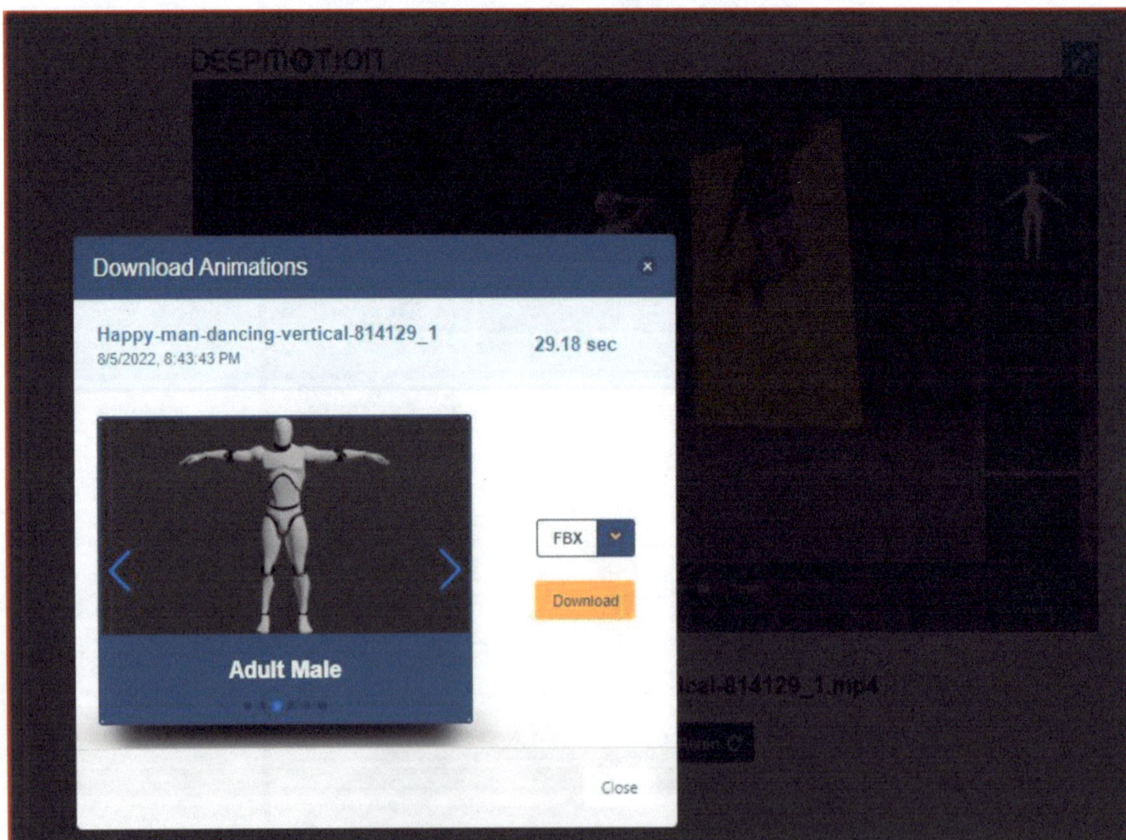

Figure 6.10: Download Animations

Before downloading the animation, the dialog box gives us the option to switch or confirm which body type we want to use: it gives you two adult females, two adult males, and a generic child to choose from. When you're happy with the correct preview mesh, make sure you have selected the correct download file time, **FBX**, from the dropdown menu (the **BVH** and **DMPE** solutions won't work for what we need to do in Unreal). Then, click on the yellow **Download** button and save your file somewhere in your project folder.

When you download your animation, you'll see two FBX files and a folder, as per *Figure 6.11*:

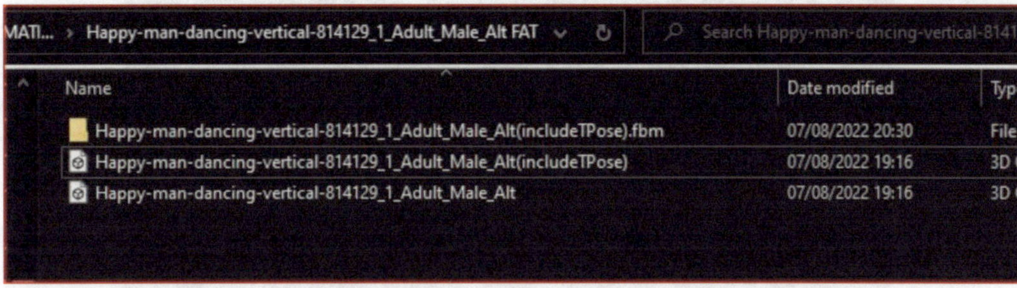

Figure 6.11: Saved files from DeepMotion and naming conventions

The FBX file that has `TPose` at the end of the filename (`Adult_Male_Alt(includeTPose)` is given to the file that uses an actual T-pose at the beginning of the animation. The other file, `Adult_Male_Alt`, has no such T-pose at the beginning and, therefore, kicks in with the animation at the very first frame. Choosing one over the other isn't critical as you can always remove the T-pose section from the animation, but the T-pose could become useful in instances where you need to align it for the purposes of retargeting. We will look at that at the end of this chapter.

Now that we have downloaded the relevant files, in this next section, we are going to import the DeepMotion motion capture file into Unreal so that we can retarget it to the MetaHuman IK Rig.

Importing the DeepMotion animation into Unreal

As mentioned at the very beginning of this chapter, we are building on what we have learned from the previous chapters, but don't worry, we'll use this section as a bit of a recap on how to import a character into Unreal.

The first thing you will need to do is to create a folder in your Unreal project called `Deepmotion`. Make sure that you are working in the project that you used in the previous chapter where you have both a source and target IK Rig for your Mixamo character and your MetaHuman character.

Once you've created the `Deepmotion` folder, right-click anywhere within the **Content** browser of your `Deepmotion` folder and look for your new DeepMotion FBX files. Choose the one that has the name `TPose` included. When you select it, you will then be greeted by the **FBX Import Options** dialog box, as shown in *Figure 6.12*:

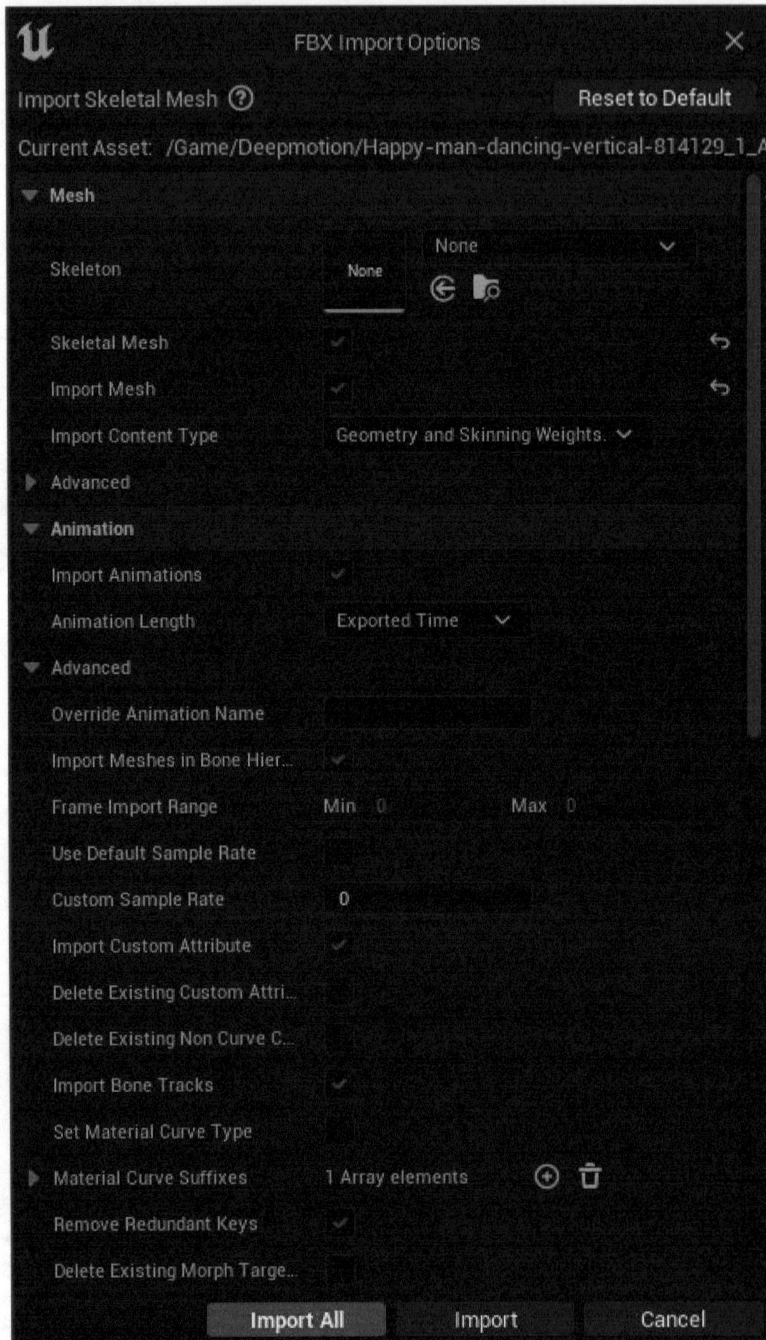

Figure 6.12: FBX Import Options

There are two things to consider here:

- First, we don't want to assign a skeleton to this import; we want to use one that is embedded in the file that we are about to import. So, under **Mesh**, leave **Skeleton** to its default position of **None**, and make sure the **Skeletal Mesh** option is selected so that it knows to choose the skeletal mesh from the file.
- Second, while it sounds obvious, make sure you tick the **Import Animations** option under **Animations**.

After those considerations, click on the blue **Import All** button. Don't be alarmed by the error that mentions smoothing that pops up; you can dismiss that.

Now, when you look at your `Deepmotion` folder in your **Content** browser, you should see something similar to *Figure 6.13*:

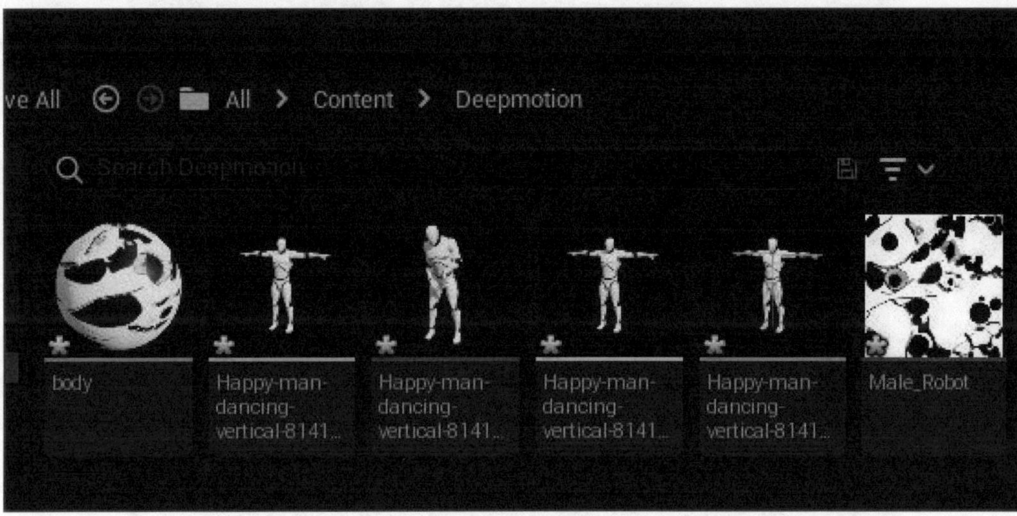

Figure 6.13: Deepmotion Content folder

Much of what you see here should be familiar; from left to right, you will see the following:

- A material shader for the body
- A T-pose skeleton without animation
- The DeepMotion skeleton with animation
- The DeepMotion skeleton physics asset

- A T-pose skeleton without animation for editing
- A texture file used in the aforementioned material shader used for the body

In this section, we have successfully imported the `Deepmotion` file into the Unreal Engine. In the next section, we will use the DeepMotion animation with our character.

Retargeting the DeepMotion motion capture

As in previous chapters, you'll need to create an IK Rig as the source. So, while in the `Deepmotion` folder, right-click anywhere and choose **Animation**, followed by **IK Rig**, as per *Figure 6.14*:

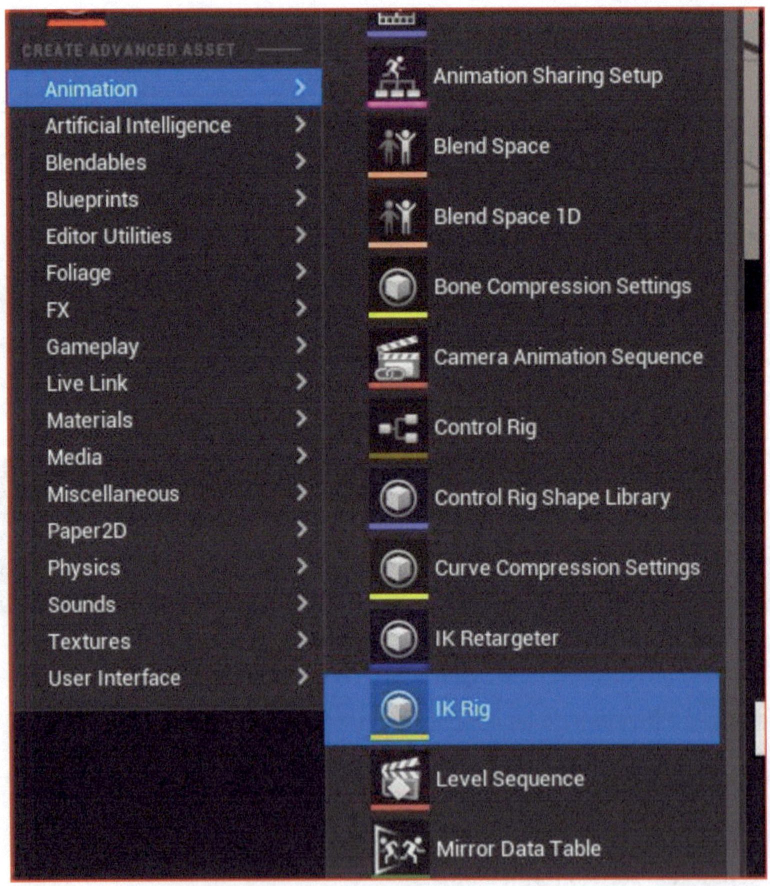

Figure 6.14: Creating an IK Rig

To avoid confusion, call this IK Rig `Source_DM_Happy` (this will help us later when we are looking for it).

Then, as we have also done before, follow the same process to create IK chains. Again, we will need to create six separate IK chains corresponding to the following:

- The root to the hip
- The spine and head
- The left arm
- The right arm
- The left leg
- The right leg

The only thing that is different, and you should expect this when importing motion capture from different sources, is the naming convention. The DeepMotion naming convention can be seen in *Figure 6.15*, where they use the **JNS** abbreviation for joints and start each appendage with the **l_** or **r_** prefix referring to either the left or the right:

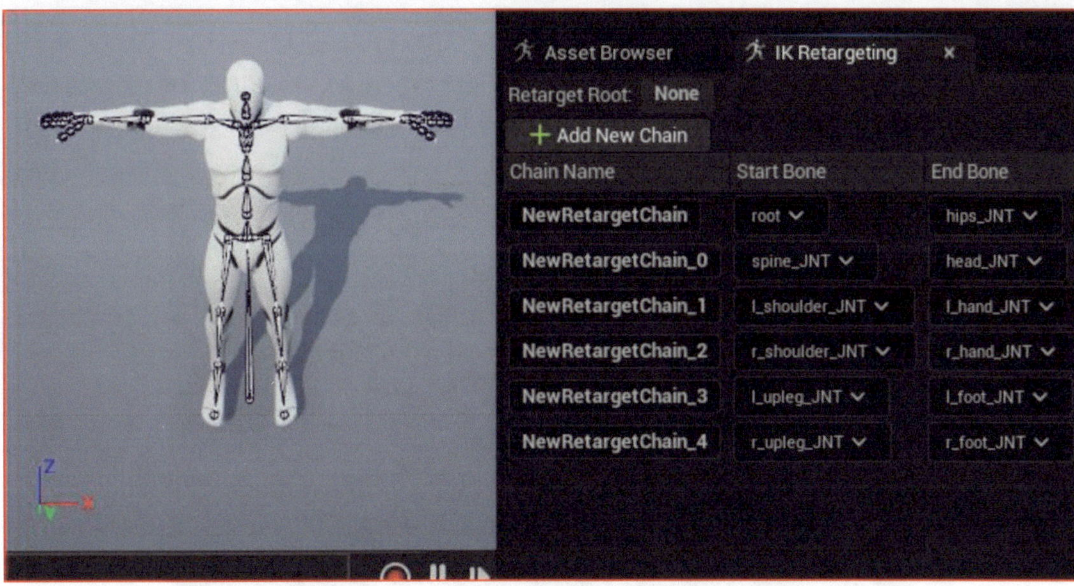

Figure 6.15: IK chains

Notice that the order of these chains (starting from **Root** to **hips_JNT** and ending at **r_upleg_JNT** to **r_foot_JNT**) corresponds to my list of IK chains; having the same order in both the IK source and IK target reduces errors.

Now it's time to create a new IK Retargeter, where we use our new IK Rig as the source. While still inside the `Deepmotion` folder, right-click anywhere in the **Content** browser, go to **Animation**, and select **IK Retargeter**, as shown in *Figure 6.16*:

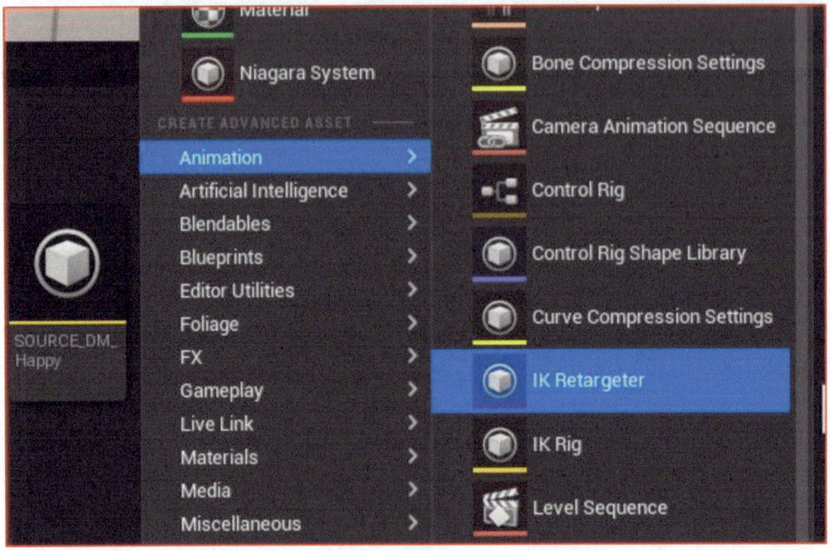

Figure 6.16: Creating a new IK Retargeter

Once you have created a new IK Retargeter, double-click on it to open it and you'll see a list of potential sources to choose from. You can see, in *Figure 6.17*, that I have a list of all the IK Rigs that are saved in my project folder:

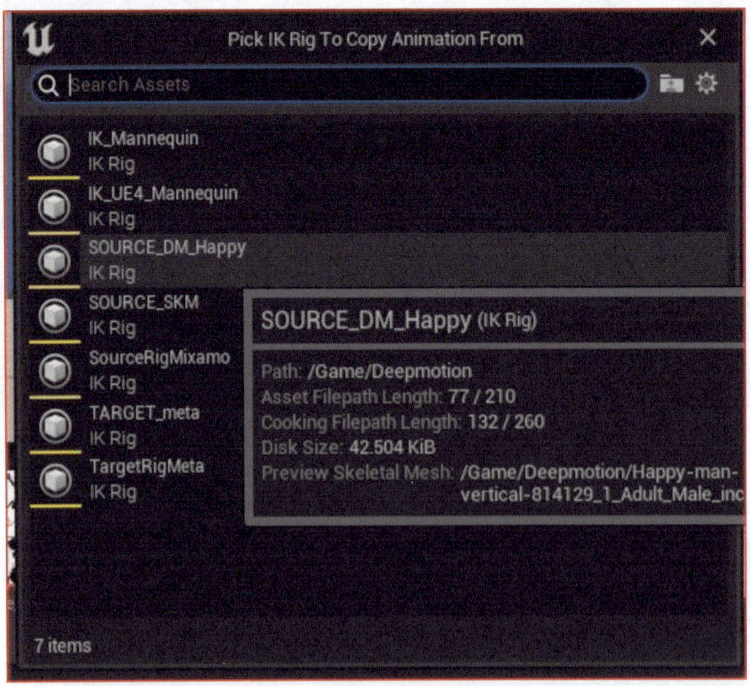

Figure 6.17: Pick IK Rig To Copy Animation From

You'll see that I have a source IK Rig titled **SourceRigMixamo**. As you practice with Unreal, you will soon end up with multiple source IK Rigs. You should still have a source IK Rig that you used from the previous chapter. This is why it's important to label these IK Rigs appropriately so that you don't inadvertently choose the wrong one.

You *don't* want to use the Mixamo rig from the previous chapter, so select **Source_DM_Happy** as that is the rig from which we want to copy the animation. Then hit **OK**.

> **Note**
> If you choose the wrong IK Rig, you will need to delete this Retargeter and create a new one, hence why labeling the IK source rig is important.

Once you've created an IK Retargeter using the **Source_DM_Happy** rig, open it up by double-clicking on it. This will bring up the following interface:

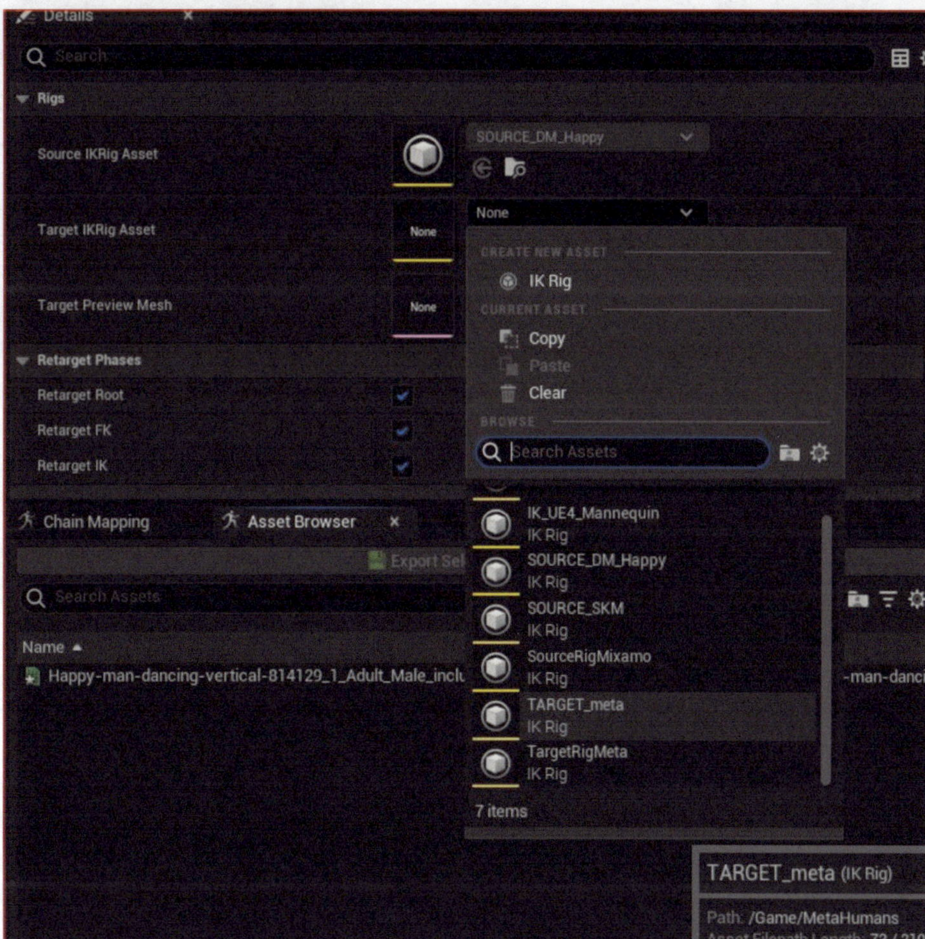

Figure 6.18: Choosing the target in the IK Retargeter

Now, you want to choose the IK target to apply the DeepMotion motion capture to. You can see from *Figure 6.19* that **Source IKRig Asset** is locked but **Target IKRig Asset** still has a drop-down list. Choose your MetaHuman target rig; in my case, it's **TARGET_meta**.

It's at this point that we also have the option to choose the appropriate **Target Preview Mesh** too. In my case, the target preview mesh is the **Female Medium Overweight** mesh, which is titled **f_med_ovw_body_preview_mesh**, as per *Figure 6.19*:

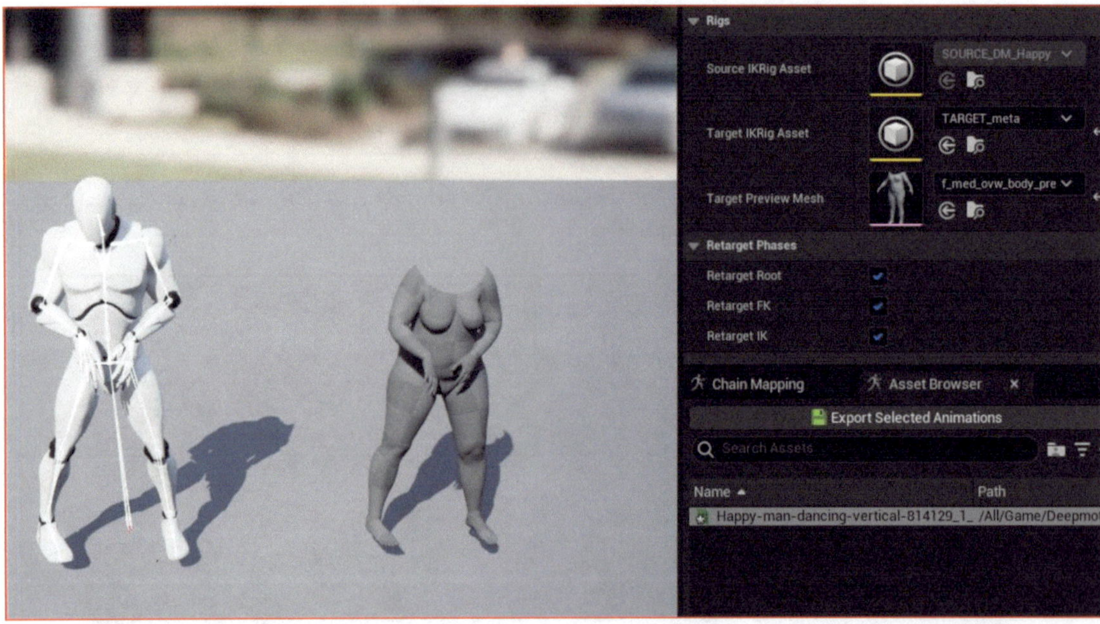

Figure 6.19: Target Preview Mesh

At the bottom of *Figure 6.19*, under the **Asset Browser** tab, you can see that the DeepMotion animation is now available for us to export. So, if you are happy with the animation, just click on the green **Export Selected Animations** button.

As a reminder, clicking on the **Export Selected Animations** button will create an animation file that will now work with your MetaHuman character. You will be given the option of where to save the animation to choose your `Deepmotion` folder.

Next, add your MetaHuman character to your scene by dragging and dropping it from your **Content** folder to your viewport. Then, ensure your MetaHuman blueprint is selected in **Outliner**.

After that, go to the **Details** panel, select **Body**, and under **Animation Mode**, choose **Use Animation Asset**. Run a search for your new retargeted animation file and click on it. In *Figure 6.20*, you can see that I picked the **Happy Animation** file from the drop-down list:

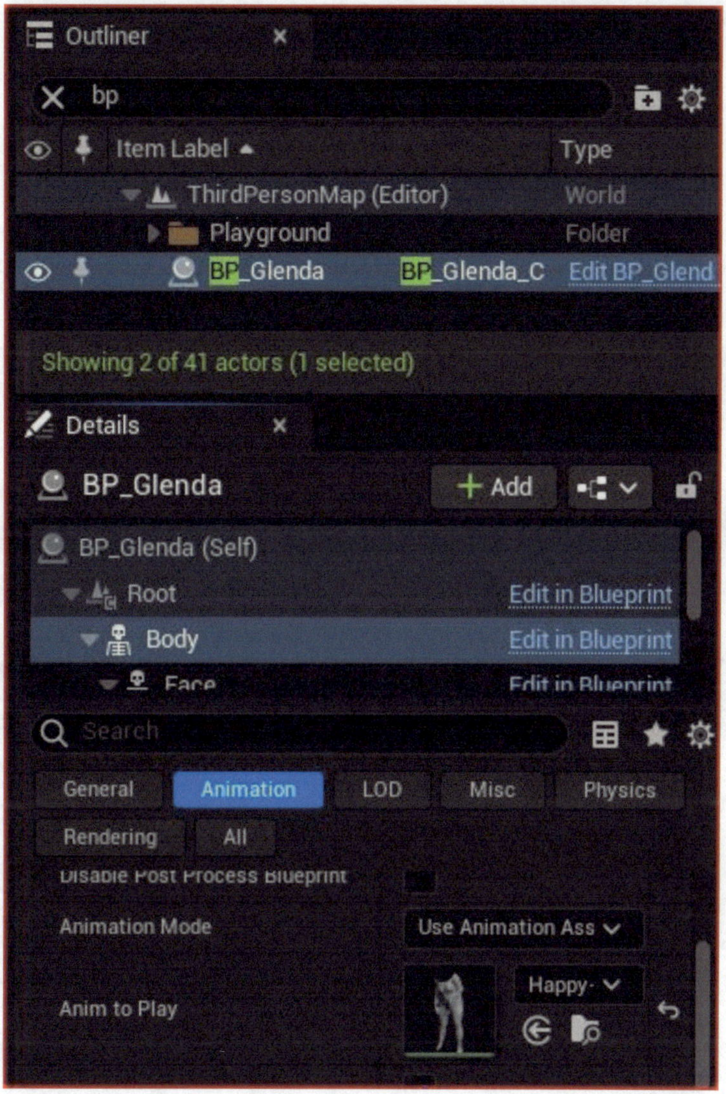

Figure 6.20: Applying the animation

With your file selected, run **Play** in your viewport and you'll see your character come to life.

Now that you have successfully gone through the whole process of creating motion capture data from video and retargeted it to your MetaHuman character, we'll take a look at troubleshooting a common problem in the next section.

Fixing position misalignment issues

It's unlikely that your animation is going to perfectly match your video, and it's just as unlikely that the retargeting process is going to be smooth sailing either. There's always a slight mismatch between the source and target rigs. One of the most common problems is the arm positions, which mostly boils down to the T-pose and the A-pose.

As MetaHumans are set in an A-pose, and our DeepMotion rig was set to a **T-Pose**, this is where there's a problem. In the event that you chose **T-Pose** in DeepMotion, there's a handy little fix that saves you from having to go through the download and retargeting process again.

As you can see from *Figure 6.21*, showing the **IK Retargeter** interface, we can see the problem: the source DeepMotion character is in a **T-Pose** and the target MetaHuman character is in an **A-Pose**. In this scenario, because of the misalignment, the arms will not animate properly and will most likely intersect with the body:

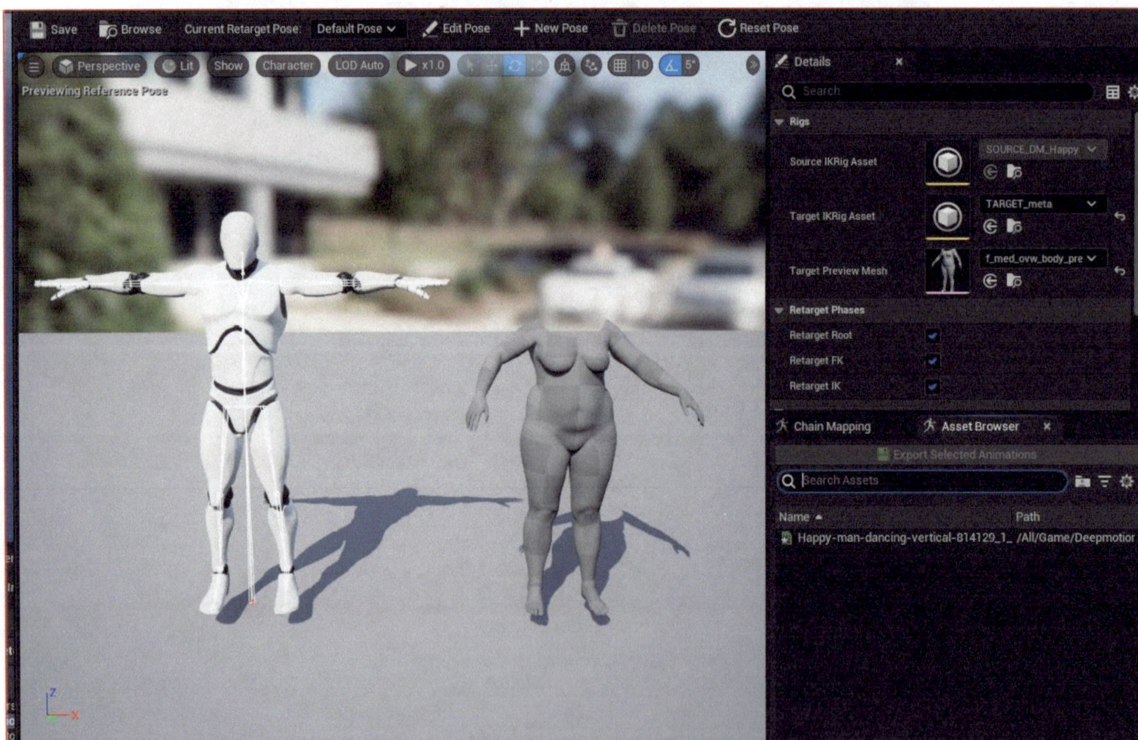

Figure 6.21: IK Retargeter T-pose versus A-pose

The only option we have here is to change the pose of the target, which is the MetaHuman. To do this, click on the **Edit Pose** button at the top of the screen, as shown in *Figure 6.22*. This will allow you to rotate the joints of your MetaHuman character from within the IK Retargeter:

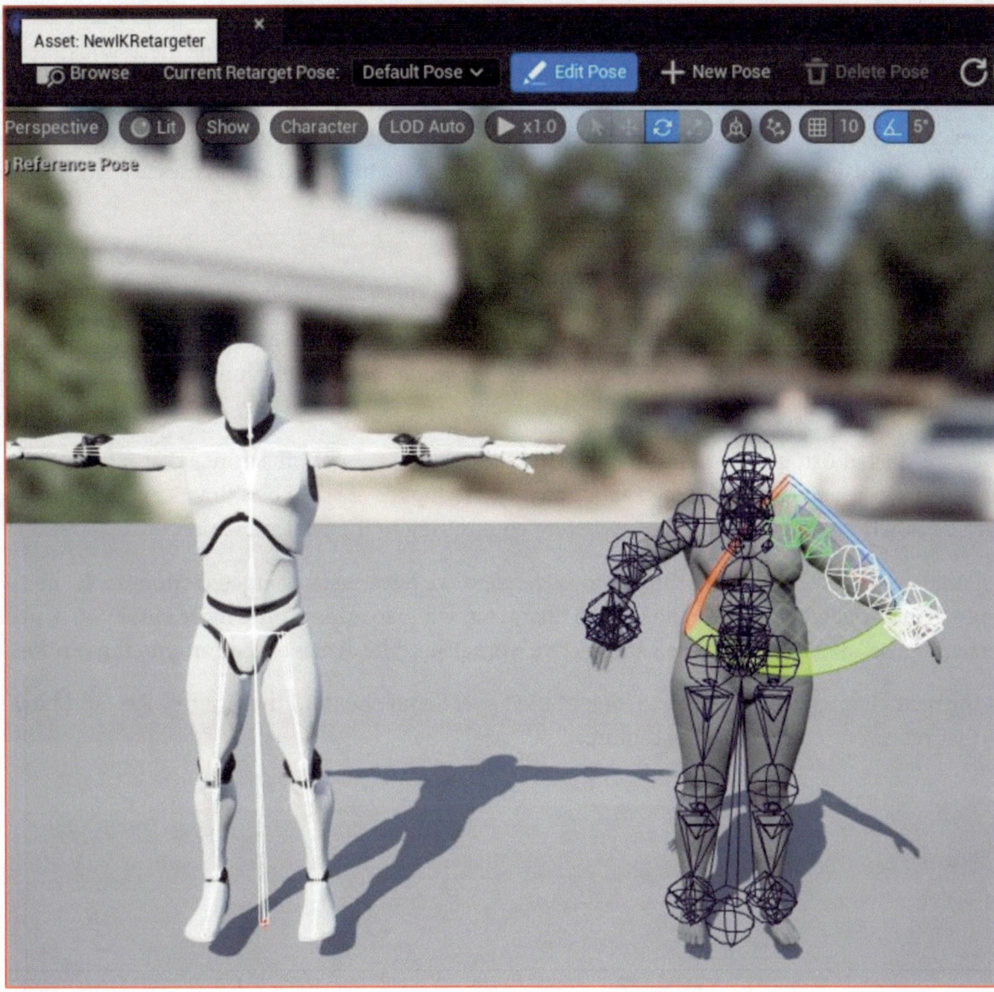

Figure 6.22: Edit Pose in the IK Retargeter

I strongly advise that you use rotational snapping, which is highlighted at the top-right of *Figure 6.22*. I found that the difference between the T-pose and the A-pose in terms of arm rotation was about 45 degrees. Currently, the snapping is set to increments of five degrees; however, you can change that to your liking.

The MetaHuman also has a slight rotation on the elbow joints that you will need to straighten to match that of the source; using the snapping tool allows you to get a much more uniform result. Be sure to change the angle from the front when you make corrections to the elbow joints so that you can see what you are doing.

When you are happy, click on the **Edit Pose** button again. This will allow you to press **Play** again, to view how well the animation is retargeted. You can keep going back to fine-tune these adjustments.

You may also find that you have exported the correct pose, but the animation is still causing slight issues, particularly with collision. In terms of DeepMotion, this could easily be attributed to the fact that you were using preset preview meshes as opposed to specific MetaHuman meshes. We will look at how to fix these issues in the next chapter.

Summary

In this section, we covered how we can create our own animation with as little as a single video camera. First, we looked at some of the major considerations when it comes to filming, what to avoid, and what steps we can take to bring even more accuracy.

Then we started using DeepMotion, exploring the various animation settings that it can offer us, including some artificial intelligence functionality. We looked at some best practices when it comes to these functions and the use of reruns before committing to the final animation.

Building on what we learned in the previous chapters, we once again retargeted our bespoke motion capture and applied it to our MetaHuman character, while looking a little more closely at A-poses versus T-poses. Finally, we covered an effective workaround for issues arising around those poses.

In the next chapter, we are going to look at the Level Sequencer and the Control Rig, and how to further refine our custom motion capture.

Part 3: Exploring the Level Sequencer, Facial Motion Capture, and Rendering

In *Part 3* of this book, we will look at the Level Sequencer, where we can play and render out our animations. Here, we will focus on facial motion capture solutions such as using an iPhone, but we will also explore professional facial capture solutions. In addition, the rest of *Part 3* will explore rendering, but we will finish with a bonus chapter featuring the Mesh to MetaHuman plugin.

This part includes the following chapters:

7

Using the Level Sequencer

In the previous chapter, we learned how to bring our own motion capture data into Unreal and retarget it to a MetaHuman. However, there are times when we need to make adjustments that are required to fix issues or add an extra level of creativity to its performance.

One issue we came across in the last chapter was caused by the discrepancies between using A-Pose and T-Pose, and we were able to fix that by editing the A-Pose of our MetaHuman inside the MetaHuman Blueprint.

In this chapter, we are going to look at another way to make changes to our character's pose to fix minor issues, such as an arm colliding with the torso of the MetaHuman, but will also look at how we can refine the motion of the character. For this, we will use the **Level Sequencer**, which is the tool we use for animating anything in Unreal Engine, and in many ways, works like a timeline in a video editing application.

So, in this chapter, we will cover the following topics:

- Introducing the Level Sequencer
- Creating a Level Sequencer and importing our character Blueprint
- Adding the retargeted animation to the character Blueprint
- Adding and editing the Control Rig
- Adding a camera to the Level Sequencer
- Rendering a test animation from the Level Sequencer

Technical requirements

In terms of computer power, you will need the technical requirements detailed in *Chapter 1* and the MetaHuman plus the Unreal Engine Mannequin that we imported into UE5 in *Chapter 2*. Both of these will need to be saved in the same project in UE and you will need to have UE running for this chapter.

For this chapter, you will also need to have access to the motion capture data that you just retargeted in *Chapter 6*.

Introducing the Level Sequencer

Until now, you've only been able to preview your animation either within the character Blueprint or within the viewport using the **Play** button. The **Play** button is effectively simulating gameplay, which is purely for an interactive experience.

The Level Sequencer can be used in gameplay, but for the purpose of this book, we want to focus on using the Level Sequencer to make the most of our motion capture animation. A Level Sequencer is a timeline within our level where we can control our animations. It is similar to any other timeline in an editing program, except that instead of adding video clips, we add elements to our scene, and then apply animatable attributes.

When using Unreal Engine for animation, anything you want animated needs to be added to a Level Sequencer, including lights, cameras, actors, vehicles, and even audio, and you can have more than one Level Sequencer in any given project.

The beauty of the Level Sequencer is that it allows you to only focus on the animated objects, and also allows us to effectively tweak animation by adding independent keyframes without being overwhelmed by all the keyframes that come with the motion capture data. Using it, we can make changes to the motion capture animation without having to depend on getting absolutely perfect takes when working with a motion capture solution such as DeepMotion or motion capture library files such as Mixamo.

In the next section, we'll go through the process of getting a character into a Level Sequencer.

Creating a Level Sequencer and importing our character Blueprint

So, let's get started with creating a Level Sequencer (there isn't a lot to it).

First, you need to right-click anywhere within your **Content** folder; in my case, I did just that within my **MetaHumans** folder, which you can see in *Figure 7.1*. Then, go to **Animation**, and then click on **Level Sequencer**.

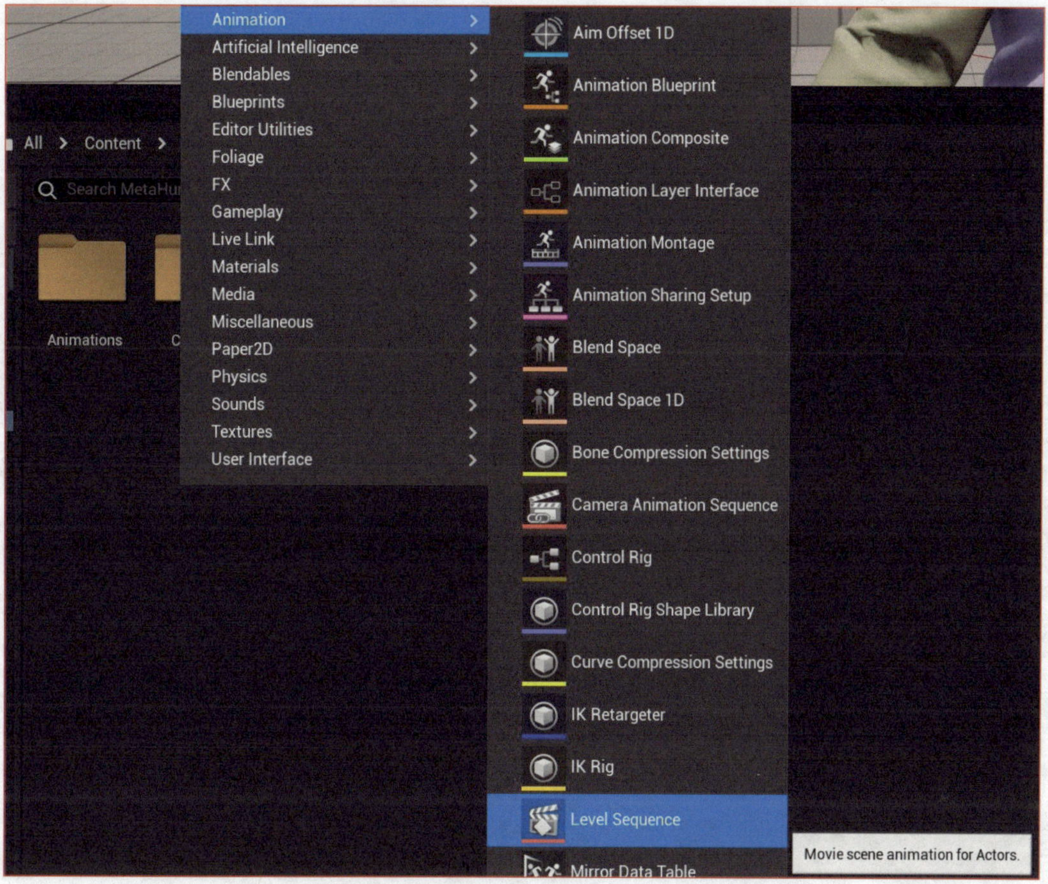

Figure 7.1: Creating a Level Sequencer

With the Level Sequencer created, you'll see a **Level Sequencer** clapper icon in the **Content** folder. Double-click on the Level Sequencer icon to open it. You will see an empty Sequencer as per *Figure 7.2*:

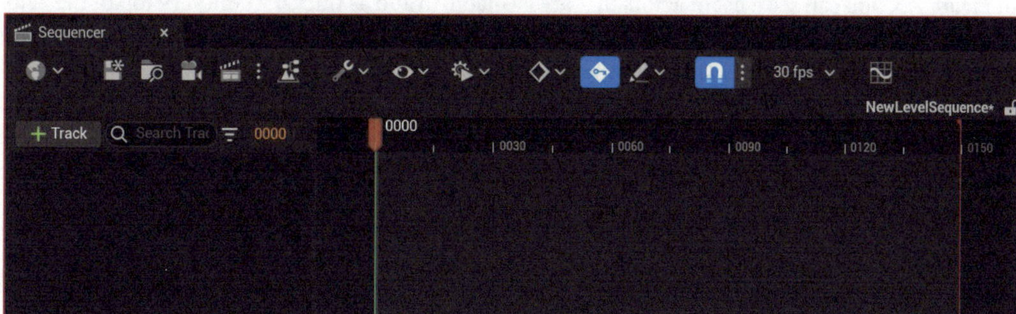

Figure 7.2: An empty Level Sequencer

In order to animate using the Level Sequencer, you need to add an actor. An actor can be pretty much anything that you want to animate. Once an actor is added to a Sequencer, an animation track is created.

Because we want to animate our MetaHuman character, we will need to add the MetaHuman Blueprint as our animation track. To do this, simply click on **+ Track** and then **Actor To Sequencer**:

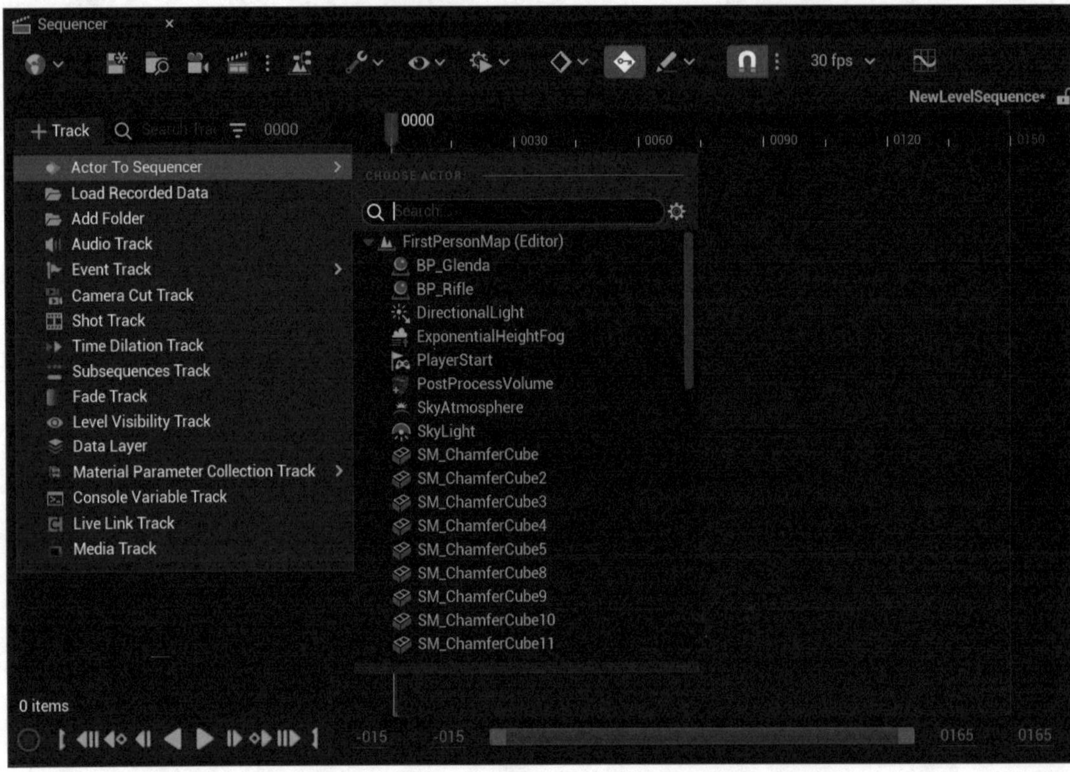

Figure 7.3: Adding an Actor to the Sequencer

In *Figure 7.3*, you can see a list of actors that are available to add as tracks. At the very top of the actor list is **BP_Glenda**, which is my MetaHuman character. Click on your MetaHuman Blueprint to import it into the Level Sequencer as an animation track.

Once you add the Blueprint to the Sequencer, you will get two tracks: one for the body and one for the face. As you can see from *Figure 7.4*, each of these tracks has a Control Rig. Initially, the **Face** Rig should be selected, which will reveal a yellow interface on the viewport with controls to animate the face (although we won't be looking at these).

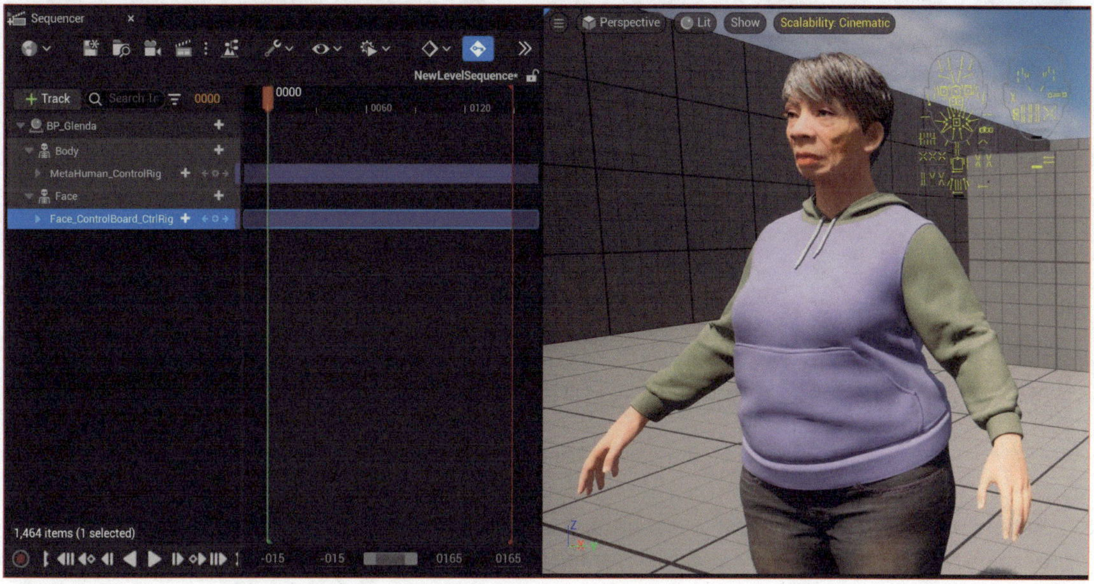

Figure 7.4: Adding the MetaHuman Blueprint

The other rig available to us is the **Body** Rig. If you select the **Body** track in the Sequencer, the rig will become visible in the viewport, now demonstrated in *Figure 7.5*:

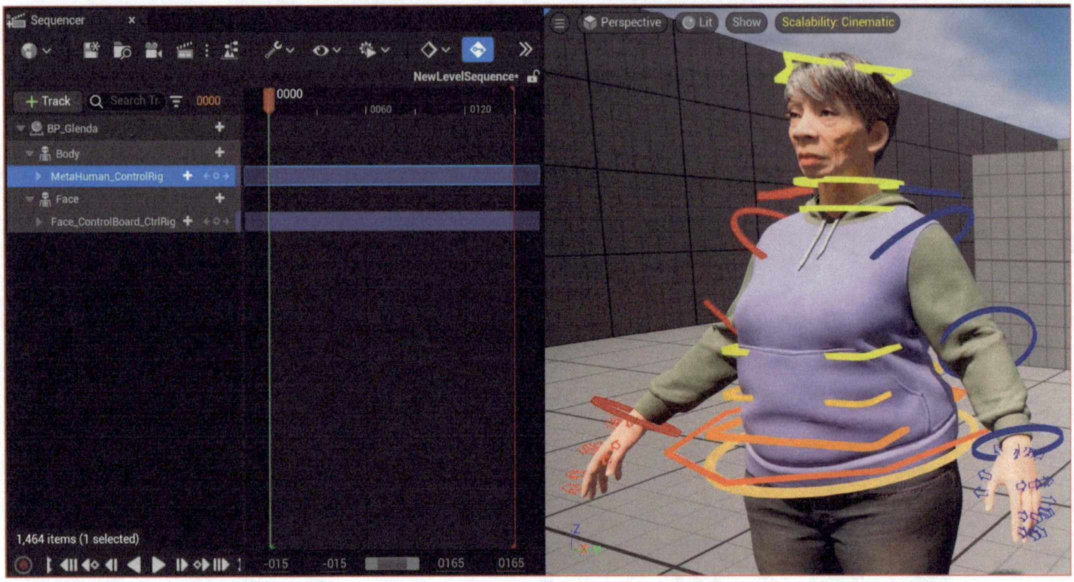

Figure 7.5: The MetaHuman Control Rig

At this point, you have just gained a vast amount of control over your MetaHuman Character in terms of animation. Whether you are a seasoned animator or a novice, I recommend you experiment with these animation controls. In particular, experiment with rotating any of the colored components of the MetaHuman Control Rig as per *Figure 7.5*, before you move on to the next section.

With the character Blueprint added to the Level Sequencer as an actor, we are now ready to bring in some motion capture data, which we will do in the next section.

Adding the retargeted animation to the character Blueprint

Before we continue to our DeepMotion animation into the Sequencer, I need to warn you that we are going to take a step that will seem somewhat counter-intuitive: we will delete the Control Rigs for both the body and the face only to end up adding a body Control Rig back in again. In this chapter, our aim is to add the motion capture data and then add an additional track of keyframe animation. However, to do that, we need to have the motion capture data baked into the control rig and then we need to have another control rig for additional animation.

So, let's delete the two current Control Rigs. You can do this by simply clicking on **Metahuman Control Rig** and **Face_ControlBoard_CtrlRig** in the Sequencer and hitting *Delete* on your keyboard.

Now, with **Body** selected in the Sequencer, click on the + icon, and then from **Animation**, search for `Retargeted`. This should call up the retargeted data created by the IK Retargeter from the previous chapter, which you can see in *Figure 7.6*:

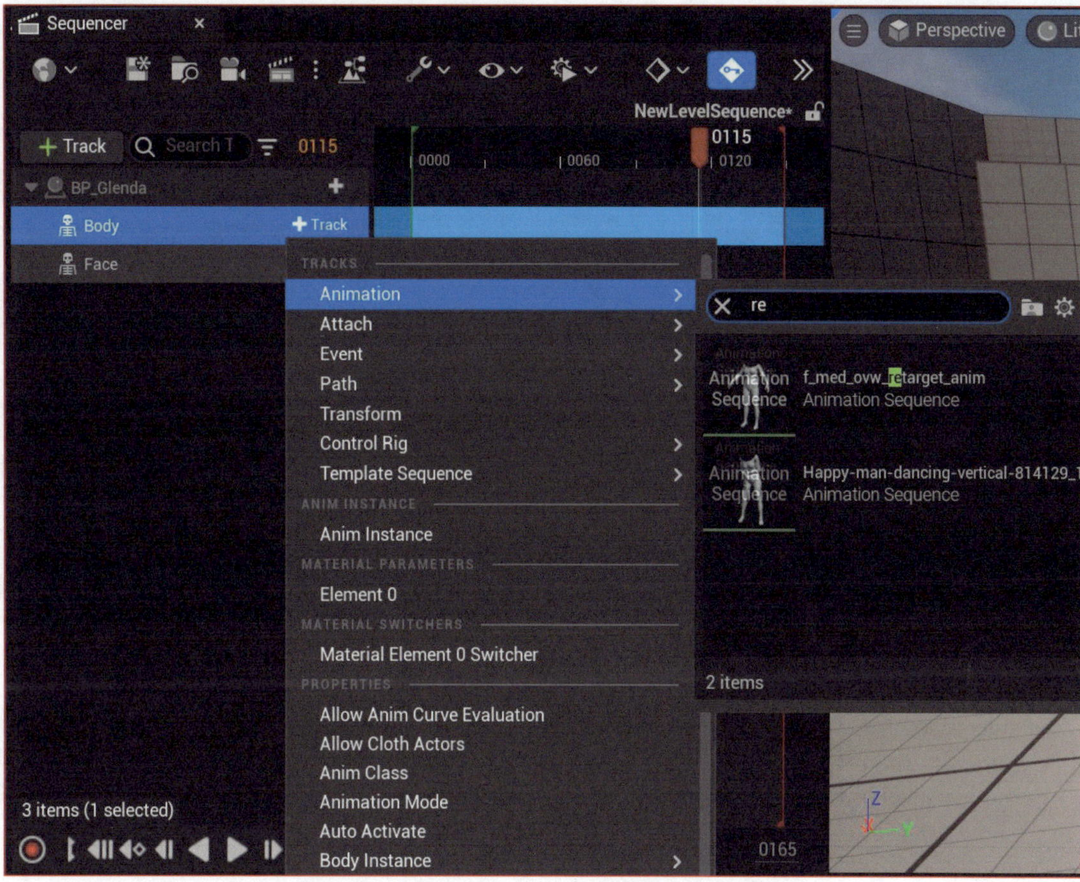

Figure 7.6: Adding the retargeted mocap data

Once you have selected the retargeted mocap, it will appear on the timeline within the Sequencer.

> **Note**
>
> The animation will start at wherever your **play head** is on the timeline. The play head is the position on the sequencer timeline that it's currently paused at, and the frame the animation will start from. In *Figure 7.6*, my play head is at the frame numbered **0115** (indicated by the red arrow).

When you have imported the mocap animation as a track, you can reposition this track to start at any time by simply dragging the track left or right. The track itself includes the title of the animation displayed within it. In *Figure 7.7*, you can see the animation track under the horizontal blue line.

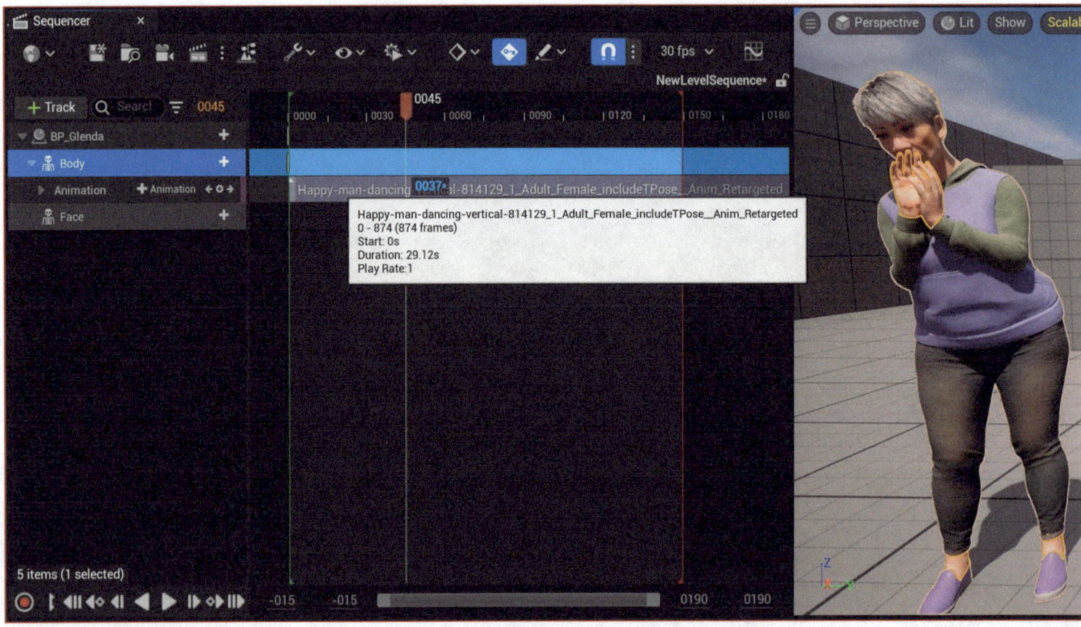

Figure 7.7: The animation track

In order to modify the animation, we must convert the motion capture data into keyframe data on a Control Rig. This process is called **baking**, and we can do this by simply right-clicking on the body track, choosing **Bake to Control Rig**, and selecting **Metahuman_ControlRig** as seen in *Figure 7.8:*

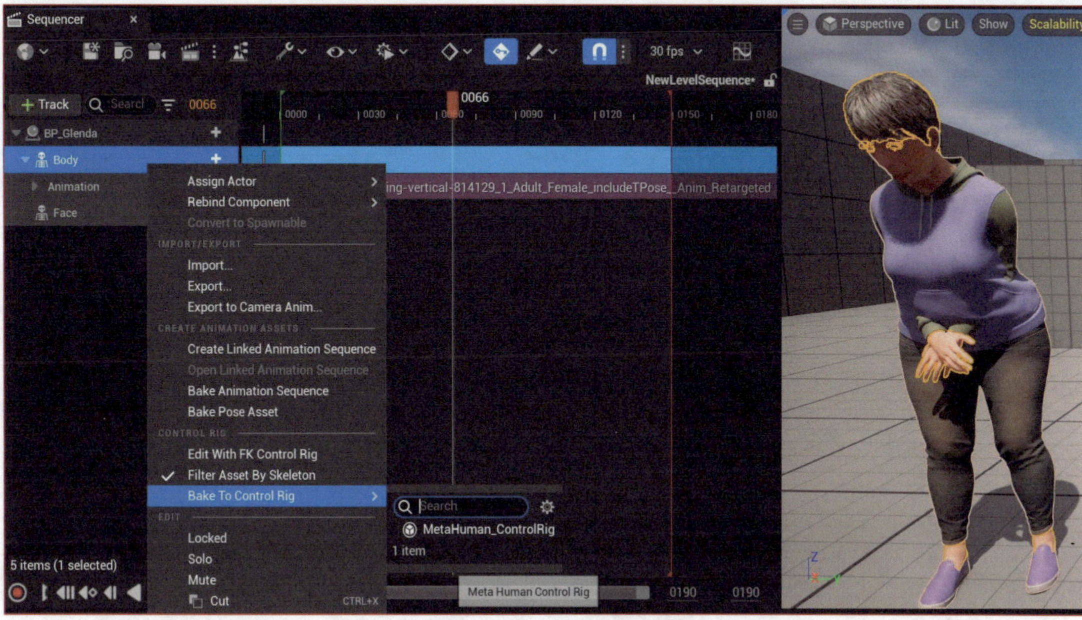

Figure 7.8: Baking to the Control Rig

Once you have started the baking process, you will see the **Options for Baking** dialog box. Because we don't need to reduce keys, you can keep the default settings and just click **Create**.

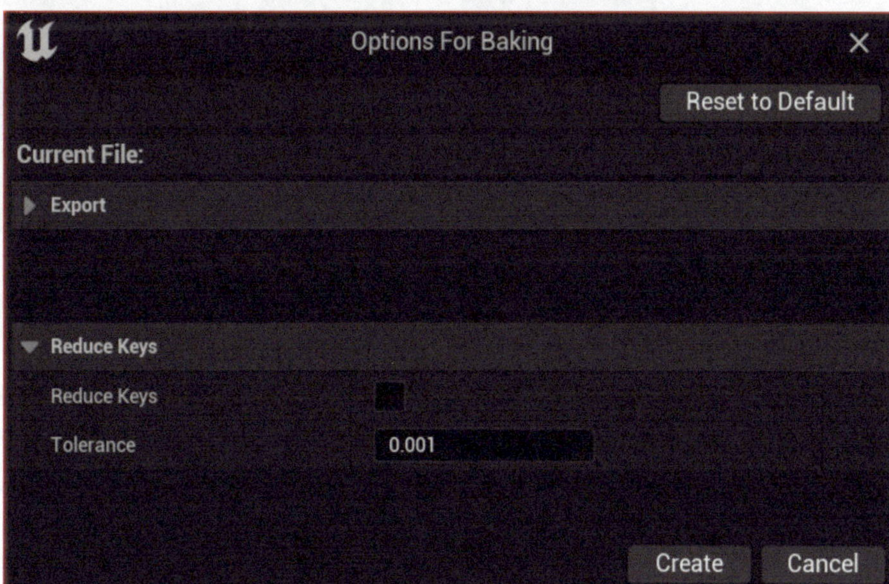

Figure 7.9: Options for baking

In *Figure 7.10*, you can see that the mocap animation I imported is now baked into the MetaHuman Control Rig and the character in the viewport is now animated.

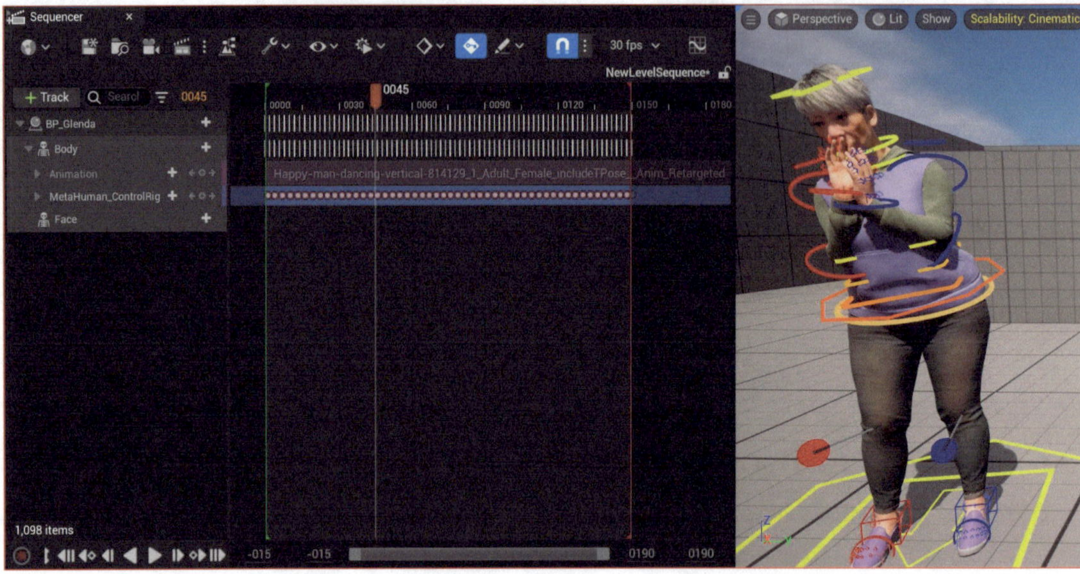

Figure 7.10: Mocap baked into MetaHuman Control Rig

Now, you can activate the play function by either hitting the *spacebar* or using the **Play** button at the bottom of the **Sequencer** tab.

With the mocap animation working in the viewport, the next step is to set up a way to make edits to the animation. Because there is now a keyframe on every single frame for every bone in the MetaHuman body, attempting to make any changes to the current MetaHuman Rig would be practically impossible. For example, if we choose to go to frame **100** and change the pose on that particular frame, only frame **100** would be affected as all the other frames have poses based on the mocap data we converted earlier. Let's see how to get around this.

Adding and editing the Control Rig

To get around our keyframes problem, we need to create another MetaHuman Control Rig with no keyframes, so that any keyframes that we do add will have an **additive** effect.

What do we mean by additive? For example, if a rotation of a shoulder joint on the *x*-axis was 100 degrees as a result of motion capture, then using an additive workflow, rotating a shoulder by a further 20 degrees on the *x*-axis would result in the final rotation being 120 degrees. We get to 120 degrees because we are simply adding 100 + 20 degrees.

> **Note**
>
> Keyframes on the additive section will not affect the original keyframes of the baked Control Rig. However, they do affect the end result.

In order to gain an additive effect, we must create an **Additive** section in our Sequencer, as seen in *Figure 7.11*:

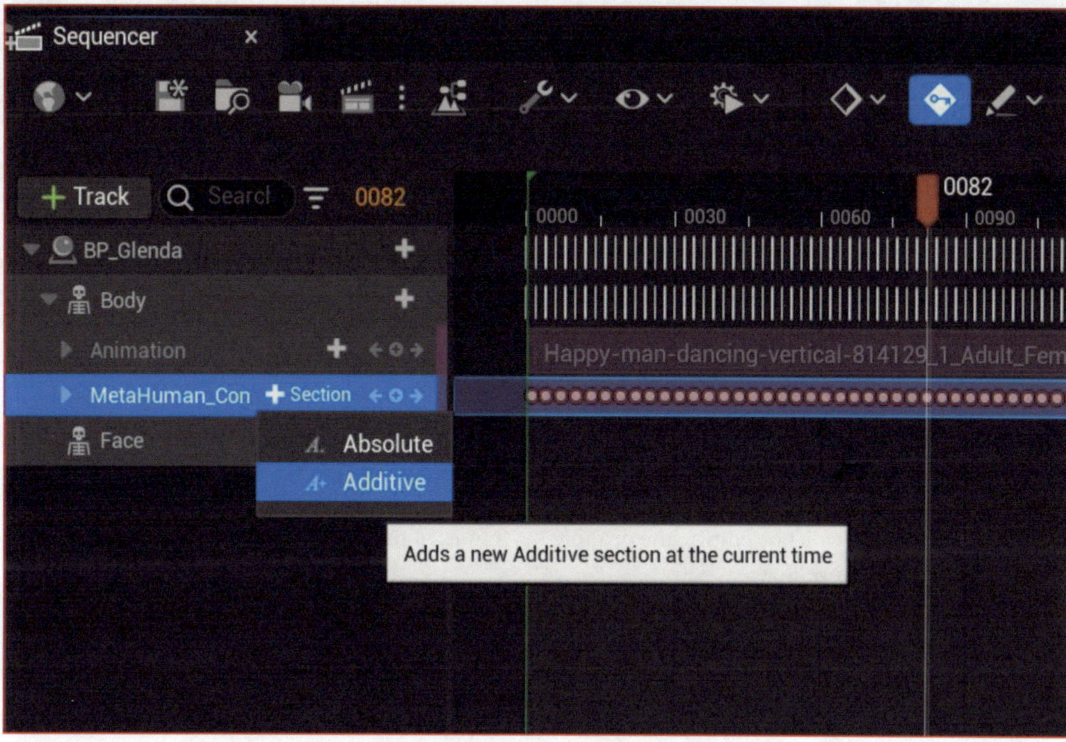

Figure 7.11: Adding an Additive section

As per *Figure 7.12*, the **Additive** track is added, which is a sub-track of the Control Rig we just created. This is where we can address animation issues or add changes to the animation without affecting the original motion capture:

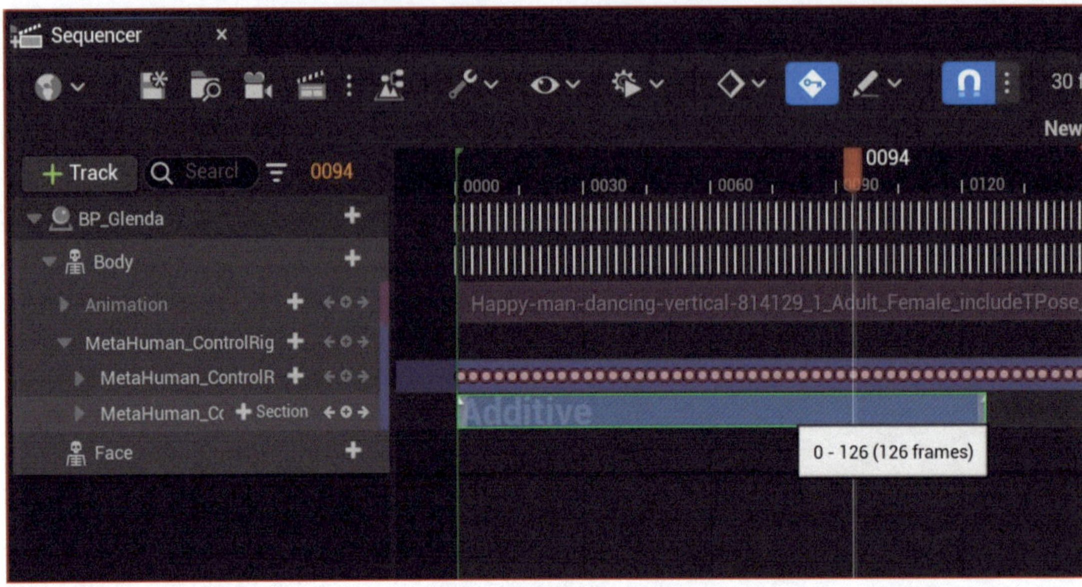

Figure 7.12: The Additive section track

At this point, we effectively have two rigs, each with its own track: one track has keyframes for every bone on every frame and the other has zero keyframes. In the next section, we will be adding keyframes to the additive section/track only. Even though we are making changes to the animation as it appears in the viewport, we won't be editing the original keyframes of the motion capture. In essence, this is a non-destructive workflow.

> **Note**
>
> The use of the words section and track are synonymous in the case of adding an **Additive** or absolute section/track.

To edit the **Additive** section, make sure that you have the **Additive** section selected in the Sequencer, which I have done in *Figure 7.13*:

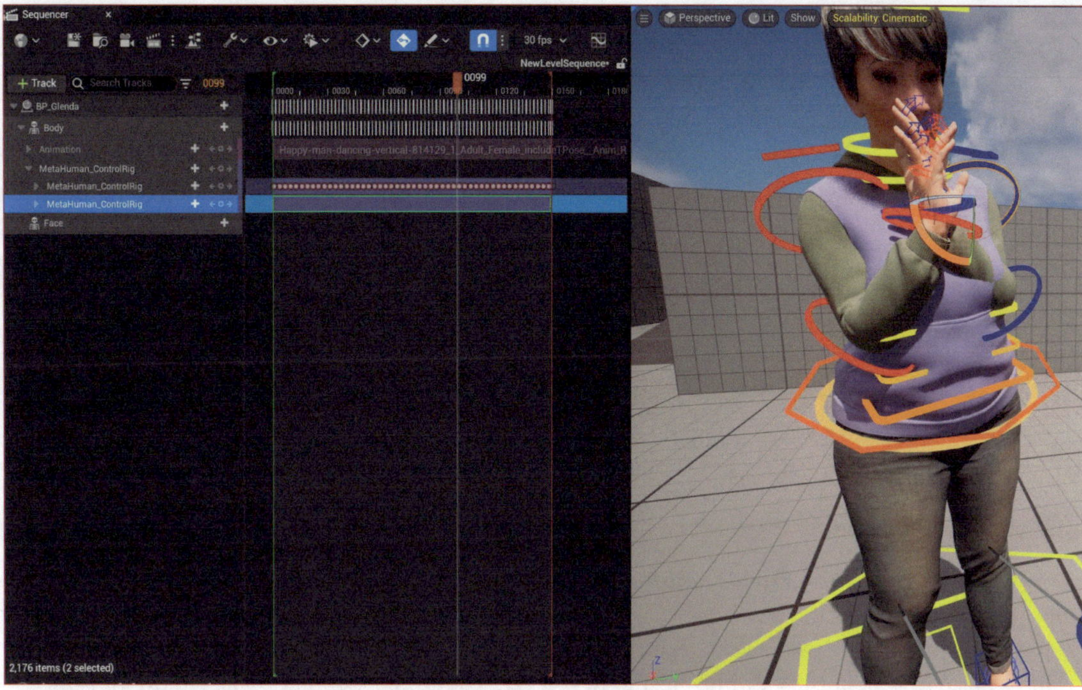

Figure 7.13: Adjusting the Additive control track

You can also see that this is a problematic clip because the mocap has collision issues with Glenda's left arm – it's colliding with her body, which is most likely due to the source character being much leaner than the target. However, with the additive workflow, we can just concern ourselves with fixing the time frame where that becomes an issue.

Figure 7.13 shows us that, in frame **0099**, Glenda's arm intersects with her body, so we need to fix that frame. We can do that by rotating one of the arm joints.

To do this, hit the *E* key to use the **Rotate** function. Then, click on the drop-down arrow on the left of **Metahuman_Control Rig** in the Sequencer. In *Figure 7.14*, you can see the drop-down list that allows me to gain access to all the different bones. For this issue, in particular, I want to just alter the left upper arm and left lower arm.

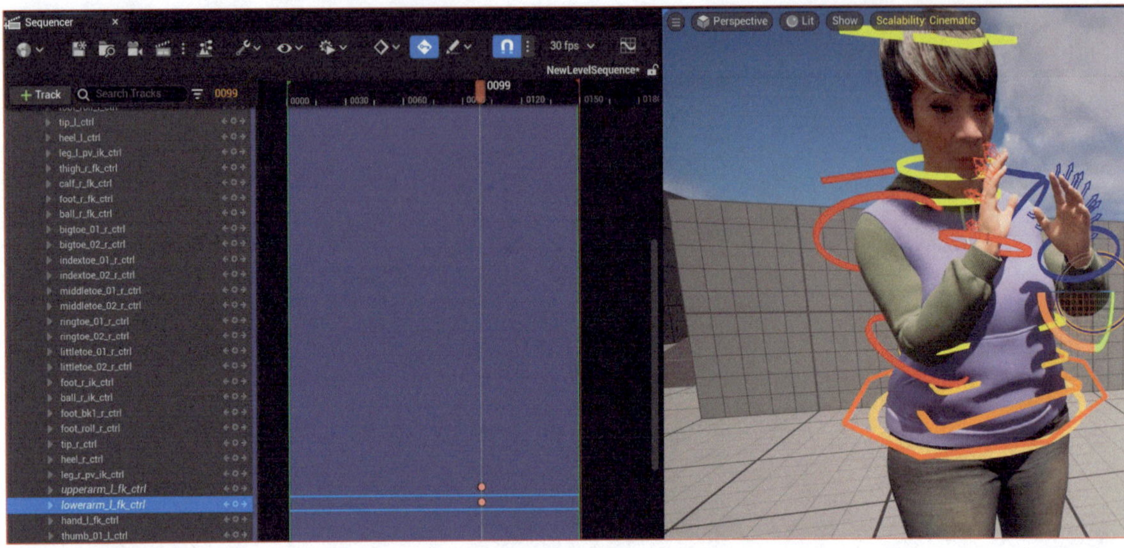

Figure 7.14: Setting keyframes on the Additive track

By default, as soon as you make a change, a keyframe is set. You can see the keyframe highlighted in *Figure 7.14* and, in the viewport next to it, you can see the effect of that change in the viewport. Because I have no other keyframes set in the additive track, the effects of that change will be apparent for the whole duration of the clip.

If I wanted to just adjust to a specific time period such as 2 seconds, I would need to create 3 keyframes. The 1st and 3rd keyframe would be to preserve the original pose and the 2nd (middle) keyframe would be where the change would take place.

Take a look at *Figure 7.15* and you will see how I have added extra keyframes:

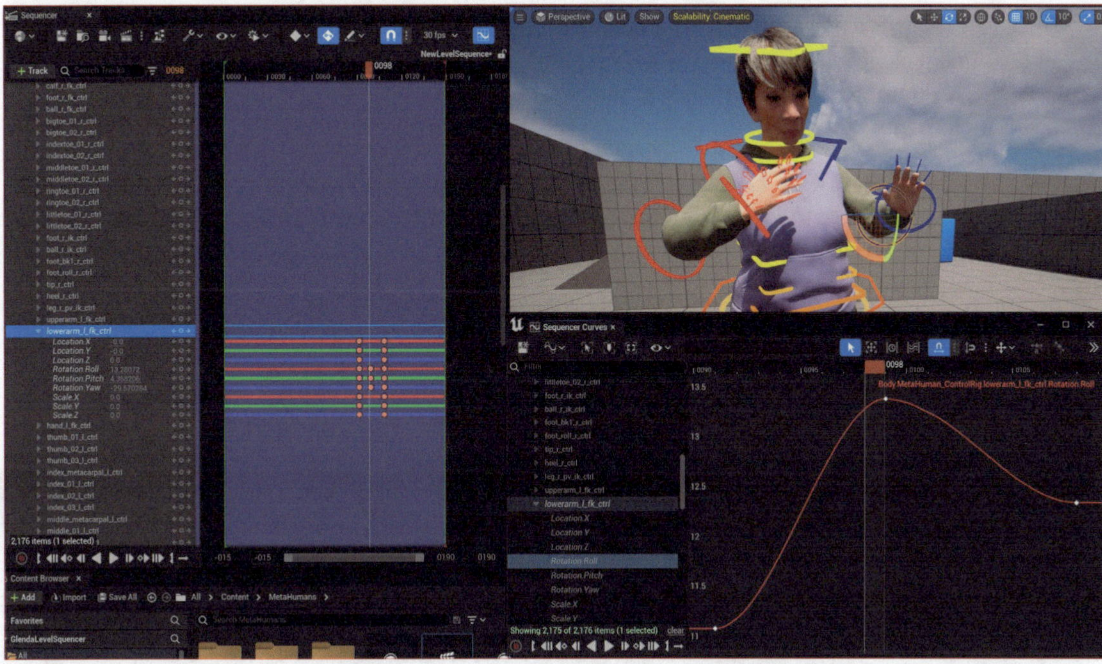

Figure 7.15: Adding extra keyframes to the Additive track

The middle keyframe is where the most extreme change has been made because this was the problem area. As you can see in *Figure 7.15*, I have numerical control over the **Location**, **Rotation**, and **Scale** settings, which is what I used to rotate the shoulder so that the arm isn't penetrating through the torso anymore, thus fixing the problem. You could use the spline for editing, as shown in the graph on the right of *Figure 7.15*, but I personally find it cumbersome, albeit useful for visualizing changes.

There are endless possibilities when it comes to adding keyframes to fix animation or to add a level of creativity. You may decide to add a head turn, a blink, a wave, or something else you didn't get at the motion capture stage. All this is now possible with the Additive selection within the Level Sequencer.

> **Note**
>
> When you want to edit a particular joint, use the search option to find the joint. This will show just the joint you searched for, which allows you to focus just on that should you find the list of joints distracting.

Now that we've got our character into the Level Sequencer and made some tweaks, the next thing we need to do is to create a camera in order for us to render out a movie.

Adding a camera to the Level Sequencer

The UE5 camera is a powerful tool, as it operates just like a real camera. I could write a whole book on the camera alone, but in the interest of completing this chapter, you'll just learn about some very basic camera tips that relate specifically to the Level Sequencer.

For simplicity, we are going to create a camera using the Level Sequencer. We also need a **Camera Cut**; this is like a master track, mainly designed for the use of multiple cameras, but we still need it for just one camera. The Camera Cut is only automatically generated when we create a camera from within the Level Sequencer.

Before we can do that, first we need to create a playback range. You can do this by right-clicking anywhere on the timeline within the Level Sequencer, choosing **Set Start Time**, and then clicking where you want to start the animation. Then, do the same with our **Set End Time**. The difference between these two times is the playback; however, this range is also used for defining the range of frames to render at a later stage.

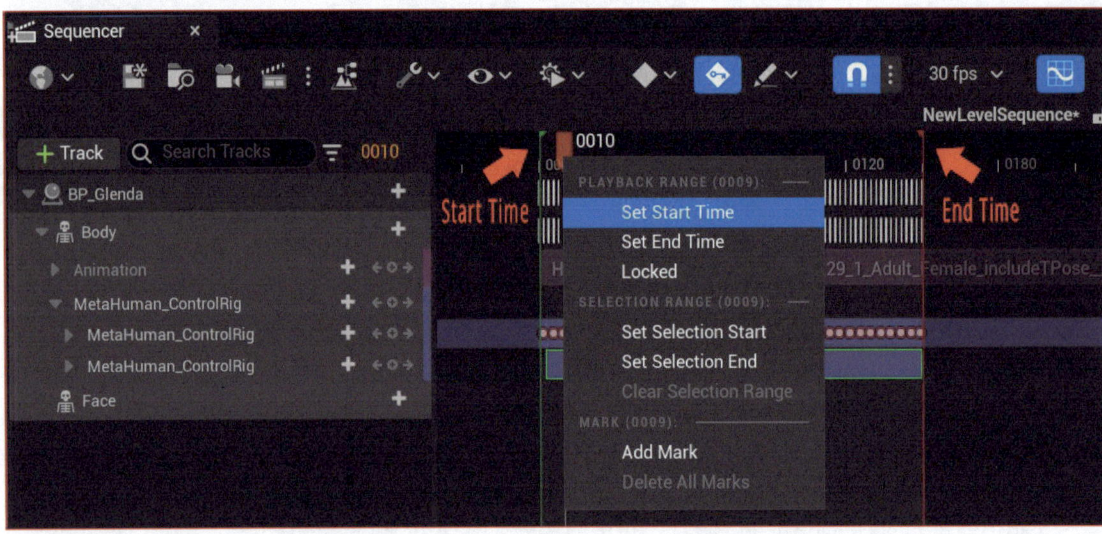

Figure 7.16: Setting a start frame for the playback range

You will know when you have created a playback range because you will see both a green and red line, as per *Figure 7.16* – I have selected the start time at the beginning of the keyframes that I baked earlier, and the end time is just where the keyframes end. This ensures that my playback range is the same length as the entirety of the animation. You can always extend your playback range by simply dragging the red line to the right-hand end of the timeline.

With the playback range created, now we can create a camera that will automatically create a Camera Cut to fill the playback range that we created. Very simply, click on the camera icon at the top of the Sequencer:

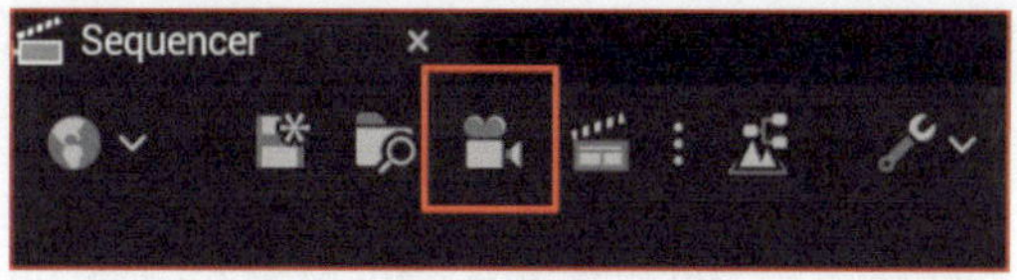

Figure 7.17: The camera icon

A camera will be created, and more tracks will have been created within the Sequencer:

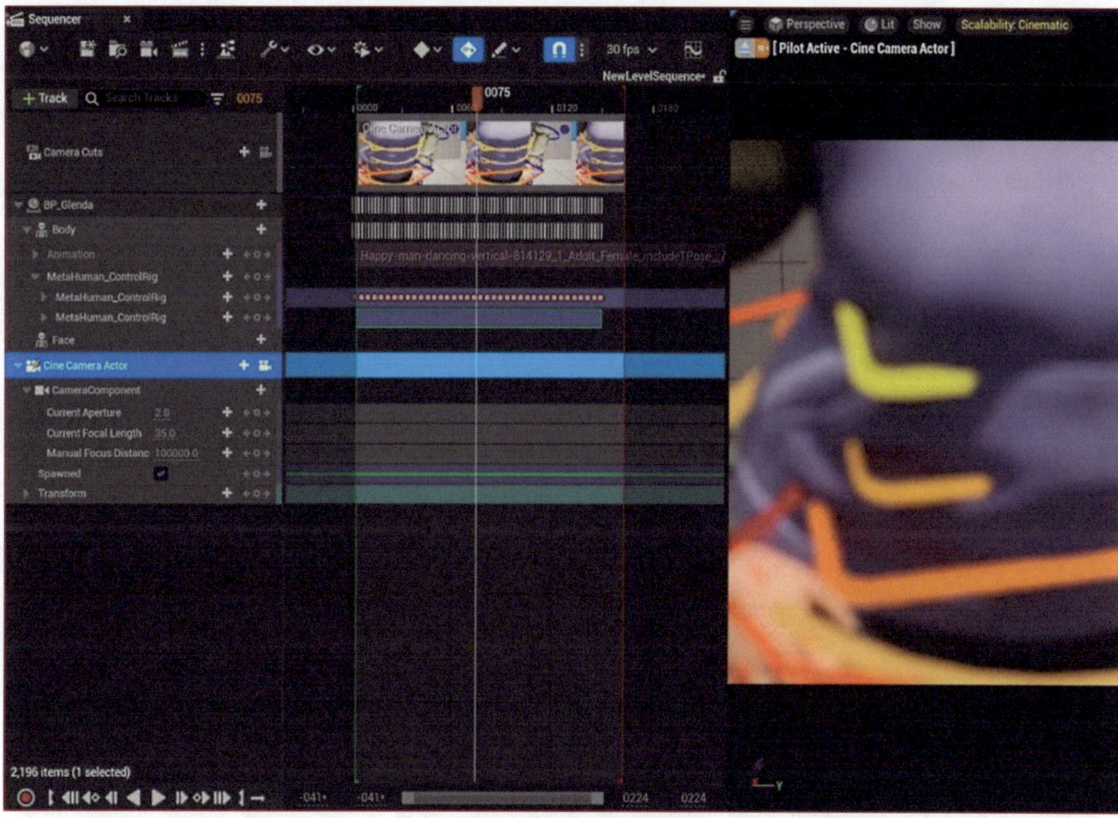

Figure 7.18: The camera created

You can see from *Figure 7.18* that we have now obtained a **Cine Camera Actor** (which is a virtual version of a real camera). With the camera, we also have a number of parameters, such as the following:

- **Aperture**: This is how wide the iris of the lens is. A lower number means that more of the picture will be out of focus, while a higher number provides a sharper image. This realistically mimics how cameras work in terms of depth of field, but not exposure.

- **Focal Length**: Just like with a real camera, the focal length is measured in millimeters. A lower number creates a wider-angle lens and a higher number creates a telephoto or long lens.
- **Manual Focus Distance**: Again, just like a real camera, the focus area is set to a given distance from the camera. For example, you may only want to be focused on objects that are 5,000 mm away from the camera.
- **Spawned**: A feature aimed at game simulation. If checked, the game engine will spawn the camera when the game starts.
- **Transform**: An editable parameter for moving, rotating, and scaling the camera.

For the most part, you will only want to animate the following parameters: **Moving** and **Rotating** in **Transform**, along with **Focus Distance**.

Before you go about setting keyframes, a useful function is to pilot the camera to animate. In other words, you can see through the viewport to make sure you've got the best composition. In *Figure 7.19*, I have highlighted the camera icon on both the **CameraComponents** track and the **Cine Camera Actor** track. These need to be toggled until you get the **Eject** icon (the triangle), which I have also highlighted.

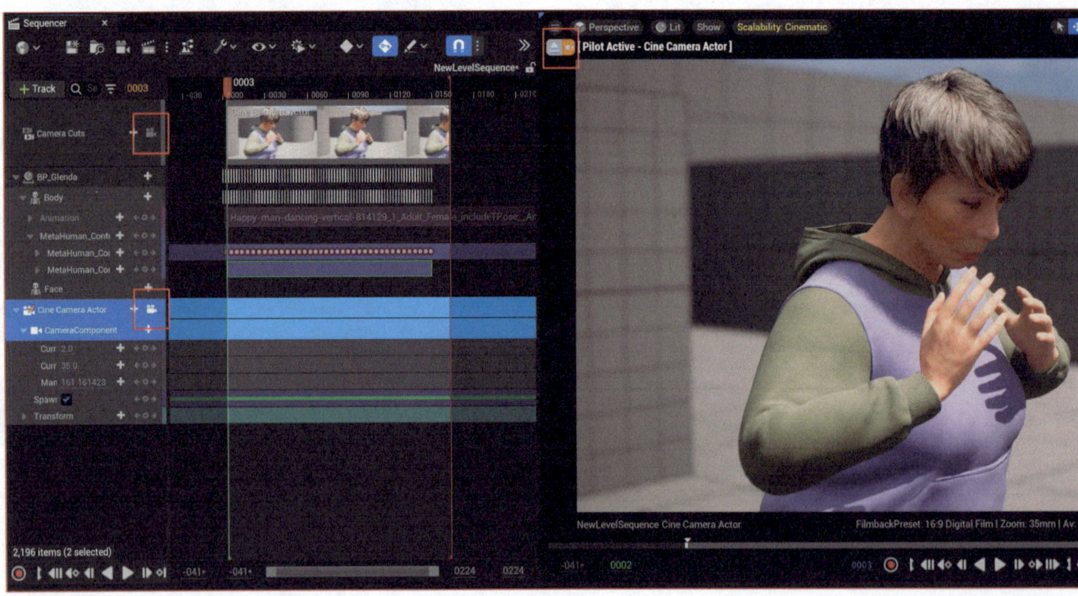

Figure 7.19: The camera created

Figure 7.19 demonstrates that the camera is now being piloted, which is a far more efficient way of controlling your camera. If you're familiar with 3D programs or first-person games, you will find that the navigation with the camera is very intuitive:

- *Alt* + *left-click* to orbit (move around)
- *Alt* + *middle click* to track (move left to right and up and down)
- *Alt* + *right-click* to dolly (move forward and backward)

When you are familiar with navigating your scene with the camera, let's create your first animation of a camera:

1. Click on **Transform** under **CameraComponent** inside the Sequencer.
2. Then, ensuring your play head is parked close to the beginning of **Play Range**, hit *Enter*. This will create a keyframe for all of the transform parameters, such as **Location**, **Rotation**, and **Scale**.
3. Do the same with the **Focus Distance** attribute after first ensuring your MetaHuman is in focus just like in *Figure 7.19*. You will need to click on **Manual Focus Distance**, change the value, and hit *Enter* to create a keyframe.
4. When you're happy with both your composition and your focus, park your play head at a different frame.
5. Once you reposition your camera, a keyframe will automatically be placed. If it doesn't get placed automatically, just click on the **Transform** attribute as before and hit *Enter*.

You've now created your first animation of a camera while filming a MetaHuman. You may have to edit the **Focus Distance** attribute to make sure your MetaHuman remains in focus throughout the shot.

It takes a little while to plot camera moves and you may find that you are creating keyframes only to have to delete them again and again. This is perfectly normal. Once you feel you've got a reasonable camera movement, it's time to render some animations.

Rendering a test animation from the Level Sequencer

To render out an animation, first, click on the **Movie Scene Capture** button (it's the clapper board icon) at the top of your Sequencer:

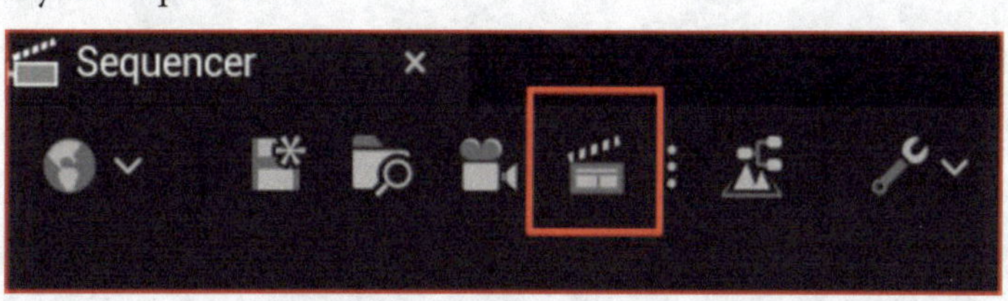

Figure 7.20: Clapper board icon

> **Note**
>
> If you have installed the Movie Render Queue plug-in, you will be given a choice of which renderer to use. If so, choose **Movie Scene Capture (Legacy)**.

You will then get the following **Render Movie Settings** dialog box:

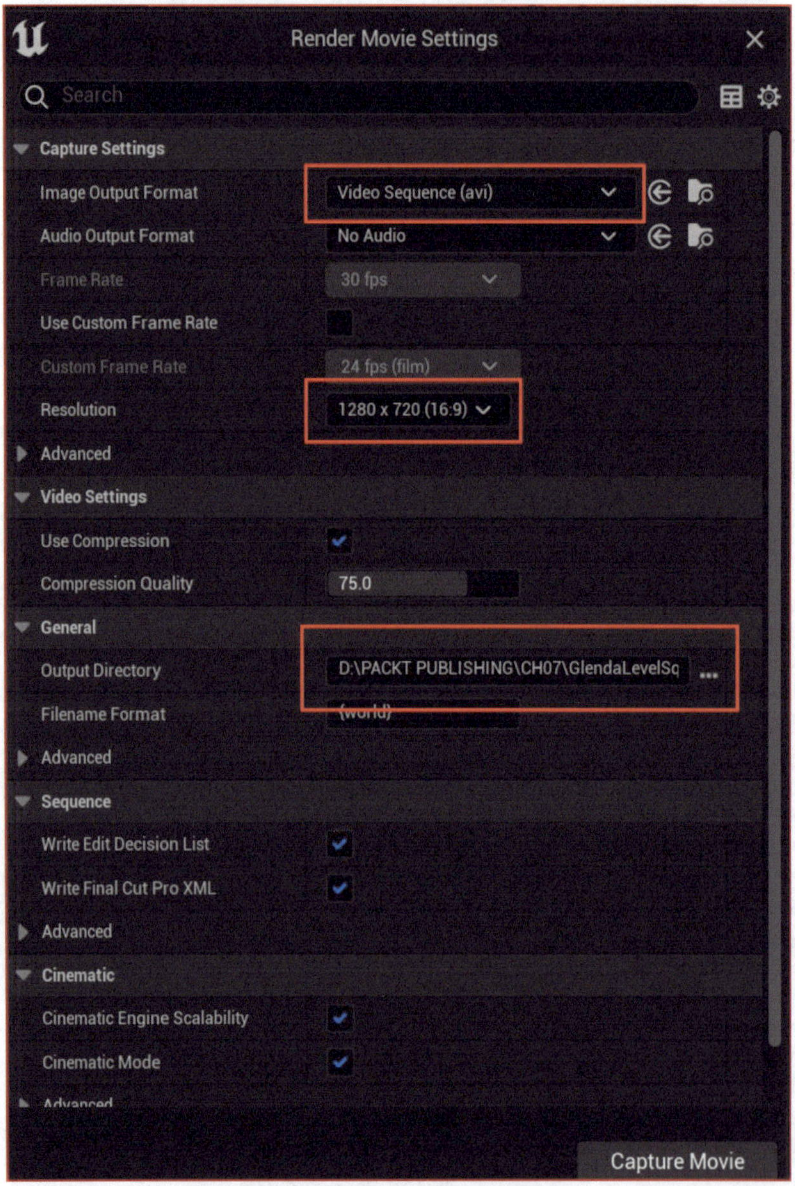

Figure 7.21: Render Movie Settings

In *Figure 7.21*, I have left all the settings with their default values. Three important settings to note are:

- **Image Output Format**: You need to render a movie in a format that your system can play. The default is **AVI** but you can change it to a **QuickTime Pro Res** file.

> **Note**
>
> To ensure that you can render Apple Pro Res, go to **Edit**, then **Plugins**, search for `prores`, and check the **Apple ProRes Media** checkbox. Then, you will need to restart Unreal.

- **Resolution**: The default resolution is **1280 x 720 (16.9)** pixels, but you can change it to a higher resolution if you like.
- **Output Directory**: By default, the **Render Movie** renderer will try to render the file to your project folder to use as the output directory. You can choose another directory if you prefer.

Once you are happy with your render settings, click on **Capture Movie**. It will take a few minutes to render your file – while you wait, you can see a preview of your render, as seen in *Figure 7.22*. You can see that my file is being written to a bespoke directory that I created for this book.

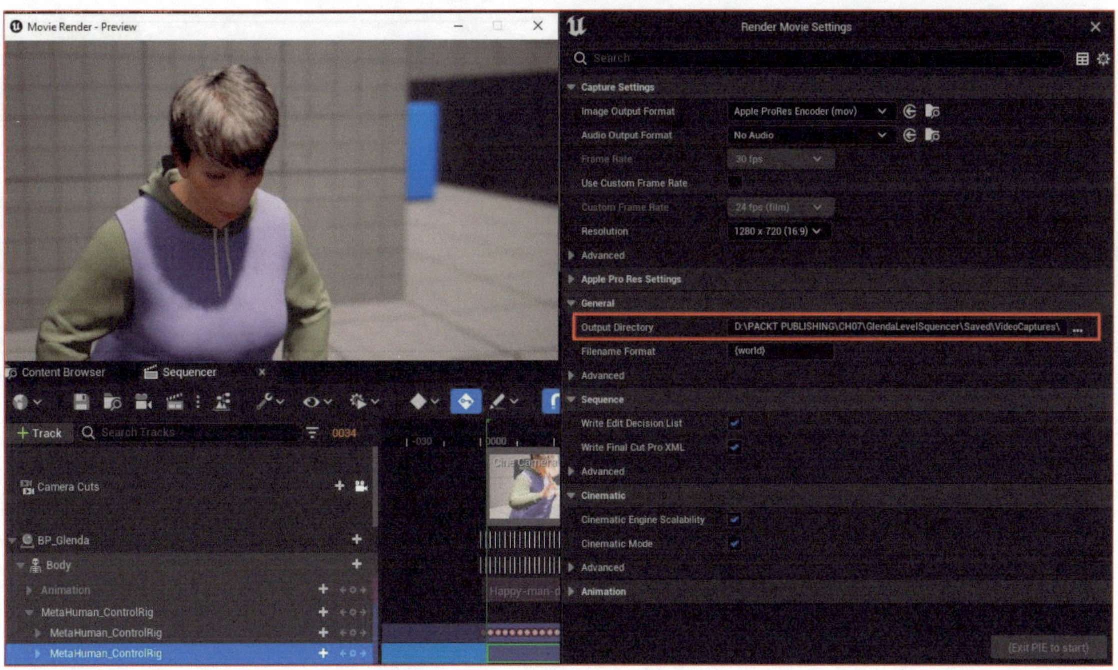

Figure 7.22: The movie render – preview window

To view your finished video, go to the output directory on your PC and click on the **MOV** file created to play your animation.

> **Note**
>
> On slower systems, when your render looks like it has finished rendering, the render preview window will remain open. The renderer goes through a process of writing all the frames and then through another process of containing the frames within the QuickTime file. At higher resolutions, with bigger files, and slower machines, this process can take almost as long as the initial render.

Summary

In this chapter, we learned how to create a Level Sequencer and add our character to it. We also learned how to create a keyframed MetaHuman Rig based on our mocap data from the previous chapter and an Additive section to apply additional keyframes for the purpose of fixing issues.

Then, we briefly covered keyframing within the Level Sequencer before moving on to creating a camera and animating it in the Level Sequencer. Finally, we learned how to export video files from UE5.

In the next chapter, we are going to work with Facial Motion Capture using an iPhone.

8

Using an iPhone for Facial Motion Capture

In the previous chapter, we took our body motion capture to the next level by learning how to make adjustments to the animation and render video using the Level Sequencer. The Level Sequencer plays an integral part when it comes to managing animation and we will use it again here as we explore facial motion capture.

In this chapter, we are specifically looking at facial motion capture for our MetaHuman, taking advantage of the iPhone depth camera and facial tracking features. MetaHumans come with dozens of intricate facial controls that respond to facial capture tools, giving you the power to create incredibly realistic facial performances including speech. This can capture your own performance or an actor's performance to such a degree that even very subtle nuances are reflected, thus making the overall result incredibly realistic.

So, in this chapter, we will cover the following topics:

- Installing the Live Link Face app
- Installing Unreal Engine plugins (including Take Recorder)
- Connecting and configuring the Live Link app to Unreal Engine
- Configuring and testing the MetaHuman Blueprint
- Calibrating and capturing live data

Technical requirements

In terms of computer power, you will need the technical requirements detailed in *Chapter 1* and the MetaHuman plus the Unreal Engine mannequin that we imported into UE5 in *Chapter 2*.

You will also need an iPhone and a stable Wi-Fi connection to install plugins.

Let's look at that iPhone requirement a little more. You will need to have an iPhone X or newer, or an iPad Pro (3rd generation) or newer. This is because (unlike other phones, such as Android ones) they have a built-in depth camera, which is necessary for motion capture.

You will also need a long cable – approximately 2 meters – because it is best to have your iPhone on charge during motion capture sessions as the process is quite battery consuming.

Installing the Live Link Face app

The Live Link Face app is a free app that you can download onto your iPhone or iPad directly from the App Store. Its sole purpose is to utilize the iPhone's built-in depth camera, along with facial recognition and pixel tracking technology, to produce data that works within ARKit. In addition to collecting facial motion capture data in real time, it also transmits the data via **Internet Protocol** (**IP**) to your desktop computer using a Wi-Fi connection; this data is then picked up by the Live Link utility in Unreal Engine, which we shall delve into later.

Figure 8.1 shows the Live Link Face app in the Apple App Store:

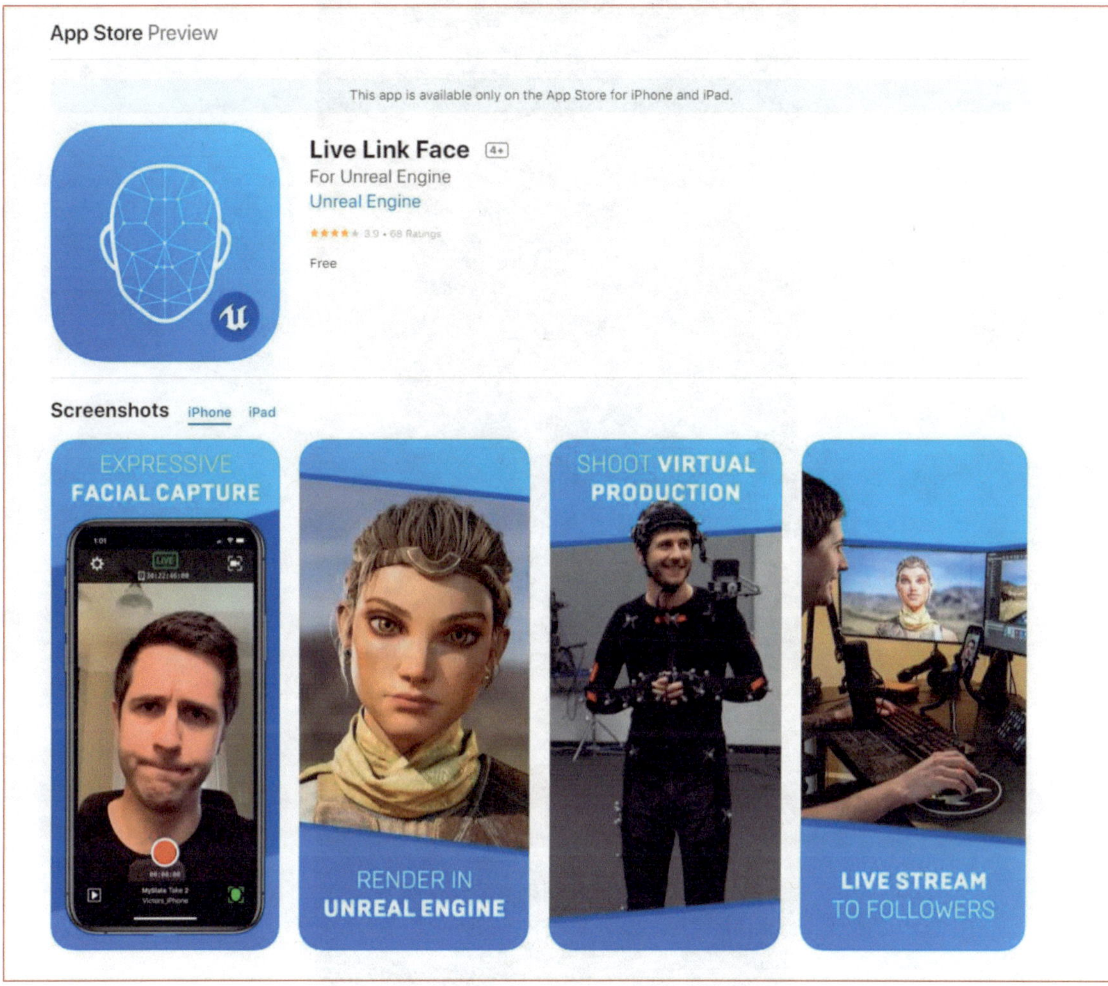

Figure 8.1: The Live Link Face app in the App Store

Once downloaded and installed, open the app to test that it is working. While looking at the display, you should immediately see your face. By default, the mesh overlay is enabled as seen in *Figure 8.2*, and you'll see that the mesh very accurately tracks your face.

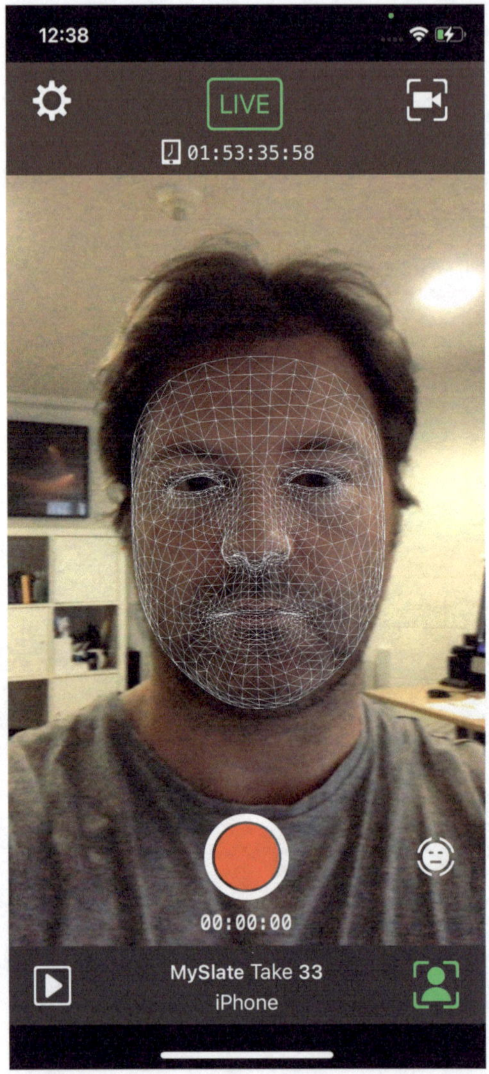

Figure 8.2: Opening up the Live Link Face app

As soon as our face is being tracked, we know the app is working. There is no need to do any more with the application for the time being. In the next section, we will install a number of Unreal Engine plugins, such as Live Link, which will allow us to receive the motion capture streaming data from the iPhone.

Installing Unreal Engine plugins (including Take Recorder)

As just mentioned, there are a number of plugins that you will need to have installed. The good news is that upon downloading and importing your first MetaHuman character, you will have inadvertently and automatically installed them without realizing it. However, you will need to make sure that the following plugins are enabled:

- Live Link
- Live Link Control Rig
- Live Link Curve Debug UI
- Apple ARKit
- Apple ARKit Face Support
- Take Recorder

To easily find the plugins, go to **Edit**, then **Plugins**, and we'll start installing the required plugins.

Live Link, Live Link Control Rig, and Live Link Curve Debug UI

To find the Live Link plugins, search for **Live Link** as demonstrated in *Figure 8.3*. You can see that I have enabled the following plugins, which are indicated by the checkboxes and the blue ticks:

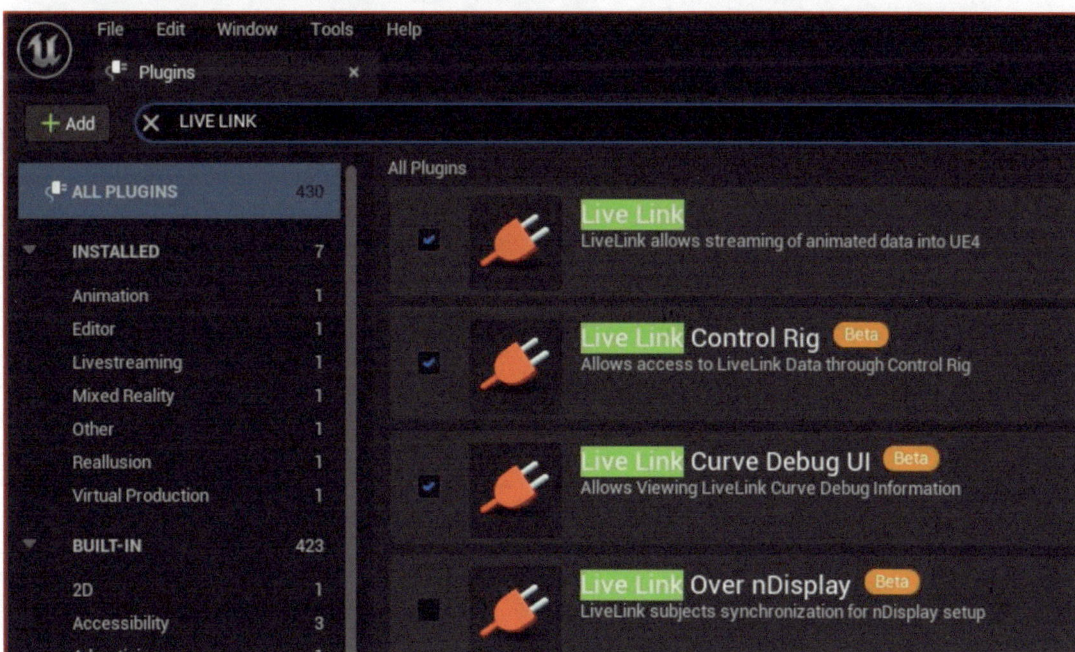

Figure 8.3: Enabling the Live Link plugins

Some of these plugins are essential for using the app and I will now briefly outline their importance.

Live Link

Live Link is the core plugin that allows third-party applications to stream animation data directly into Unreal Engine. Applications such as MotionBuilder and Maya permit users to make changes to these applications and see the results updated in the Unreal Engine viewport in real time. This functionality in the context of this book permits users to use other applications such as the Live Link iPhone app to stream data directly into Unreal Engine.

Live Link Control Rig

Live Link Control Rig allows the incoming data from a third-party application to communicate with the animation controllers of a character. For instance, a MetaHuman has a control rig that allows users to manually animate it. Live Link Control Rig harnesses the same control rig protocol.

Live Link Curve Debug UI

For the purpose of debugging and viewing the connection from a third-party animation data source into Unreal Engine, we will use the Live Link Curve Debug UI plugin.

> **Note**
>
> Live Link Curve Debug UI, while not essential, is a convenient interface for troubleshooting issues when it comes to advanced refinement; however, discussing it in detail is beyond the scope of this book as it looks at every single control point of the face.

ARKit and ARKit Face Support

Next, we need ARKit and ARKit Face Support. ARKit is an AR solution designed to work exclusively on an Apple iOS camera device. It ensures that Unreal is able to understand the incoming data. ARKit Face Support connects specifically to the face tracking solution via depth and RGB cameras on the iPhone.

So, in the **Plugins** tab, run a search, but this time for **ARKit**. You will see a list of the available ARKit plugins that you need to enable:

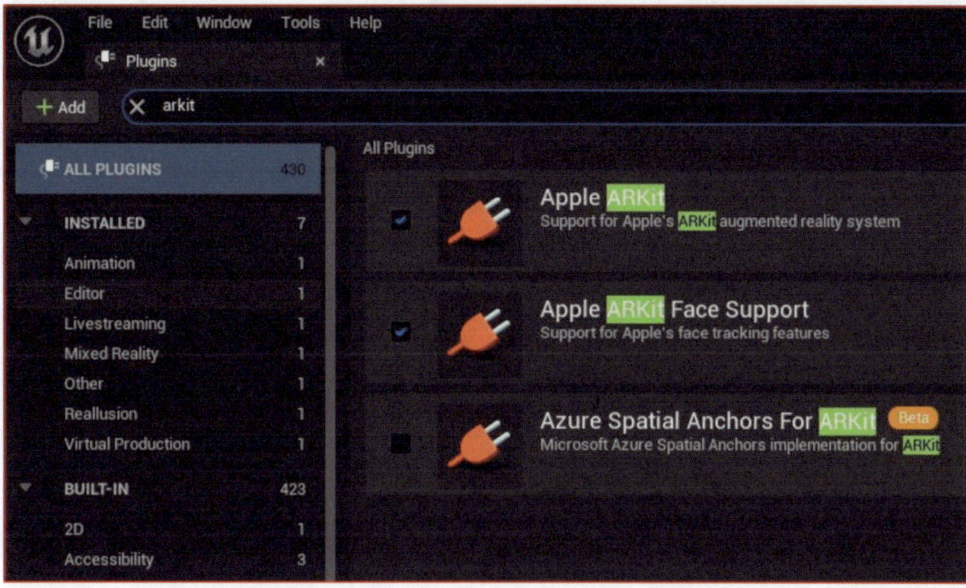

Figure 8.4: Enabling the Unreal Engine ARKit plugins

Take Recorder

We have one more plugin to enable, which is Take Recorder. Try to think of Take Recorder as a video camera. Effectively, it records the motion capture data received by Live Link and stores it for playback, which in turn is imported into the Level Sequencer. Just like a video camera, we can record multiple takes until we are happy that we have got the best one (or at the very least, as close as possible to the best!).

To enable **Take Recorder**, search for the plugin as per *Figure 8.5*:

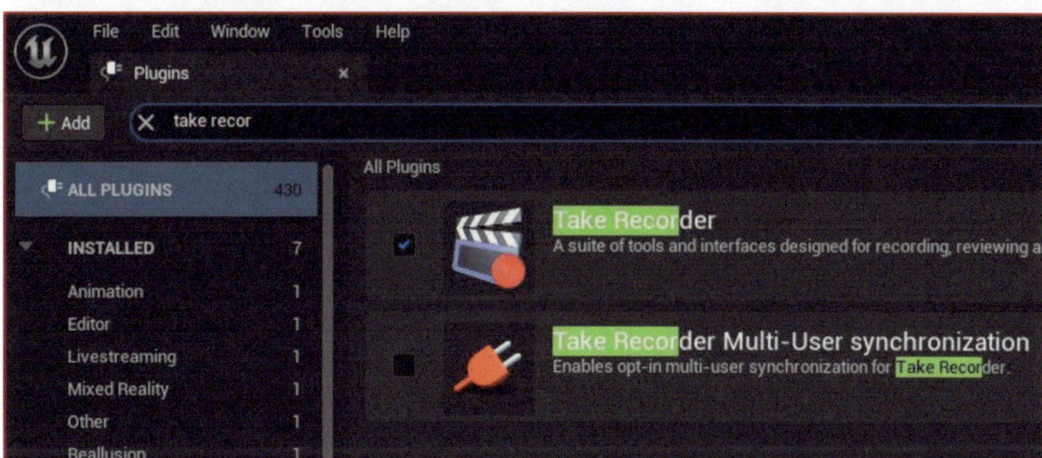

Figure 8.5: Enabling the Unreal Engine Take Recorder plugin

> **Note**
>
> You may need to restart Unreal Engine if you have enabled any of these plugins for them to take effect.

With all of the necessary plugins enabled, we can now move on to the next section where we will configure the Live Link Face app so that it can send data into Unreal Engine.

Connecting and configuring the Live Link Face app to Unreal Engine

With the Live Link Face app installed on the iPhone and the Live Link plugin enabled in Unreal Engine, we now need to get them to talk to each other (figuratively speaking, of course). Our goal is to send motion capture data from the iPhone to the PC and/or the Live Link app to send this data into Unreal Engine.

To do this, we first need to configure the app by finding our computer's IP address:

1. Hit the Windows key and search for `Command Prompt`.
2. In the Command Prompt, type `ipconfig`.
3. You'll see a list of all the IP configurations. On the top line you'll see the **IPv4** address, which should be similar to the following:

   ```
   192.168.100.155
   ```

   Make a note of that number, which will be unique to your machine.
4. Next, open up the Live Link Face app.
5. On the top left of the screen, you will see a cog icon, as illustrated in *Figure 8.6*:

Figure 8.6: Clicking on the settings icon

6. Pressing the cog will bring you to the **Settings** page. When there, click on the **Live Link** option:

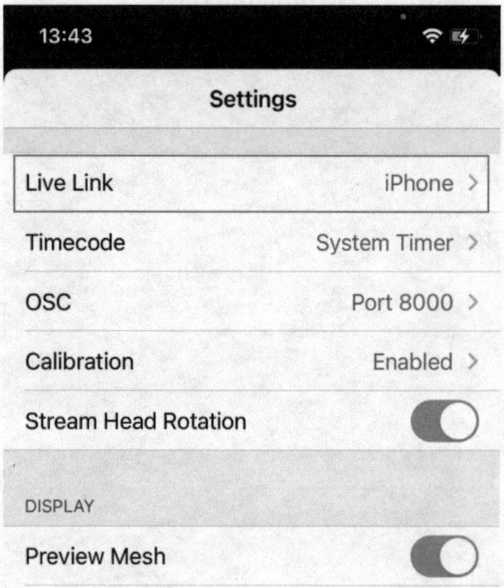

Figure 8.7: Clicking on Live Link iPhone

7. Now click on **Target** and type in the IP address of your computer.

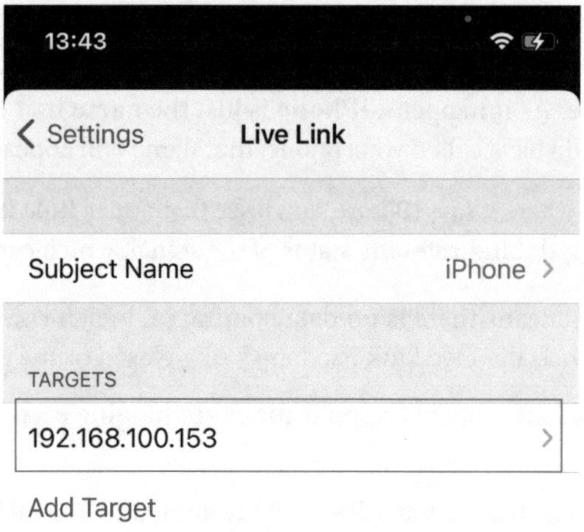

Figure 8.8: Clicking on the IP target

Once you have set your IP address in the app, you need to switch over to Unreal Engine again to see whether you are receiving a signal.

8. In Unreal Engine, go to **Window**, then **Virtual Production**, and click on **Live Link** where you will be brought to the following Live Link interface:

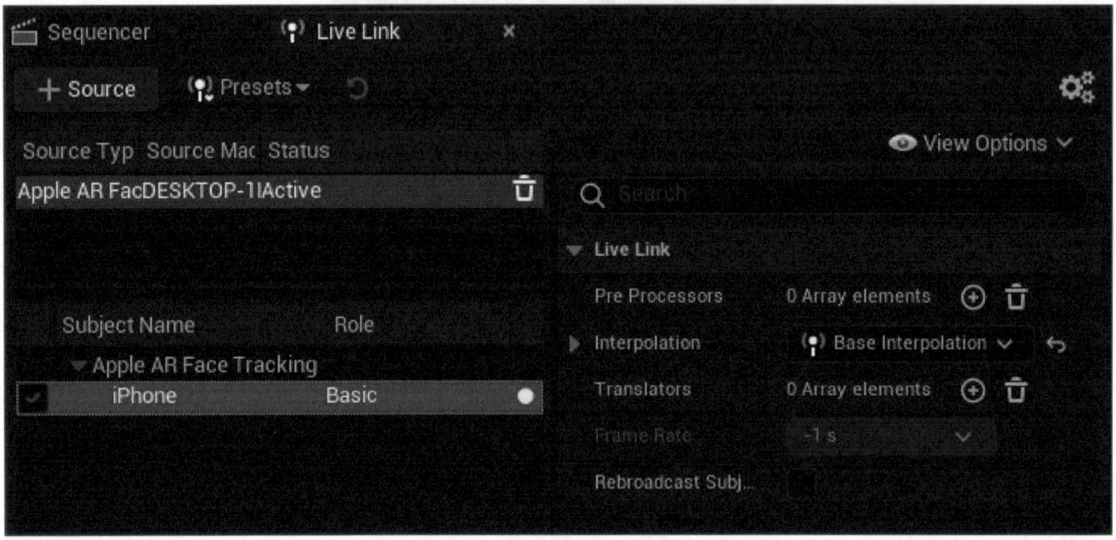

Figure 8.9: The Live Link interface

In *Figure 8.9*, you can see that Live Link has automatically picked up a signal. It recognizes that the type of signal is **Apple AR Face Tracking** and shows the name of the subject that the signal is coming from, in my case, **iPhone**. As it happens, **iPhone** is just the name that I gave to the phone after I purchased it. Whatever you have called your phone, that name will appear under the subject name.

Also in *Figure 8.9*, next to where it says **iPhone**, you'll see that under **Role** it says **Basic** and to the right of that is a yellow dot. This dot indicates the status of the signal, which can be interpreted as follows:

- If the dot is red, it means there is no data coming in, which could be caused by improper configurations such as the Live Link Face app being closed or the phone being off
- The yellow dot indicates that both applications are pinging each other but no active ARKit data exists
- A green dot indicates that there is ARKit data coming into Unreal Engine from the Live Link Face app

Knowing that both apps are effectively speaking to each other means that we can go on to the next step and configure our MetaHuman to receive data.

Configuring and testing the MetaHuman Blueprint

We must now tell the MetaHuman Blueprint to receive data from Live Link. As it happens, this is very simple:

1. Open up the MetaHumans Blueprint from within your **Content** folder.
2. In the **Components** tab on the left-hand side, click on the top of the hierarchy where it says **BP_ (your MetaHuman Name)**. In my case it is **BP_Glenda**. This will let you see the settings you need to edit in the **Details** panel, as per *Figure 8.10*:

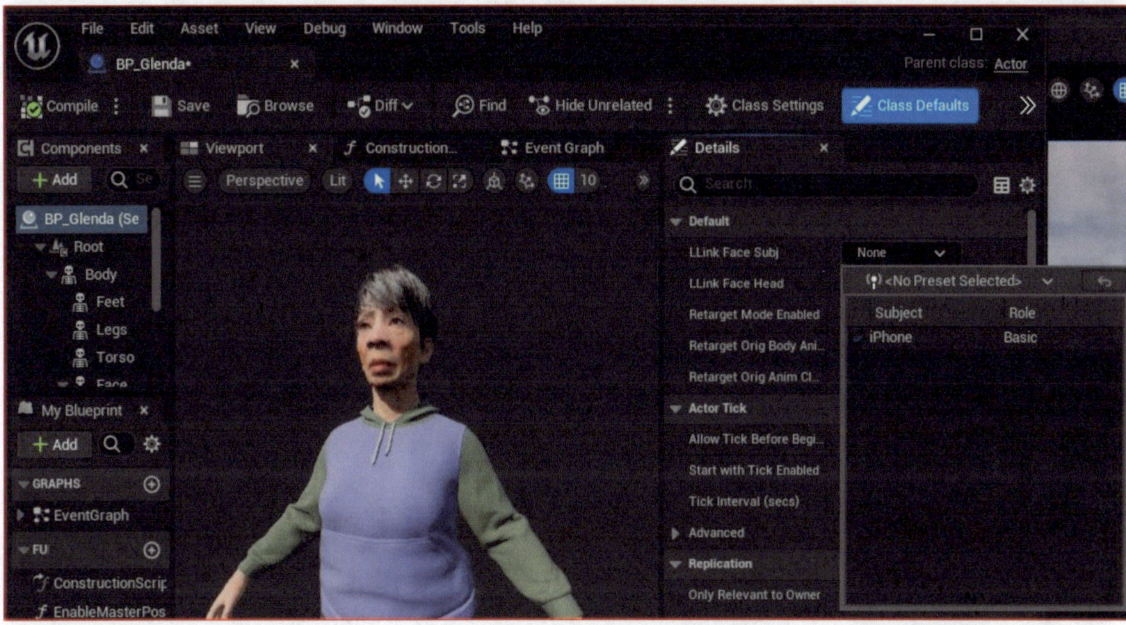

Figure 8.10: Creating a Level Sequencer

3. Go to the **Llink Face Subject** drop-down list and select the name of your phone. Again, in my case, it's just called **iPhone** but your phone may have a more specific name.
4. Also, tick the **Llink Face Head** option, which enables head movement data to be accepted by the Blueprint.

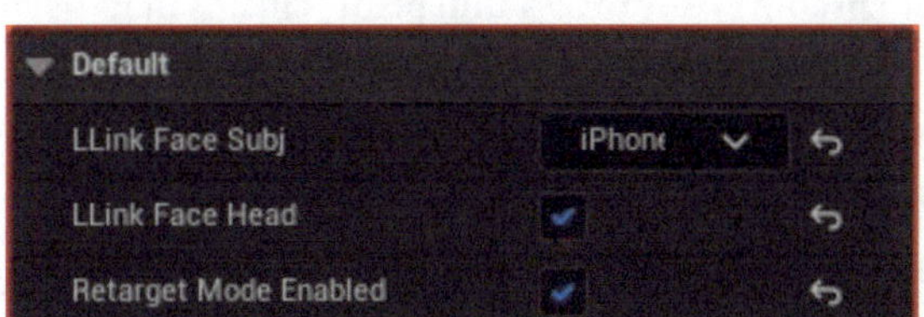

Figure 8.11: Enabling the Llink Face Head option

Next, click on **Face** within the **Components** tab. Then, in the **Details** panel, go to **Animation**, as seen in *Figure 8.12*:

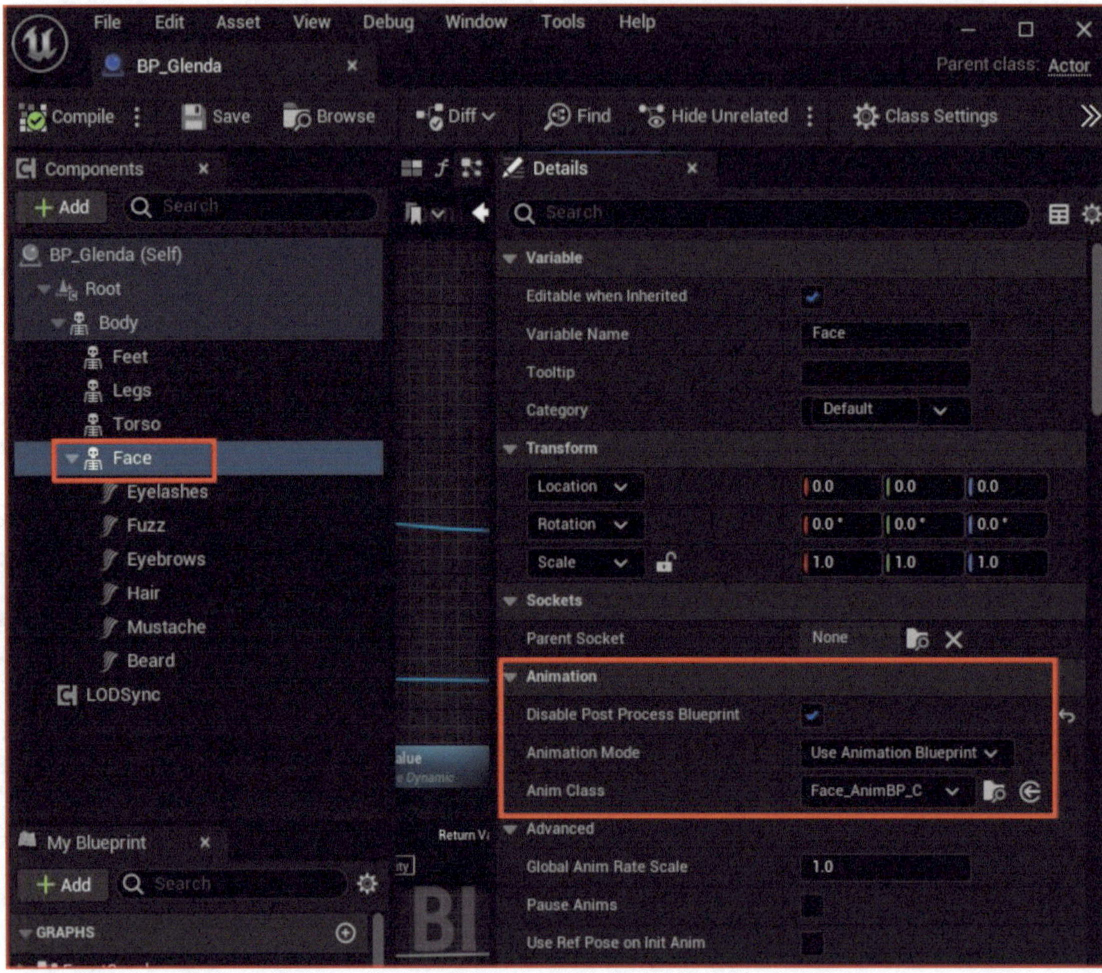

Figure 8.12: Changing Animation Mode and Anim Class

5. Here, ensure that **Disable Post Process Blueprint** remains in its default ticked position. If the box isn't ticked, please tick it.
6. Then, change **Animation Mode** to **Use Animation Blueprint** and change **Anim Class** to **Face_AnimpBP_C**.
7. Now, be sure to hit **Compile** and then save the Blueprint otherwise these changes won't take effect.

With these changes made to the blueprint, it's time to test the mocap data as it streams from the Live Link Face app and into your MetaHuman Blueprint. Before testing, make sure you go through the following checklist:

- The IP address is correct in the app
- Live Link is enabled and open
- The MetaHuman Blueprint is receiving the iPhone signal, next to **LLink Face Subj** in the **Default** parameter within the **Details** panel
- The MetaHuman Face Blueprint is set to **Use Animation Blueprint** for **Mode** and **Face_AnimpBP_C** for **Anim Class** as per *Figure 8.12*

If you have followed the checklist, the next thing you need to do is to run a simulation by hitting *Alt + P*. At this point, you should see a live facial capture of your character in the viewport.

If you have continued on from the previous chapter and have the Level Sequencer open, you will see the new facial animation on top of your character's body as acquired through DeepMotion Animation 3D. Note that you can even play the body animation from the Level Sequencer while previewing the Live Facial capture simultaneously.

It won't take long to realize that the iPhone motion capture result is not perfect. However, it is a very powerful and complex tool with plenty of scope to refine the data as it comes in and refine it again after the data has been recorded.

> **Note**
>
> If you are experiencing problems with the facial animation, such as the head rotation working and nothing else, there was a known bug that was fixed with an update of Quixel Bridge. If you are running Unreal Engine 5.0.3 or above, ensure that you have updated the Quixel Bridge plugin to version 5.0.0 or above. You will then need to re-download and re-import your character.

In the next section, we will look at calibrating the Live Link Face app to get us a better result.

Calibrating and capturing live data

To get a better result, the ARKit capturing process needs to acquire data that takes the performer's characteristics into account. As you can see from *Figure 8.13*, the app has done a good job of capturing the performer's facial proportions, clearly outlining the eyes, nose, mouth, and jaw. However, giving the app a baseline of information (such as a neutral pose) would really help to refine the overall outcome.

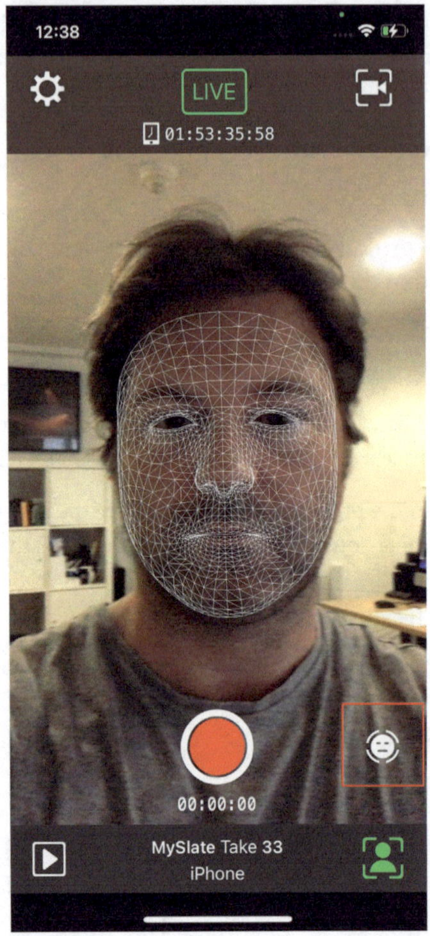

Figure 8.13: Calibrating the Live Link Face app

To understand how and why baselines and neutral poses work, let's take a look at the eyebrows as an example using an arbitrary unit of measurement. If in the resting or neutral position the eyebrows are at *0* and a frown is at *–10*, and a surprised expression raises the eyebrows to *+15*, then knowing what the neutral pose is would give the app a better idea of where to determine the frown or surprised expressions to coincide with its tracking capability.

The calibration process in the Live Link Face app is incredibly simple as it relies only on a neutral expression. In *Figure 8.13*, I've highlighted the face icon on the right of the record button – click on the face icon, hit **Recalibrate**, and a short countdown will commence before taking a picture of your neutral pose for calibration.

Once calibrated, it's time to prepare for capturing a facial performance. For this, there are three main considerations:

- **System performance**: We need to streamline as much as possible so that our systems and Unreal Engine are only concerned with getting as much data at the highest possible frame rate as possible. Therefore, processor-intensive tasks such as photorealistic lighting, high levels of lighting, and camera effects need to be scaled down. Also, ensure that no shaders are prepared in the background and that no other applications are running.
- **Take Recorder**: We'll be using the Take Recorder plugin to record the facial motion capture, so you need to ensure it is enabled.
- **The Level Sequencer**: We'll be using the Level Sequencer to import and play back the facial mocap and for refining any animation with it if need be.

I'll guide you through the process of capturing the facial capture with your phone step by step:

1. Ensure your phone is in a fixed position with plenty of light and that the front camera is looking directly at the performer.
2. Ensure that Live Link is receiving the signal (remember that you want to see a green dot next to the name of your phone).
3. Then, make sure that all rendering settings are turned to **Low** and complex scene actors are either hidden or removed from the scene. See *Figure 8.14* as an example of a scaled-down viewport setting using the **Unlit** and **Low** settings:

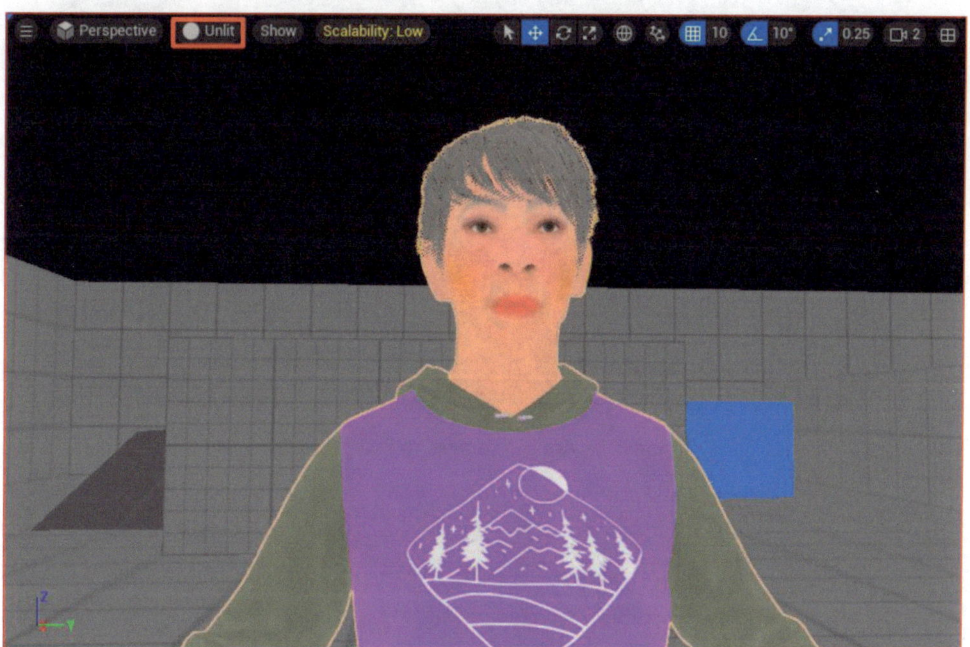

Figure 8.14: Scalability set to Low and Unlit

4. Open **Take Recorder** by going to **Window**, then **Cinematics**, and then **Take Recorder**.
5. Then, add the character blueprint by clicking on the **+ Source** button. Run a search for your character's blueprint under **From Actor** and add your phone from the **From LiveLink** option, as per *Figure 8.15*.

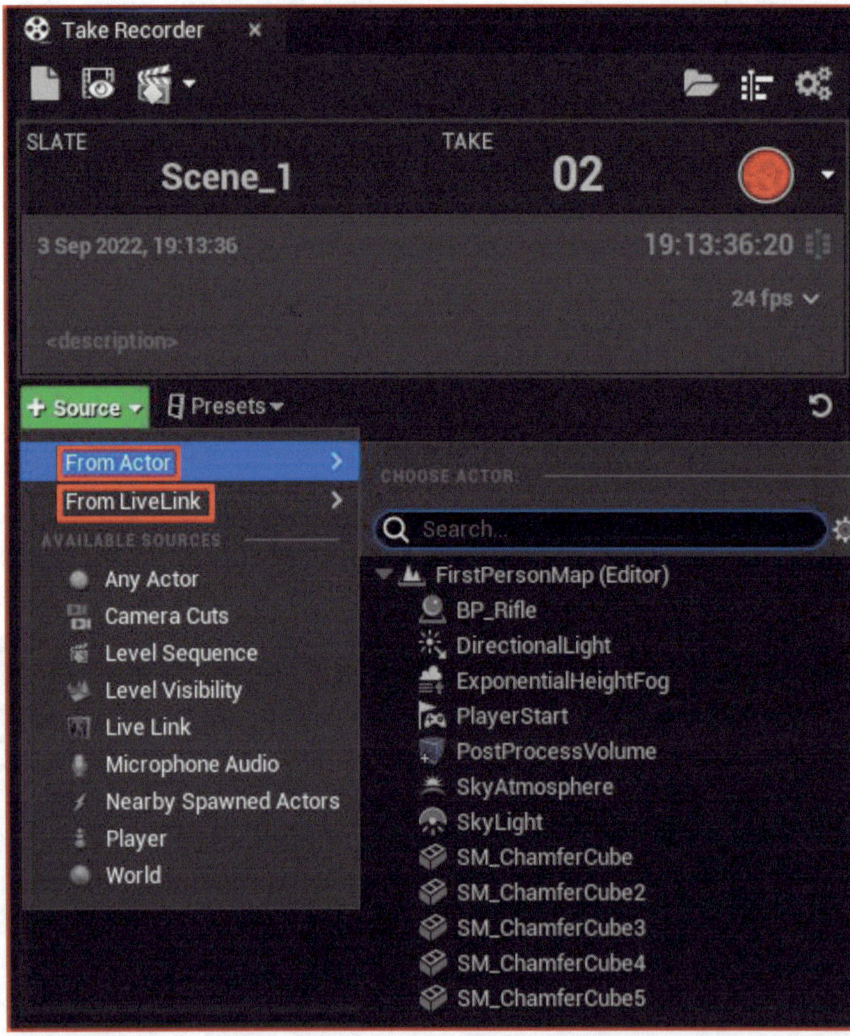

Figure 8.15: Adding sources to Take Recorder

6. When you're ready, first run a simulation by hitting *Alt* + *P* and then hit the large red record button.

   As soon as you run the simulation, the motion capture will begin, along with a 3-second countdown, similar to *Figure 8.16*:

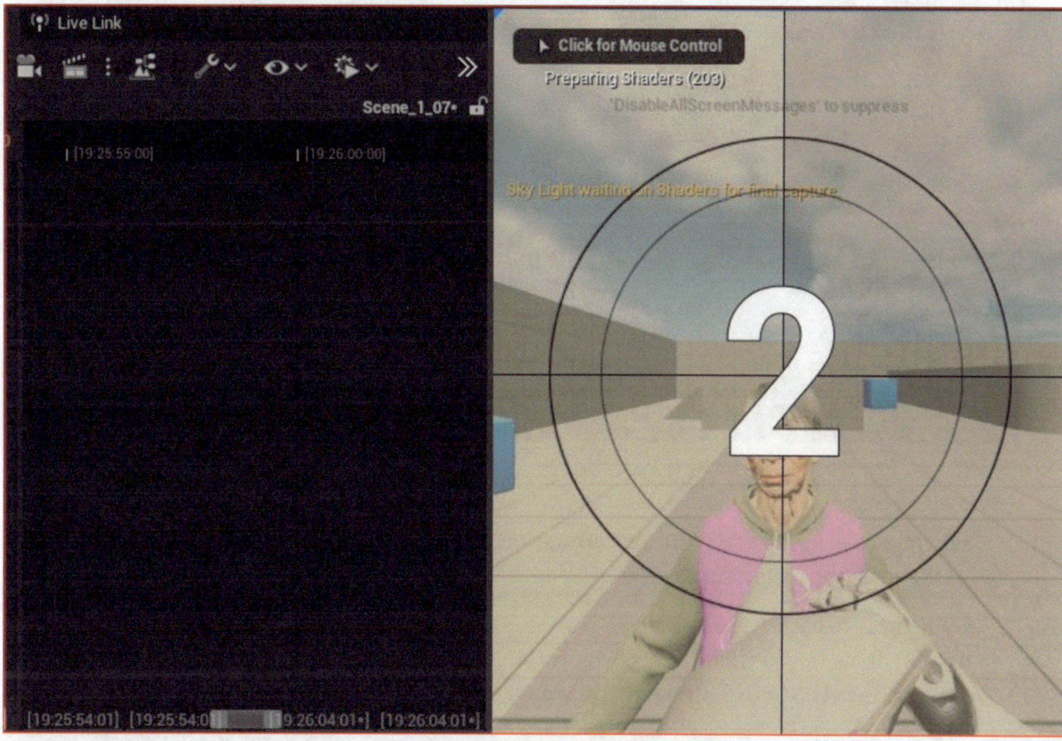

Figure 8.16: The 3-second countdown

Immediately upon recording, the Blueprint track and the iPhone track will be written as a take and a reference of this will temporarily occupy the Level Sequencer to show which tracks are actively recording:

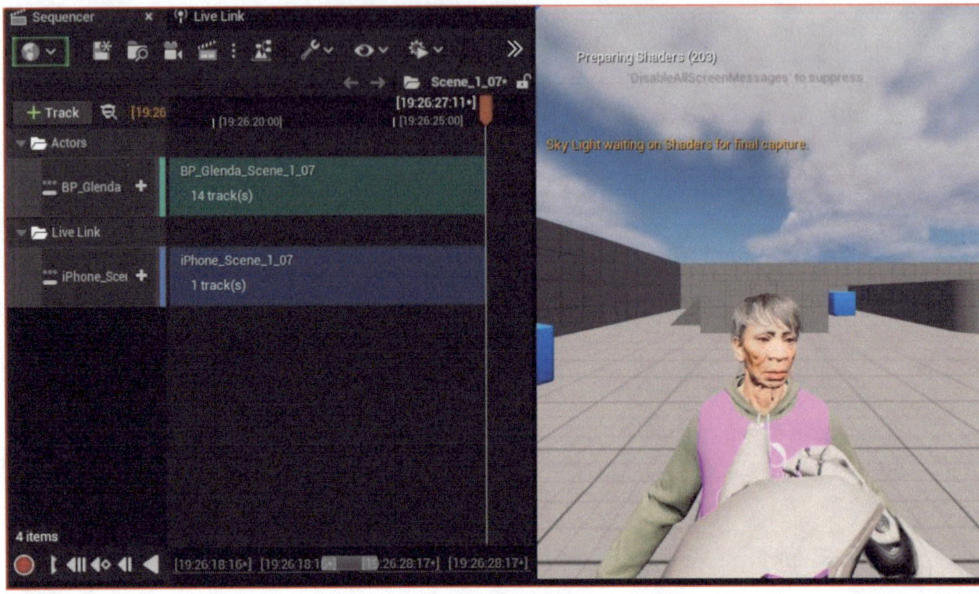

Figure 8.17: The tracks being recorded

When you are happy with your mocap session, hit the stop button on Take Recorder and stop your simulation by hitting *Esc*.

7. Going back to the Level Sequencer, you can now take a look at your facial mocap. If you don't have anything in your Level Sequencer, you will need to add your character Blueprint, click on **+ Track**, then **Actor to Sequence**, and search for your character as per *Figure 8.18*:

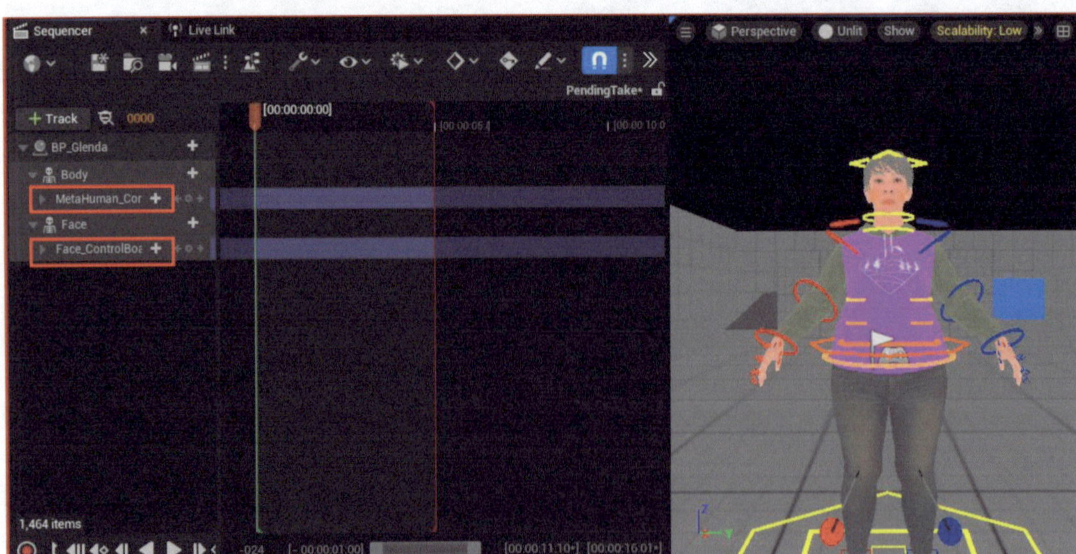

Figure 8.18: Importing the character Blueprint into Level Sequencer

Note that in *Figure 8.18*, when you bring in your character, you also bring in a rig for both the face and another for the body. However, because we are driving the character with mocap, you need to delete these rigs.

8. Once you've deleted the rigs from Level Sequencer, click on **Face**, then **+Track**, then **Animation**, and the most recent mocap session will be at the bottom of the list. In my case, I'm choosing the first take, `BP_Glenda_Scene_1_01_0`.

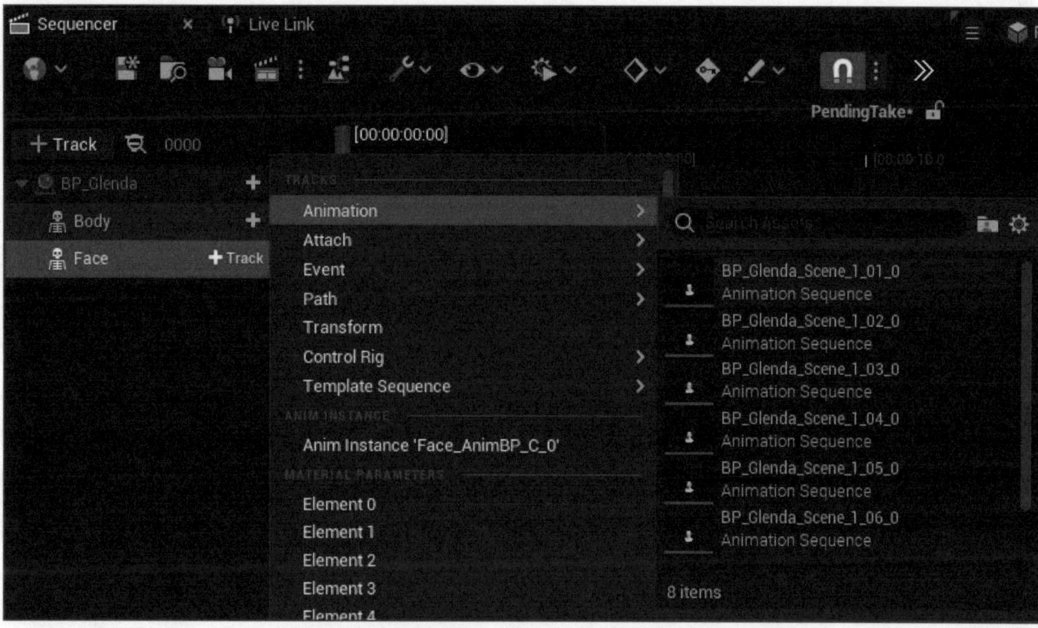

Figure 8.19: Adding an actor to the Level Sequencer

9. Once you have selected a take, press the play button on the Level Sequencer to watch your motion capture play back in real time.

If you still have the character Blueprint from the previous chapter with the retargeted animation, you can import the body animation. In addition, if your performance requires speech, the Level Sequencer is capable of playing back audio if you wanted to test your performances inside Unreal Engine. This is useful when ensuring that the facial capture is in synchronization with the audio of the speech recorded.

Note

It is advised that you capture the body and face simultaneously because most performers lead with their heads and the head leads the body. Getting both the body and head in sync can only really be done properly when both elements are captured at the same time.

The iPhone solution can work simultaneously with DeepMotion Animate 3D. To do this, you need a facial capture rig to ensure that the iPhone's depth camera is facing you at all times and that your hands are free. Ideally, the camera needs to be at a consistent distance at all times. Any movement of the camera separate from the head will be understood as a head movement and will lead to inaccurate data.

Companies such as MOCAP Design specialize in creating helmets that work with iPhones. You can see some of their iPhone and GoPro camera solutions at `https://www.mocapdesign.com/m2-headcam`.

This solution may be expensive to most so, alternatively, a DIY solution or 3D printed solution may be more cost-effective. Additionally, there are now solutions for live streamers to keep their phone cameras at a consistent distance. While not perfect, they are certainly better than holding a phone in one hand or on a tripod.

Summary

In this chapter, we have explored the iPhone's facial motion capture solution for MetaHumans in Unreal Engine. We used the Live Link app, along with Live Link and ARKit plugins, to capture live data. Additionally, we got to use the Take Recorder plugin in conjunction with the Level Sequencer as a way to record and manage our mocap.

In the next chapter, we will continue our facial motion capture but on a much more professional level, using Faceware.

9

Using Faceware for Facial Motion Capture

In the previous chapter, we used an iPhone to capture facial data via the Live Link Face App. While that is a great solution, it does have its limitations. One such limitation is how little control we had with regard to calibration; we were only able to calibrate to a neutral pose.

In this chapter, we're going to look at a more professional solution that is used in both AAA games and film projects. Unlike the iPhone's depth camera, we are looking at a video camera-based solution that provides us with a lot more calibration control: the solution is Faceware Studio.

Not only will we be taking advantage of the improved calibration when it comes to facial motion capture for our MetaHuman, we will also be looking at the additive tool in the Level Sequencer too.

So, in this chapter, we will cover the following topics:

- Installing Faceware Studio on a Windows PC
- Installing Unreal's Faceware Plugin and the MetaHuman sample
- Setting up a webcam and the streaming function
- Enabling Live Link to receive Faceware data
- Editing the MetaHuman Blueprint
- Recording a session with a Take Recorder
- Importing a take into the Level Sequencer
- Baking and editing facial animation in Unreal

Technical requirements

In terms of computer power, you will need the technical requirements detailed in *Chapter 1* and the MetaHuman plus the Unreal Engine Mannequin that we imported into UE5 in *Chapter 2*.

You will also need:

- A webcam and a well-lit room
- A stable internet connection as you will be downloading plugins
- Faceware Studio

> **Note**
>
> A word of warning: Faceware Studio is not a free solution; however, it is cheaper than a second-hand iPhone X. For individual users, there is an Indie pricing plan, which is €15 per month (at the time of writing). Alternatively, you can request a free trial.

Installing Faceware Studio on a Windows PC

To install Faceware Studio, head over to `https://facewaretech.com/` and navigate to the **Pricing** page. There are two options for the Faceware Studio software that you could download, depending on your budget. The first is the **Faceware Studio (Indie)** version, which is currently priced at $179 annually; the second is the free trial version of Faceware Studio.

Let's assume you do the latter – click **Try Now** under **Faceware Studio**, as per *Figure 9.1*.

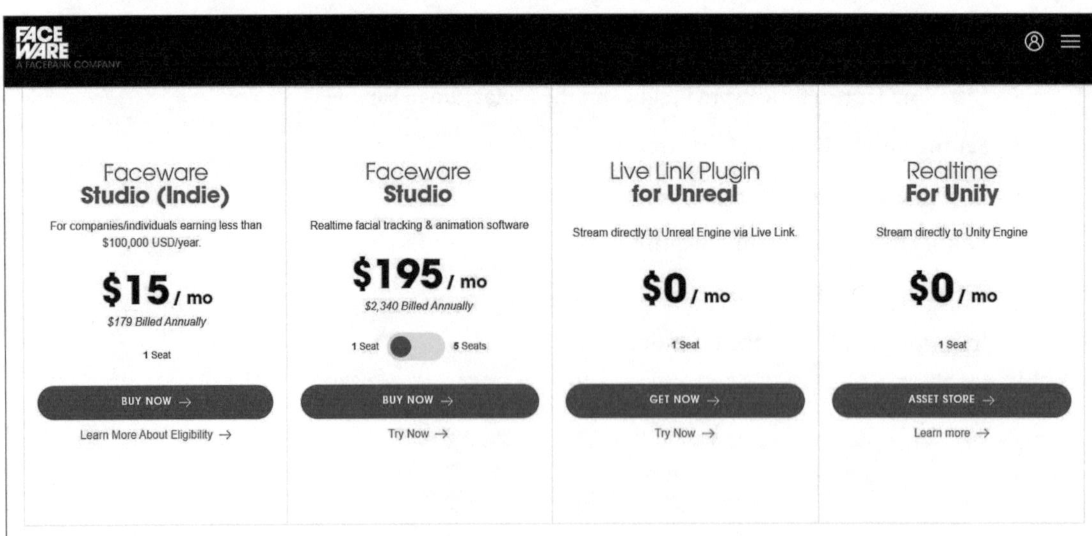

Figure 9.1: Faceware pricing options

You'll be invited to register for a Faceware account as per *Figure 9.2*:

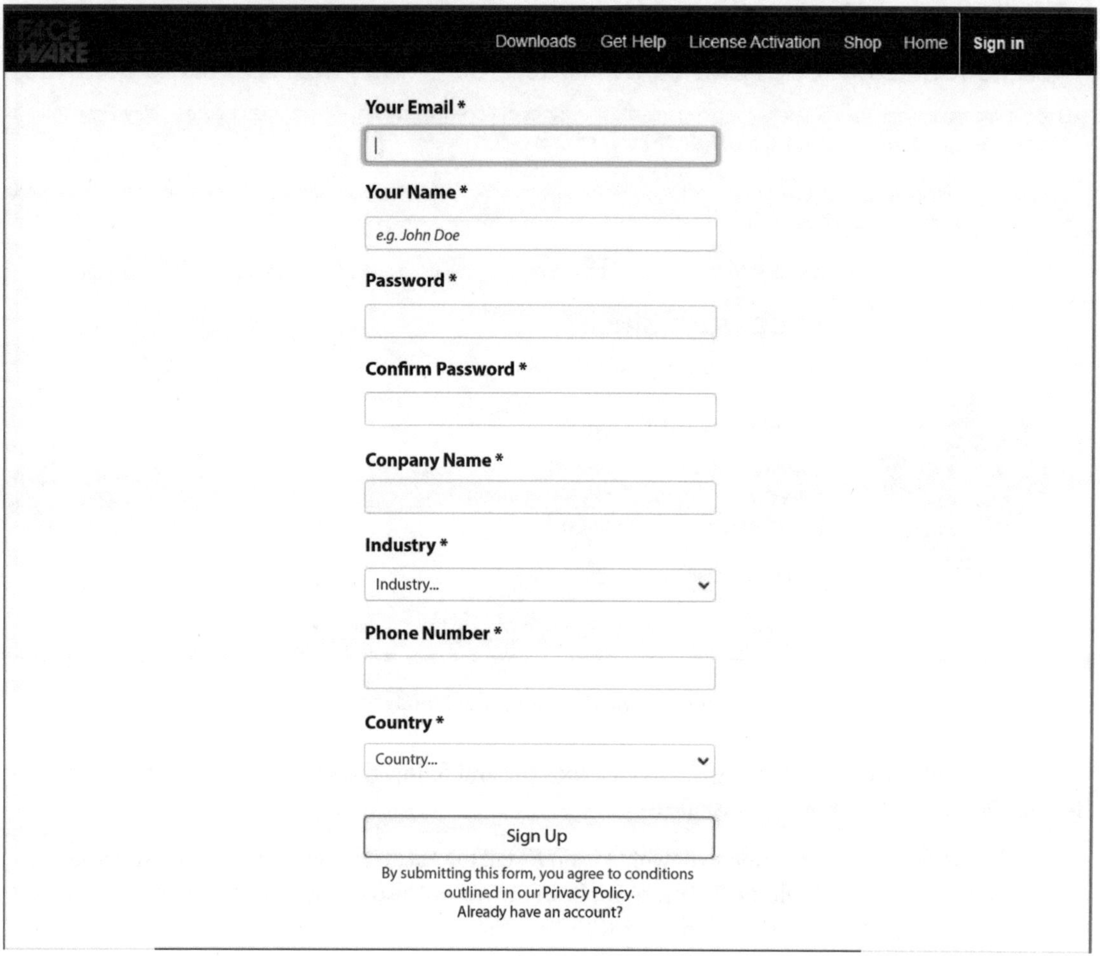

Figure 9.2: Sign up for an account

Once you have an account set up, navigate to and click on **Downloads** at the top of the page. This will take you to a list of available downloads. From *Figure 9.3*, you can see that Faceware Studio is available (if you don't see it, just scroll down the page). Here, you can click the **Download** button.

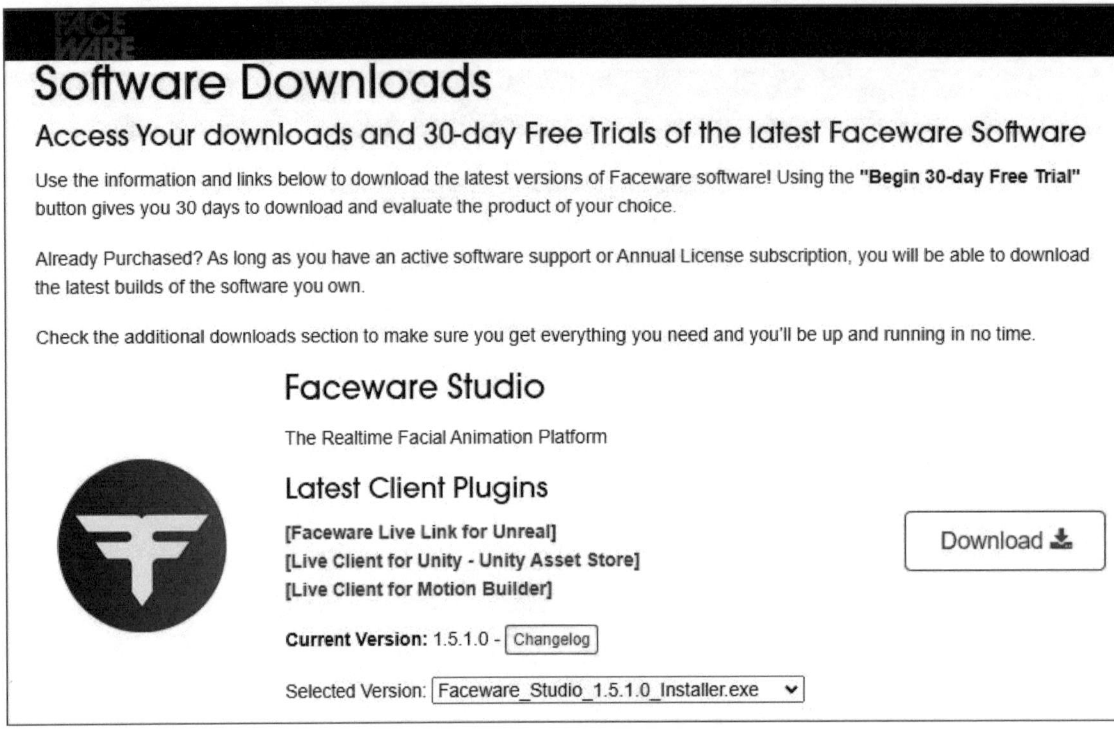

Figure 9.3: Downloading your 30-day trial

Once downloaded, open the `installer.exe` file and follow the simple onscreen instructions, then Faceware Studios will be installed!

In the next section, we are going to download and install the Faceware Live Link plugin, which allows Unreal to receive data from the Faceware application. We will also download a MetaHuman sample from Epic Games that is designed to work with Faceware.

Installing Unreal's Faceware plugin and the MetaHuman sample

To install Unreal's Faceware plugin, open up your project from *Chapter 8* and then open up the Epic Games Launcher. Search for the **Faceware Live Link** and then click on **Install to Engine**, as shown in *Figure 9.4*:

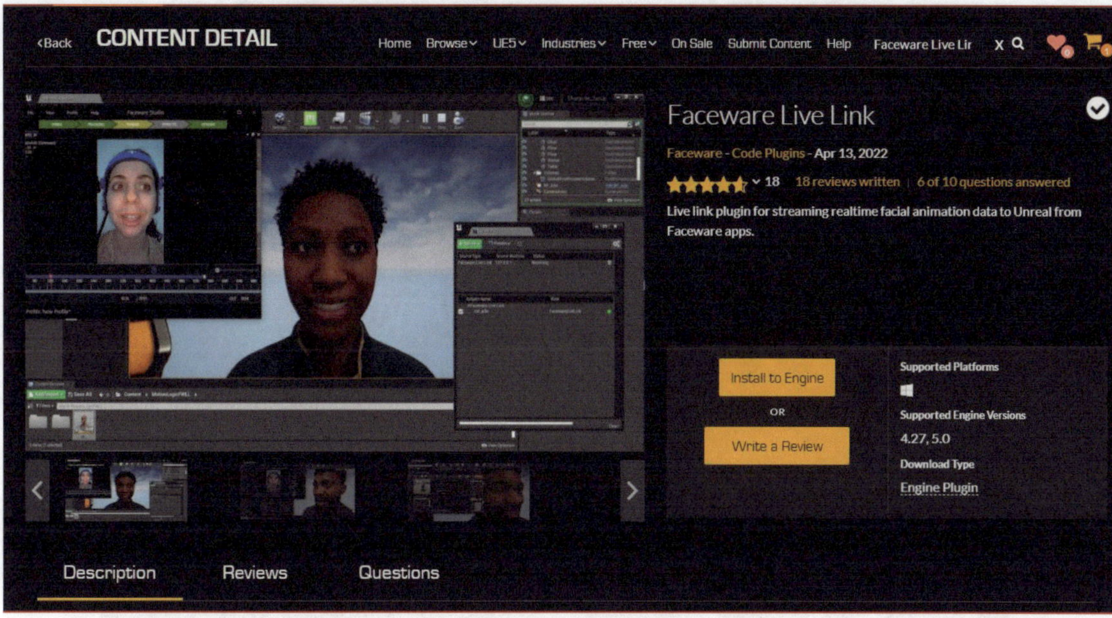

Figure 9.4: Epic Games Launcher Faceware Live Link page

After the installation of the plugin has finished, scroll down on the Faceware plugin page until you see the link for the Sample MetaHuman Blueprint, as shown in *Figure 9.5:*

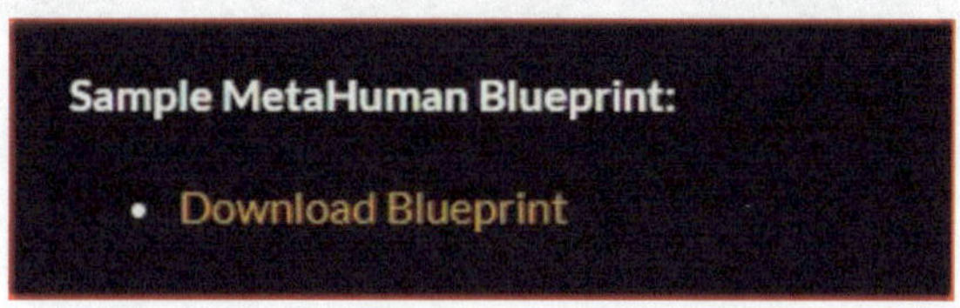

Figure 9.5: Sample MetaHuman Blueprint

Click on the **Download Blueprint** link. This will open a new browser, taking you away from Epic Launcher and you will see the following message:

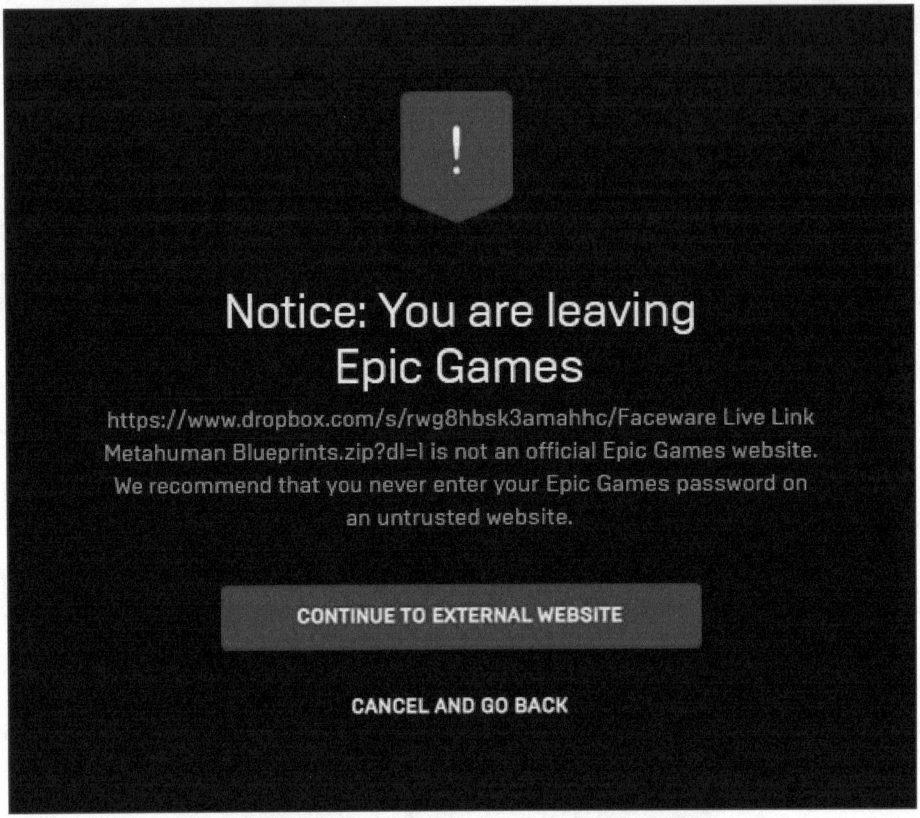

Figure 9.6: CONTINUE TO EXTERNAL WEBSITE button

Click on **CONTINUE TO EXTERNAL WEBSITE**. At this stage, you will be asked where you want to download the Sample MetaHuman Blueprint to.

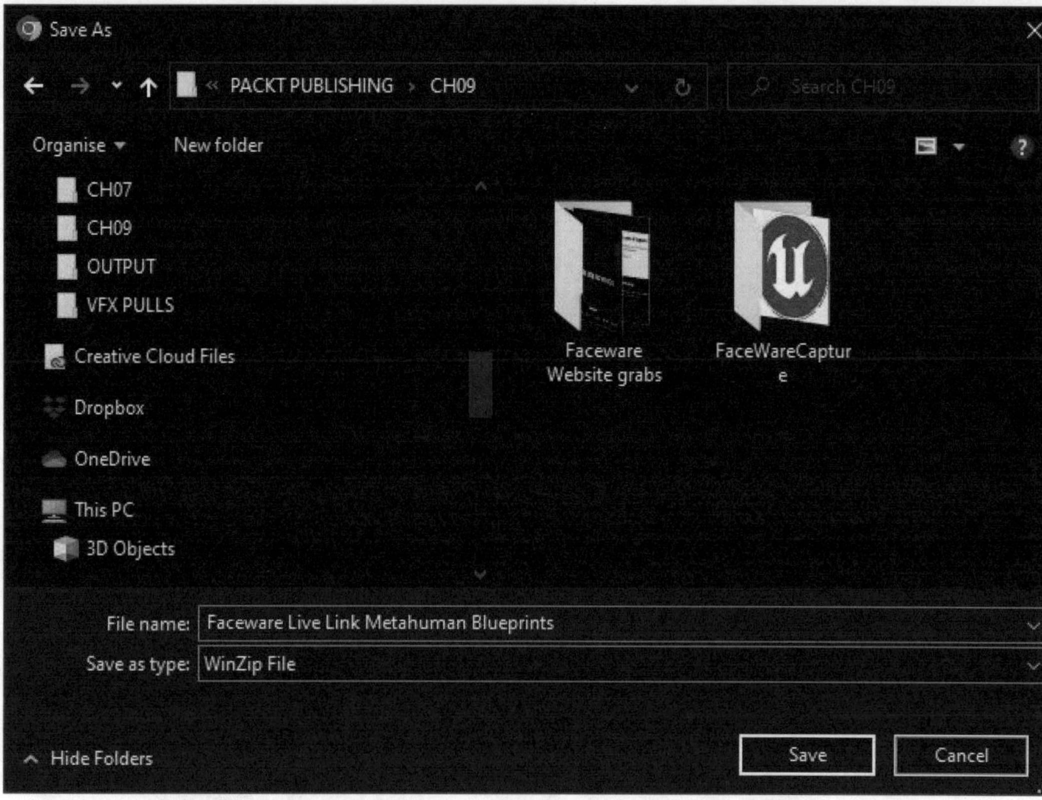

Figure: 9.7: Saving the Sample MetaHuman Blueprint

You can download it to a temporary location for the moment, or alternatively download it directly to your `MetaHumans` folder inside your project. If you don't know where on your computer your project folder is, you can find it by jumping back into your Unreal project and going to the Content Browser. From there, right-click on the `MetaHumans` folder and choose **Show in Explorer**, as shown in *Figure 9.8*.

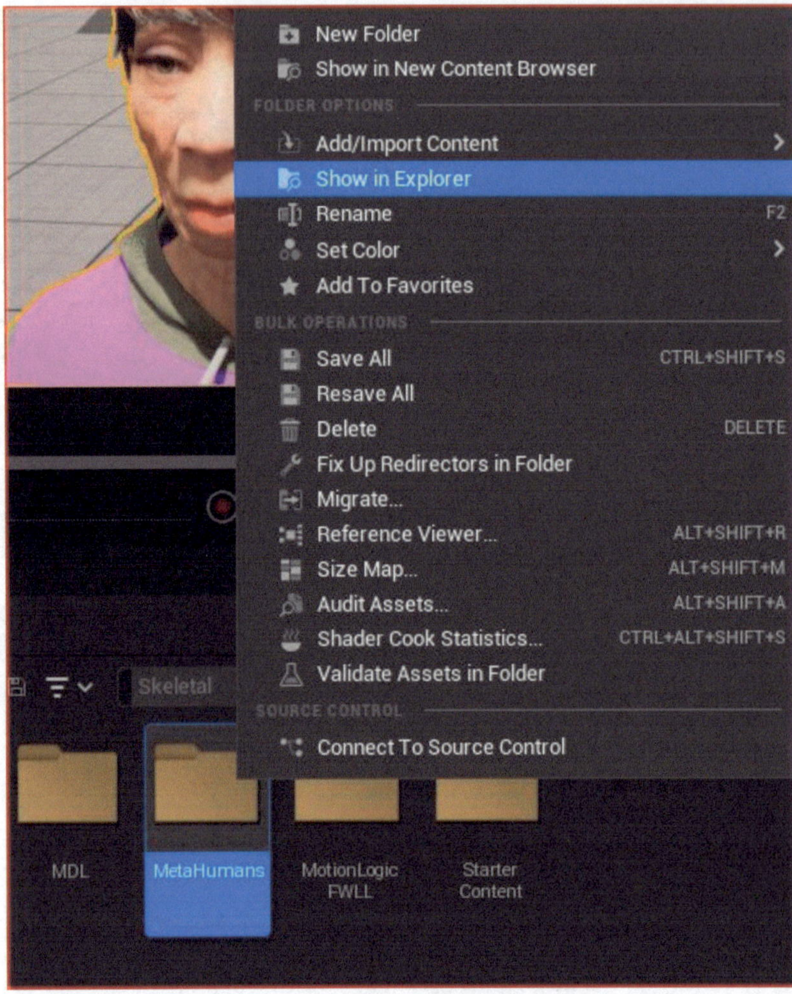

Figure 9.8: Locating your project folder

Clicking on **Show in Explorer** will open Windows Explorer so that we can see where our project files are independently of Unreal. Similar to what I have done in *Figure 9.9*, copy the file path of the `MetaHumans` folder location on your machine. Now we're going to save the Sample Blueprint into the project's `MetaHumans` folder we created in the previous chapter.

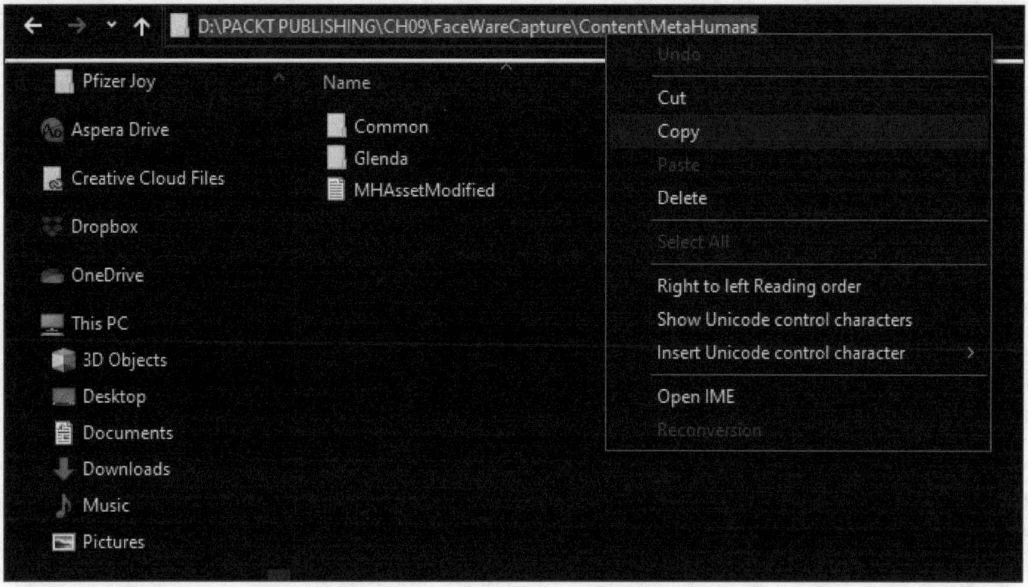

Figure 9.9: Copying the project location

Doing this will save the Blueprint into your project folder; however, it will be in a zipped file; you will need to extract it to the same folder. Once you do that, restart Unreal. During the restart, the MetaHuman Sample will update your project to ensure that MetaHumans will work with the Faceware plugin.

In the next section, we will move on over to the Faceware Studio software and use a webcam to track our face.

Setting up a webcam and the streaming function

The next step is to ensure that you have a working webcam or another camera with a working connection to your computer. If you have a camera that you've used in applications such as Zoom or Teams, it will also work with Faceware.

- So, boot up the Faceware Studio software. You should be greeted by an interface similar to what is shown in *Figure 9.10*:

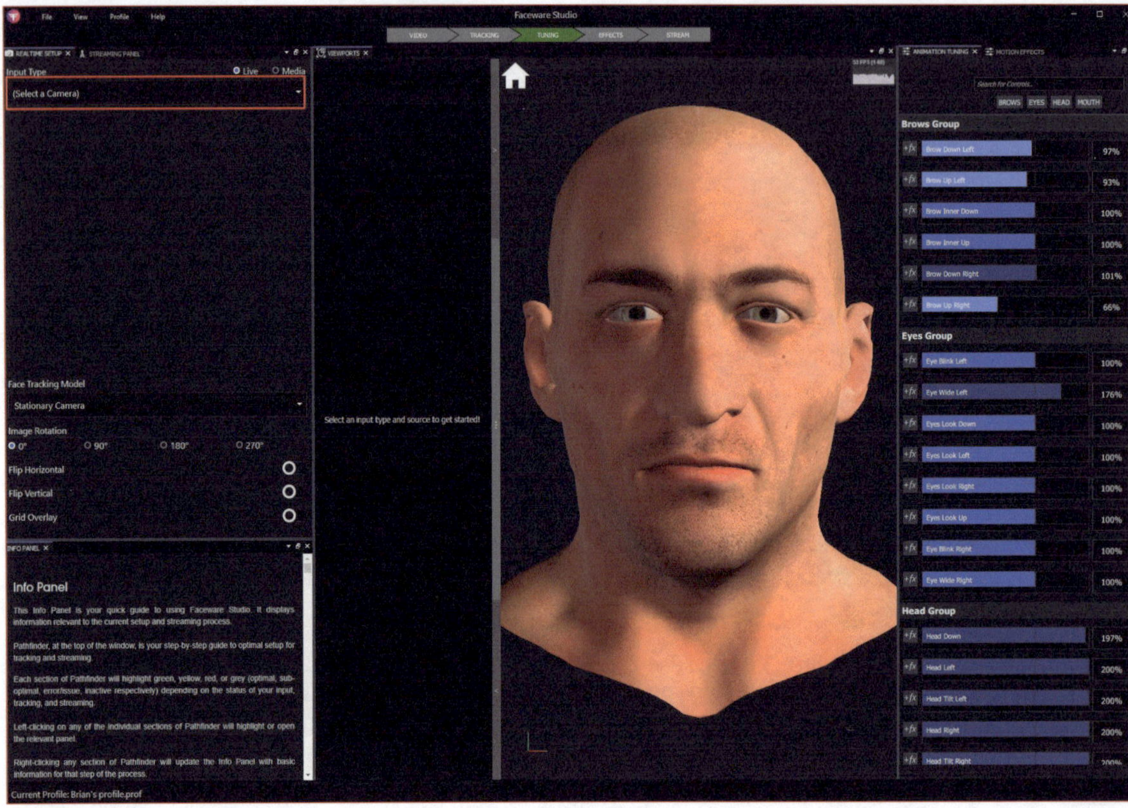

Figure 9.10: The Faceware interface

To set up our webcam and the streaming function, we will need to explore the **Realtime Setup** panel and the **Streaming** panel.

Realtime Setup panel

On the left side of the screen is the **REALTIME SETUP** panel. Under **Input Type**, click the drop-down menu and select your webcam. As soon as you select a working webcam, you will get more options, as shown in *Figure 9.11*:

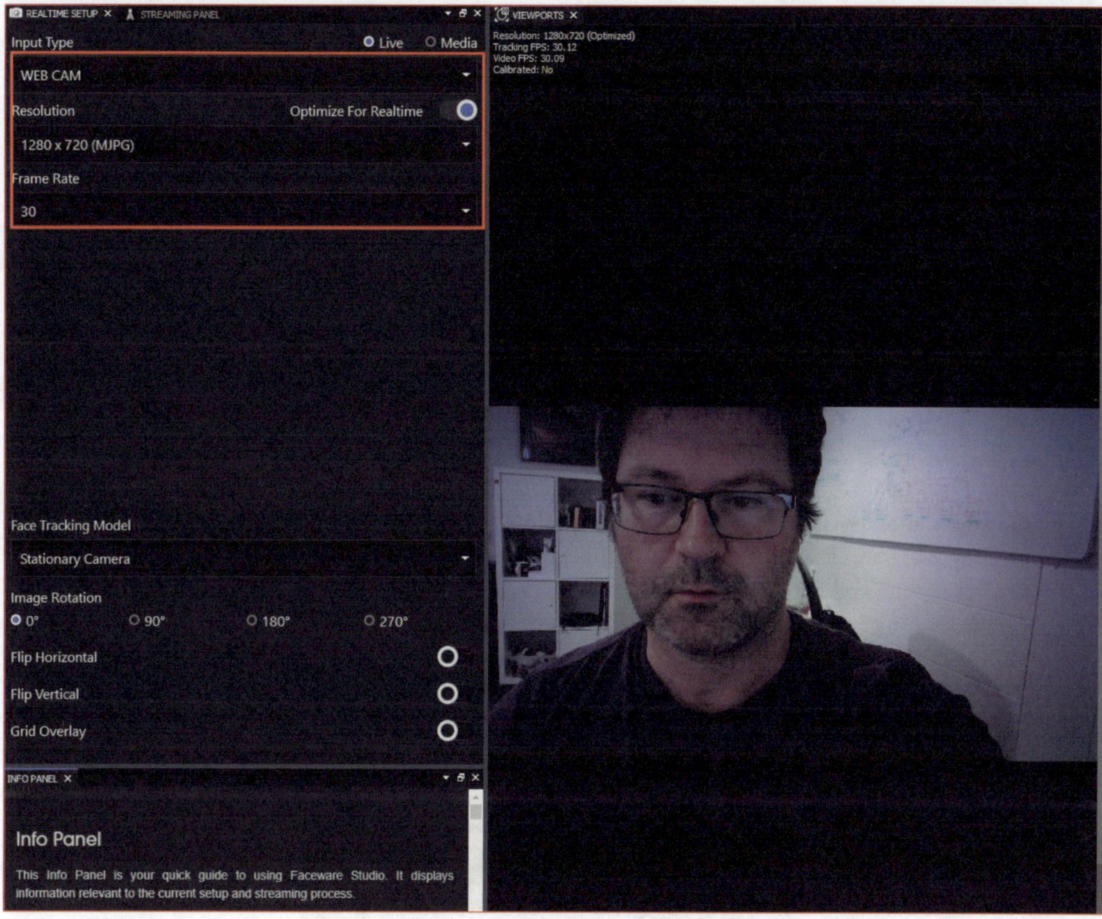

Figure 9.11: Realtime Setup panel

Let's look at the options available:

Input Type

The **Input Type** panel allows you to choose what kind of video you want to use. As our goal is to stream live facial capture data into Unreal, we will pick **Live**. Should you wish to use pre-recorded footage located on your machine, you can select **Media**, but we won't be exploring that option.

Resolution

Resolution can be as large as the video signal coming in. So, if your webcam and computer are capable of handling an ultra-high-definition webcam, Faceware won't have any issues with it. In my case, my webcam had a resolution of 3840 X 2160. However, that high resolution gives no advantage and actually works against us due to the processing required for all that high-resolution data. I've reduced the resolution to a more practical **1280 X 720**, as this resolution holds all the information required for a good track but isn't as data heavy as my original option.

You are also given the option to choose either **(MPG)**, which uses the **Motion JPEG (MJPEG)** compression/decompression codec algorithm, or **(H264)**, which uses the H264 codec algorithm. Ultimately, choose whichever one works best for your machine in terms of frame rate, which I will explain in the next section.

Frame Rate

Frame rate is an important factor for accurate motion capture. You may remember from *Chapter 5, Retargeting Animations with Mixamo*, that motion capture was available to us at frame rates of 30 frames per second and above. Our goal is always to achieve a frame rate of 30 frames per second or above, which you can see I have done in *Figure 9.11*.

To further reduce processing time, you can switch on **Optimize for Realtime**, which will reduce the resolution and in turn increase the frame rate. If you look again at *Figure 9.11*, you can see a difference in resolution occurs in the top left of the viewport that features the webcam signal. I have also provided two examples of this signal information in *Figure 9.12*:

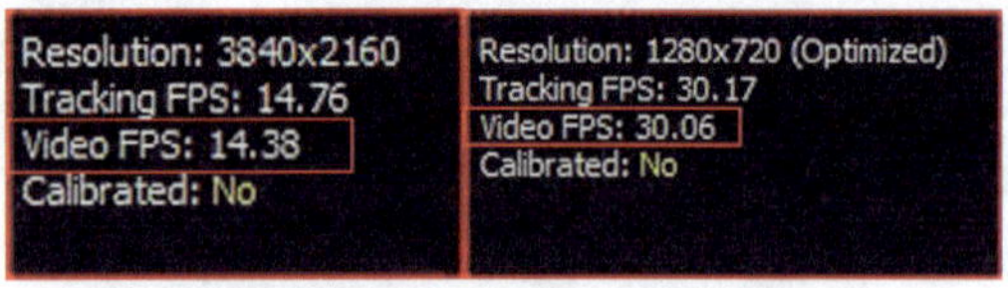

Figure 9.12: Resolution versus frame rate

You can see that the 3840x2160 resolution on the left gives us a video frame rate of just 14.38, which is bad, whereas the 1280x720 signal is giving us a video frame rate of 30.06, which is better (considering our target of 30 fps).

You may also notice that the **Tracking FPS** is generally the same as the **Video FPS**. If the **Tracking FPS** is lower, it means there's something wrong with the software; possibly other applications are running, causing Faceware to be under-resourced. Try closing down any other applications that are running to help out with this.

> **Note**
>
> The difference between Tracking FPS and Video FPS is quite simple. Tracking FPS is how fast the software can correctly identify areas of the face and where they are in the picture, whereas Video FPS is simply how many frames the software is receiving from the webcam per second.

Face Tracking Model

Referring back to *Figure 9.11*, below **Frame Rate**, the next field is **Face Tracking Model**. The drop-down menu provides two options:

- **Stationary Camera**: Suitable for webcams where the camera is stationary, but the user's head is moving.
- **Professional Headcams**: Suitable for professional solutions where the camera is fixed to a head rig and only captures facial expressions rather than head movements. Headcams aren't capable of tracking neck movement, so if the user nods or shakes their head, the data isn't recorded. In this scenario, a motion capture suit is relied upon to capture body motion, including head and neck movement. Typically, both body and facial captures are done simultaneously when professional headcams are being used as it produces a more natural result.

In our case, we are picking **Stationary Camera**.

Image Rotation

In cases where your camera is upside down or turned to the side, you can rotate the video signal in increments of 90 degrees to fix it. I don't need this, so the **Image Rotation** option is set to **0** degrees.

Flip Horizontal and Flip Vertical

Again, if you are dealing with an upside-down camera or if you have a personal preference for a mirror image, you can choose to flip the image horizontally or vertically. I won't be using these either.

Grid Overlay

This is a somewhat helpful tool to ensure your face is in the middle of the frame. I haven't enabled this.

Now, before we go over to the **Streaming** panel, make sure that you have a video signal coming into Faceware, that your input is set to **Live**, and that your face is being tracked, with tracking markers moving in tandem with your face. You can see from my example in *Figure 9.13* that I have orange tracking markers around my eyebrows, eyes, nose, and mouth:

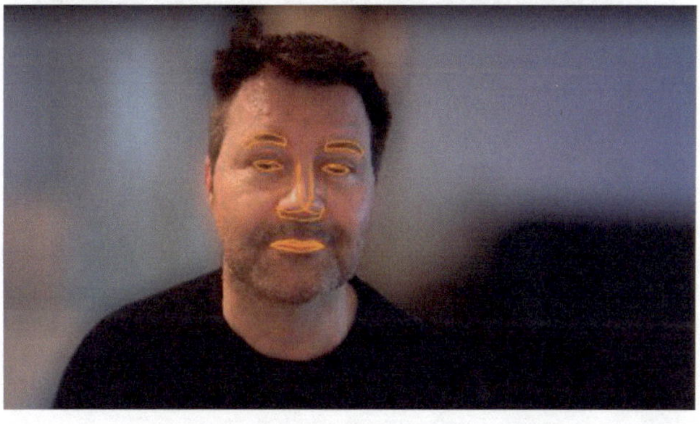

Figure 9.13: Tracking markers working

Once your face is being tracked, then you need to ensure that Faceware is able to send data out in the **STREAMING** panel.

Streaming panel

Switch over to the **STREAMING** panel, and you will see the following options shown in *Figure 9.14*:

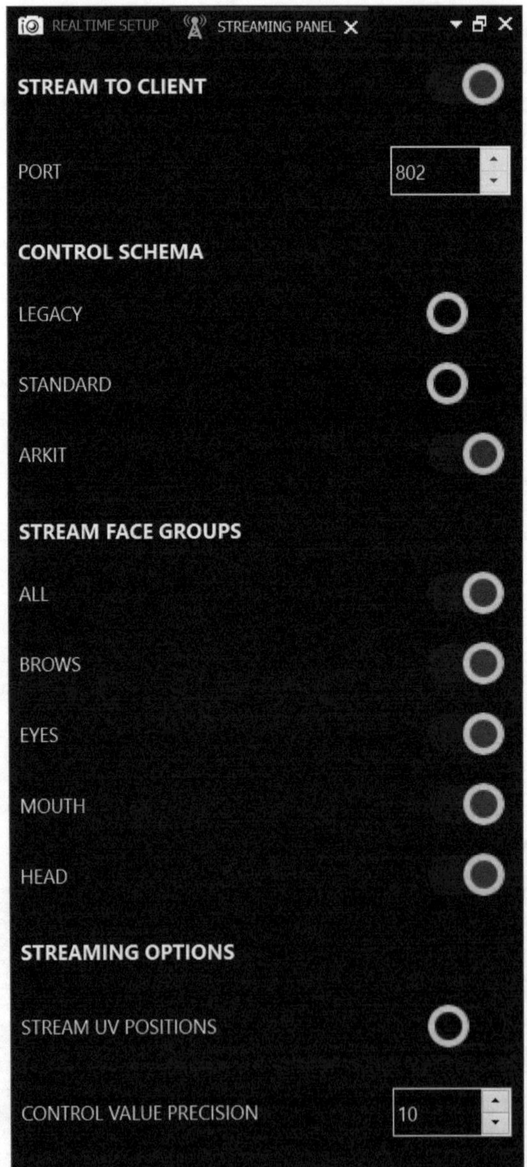

Figure 9.14: The Streaming panel

Let's take a look at each section of the panel.

Stream to Client

The first option in **STREAM TO CLIENT** is the **STREAM TO CLIENT** toggle button itself, which I have toggled to the right to turn it on. Effectively, the button is just an on-and-off switch. When it's on, Faceware will stream live motion capture data to the client. The client in this instance is the Unreal Engine, which is enabled to receive the streaming data via Live Link.

Note that if you don't have a live video signal, you won't be able to enable **STREAM TO CLIENT**.

The second option is **PORT** – these ports are set up automatically when the Live Link plugin is installed. During the installation of Faceware, Faceware detects which ports are available for streaming to; however, do make note of the port number just in case. You should leave **PORT** as the default value; in my case, that is **802**.

Now you are ready to start the face tracking. Get your face into a neutral pose, so no smiling or pouting, and click on the **CALIBRATE NEUTRAL POSE** button as per the bottom left of *Figure 9.15*:

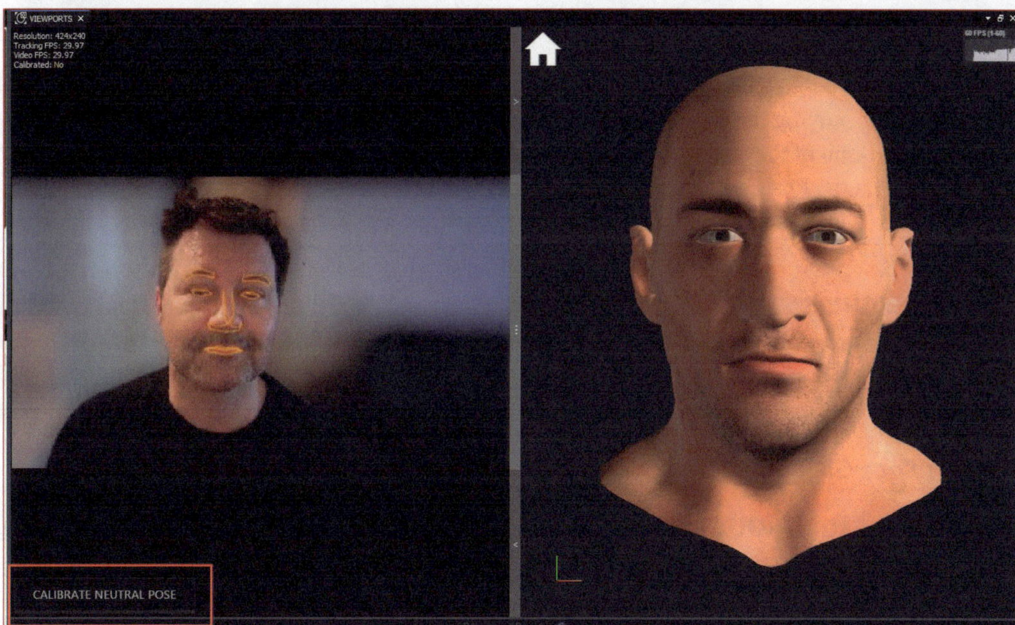

Figure 9.15: Calibrating neutral pose

Be sure to look directly into the webcam when you do this and expect to hold that pose for about 5-10 seconds while Faceware recalibrates to your face. When it is done, it will automatically track your face. Take a look at *Figure 9.16*, where you can see that the CGI character is following the movement of my own head and facial expressions.

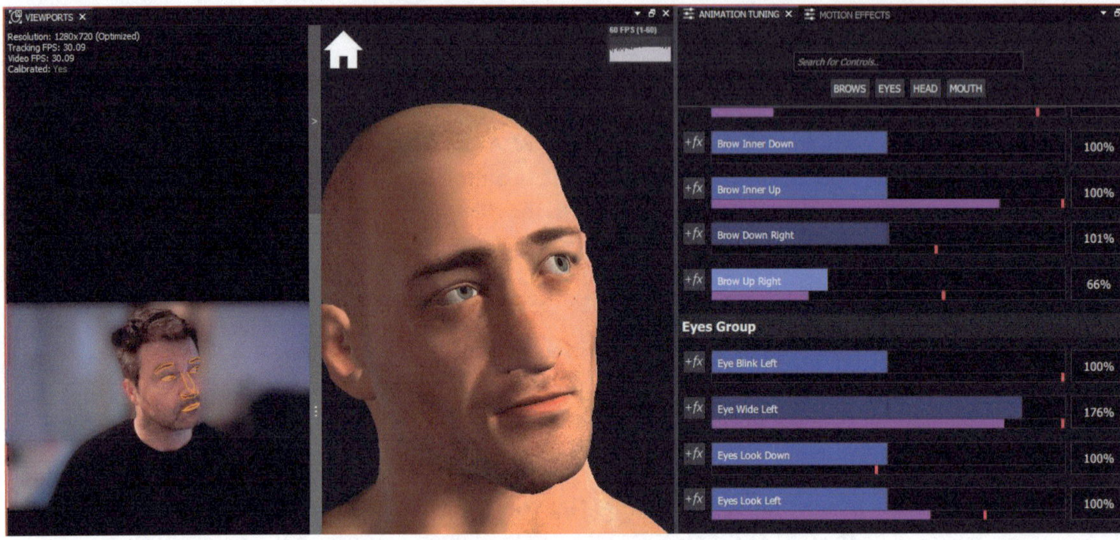

Figure 9.16: ANIMATION TUNING panel

You'll also notice the **ANIMATION TUNING** panel on the right of the screen; you'll see a lot of horizontal bars moving in response to your head moving. These are all the ARKit controls being animated as a result of the face tracking. We will go into this in further detail later. For now, let's take a further look at the Realtime Setup features.

Control Schema

CONTROL SCHEMA refers to the naming conventions used for the streaming data from Faceware studio. Because we are utilizing ARKit, make sure you enable **ARKIT**. **LEGACY** and **STANDARD** are good, but they don't have the fidelity of ARKit, which is used in the design of MetaHumans, and for this book, they are redundant.

Stream Face Groups

The **STREAM FACE GROUPS** feature allows us to remove certain parts of the face from streaming. If we were using a professional head cam that doesn't record head rotation, I would suggest disabling the head from **STREAM FACE GROUPS**. In that scenario, we would be capturing the head rotation using a body motion capture solution.

In our example, let's assume that we want to record the head rotation and all the facial movement. To do this, under **STREAM FACE GROUPS**, ensure to enable **ALL**. However, if you just wanted to capture one face group, for example, you just want to move eyebrows, you could just enable the **EYEBROWS** option.

At this point, we should be streaming, but let's just look at one final part of the Faceware interface: the status bar.

Status bar

In *Figure 9.17*, you can see that the top toolbar is a color-coded tab list providing a way to troubleshoot and rectify issues quickly as they arise:

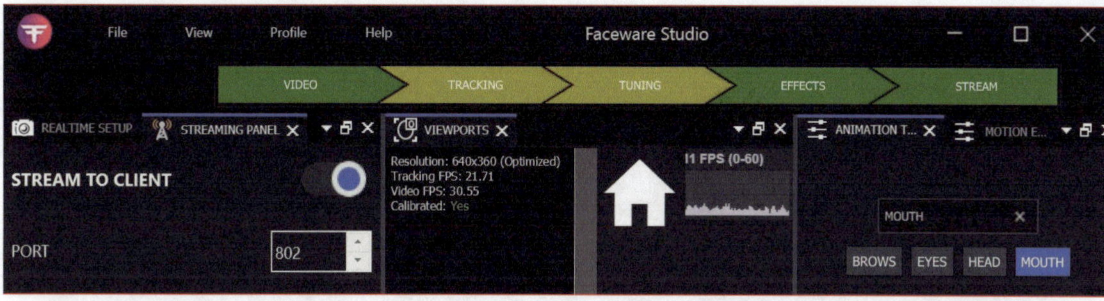

Figure 9.17: Top toolbar

They are in the order of left to right:

- **VIDEO**: This is a shortcut to the **REALTIME SETUP** panel, which we have just covered.
- **TRACKING**: This is a shortcut to the viewports, as seen in *Figure 9.17*, so that we can visualize how well the tracking is going. You can see in *Figure 9.18* that not only is my head movement being tracked, but the tracker is even able to detect a wink through my glasses.

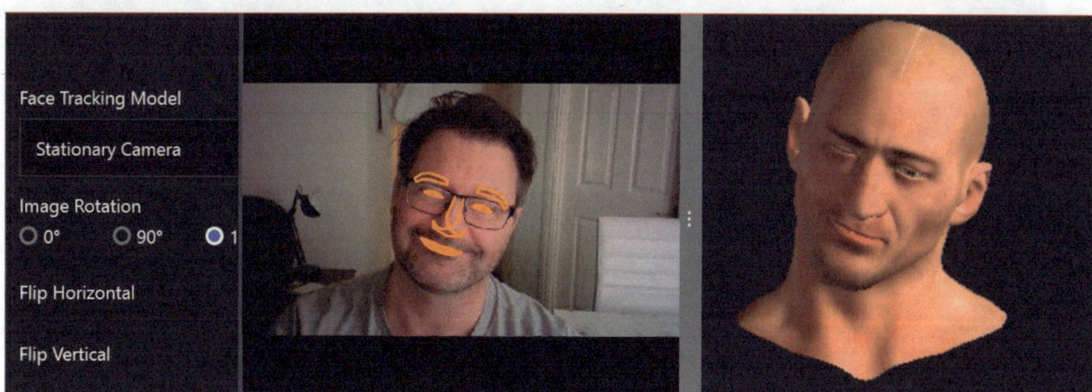

Figure 9.18: Viewports

- **TUNING**: This is a shortcut to the **TUNING** panel, where we will do most of the tweaking and fixing of issues. You can see that we have a lot of control over refining the brows, eyes, head, and mouth. As daunting as this may look, these controllers are relatively simple to use.

  For example, if you look at the CGI head and its jaw doesn't open as wide as your jaw in the webcam, you can increase the **Jaw Open** parameter to as much as 200% by dragging the blue slider to the right. I made similar adjustments in *Figure 9.19* by dragging some of the mouth sliders to the right as much as 200%.

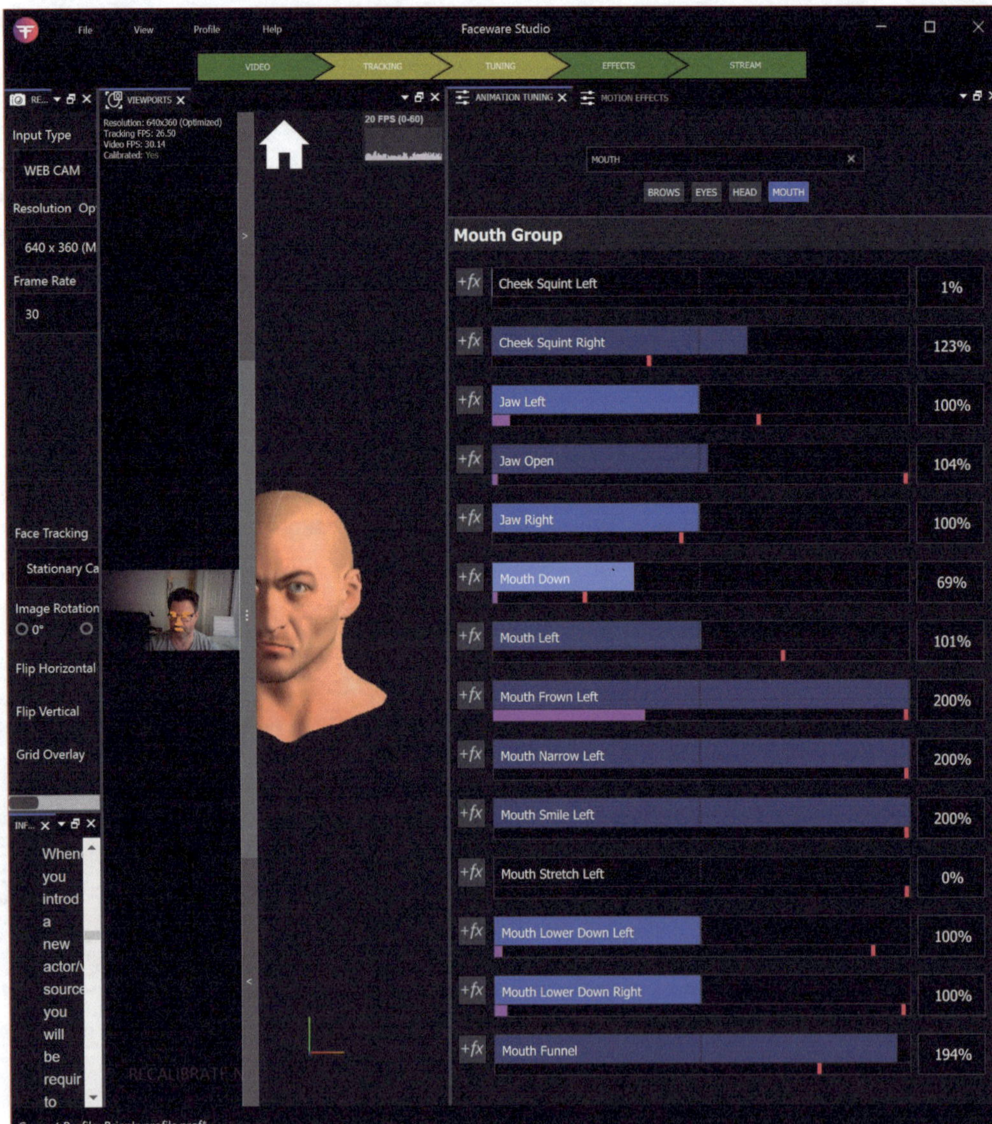

Figure 9.19: Tuning

If the jaw opens too much in the CGI character compared to your webcam video, then drag the slider to the left to decrease the amount. The same can be said for all of the parameters in the **TUNING** panel.

- **EFFECTS**: While not a common panel to use, **EFFECTS** does come in useful if you've found that you're just not getting the desired result using **TUNING** alone. An example would be where the **Mouth Smile Left** is appearing just a little too high on the CGI face. To fix this, we can manually add an **Offset** with a negative value to counteract that, illustrated in *Figure 9.20*:

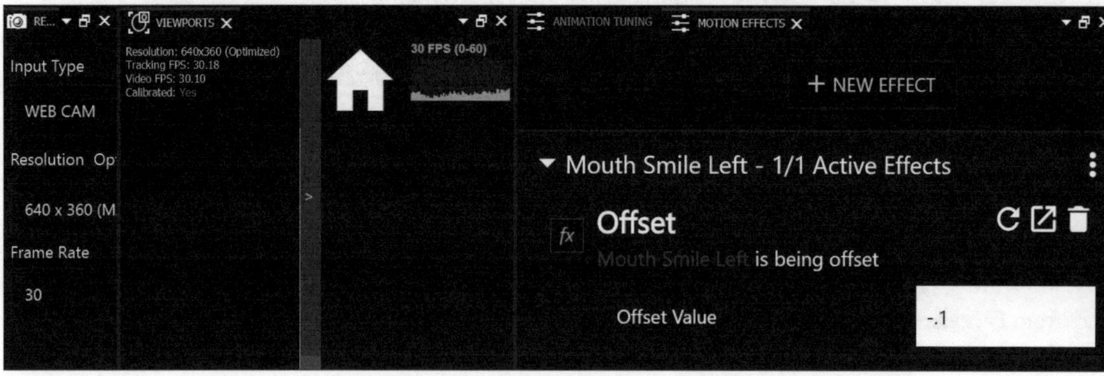

Figure 9.20: Effects

- **STREAM**: This is a shortcut to the **STREAMING** panel, which we also covered earlier.

Ideally, all of these buttons are green in the top menu. If they go between yellow and green, the settings are effective but not optimal. If they go into the red, then you'll certainly need to make changes.

The most common circumstance that results in a red button is when we move our face out of the webcam's range. The face tracking is generally very good but once we go out of frame, it can't track and will immediately give us a red tracking button. The second most common red button instance is low frame rates, which in turn will result in a poor track.

Before we go into any more detail on any of these additional panels, especially **TUNING**, we must first go back to Unreal to make sure we are getting live facial capture data, and we will also need to jump into our MetaHumans Blueprint. The reason for this is that it is better to view how our MetaHuman is responding to the facial tracking and make our adjustments with that information rather than looking at the default head inside Faceware.

Enabling Live Link to receive Faceware data

Before we jump into the MetaHuman Blueprint, let's just double-check to see that Live Link is receiving a signal.

To open up the Live Link plugin inside Unreal, go to **Window**, then **Virtual Production**, and choose **Live Link**, as per *Figure 9.21*:

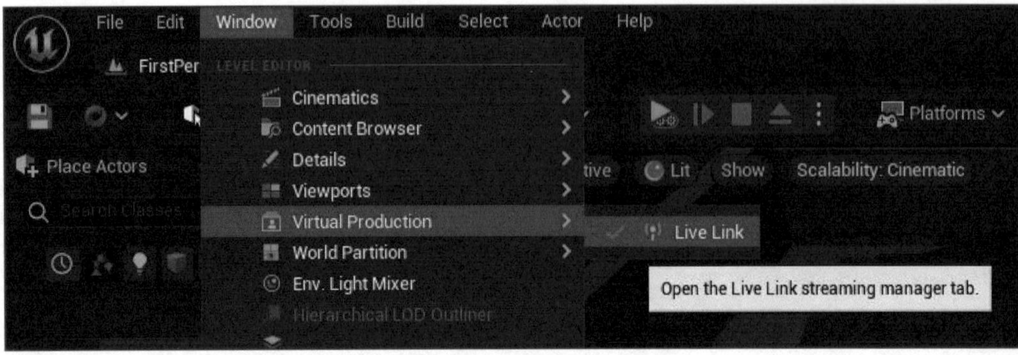

Figure 9.21: Opening Live Link

In *Figure 9.22*, you can see that I've clicked on **Faceware Live Link** to select the incoming signal from Faceware. Make a note of the **Port Number**: it is the same port number I was able to detect in the Faceware **STREAMING** panel, as per *Figure 9.14*. If the Live Link port number is different to the Faceware port number, you can change it in either application to match.

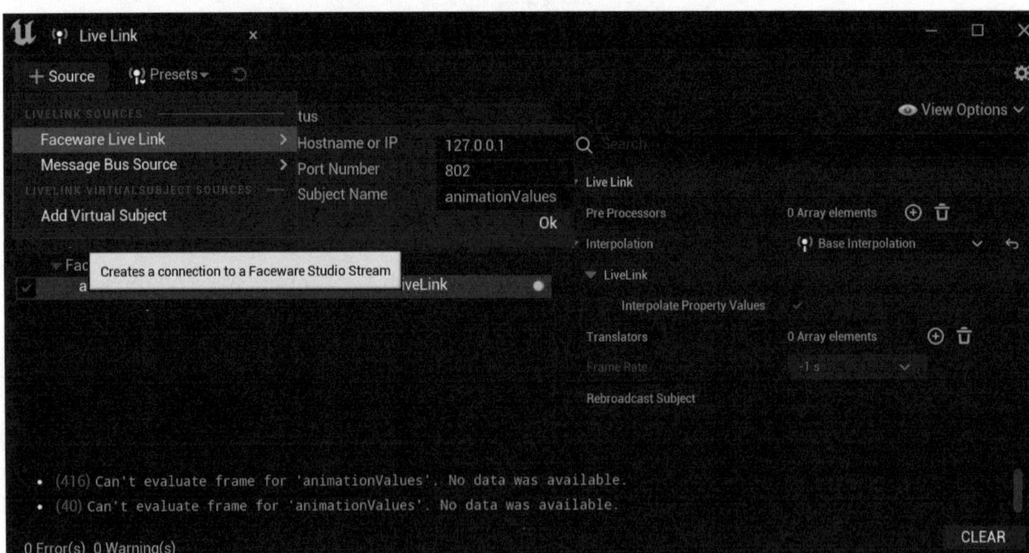

Figure 9.22: Live Link Port Number

Now, with the **STREAM TO CLIENT** enabled in Faceware, we should have a good face track working. A good face track means we get no red warnings. It also means that we are receiving a live signal in Live Link, giving us a green button, as shown in *Figure 9.22*. Once we get that green button, we are good to start working with the MetaHuman Blueprint.

Editing the MetaHuman Blueprint

To start, we need to create a new Level Sequence because we're going to add our MetaHuman Blueprint to the Level Sequencer:

1. Just like in the last chapter, drag and drop the MetaHuman Blueprint from the Outliner and onto the Level Sequencer. Again, you'll notice that a **Metahuman_ControlRig** and a **Face_ControlBoard_CtrlRig** have been created. Delete both of these as we don't need them.
2. Next, click on **Face** from the Blueprint in the Level Sequencer. In *Figure 9.23*, you'll see how the **Details** panel has given me parameters for me to edit, namely the **Animation Mode** and **Anim Class**.

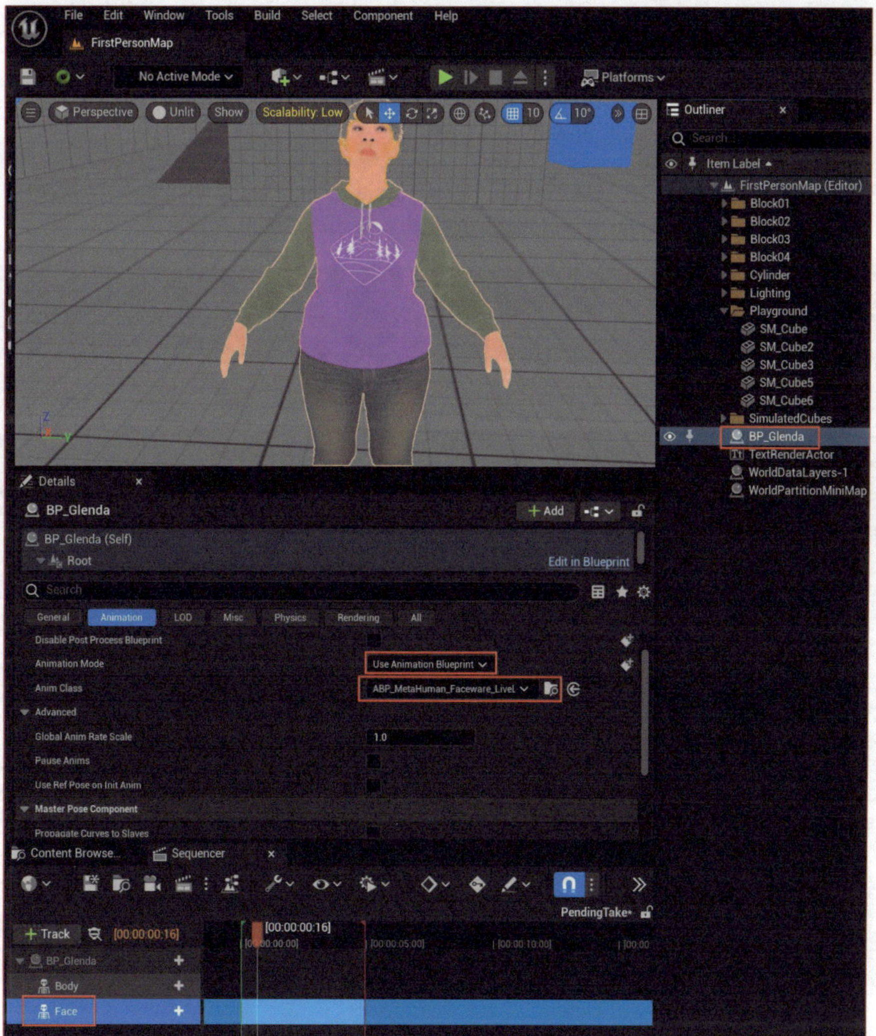

Figure 9.23: Selecting Face from the MetaHuman Blueprint

Ensure **Animation Mode** is set to **Use Animation Blueprint** and that **Anim Class** is set to **ABP_Metahuman_Faceware_LiveLink Face**.

3. Now test your facial motion capture data by hitting the **Play** button at the top of the Unreal Engine interface. This will run a game simulation where you can see the facial animation come to life.

Make sure to hit **Stop** to stop the simulation. You need to do this before you can start the **Take Recorder**, which we use in the next section.

Recording a session with a Take Recorder

In the previous section, I mentioned running a simulation to test the facial motion capture data. That's fine for just doing quick tests, but for animation production, we need to record the motion capture data, and to do that, Epic Games have created the Take Recorder. This will allows us to record mocap sessions and play them back from the Level Sequencer.

To use a Take Recorder instead, follow these steps:

1. Go to **Take Recorder** tab and add the MetaHuman Blueprint. You can see in *Figure 9.24* that I've done this by clicking the **+ Source** option, and then **From Actor**.

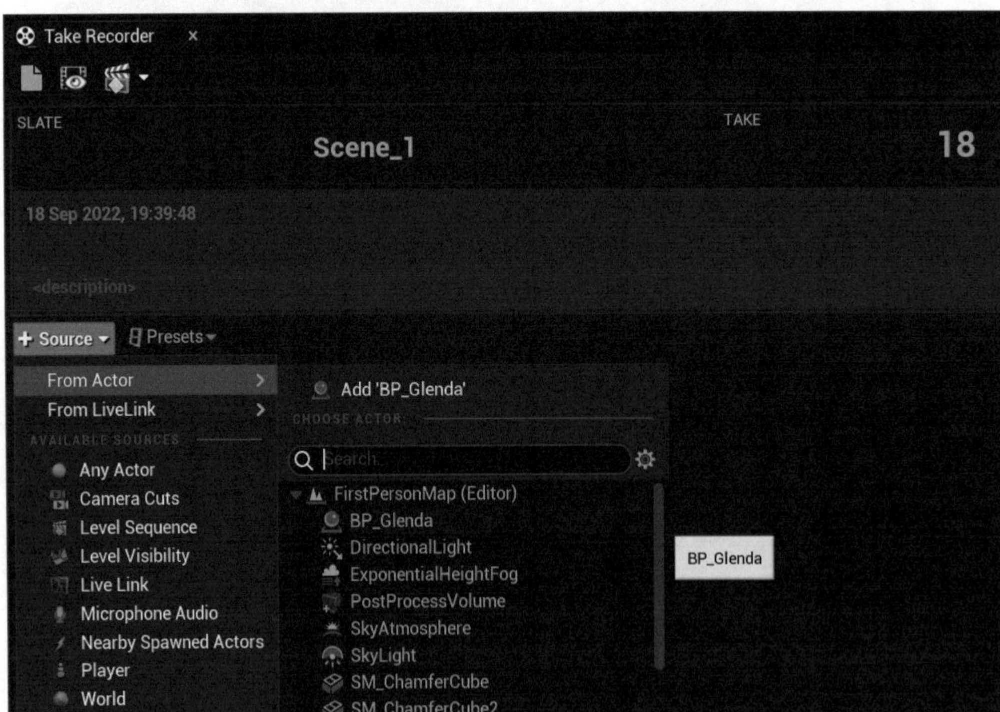

Figure 9.24: Adding the MetaHuman Blueprint to the Take Recorder

2. Still in the **Take Recorder** tab, add another asset by using the **From LiveLink** option, as per *Figure 9.25*. Here, we are going to add **animationValues**. The values referred to here are all the ARKit data values as they are being streamed from Faceware, such as rotation of the head, blinking of eyes, and opening of mouth.

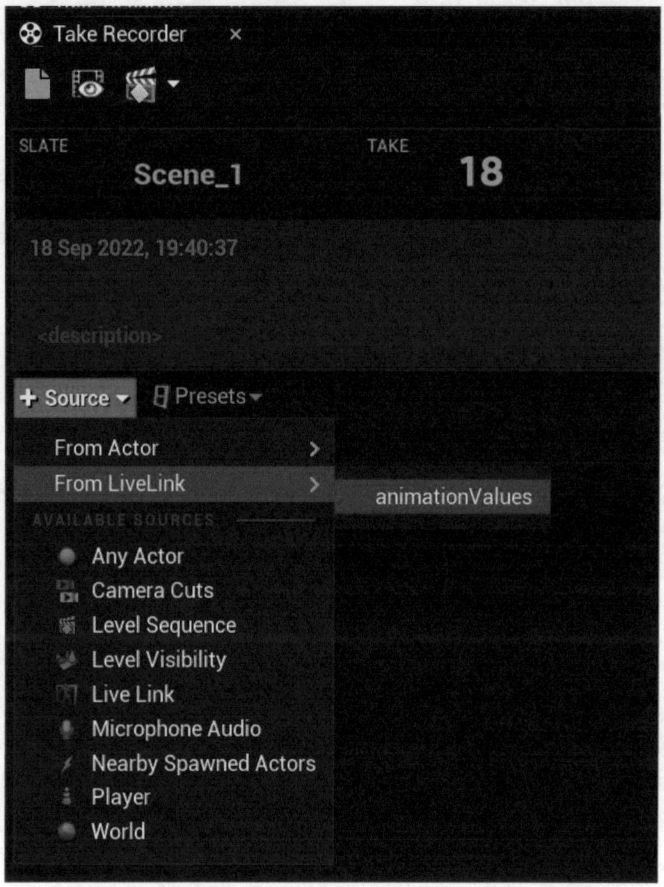

Figure 9.25: Adding animationValues to the Take Recorder

3. Note the **Take** number. In my case, it's **Scene_1 Take 18**. Whenever we want to play back a take, it is convenient to know in advance which take was the good take.
4. Hit the **Record** button on the **Take Recorder** (yes, it's the big red button!).
5. Run the simulation again by pressing **Play**. Your animation is coming to life again as you stream from Faceware into Unreal.
6. Hit **Stop** on the **Take Recorder** and note the new **Take** number.

7. In order to play back the take we just captured, we first need to change the Animation Mode. Select **Face** to edit the **Animation Mode**. Then change the mode from **Animation Blueprint** to **Use animation Asset**, as per *Figure 9.26*:

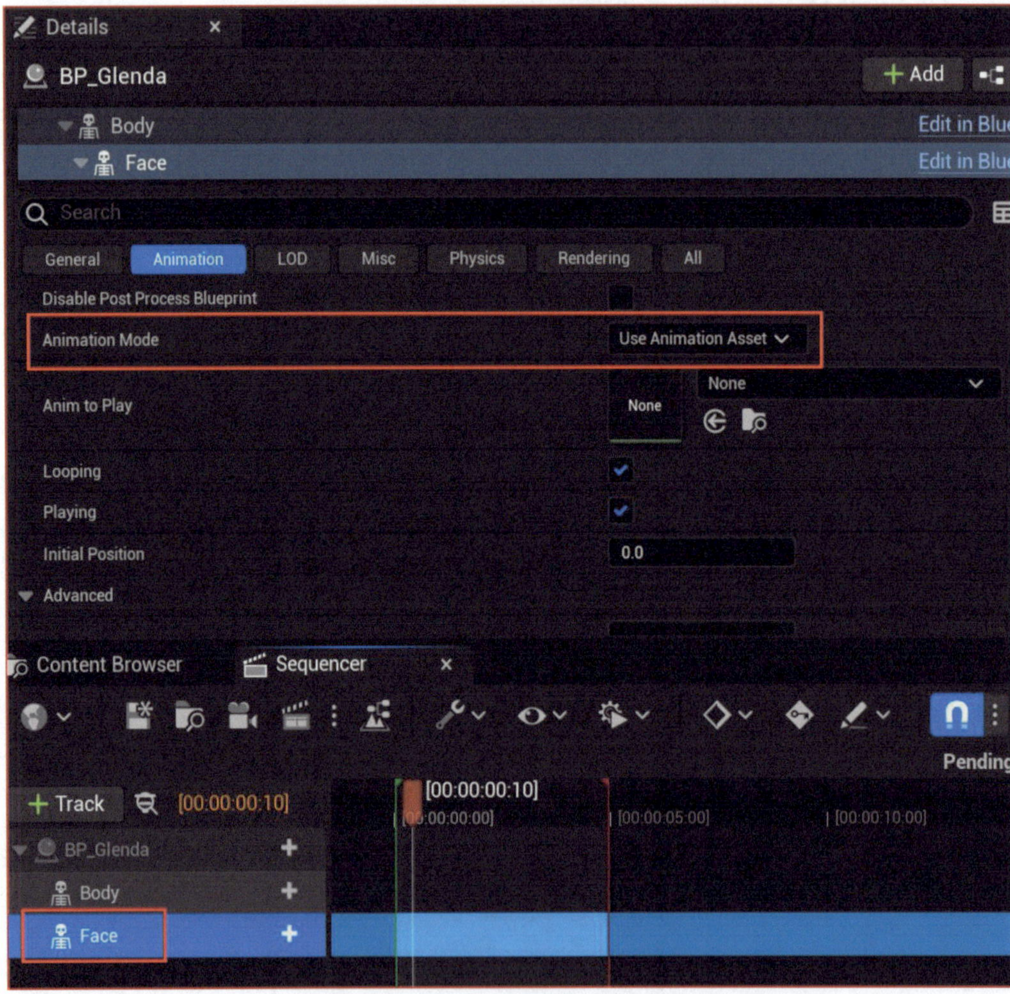

Figure 9.26: Changing the Animation Mode to Use Animation Asset

We change the animation mode to **Use an Asset** when we want to play back a take and revert to **Blueprint** when we want to record a take.

In the next section, we will go back to the Level Sequencer in order to play back our facial motion capture recording.

Importing a take into the Level Sequencer

To play back our facial capture take, we need to add it to the Level Sequencer. To do this, follow these steps:

1. Click on the + icon next to **Face** to add the animation. In the context menu, go to **Animation** and run a search for your most recent take. In my case, I am looking for take 19, as shown in *Figure 9.27*:

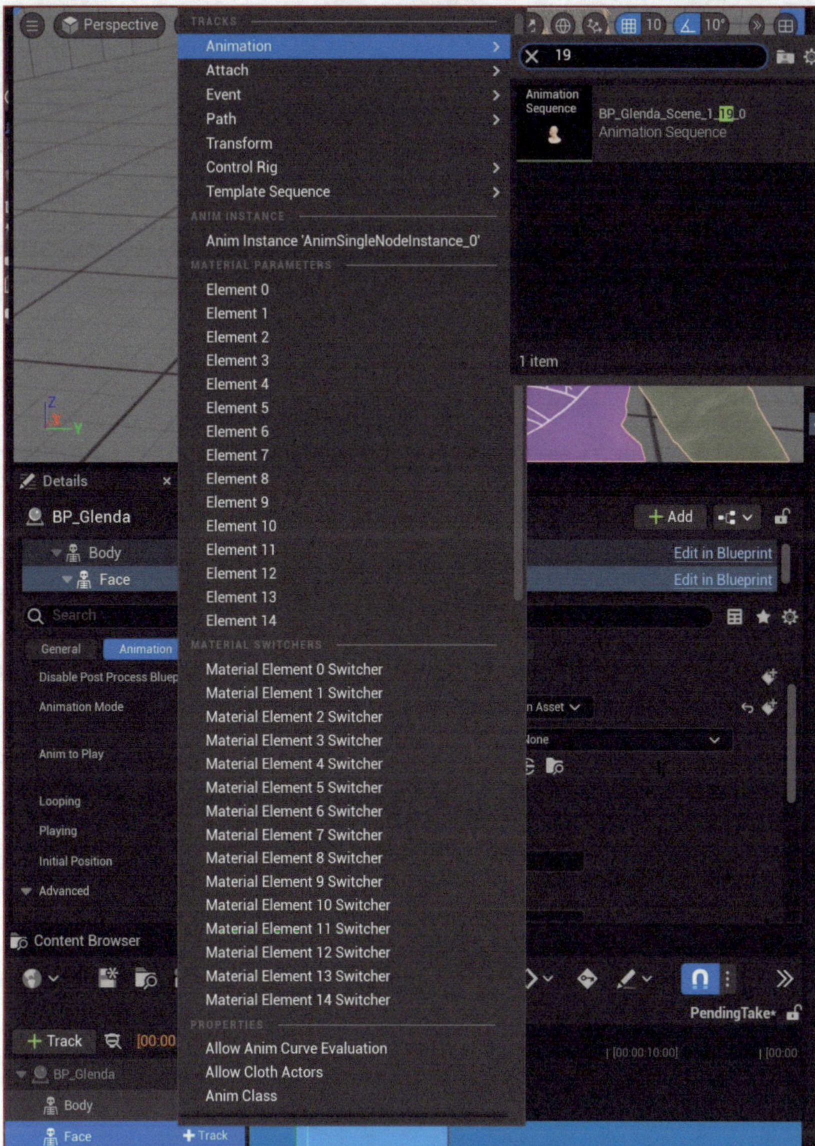

Figure 9.27: Adding the Animation Asset to the Face as a track

2. Click on the desired track and it will automatically populate the **Face** track inside the Level Sequencer, as per *Figure 9.28*:

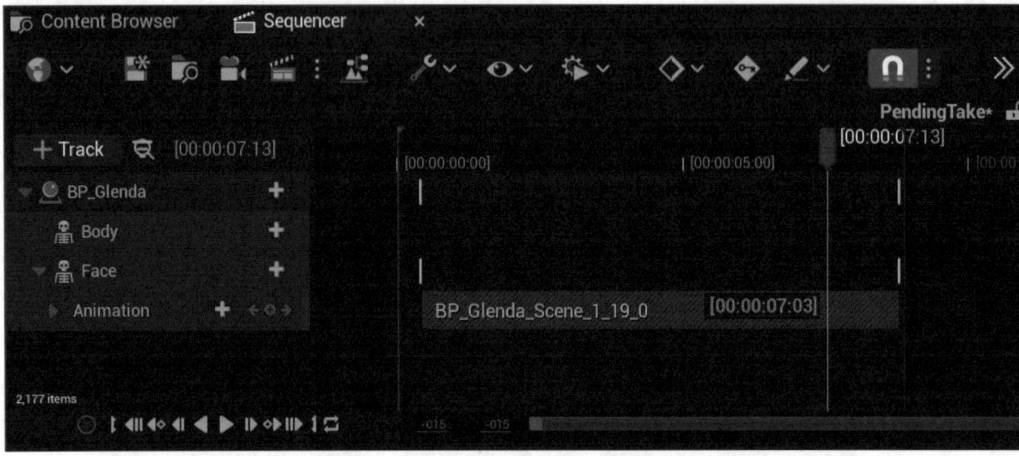

Figure 9.28: Adding the Take Recorder track to the Level Sequencer

3. To play back the animation, click anywhere in the timeline where the playhead is and hit the *spacebar*.

Now we have added the Motion Capture data directly into the Level Sequencer. However, that is raw data and, in all likelihood, it will need a little editing. In the next section, we will look at some of the MetaHuman controls that we can take advantage of to further push the creative control of our characters.

Baking and editing facial animation in Unreal

Building on the previous chapter, where we added facial motion capture using the iPhone, we will apply the process of baking animation keyframes to the Faceware Studio Capture.

Similar to how we baked motion capture data onto a body control rig, we are going to do the same with the face rig and then create an additive section to make animation adjustments:

1. With **Face** selected, right-click and choose **Bake to Control Rig**, followed by **Face_ControlBoard_CtrlRig**, as per *Figure 9.29*:

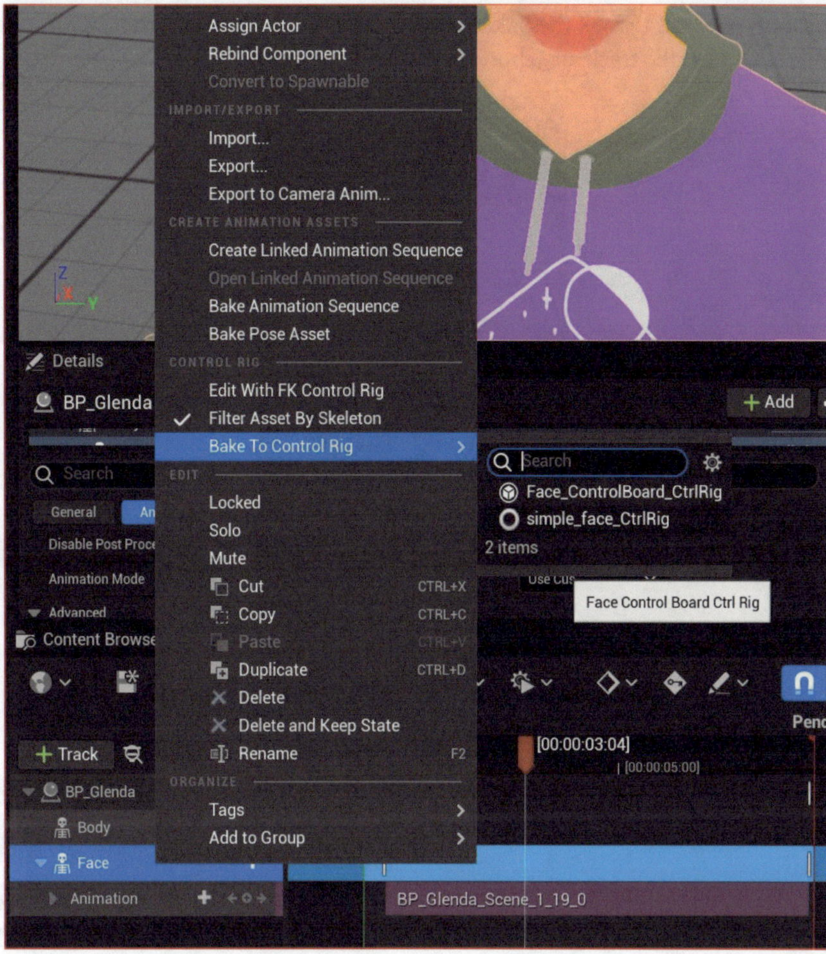

Figure 9.29: Baking the facial capture Animation Asset to the control rig

Once we've baked to the control rig, we should see the track looks similar to *Figure 9.30*:

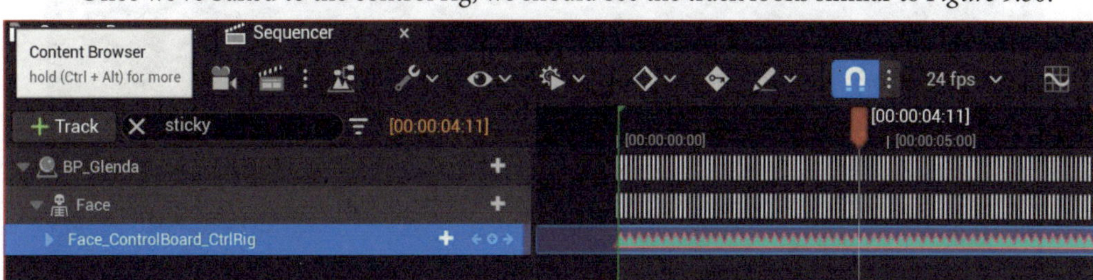

Figure 9.30: The mocap data baked into the control rig

2. For safety, we want to lock the baked track so that we don't inadvertently edit it. Do this by right-clicking on the track and choosing **Locked**, as per *Figure 9.31*:

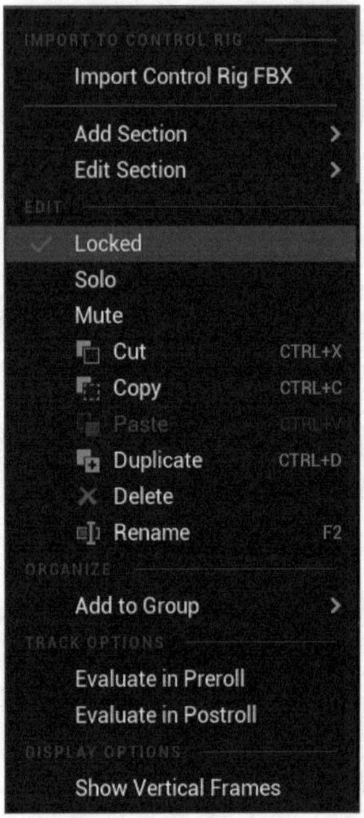

Figure 9.31: Locking the baked track

3. With the control rig track locked, we can create an additive track for adding additional animation. It is effectively a duplicate track without any keyframes. To do this, click on **+ Section** next to **Face_CcontrolBoard_CtrlRig** and choose **Additive**, as per *Figure 9.32*.

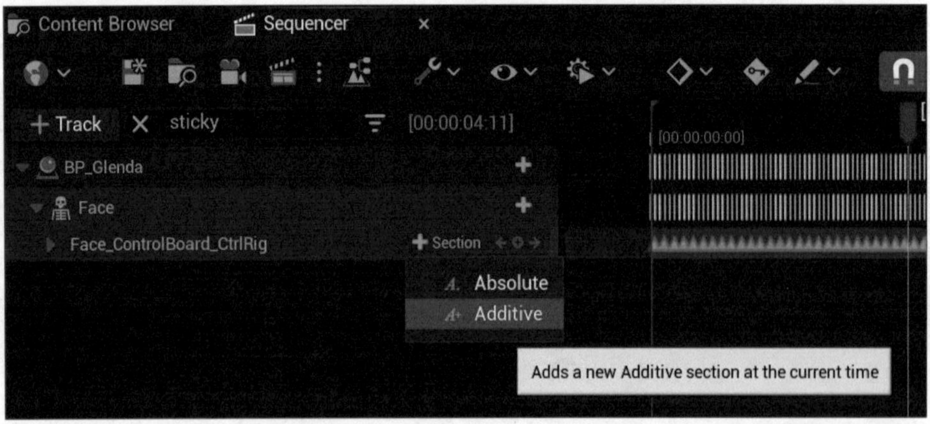

Figure 9.32: Creating an additive section

4. Once you've created the additive track, the next step is to add keyframes to it. However, before doing that, you might want to double-check to see that the original motion capture track is locked. It will have a red border around it, as shown in *Figure 9.33*, if it is locked.

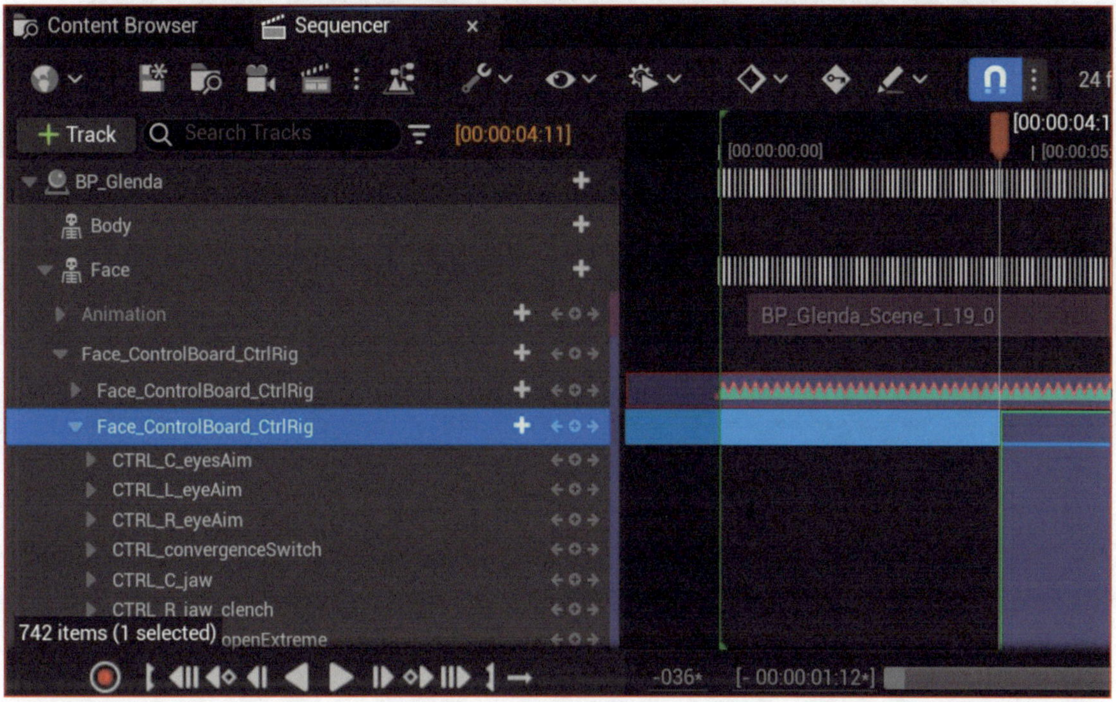

Figure 9.33: Locked track and new track

Also, take notice of the fact that there are no keyframes next to all of the controllers in the new additive track. This is exactly what we want.

Now let's look at editing the face. During the **Take Recorder** session, and after I played back the mocap in the Level Sequencer, I noticed that on occasion, the right eye would blink out of time with or randomly on its own. This isn't a physical effect of me writing this book but more than likely due to my wearing glasses during the recording.

To fine-tune this issue, you can run a search in the Sequencer for something simple, such as `eye blink`. This will come up with a list of the parameters related to this movement:

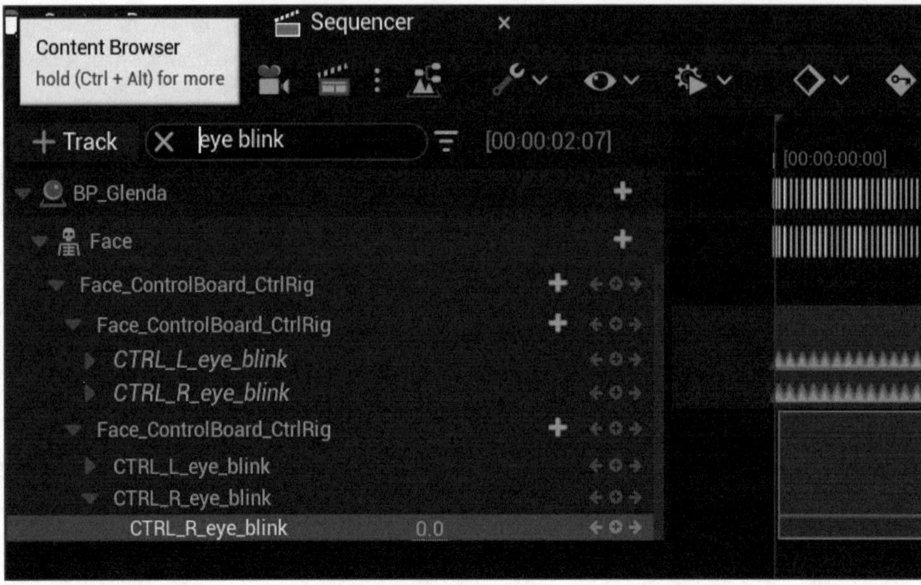

Figure 9.34: Picking a controller to edit

Using the Unreal MetaHuman controllers, I was able to set just a few keyframes to fix the eye issue. You can see from *Figure 9.35* that I laid down the first keyframe at a point where the mocap was correct, the third keyframe where the mocap was correct again, and the second keyframe between them to correct the problem frames.

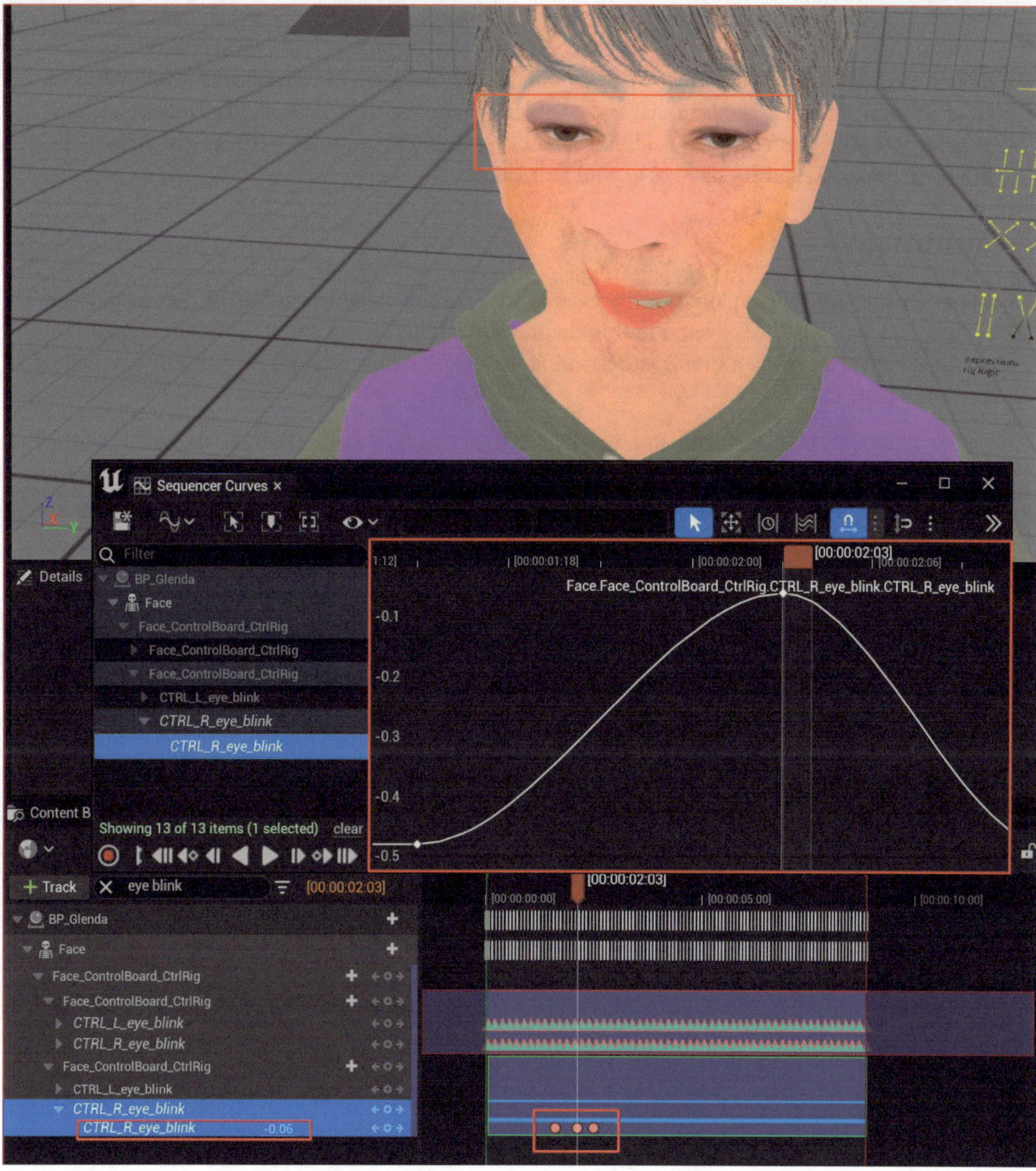

Figure 9.35: Making slight adjustments to Animation Controllers

If we only created the second keyframe, it would impact all the animation on the relevant track. We create the first and third keyframes to protect the animation outside the animation range of the first and third keyframes.

We are only touching the surface of editing motion capture data with the Level Sequencer. From the example I have given, I just used an additive section to fix a problem. It is a great function to know how to use, particularly when it comes to motion capture sessions. The reason is that you will know when a mocap session is good enough and whether it is cost effective to tweak the animation later or keep on going for a better take. In addition to just tweaking, you can use the techniques described in this section to make radical changes to your animation.

Summary

In this chapter, we have explored the Faceware Facial motion capture solution for MetaHumans in Unreal. Much of what we covered in this chapter was similar to the iPhone solution but with the bonus of being able to use a simple webcam, and we looked at how we can fine-tune our data before Unreal receives it.

On top of this, we had some time to revise what we have learned about the **Take Recorder**, and we learned how to bake our facial motion capture data into a control rig in a similar way to how we baked our body motion capture from DeepMotion. Finally, we uncovered some of the power of using the additive feature in conjunction with the MetaHumans' many facial animation controllers to fix issues.

In the next chapter, we will build on this knowledge as we look at how to merge multiple takes inside the Level Sequencer and explore further ways to render videos.

10

Blending Animations and Advanced Rendering with the Level Sequencer

In the previous chapters, you've been equipped with a choice of facial motion capture methods, be it using an iPhone or a webcam with Faceware. You've also learned how to acquire custom body motion capture with DeepMotion. One common thread in all of this is the Level Sequencer.

In this chapter, we will come back to the Level Sequencer to manage our mocap animation data. You will learn how to manage both body motion capture and facial motion capture, fix timing issues, and merge takes.

In addition, we will look at some of the more advanced industry-standard rendering techniques and explore additional items that we can use with the Level Sequencer.

So, in this chapter, we will cover the following topics:

- Adding the MetaHuman Blueprint and body mocap data to the Level Sequencer
- Adding facial mocap data to the Level Sequencer
- Exploring advanced rendering features

Technical requirements

In terms of computer power, you will need the technical requirements detailed in *Chapter 1* and the MetaHuman plus the Unreal Engine Mannequin that we imported into UE5 in *Chapter 2*.

If you have followed along with all of the chapters, you will also have Mixamo and DeepMotion data from *Chapter 5* and *Chapter 6*, respectively. We will be using that data here.

Adding the MetaHuman Blueprint and body mocap data to the Level Sequencer

In this section, you will once again add your MetaHuman to the Level Sequencer so that you can apply both body capture data and facial capture data to it.

Adding the MetaHuman Blueprint

To start, first, create a new Level Sequencer by right-clicking anywhere within your content browser, finding **Animation** in the menu, and clicking **Level Sequencer**.

Once your new Level Sequencer has been created, click on **+Track** and add your MetaHuman Blueprint as per *Figure 10.1* (if you don't see it, use the search function and type in **BP** for Blueprint):

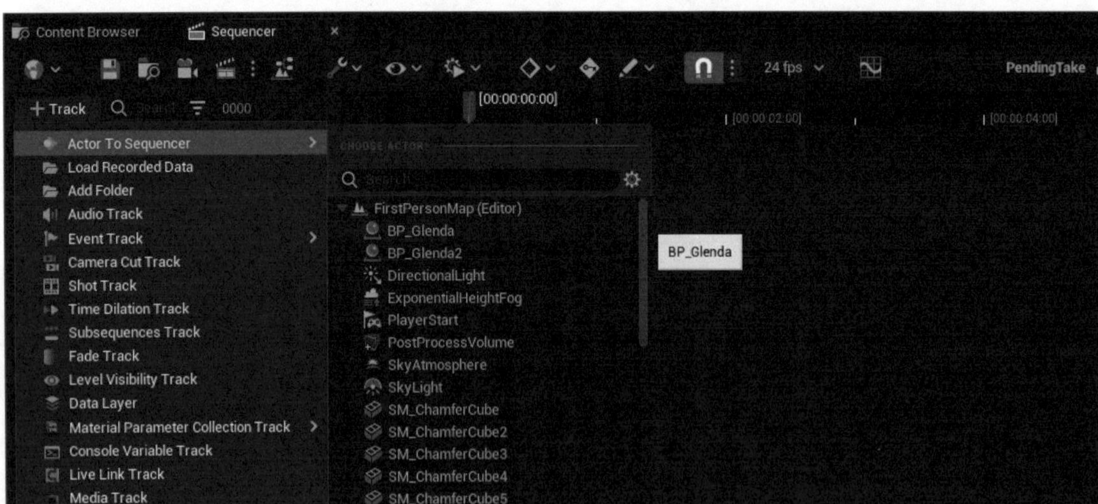

Figure 10.1: Adding the Blueprint to the Level Sequencer

As soon as you have your MetaHuman Blueprint in your Sequence, you'll notice that both the Body and Face control rigs are present, which is standard when you add a MetaHuman Blueprint to a Level Sequencer:

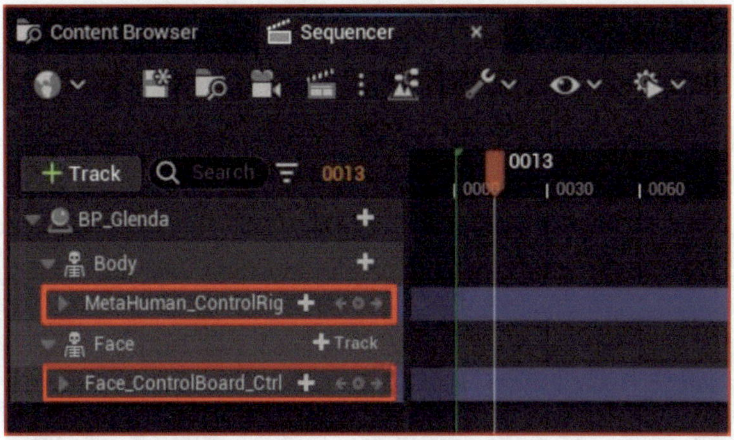

Figure 10.2: The Body and Face control rigs

For the moment, we don't need the control rigs because we're just learning how to manage our animation data, which we will add in the very next section. So, delete both rigs highlighted in the Level Sequencer in *Figure 10.2*.

With the Level Sequencer still open, we are now ready to add our body mocap data.

Adding previously retargeted body mocap data

If you have followed along with all of the chapters, you will have created body motion capture files with Mixamo and DeepMotion

To add body animation, just click on **+Track**, then go to **Animation**, as shown in *Figure 10.3*:

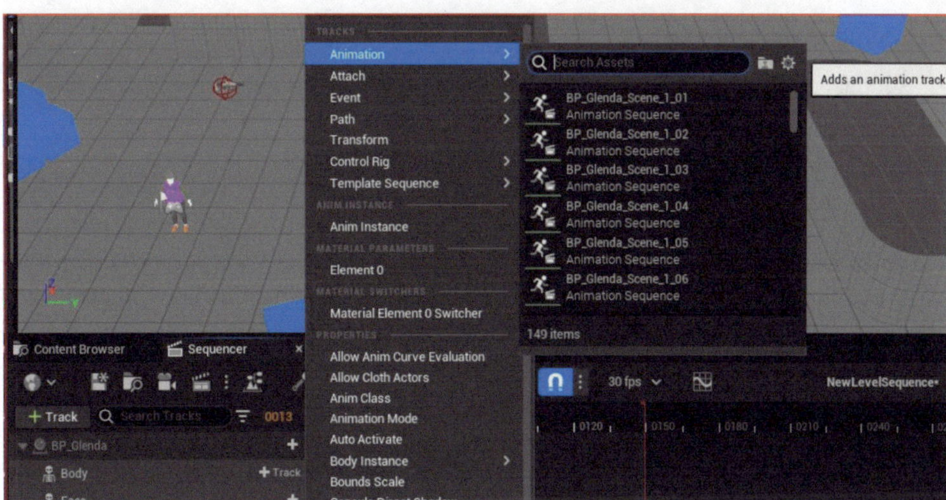

Figure 10.3: Adding an animation

If you don't see your animation in the list, use the search function. Remember, any track you are adding will have to have been retargeted, so you can always use the **Retargeted** suffix when running a search. That way, you'll be able to see all the available mocap in your project.

In *Figure 10.4*, you can see that I've added a track. You can even see that it has the track title, which can confirm at a glance that you are using the correct mocap track:

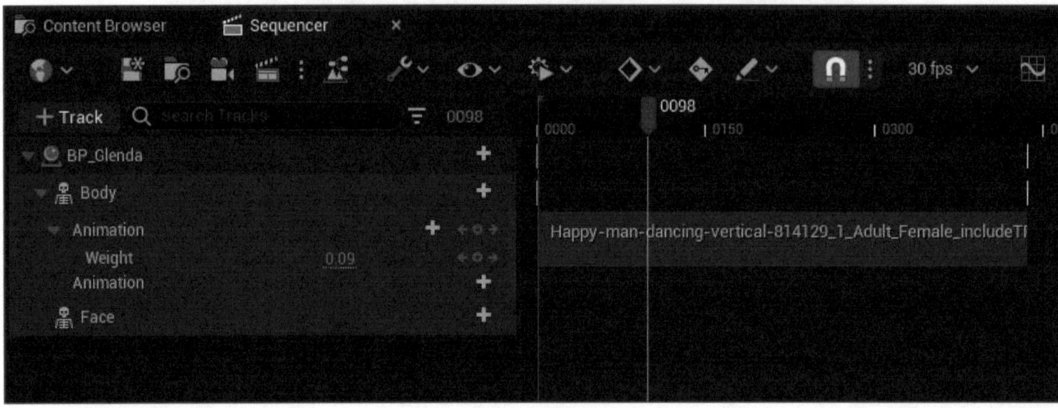

Figure 10.4: An added track

You completed this step at the end of *Chapter 8*, but in the next section, we will look at ways to bring in additional mocap tracks for the body.

Adding additional body mocap data and merging mocap clips

There are two ways to bring in additional mocap tracks:

- Adding an animation track
- Adding animation to an existing track

Let's take a look at them now.

Adding an animation track

To add an animation clip as a track in the Level Sequencer, click the + icon next to **Body**. This will create an additional animation track that you can reposition along the timeline and blend with the first track using the weight tool using keyframes.

In *Figure 10.5*, you can see that I now have two animation tracks:

- The first track is the Happy Dance file I created in DeepMotion and I have created two keyframes. The first keyframe has a **Weight** value (which is the value of influence over the character). By default, the **Weight** value is **1**, which is equal to an influence of 100%; this means that the first animation track is the most prominent. For the second keyframe, I set the **Weight** value to **0**, which is equal to 0%; this means that there is no happy dance. I know, it sounds depressing; however, all is not lost for Glenda, because I did the inverse for the new animation track.
- In the second animation track, which is the Macerena file taken from Mixamo, I keyframed the **Weight** value to start at 0% and transition to 100%, effectively blending the two dances using keyframes:

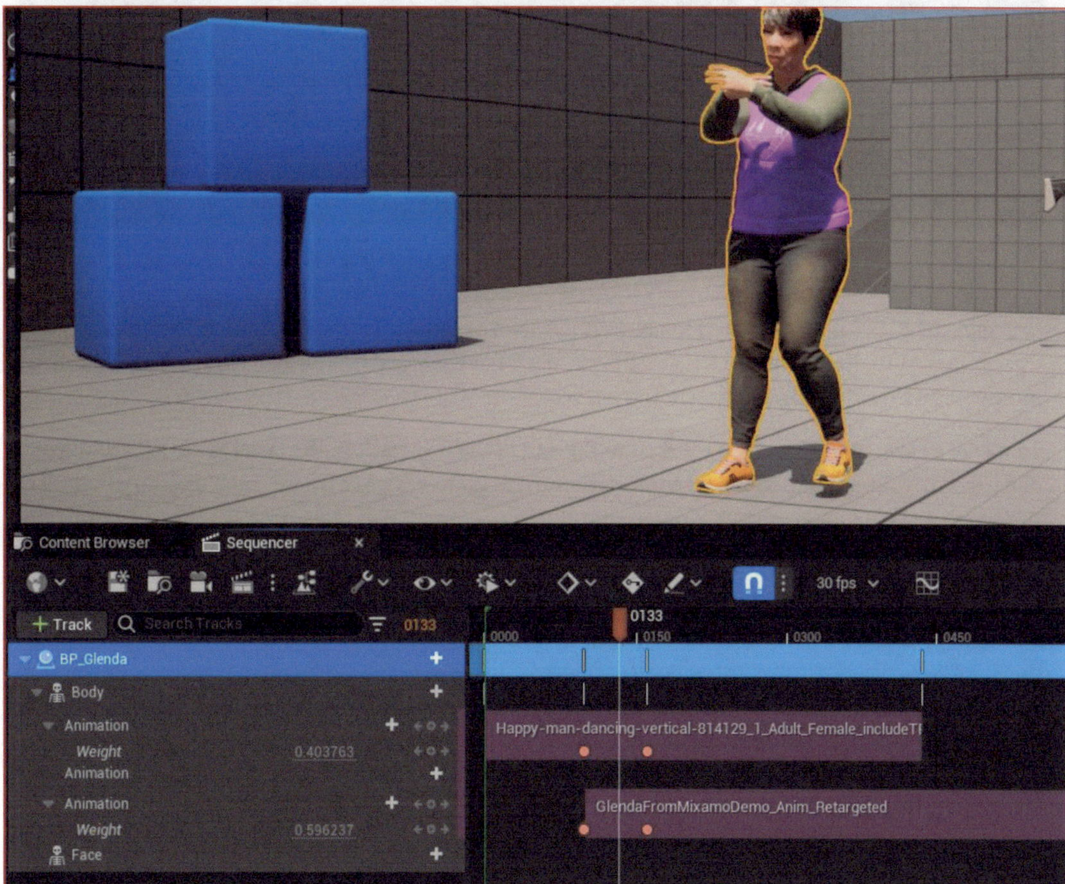

Figure 10.5: Adding another track

Adding animation to an existing track

Adding animation to an existing track doesn't create an additional track but adds new animation to the same track. Rather than clicking on the **+Track** icon beside **Body**, click on **+Animation** under **Body** instead, as you can see in *Figure 10.6*:

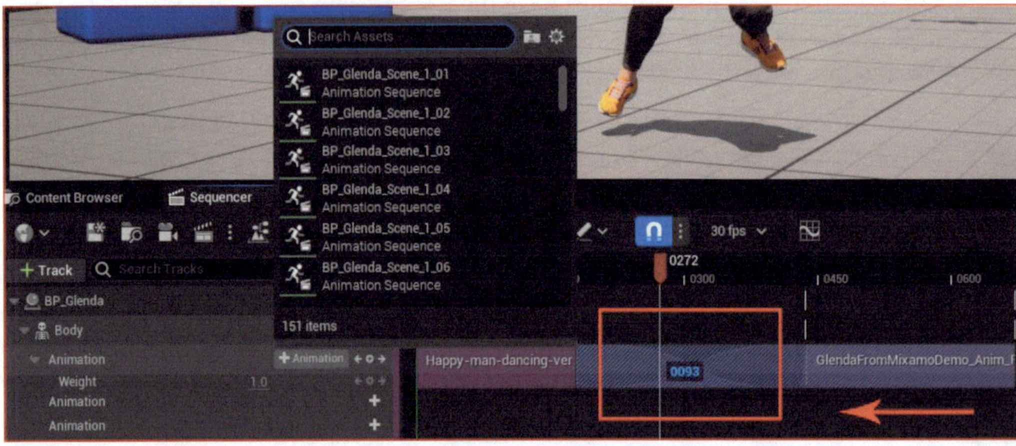

Figure 10.6: Merging two animations into one track

In *Figure 10.6*, I've already added my animation. Notice how there is a transition between the two tracks where I've drawn the red square. Effectively, I have merged one animation track into another, indicated by a descending and ascending curve.

To merge a track in this way, you must go to the end of the first track in the Level Sequencer with your playhead. If your animation is 100 frames, be sure to go to a higher frame, such as 120; otherwise, you won't be able to merge your animation to the track. Then, you must drag the second clip to the left so that it intersects with the first clip.

Note that it automatically blends from the first animation into the second animation on the same animation track. Effectively, this method has merged the two animations into one track. Take note of the number between the two animation (in the red box) clips that have merged. It reads as **0093**. This indicates that the transition length from one animation to the next is 93 frames, which is approximately 3 seconds.

In the next section, we'll take a look at a handy tip to help align animations.

Using the Show Skeleton feature for cleaner alignment

Sometimes, when we try to merge animations, we don't get great results. For example, if the first animation is of the character walking and the second animation is of the character running, often, the character will appear to have jumped into a new position dramatically from one frame to the next.

To make such an adjustment, we need to add a **Transform** track to the body in the Level Sequencer. You can do this as per *Figure 10.7*:

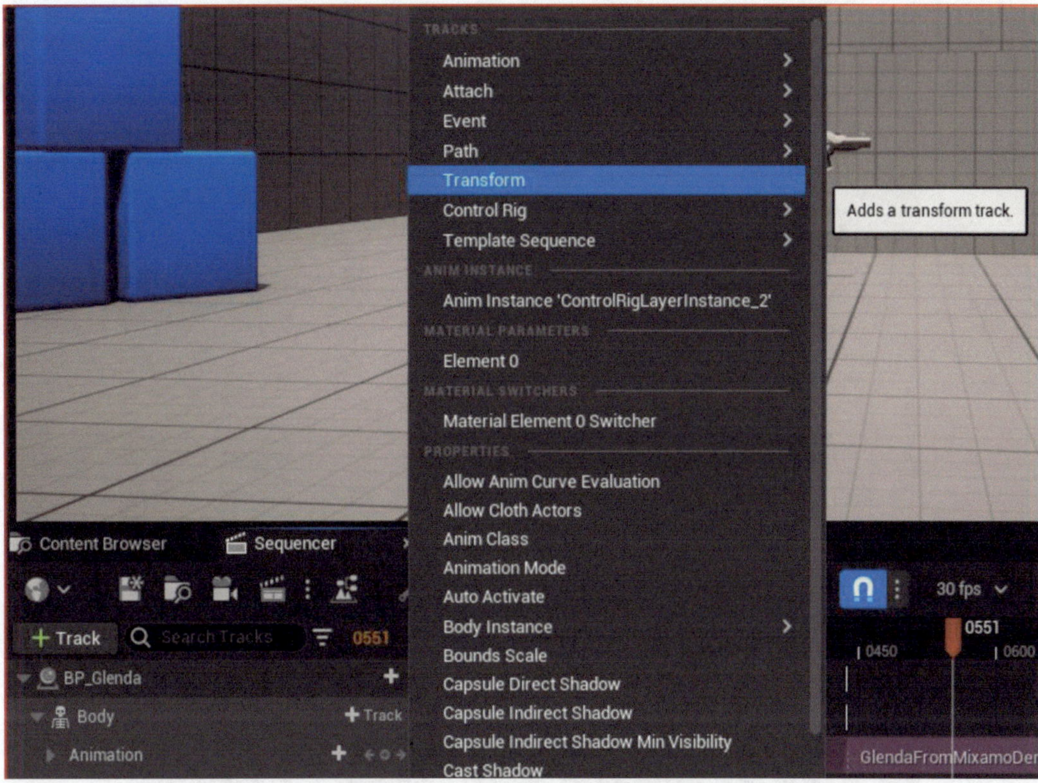

Figure 10.7: Adding a transform track

This will create a new transform track in the Level Sequencer, allowing us to create keyframes in the **Location** parameter. Now, we can move the character around to fix any character position issues without impacting any of the overall animation properties. Any movement of the character that we apply will only set keyframes on the new transform track, so we won't inadvertently lose any of the original motion capture data.

For example, imagine an animation of a character standing and waving an arm. If there is an issue with the mocap data where the body rises upwards randomly but we are happy that the character is waving, we can fix the random upward movement by adding keyframes to the **Location** parameter. We can do this without negatively impacting the waving motion of the arms.

However, it can be a little cumbersome to see the subtle adjustments when it comes to moving the character from A to B. To get around this visibility issue, Unreal has a function where we can see the MetaHuman skeleton. This allows us to focus on the exact position of our character without being confused by the mesh.

By right-clicking on the timeline, you will see the **Show Skeleton** option. Clicking on this will reveal a bright pink skeleton, which helps to make subtle adjustments, as shown in *Figure 10.8*:

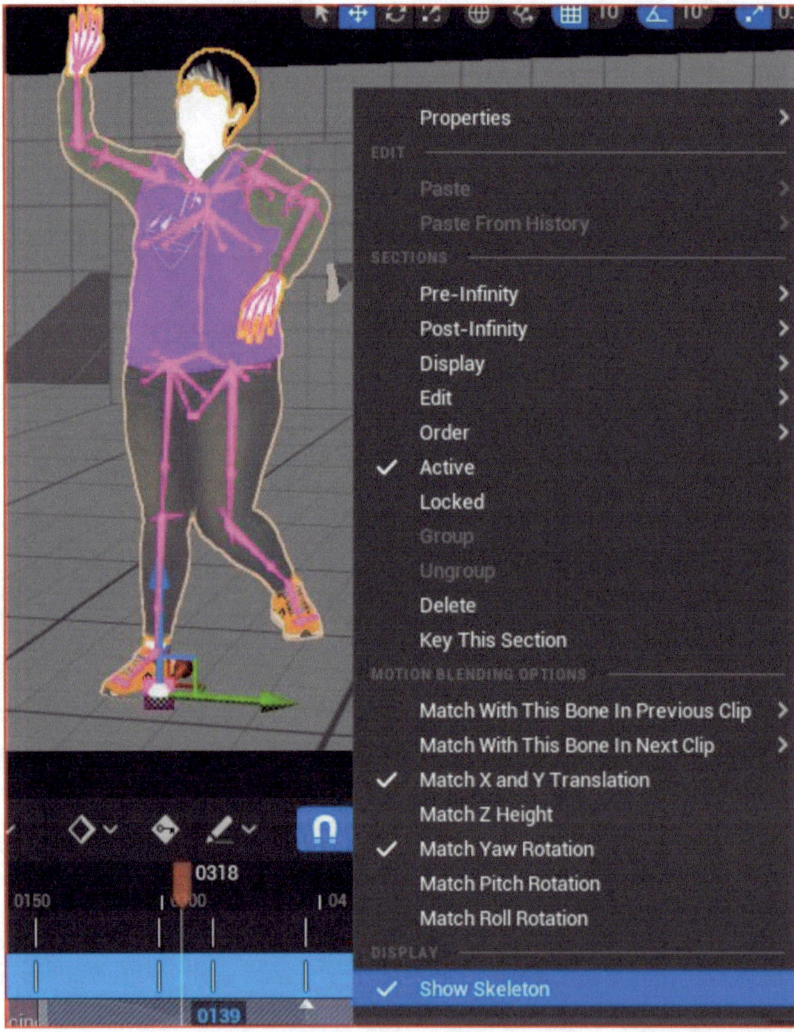

Figure 10.8: Show Skeleton

> **Note**
>
> When using the **Show Skeleton** function, both animations will be displayed with skeletons of different colors, which makes lining them up a little easier.

A common example of when to use the **Transform** track and the **Show Skeleton** functions is when you want to loop animation, such as a walk cycle.

However, if you have a character walking from position A to B, and you wish to loop the animation so that the character continues walking, we'll come across an issue. The issue is that as soon as the character reaches position B, it will return to position A if we wish it to loop.

Using the **Transform** tracks, and placing keyframes on the locator, you can create a continual animation using a loop:

1. Add a **Transform** track to your **Animation** track in the Level Sequencer.
2. Go to the very end of the track and at the last frame, add keyframes for the locator positions – that is, *X*, *Y*, and *Z*. You can also do this by hitting the *Enter* key, providing you have the transform track selected in the Level Sequencer. We are doing this to secure the position of the animation so that it isn't affected by the next step.
3. Now, extend the track so that it repeats. On the first frame of the repeated section, add a new position so that the character occupies the same space that it did at the end of the original track. Most likely, you'll just need to edit the *X* and *Y* axis positions slightly and possibly need to rotate the character on the *Z* axis if the character isn't walking in a straight line. Each clip has the option of displaying its skeleton, so the slight editing of the *X* and *Y* positions is helped by showing the skeletons because you are essentially just lining up the skeletons of each track so that they occupy the same space.

> **Note**
>
> To further edit the character's motion, you can always bake the animation to the control rig and add **Additive Section** for further editing.

Moving on from the convenient tool of visualizing your skeleton, there are other options for editing the animation clip. By right-clicking anywhere in the track and going to properties, you will see that you have more options when it comes to editing your clip:

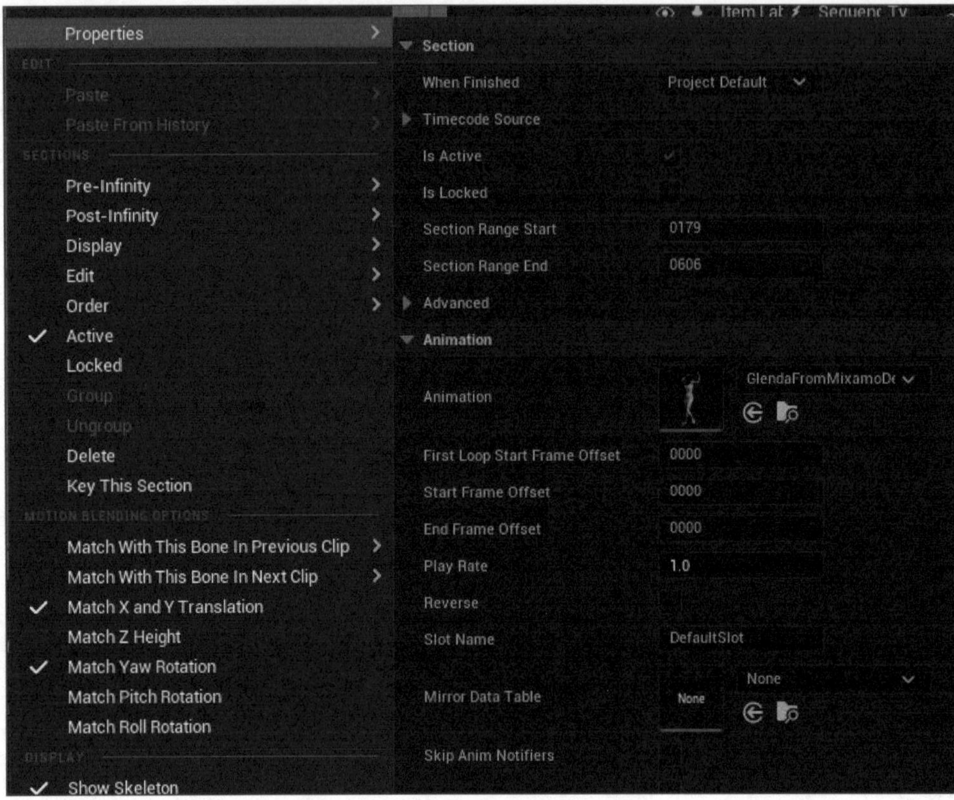

Figure 10.9: Further options

When it comes to merging animation, the most important thing is the frame rate. You may find that you are trying to blend two animations that have different speeds. The property function is a good way to tackle this problem by changing the frame rates so that they match. You can also experiment with different frame rates.

Now that we have looked at how to add mocap data related to the body, in the next section, we'll cover the same principles of adding and merging animation tracks, but this time, we will focus on the face.

Adding facial mocap data to the Level Sequencer

To add and merge the face animation requires you to follow the the exact same steps as you did for the body, by either adding a whole new Faceware track or by adding the animation to the end of the existing animation track and moving the tracks. Let's take a look in more detail.

Adding a recorded Faceware take

In this section, we are going to add the Faceware facial motion capture file to the Level Sequencer. If you are having trouble locating your Faceware facial capture file, which was recorded by **Take Recorder** in *Chapter 8*, just remember that Take Recorder added the **_Scene** suffix to the character Blueprint's name. So, in my case, I just searched for **BP+Glenda_Scene** and all my takes were listed for me to choose from.

In *Figure 10.10*, you can see that I merged Take 6, **BP_Glenda_scene_106_0**, with Take 1, **BP_Glenda_Scene_1_01_0**:

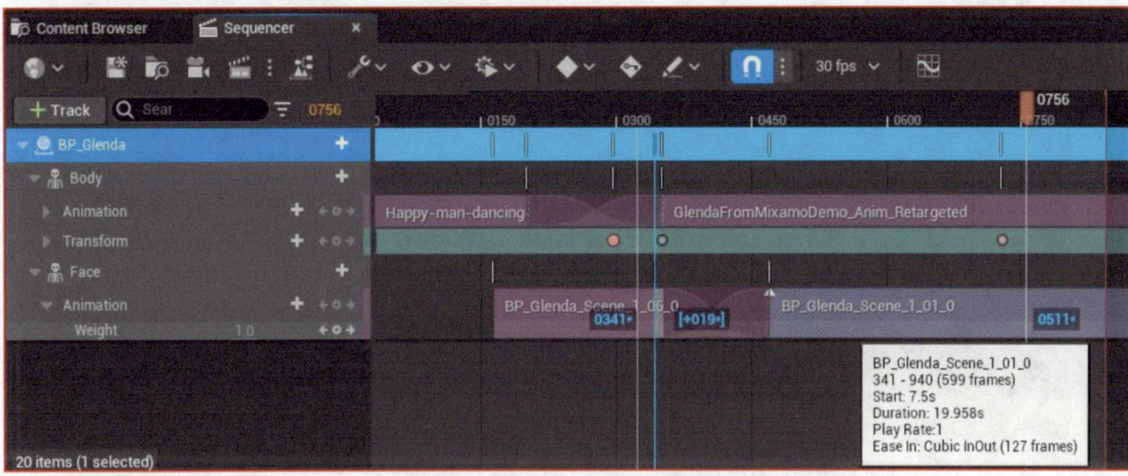

Figure 10.10: Adding Face animation to one animation track

I have selected **BP_Glenda_Scene_1_01_0**. You can see that the keyframes have appeared in blue, including **0341** and **+19**. Take note of the + icon – it means that I have moved the clip 19 frames to the right, so it will start 19 frames later.

Editing the facial mocap

The process for editing facial capture animation clips is practically identical to that of the body data, so we can use the same tools and follow the same steps from the previous section.

In addition, we can bake the track into keyframes in a control rig and add an **Additive Section** to tweak the animation, as we covered in *Chapter 8*. You can see from *Figure 10.11* that I've taken the same steps of baking the control rig, which is indicated by the triangular keyframes:

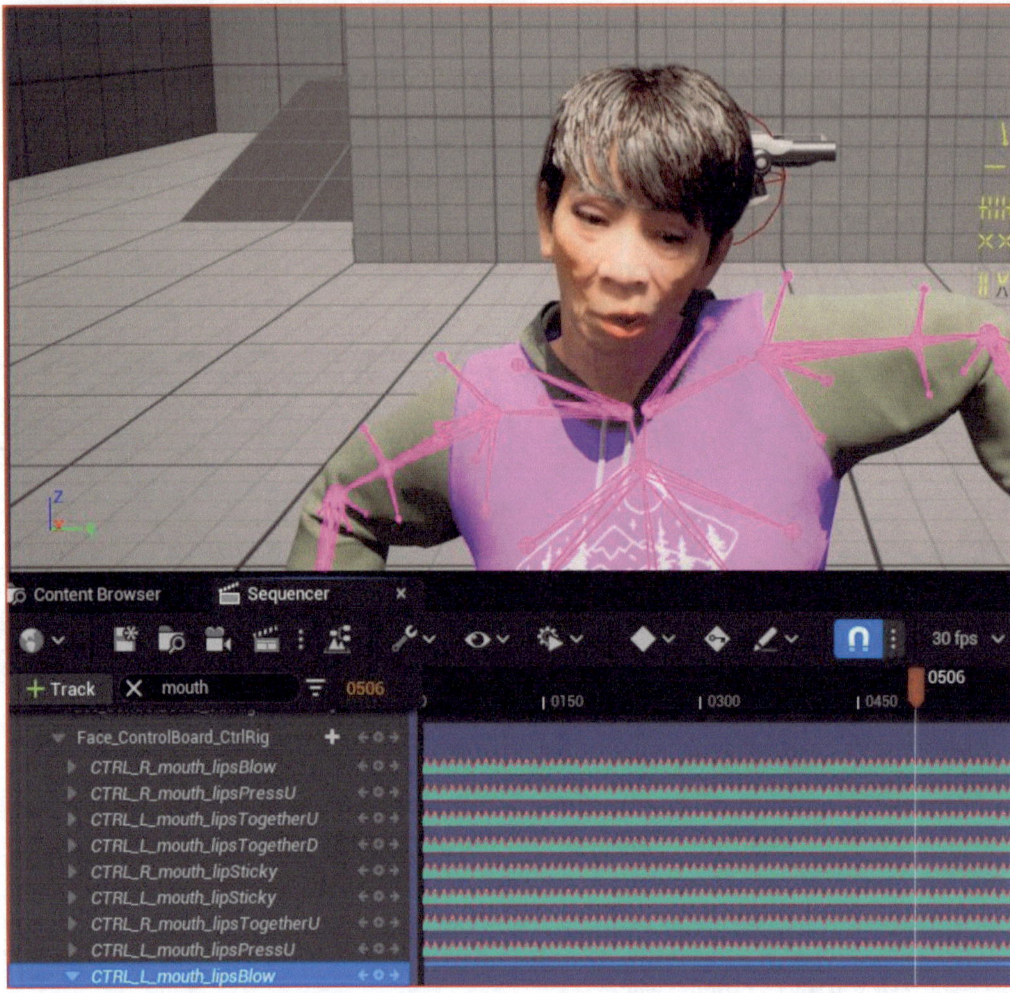

Figure 10.11: Baking the track to the control rig

A huge part of making the facial capture work with the body capture is timing. It may require just the easy step of sliding the facial mocap animation track to either the left or right; on the other hand, you may have to spend more time using the facial control rig, or even the body control rig, to make both animations match. The only way to get good at working with control rigs for the face is to experiment with them. A good practice would be to get as far as you can with the raw facial motion capture and then refine the animation using an **Additive** section with a control rig.

With some of the advanced animation features covered, it's now time to delve into some advanced rendering.

Exploring advanced rendering features

I've said this before and I'll say it again: Unreal Engine is a very powerful tool, and when it comes to rendering, it doesn't disappoint. Unreal is capable of delivering outstanding results that are comparable to traditional path-tracing renderers such as Mental Ray, Arnold, V-Ray, and RenderMan. Unreal now supports path tracing, which is the foundation of how these other renderers work.

In the context of filmmaking, Unreal has real-time rendering capabilities that should be explored to unlock its full potential. The camera and lights have features that we find in 3D programs such as Maya, Houdini, and Blender that use path tracing renderers. It's possible to export whole scenes from either of these applications with the camera and lighting settings intact and compatible with Unreal.

So, without further ado, let's take a look at some of these great rendering features.

Adding and animating a camera

In *Chapter 7*, we used a method of creating a new camera directly from the Level Sequencer; however, in this chapter, we will create the camera without using the Level Sequencer.

In *Figure 10.12*, I went up to the **Create Actor** button to quickly add an actor to the scene. From there, I chose **Cinematic**, followed by **Cine Camera Actor**. This creates a camera in the viewport of my scene:

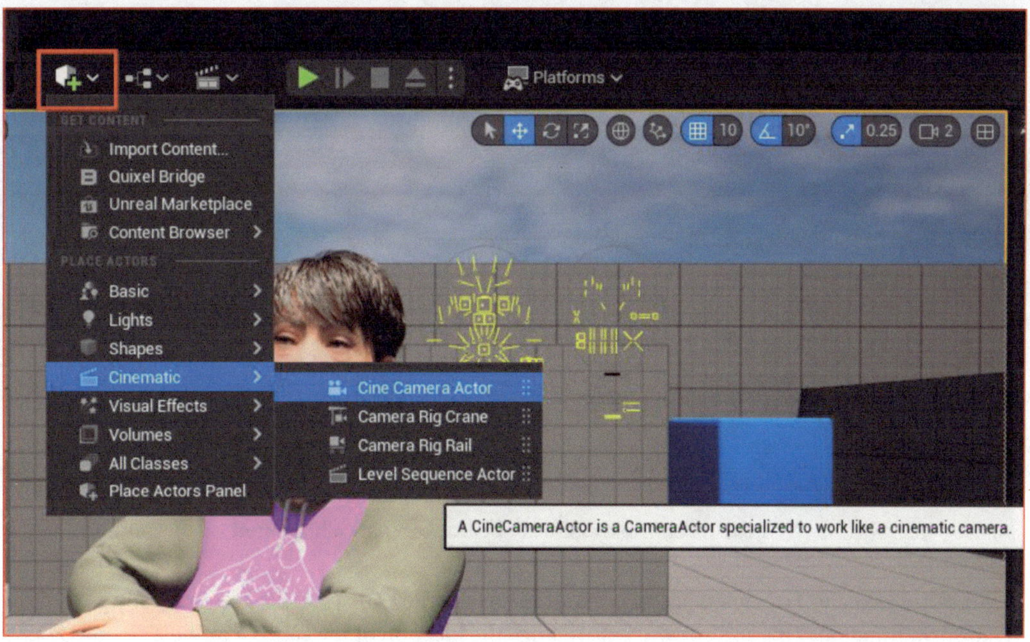

Figure 10.12: Quickly adding a camera to the scene

Next, go to the Level Sequencer and add the camera by clicking on the **+ Track** button and choosing the camera you just created.

In *Figure 10.13*, the camera cut features the grid background, as does the viewport above. This allows us to preview any camera animation from the Level Sequencer directly in the viewport:

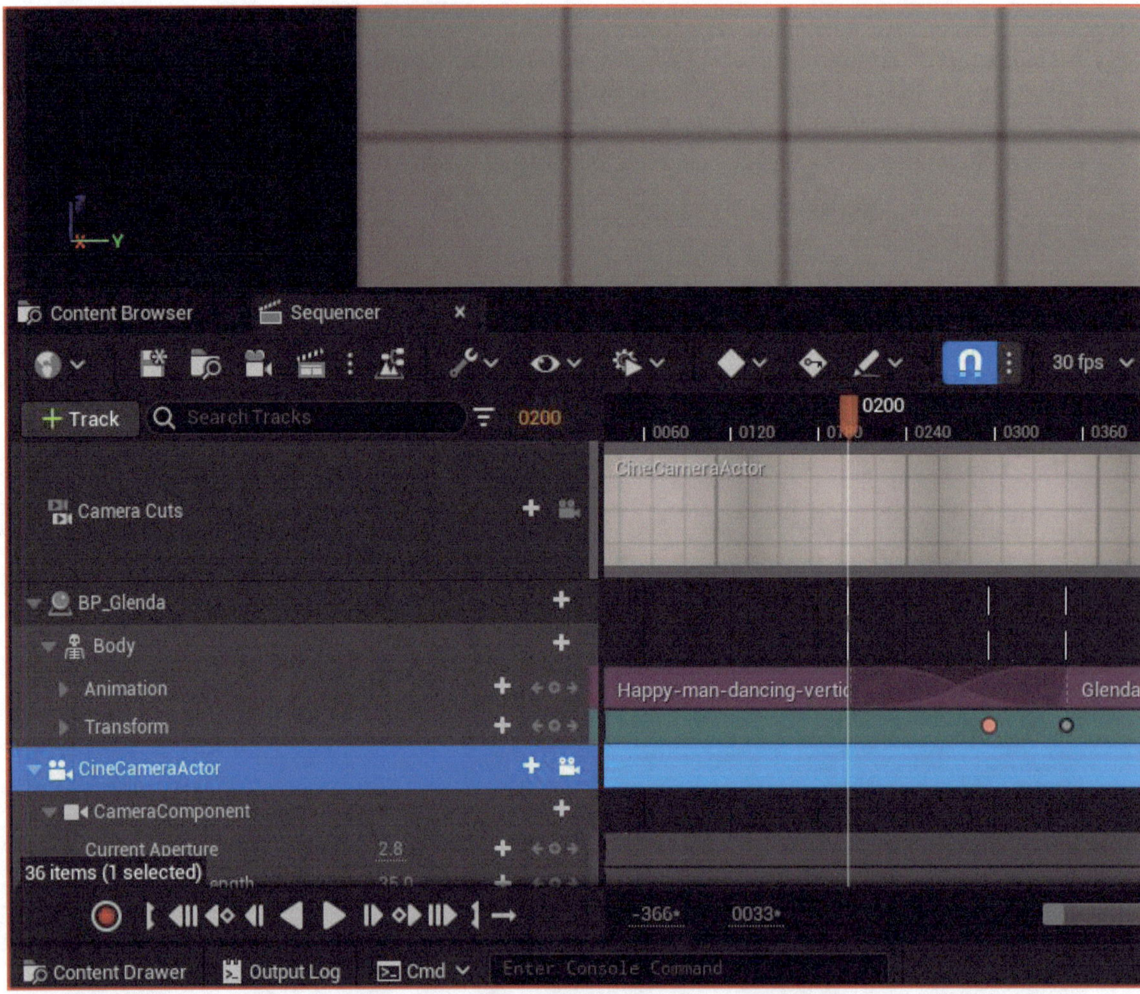

Figure 10.13: The camera cut being automatically created

Unlike the body and face of the MetaHuman Blueprints, the Cine Camera automatically generates a Transform function. This will allow you to change the location of the camera in the *X*, *Y*, and *Z* axes. You can also change the rotation of the camera in the *X*, *Y*, and *Z* axes, which change the Roll, Pitch, and Yaw, respectively.

As shown in *Figure 10.14*, you have keyframe attributes on the right-hand side. Typically, when animating the camera, you'll need to adjust the **Location** setting and edit the **Focus Distance** setting to ensure your subject is in focus:

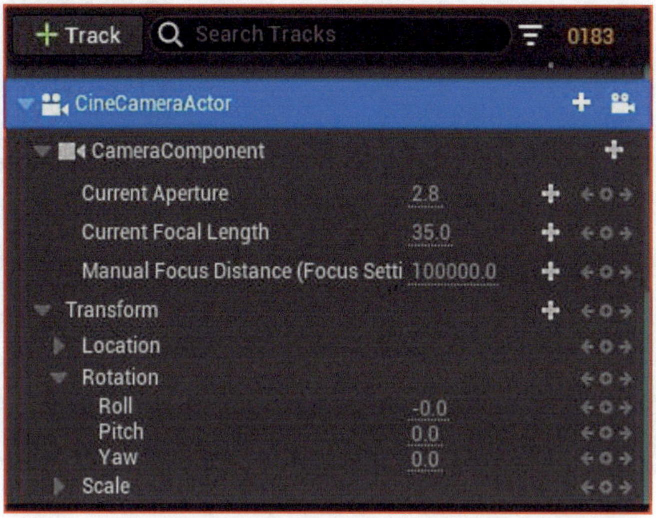

Figure 10.14: The camera transform

Rather than changing values in the Transform function within the Level Sequencer every time you want to set a keyframe in the Level Sequencer, you can always just pilot the camera inside the viewport, much like playing a first-person game using your keyboard and mouse.

Be sure to engage the autokey, as illustrated in *Figure 10.15*, which will create a keyframe every time you move the camera:

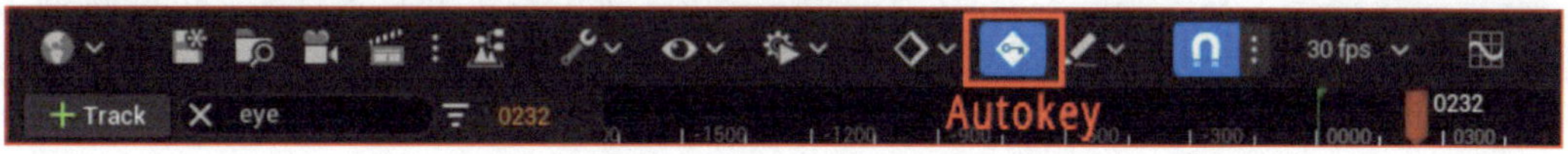

Figure 10.15: The Autokey function

In addition to just animating the camera position, you can also animate what the camera is focusing on. A very convenient tool for focus is the **Debug Focus** tool, illustrated in *Figure 10.16*. This tool gives us a clear visual indication of what is in focus. With the camera selected, tick the **Draw Debug Focus Plane** option; you'll see a pink plane appear. Anything on that pink plane is going to be perfectly in focus:

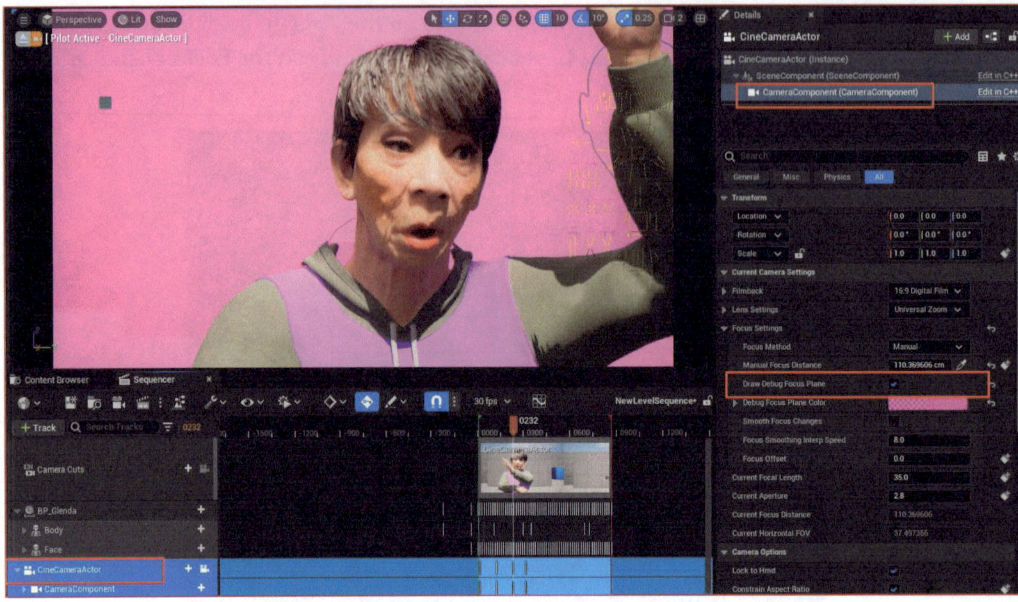

Figure 10.16: Camera debug focus

You can control the focus and animate focus distance within the Level Sequencer but use the debug plane for precision focusing.

Now, with some of the more advanced camera features out of the way, it's time to move on to lights.

Adding and animating light

For the most part, actors are added to the Level Sequencer with some attributes being animatable. It is possible to animate more attributes via the Level Sequencer, but we need to manually add them to the Level Sequencer.

Lights are also actors that we can animate. We can add a light to the Level Sequencer much the same as we added a camera earlier. By doing this, the only animatable attribute by default is the light intensity. But there are a lot of attributes for the light actor that we can add for animation purposes.

In *Figure 10.17*, you can see that by clicking on **+ Track** next to the camera component in the Level Sequencer, I have access to nearly all of the attributes featured in the **Detail** panel for animating. Click on any of these attributes in the list for them to become an animatable component within the Level Sequencer:

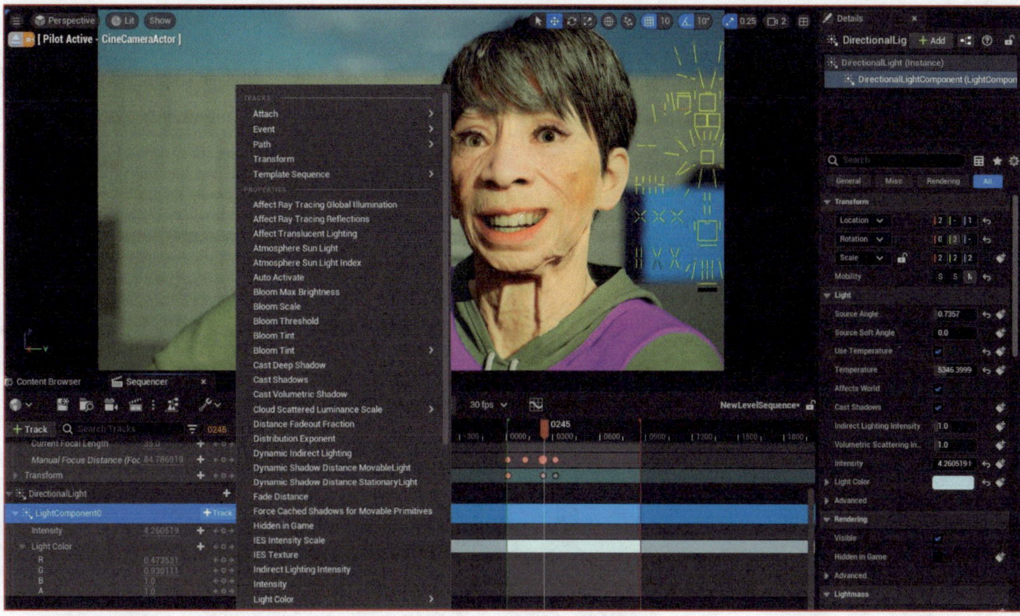

Figure 10.17: Editing lights

Generally speaking, animating lights is rare, much the same as moving lights in a live-action shoot is rare, but not unusual – perhaps you want a flashing light from a police car or a lighthouse lamp spinning around, or you want to tweak a light's intensity for when a character walks under it. I could spend a whole chapter on lighting in Unreal, if not a whole book on the subject, but we must move on to a very important feature, Post Process Volumes.

Using Post Process Volumes

Post Process Volume is an interesting tool as it gives us massive control of the final picture. Typically, Post Process Volume would surround your entire scene and is a volume in the sense that it is an area within your scene that is affected by input from an artist.

In essence, Post Process Volume is an effect and grading tool with much of the toolset aimed at the camera. For instance, we can control flares, blooms, and chromatic aberrations, which are all very specific lens characteristics, along with film grain, change exposure, white balancing, and so on. If you look at any settings inside a modern video camera or digital cinema camera, Post Process Volume pretty much has a matching feature. Epic Games have done incredible work giving artists real-world tools when it comes to their scene for real-time rendering.

In *Figure 10.18*, I have utilized some of these features:

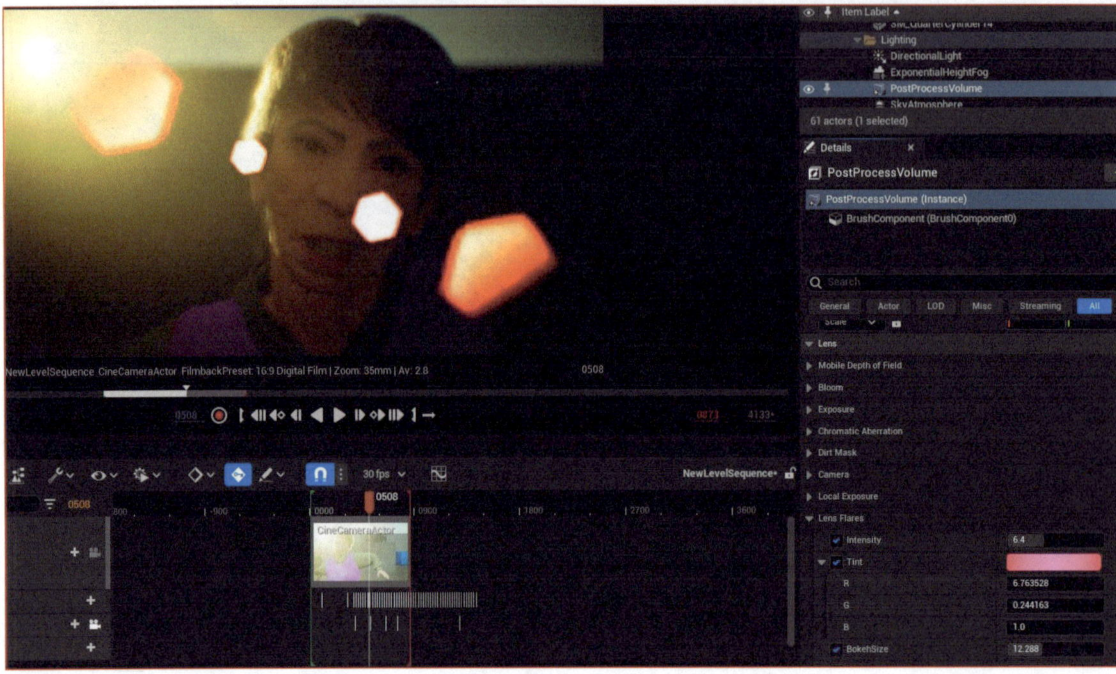

Figure 10.18: Lens effects with Post Process Volumes

Let's look at some of the features that I used:

- **Lens Flare** is obvious to see. If you're not familiar with lens flares, they're the light spots in the picture that cross over Glenda's face – they react with the light source, which is a directional light behind Glenda. I've added a pink tint to the lens flare and increased the Bokeh size, which effectively increases the size of the lens flare.
- I have also added a **Bloom** effect, which gives us a realistic light glow from her hair. A bloom effect simulates filters used on real-world lenses such as pro mist filters, which soften highlights in the image.
- In addition, I've added **Film Grain**, **Chromatic Aberration**, and a **Vignette**, which are far too subtle to see here but are commonly used to enhance realism:
  - **Film Grain** is used to simulate film stock or digital noise that is present in film or digital cameras
  - **Chromatic Aberration** is a natural phenomenon found in photographic lenses where a very subtle rainbow effect appears, particularly from highlights in the image
  - **Vignettes** are a common artifact of photographic lenses where the edges of the image are darker than the middle of the image

As the name suggests, Post Process Volume is a *post-production* tool. In terms of Unreal Engine, most of the difficult things such as lighting direction, shadow, skin shading, reflections, and so on are already set, but Post Process Volume adds an extra layer of effects over that. In a way, the Level Sequencer is like the camera and Post Process Volume is like Photoshop.

As a rule of thumb: it is best to get all of your lighting and camera work as close to the final look as possible, and rely on Post Process Volume for things you couldn't achieve otherwise.

There are quite a lot of settings in Post Process Volume and unfortunately too many to cover in a book about MetaHumans. However, they will make your MetaHumans look amazing when it comes to rendering.

> **Note**
>
> If you would like to learn more about advanced lighting and rendering techniques, I recommend you take a look at the following video tutorial, which you can purchase from the Gnomon Workshop: `https://www.thegnomonworkshop.com/tutorials/cinematic-lighting-in-unreal-engine-5`.

This brings us to the next section, where we will take a close look at rendering out files from the Movie Render Queue for compositing and color grading.

Using the Movie Render Queue

When we are setting our renders from the Level Sequencer, we are given a choice of which render queue to use. To see what render queues are available to you, click on the three dots next to the clapper icon, as per *Figure 10.19*:

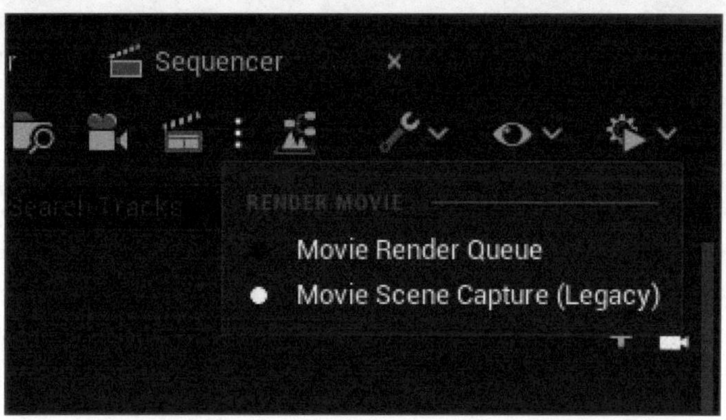

Figure 10.19: Movie Render Queue options

It is quite likely that you will only see **Movie Scene Capture (Legacy)**, but this is somewhat dated and limited. The other option that you can see is **Movie Render Queue**; however, at the time of writing, it is still only in Beta, so isn't enabled by default.

To enable it, you need to head over to the plugin section and search for **Renderer**. In *Figure 10.20*, you can see that I have already enabled both, which you should do too:

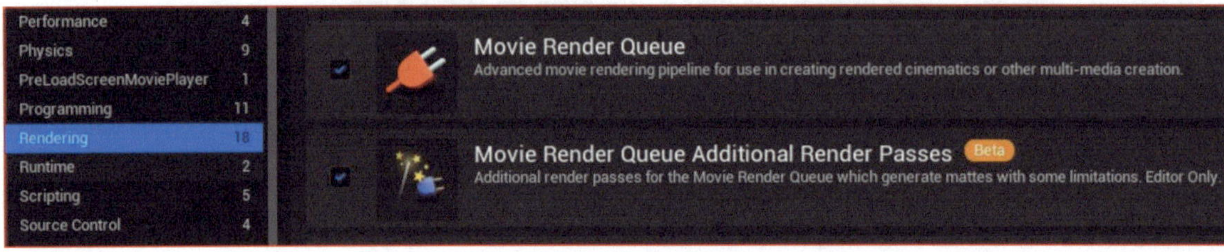

Figure 10.20: Enabling both Render Queue plugins

Now, when you click **Movie Render Queue**, as per *Figure 10.21*, you'll see the following screen:

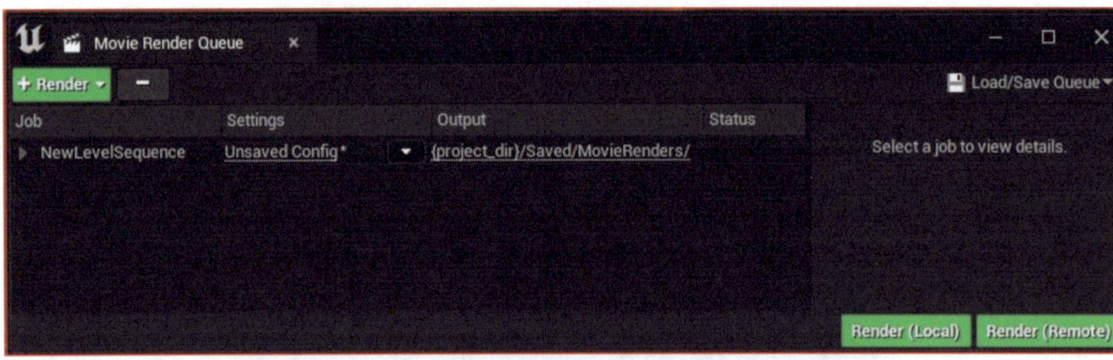

Figure 10.21: Movie Render Queue dialog box

The + **Render** button in green is for determining which sequence to render. Initializing the Movie Render Queue will assign the current Level Sequencer for rendering. However, should you have multiple Level Sequencers in your project, you can add them to the Render Queue using the + **Render** button. In this dialog box, you'll see three columns:

- **Job**
- **Settings**
- **Output**

Let's go through each of these columns.

Job

Job is the sequencer name that has been chosen for rendering. By default, it will be titled **New Level Sequence**. Keep in mind that parameters such as **Range** (how long the animation is) and **Frame Rate** are determined in the Level Sequencer.

Should you have more than one Level Sequencer in your project, they would be available under **Job** and you can select which Level Sequencer you want to render.

Settings

Settings refer to what render settings you want to apply to your sequence.

Ouput

The **Output** area displays the folder directory where your images or videos will be rendered, as set in the output setting.

There are quite a lot of options to choose from when it comes to rendering settings. Ultimately, if you are already committed to rendering a movie out of Unreal using a Level Sequencer, then you are not likely to be concerned with the real-time rendering capabilities of Unreal and are planning to do more work on the rendered sequence in post-production.

The file type, be it a movie file or an image sequence, is an important setting to consider. For example, should you plan to do additional post-production such as advanced color grading, then you should opt for an image sequence setting such as **Open EXR** that provides higher color fidelity. If you plan to just do a test render or commit a final render directly from Unreal, then a movie file such as a **Quicktime Prores** would suffice.

Let's look at the default settings, as shown in *Figure 10.22*:

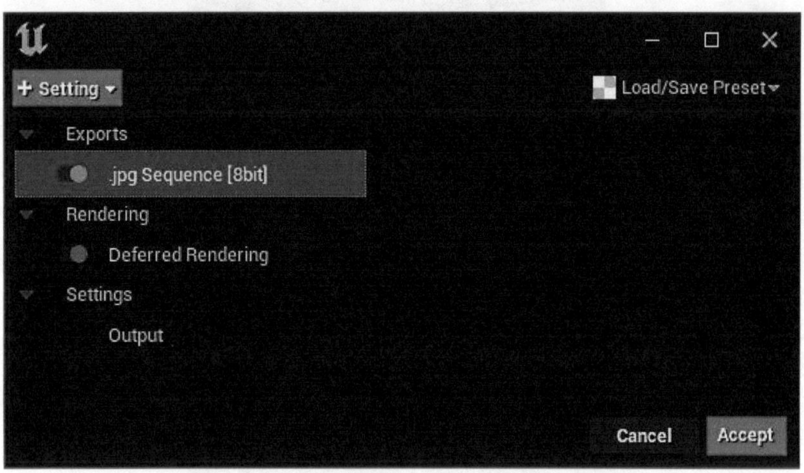

Figure 10.22: Default settings in Movie Render Queue

There are three types of default settings:

- **Exports (jpg Sequence 8bit)**: Exports allows us to choose what file format options we want, from low-fidelity and compressed formats (such as JPGs, which are only 8-bit) to high-fidelity Open EXR, which are floating-point 16-bit.
- **Rendering (Deferred Rendering)**: Deferred rendering is an optimized and default way of rendering a scene in Unreal. It renders in two passes. The primary pass includes calculations such as z depth and ambient occlusion. From the primary (base) pass, deductions can be made from the second pass regarding what needs to be calculated on a per-object basis in terms of shaders. This is to reduce processing time.
- **Settings (Output)**: When you click on **+ Setting**, you will see that there are more settings to choose from:

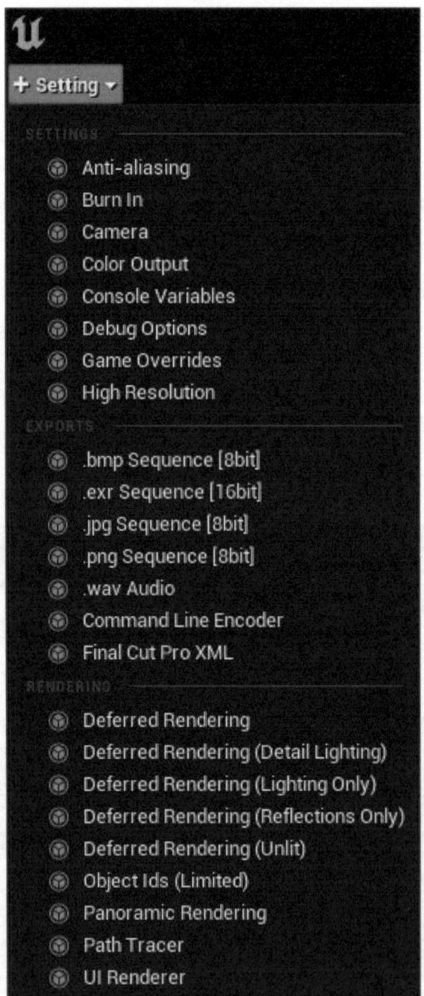

Figure 10.23: Available settings in Movie Render Queue

When rendering the Level Sequencer to a hard drive, we have various options to choose from to improve its quality:

- **Settings**: From this list, you can pick multiple options at once. For this book, I'm going to add **Anti-Aliasing** so that I can improve the quality of the motion blur.
- **Exports**: I'm going to replace **.jpg sequence [8bit]** with **.exr Sequence [16bit]**; this will significantly improve the quality of the render, particularly to refine the picture later in a video editing package. **.exr Sequence [16bit]** is exported in an **Open EXR** format – it gives us far greater ability to control what is over and under-exposed in the application, such as After Effects, Nuke, or DaVinci Resolve. Open EXR is the global visual effects standard for movies and television because it stores much more color information than other formats and also stores metadata.
- **Rendering**: Let's look at some of the rendering options available:
  - **Deferred Rendering**: The default rendering option, which uses multiple passes.
  - **Deferred Rendering (Reflections Only)**: This rendering option only renders out the reflections. This is handy if we want to control the intensity of reflections in a compositing application such as Nuke. Typically, you would choose this option as an addition to **Deferred Rendering**.
  - **Object IDs (Limited)**: Each object is given an object ID, which is represented by a unique color. When we have this option enabled, we will get an object ID video channel as part of the EXR file. When compositing in an application such as Nuke, we can then manipulate objects separately using the object ID by selecting the color associated with it. This is convenient if we want to change an object's color in Nuke without having to make changes in Unreal.

You can see the settings I have selected in *Figure 10.24*:

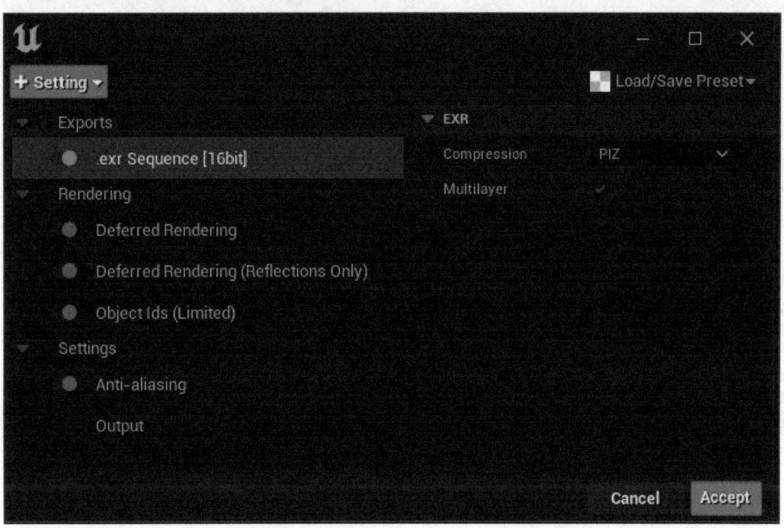

Figure 10.24: Settings selection

> **Note**
>
> The EXR file format is capable of storing multiple channels. Most image files store just three channels: Red, Green, and Blue, such as JPEG files. PNG files can store four channels: Red, Green, Blue, and an Alpha channel for transparency.

Output

Your default **Output** settings will match your Level Sequencer's default settings. However, the **Output** column is a means to override them, allowing you to control the final resolution and frame rate.

In *Figure 10.24*, I have used three render settings that will render out into one single EXR image sequence as separate channels, one channel for each of the following:

- **Deferred Rendering**
- **Deferred Rendering (Reflections Only)**
- **Object ID (Limited)**

You can see the result of that render in *Figure 10.25*. This figure represents the three extra channels that have been rendered and stored in the EXR file – the top left is **Deferred Rendering**, which appears normal, the top right is **Reflections Only**, and the bottom left is **Object ID** (in a compositing program, I can make further adjustments by manipulating these extra channels):

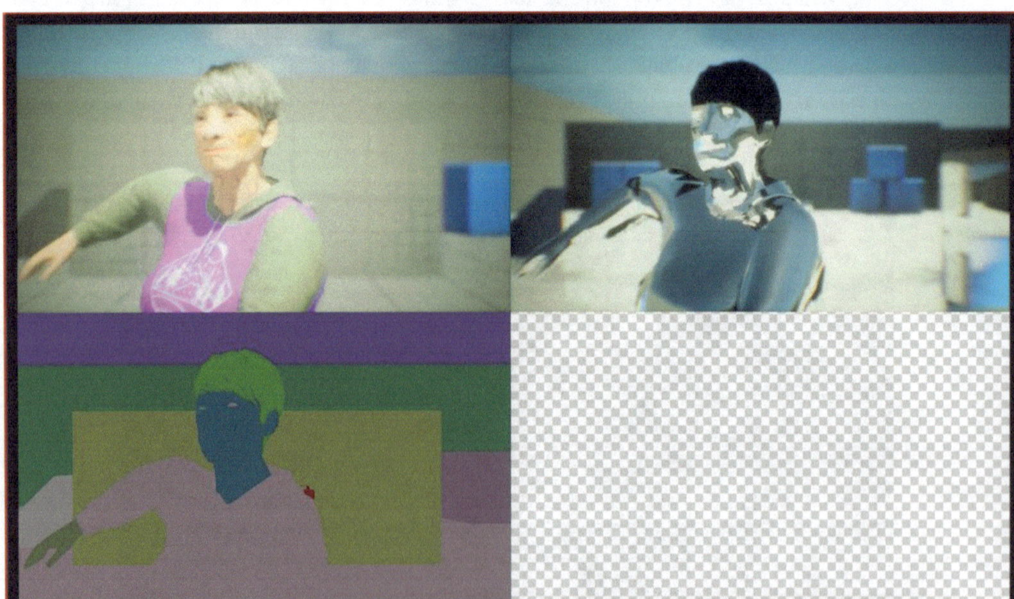

Figure 10.25: Example of rendering

The render settings in the new Movie Render Queue are very powerful and give the artist a little more control over the final images than that of a real-time render. This aligns with the results expected from traditional 3D animation productions, where compositors are given the same or more control over the 3D renders. As developments progress in Unreal, we expect that more and more 3D animation studios will adapt Unreal into their pipelines.

In the next section, we will look at some of the professional color standards that now ship with Unreal that allow MetaHumans to work within a professional studio environment.

ACES and color grading

As mentioned in the previous section, Open EXR is the professional industry standard file format used by visual effects and 3D animation studios for 3D rendering and compositing. One reason for this is that it can store a huge amount of pixel data, particularly color.

You might remember seeing **.jpeg sequence [8 bit]** as an option to render in. Well, that just doesn't cut it in the professional world simply because it doesn't represent even half of what the human eyes can see. An 8-bit image can only store 256 shades of red, green, and blue, respectively. In total, that amounts to just over 16 million colors versus the 280 trillion-plus colors in a 16-bit image.

If you take a look at *Figure 10.26*, where the widest area of color is represented by the ACES colorspace, you'll see the significant difference when compared to sRGB. The JPEG format of 8-bit is only capable of working within a small colorspace such as sRGB. Therefore, utilizing the enormous data space of the EXR file format and the enormous colorspace of ACES, Unreal Engine is capable of incredibly photorealistic renders, which is why choosing **Exr Sequence [16bit]** is preferable:

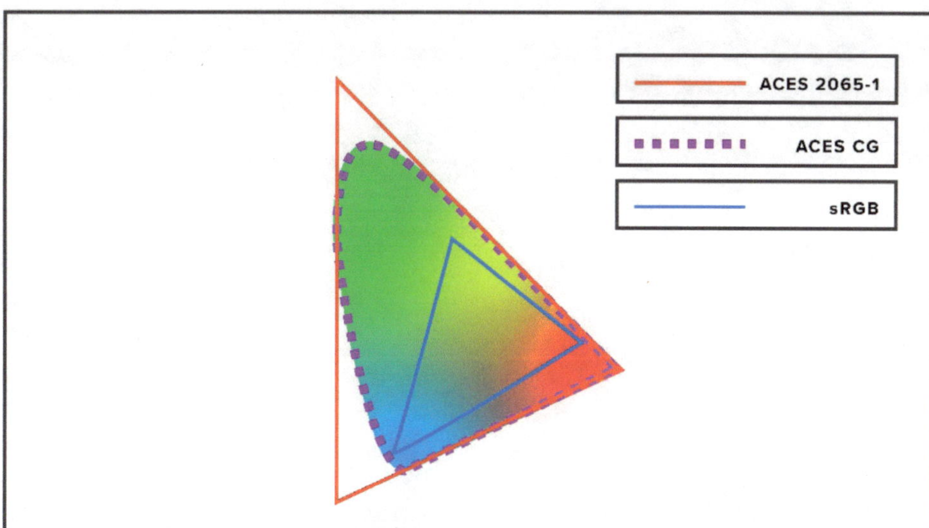

Figure 10.26: ACES colorspace versus sRGB

> **Note**
>
> For further reading on the ACES colorspace, go to `https://acescolorspace.com/`.

In this section, we uncovered some pretty advanced color theory relating to the ACES colorspace versus sRGB and how this can help you improve your MetaHuman renders.

Summary

In this chapter, we got the opportunity to revise some key elements of bringing a MetaHuman to life by applying both body and face motion capture to the Level Sequencer. We looked at alternative ways to edit movement and fix common movement issues, such as fixing the position of a character when looping an animation. We also learned how to use **Transform**, **Location**, and **Show Skeleton** to help with creating longer animations using looped tracks.

After that, we covered cameras, lights, and Post-Process Volumes, reviewing some of the very powerful and professional rendering capabilities of Unreal Engine.

In the next and final chapter of this book, we will take a look at a new feature (at the time of writing) that allows us to use our likeness or someone else's to fashion a MetaHuman around a real human!

11

Using the Mesh to MetaHuman Plugin

In the previous chapter, we reached the end of the process of creating a MetaHuman and making a video featuring our MetaHuman. While writing this book, Epic Games released version 5 of Unreal Engine – first, as an early access version, and later as a fully supported release. In addition, Epic Games also released a groundbreaking plugin that allows users to use custom meshes of faces to be used as the face of their MetaHuman. The free plugin is called Mesh to MetaHuman and at its core is the MetaHuman Identity Asset.

This opens up opportunities for artists to use all the great MetaHuman-related tools and functionality on custom face sculptors or digital scans of real people. Because we can use digital scans of real people, it gives artists the ability to create MetaHumans that have an incredible likeness to actors or even artists.

In this chapter, we will focus on how to create and utilize a digital scan of your own face and apply it to a MetaHuman. To do this, we will use an app called KIRI Engine that is available on both iPhone and Android. We will then import the digital scan to use with the Mesh to MetaHuman plugin.

So, in this chapter, we will cover the following topics:

- Installing the Mesh to MetaHuman plugin for Unreal Engine
- Introducing and installing the KIRI Engine app on your smartphone
- Importing your scanned mesh into Unreal Engine
- Modifying the face mesh inside MetaHuman Creator

Technical requirements

In terms of computer power, you will need to meet the technical requirements detailed in *Chapter 1*.

You will also need:

- An iPhone or Android phone with at least 200 MB of free space
- A stable internet connection as you will be downloading a plugin and uploading data to a server
- Access to the Epic Games Launcher used to install Unreal Engine
- The KIRI app
- The Mesh to MetaHuman plugin
- A new project in Unreal Engine

> **Note**
> You will need to be familiar with the MetaHuman Creator online application from *Chapter 2*, but you don't need to have any projects open from previous chapters.

Installing the Mesh to MetaHuman plugin for Unreal Engine

To get started, create a new project in Unreal Engine and leave it open. Then, to enable the Mesh to MetaHuman plugin, we first need to download it from the Unreal Engine Marketplace via the Epic Games Launcher.

When you have located the Mesh to MetaHuman plugin page, click on the **Install to Engine** button as seen in *Figure 11.1*:

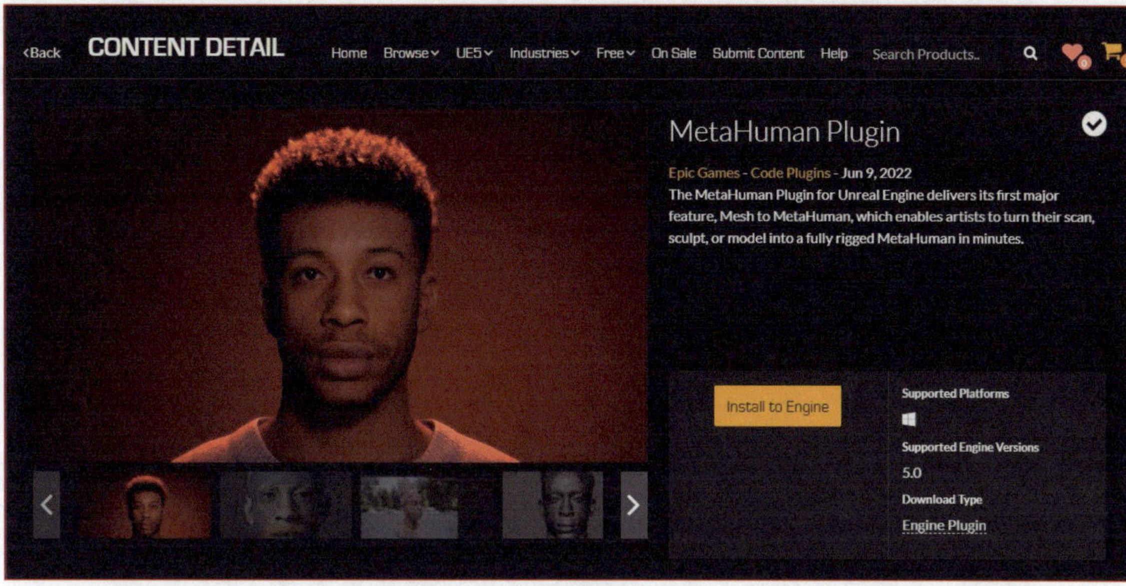

Figure 11.1: The MetaHuman plugin

With the Mesh to MetaHuman plugin installed, we'll now go to the next section to begin our journey into creating a digital scan with the KIRI Engine app.

Introducing and installing KIRI Engine on your smartphone

What is **KIRI** Engine? Well, KIRI Engine is an application that falls under the category of **photogrammetry**. Photogrammetry is the process of creating 3D geometry inside a 3D application (automatically, for the most part) using photographs.

In the context of creating a face scan for a MetaHuman, photogrammetry requires the artist to take multiple photographs in a 180-degree arc and at varying heights. From *Figure 11.2*, you can see four different angles of a head and shoulders.

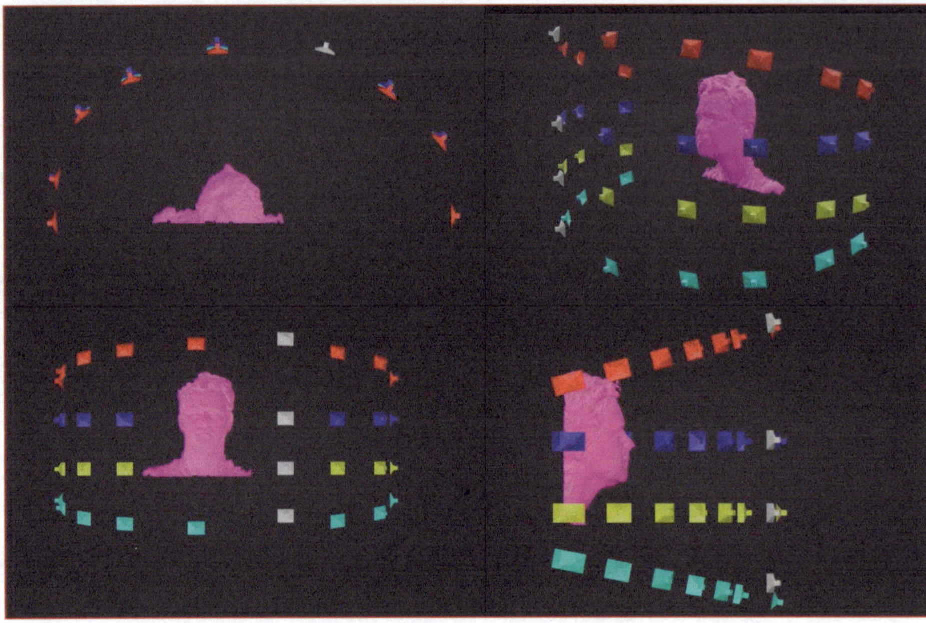

Figure 11.2: Typical camera positions

We are only interested in the front of the face, which is why we only capture within a 180-degree arc. It's also important to get high and low angles so that we get information for under the chin, nostrils, and the forehead.

Tips for shooting photogrammetry

- Use diffused (soft) lighting so there are no shadows on the face
- Have your subject sit very still with their chin tilted slightly up
- If possible, use a polarizing lens filter to minimize reflections on the skin

Now, let's get started with working with KIRI. Recently, KIRI Engine has become available for desktop when using a web browser on either macOS or Windows, which you can download here: `https://www.kiriengine.app/web-version/`. However, for the purpose of this book, I will assume that you have access to an Android smartphone or iPhone and that you are downloading the KIRI Engine app onto your smartphone.

If you have an Android device, you can install the app from Google Play for free, as seen here:

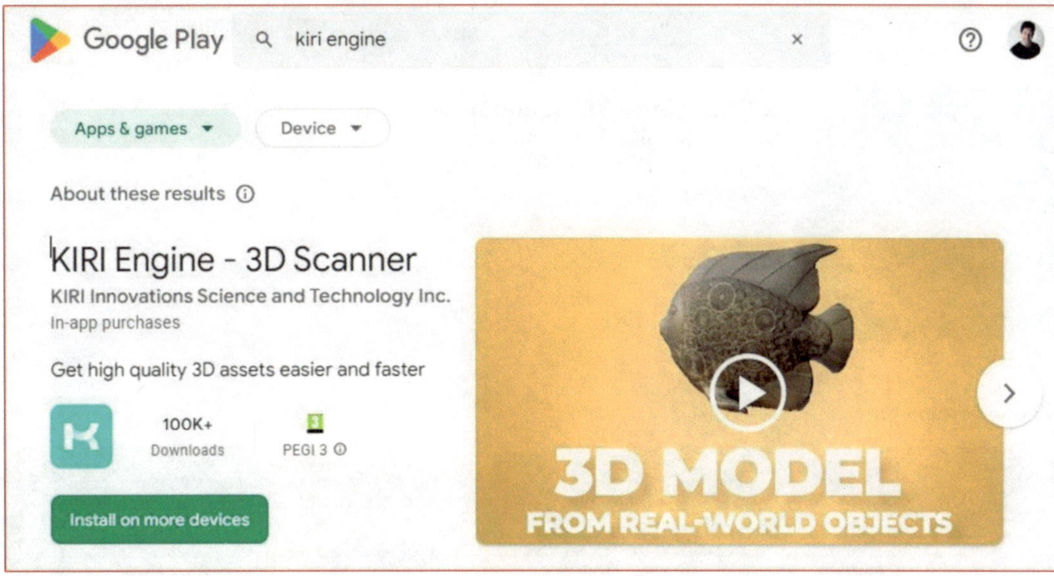

Figure 11.3: KIRI Engine on Google Play

As many of you will have used an iPhone during *Chapter 8*, *Using an iPhone for Facial Motion Capture*, you'll be pleased to know that you don't have to run off and get an Android. By going over to the App Store, you can download the KIRI Engine app on your device:

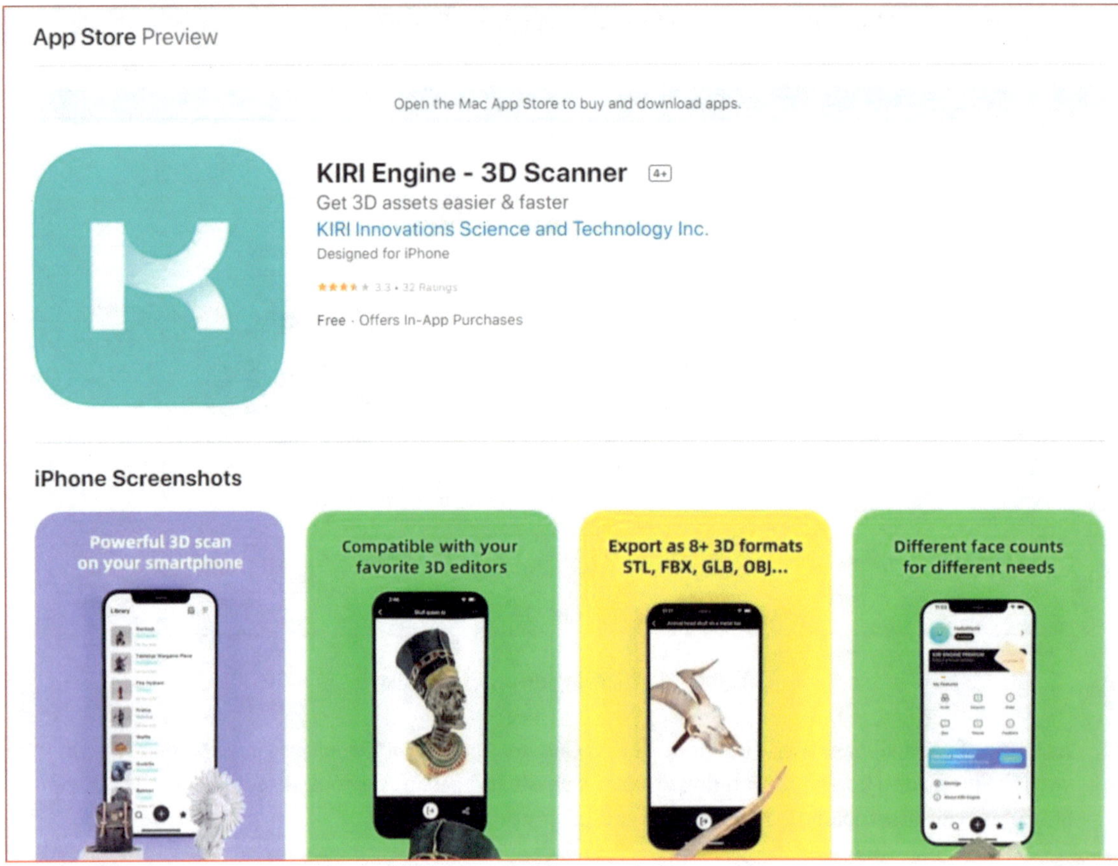

Figure 11.4: KIRI Engine on the App Store

Using KIRI Engine is very straightforward as there are very few options to choose from when running the app. When you first open KIRI Engine, whether you're on an Android or iPhone device, you'll be greeted with a simple interface as seen in *Figure 11.5*:

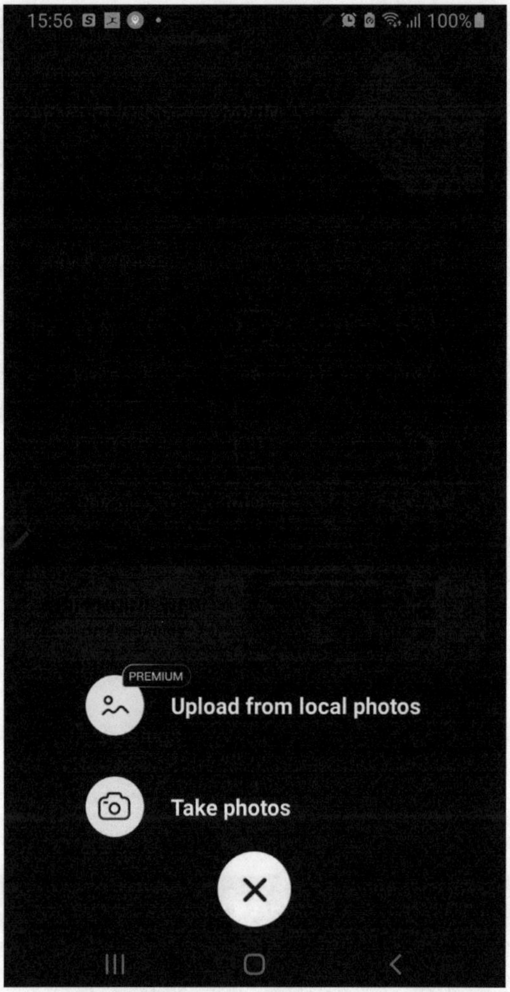

Figure 11.5: The KIRI Engine welcome screen

Here, you will be given a choice of uploading photographs that you've taken before or taking photos with the KIRI app. Choose the latter, **Take photos**, and you will see the screen change:

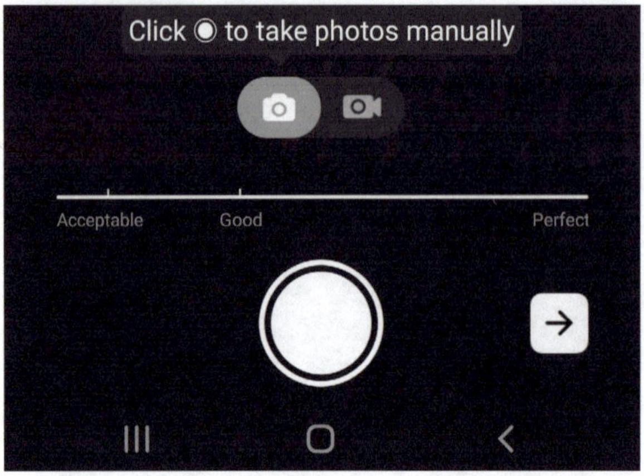

Figure 11.6: The manual option

The manual capture setting is the default setting. It is denoted by the stills camera icon at the top left of *Figure 11.6*. This is a manual capture option, which means you'll have to click on the big white button at the bottom of the screen every time you want to take a picture. The problem with this is, every time you tap the screen of your smartphone it introduces a slight camera shake, which in certain lighting conditions will give you a blurry picture.

The auto-capturing setting is accessible by clicking the movie camera icon on the right, as shown in *Figure 11.7*. With this setting, you need to click on the red button just once to start capturing. This setting takes a picture every couple of seconds (as many as 70 pictures) and will also give you warnings if you are moving the camera too fast.

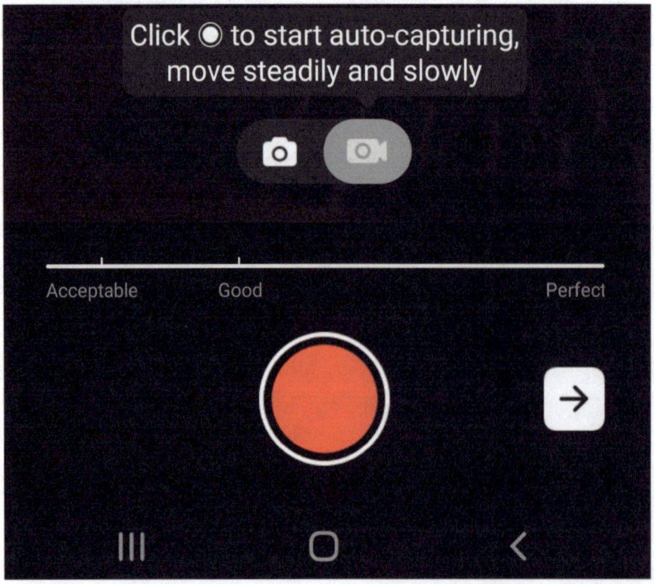

Figure 11.7: The auto-capturing option

Note the progress line above the record button; this indicates the quality of the coverage, namely, **Acceptable**, **Good**, and **Perfect**. An **Acceptable** result will get you a less detailed 3D model and will be prone to lumpiness, whereas a **Perfect** photo result will get you a more detailed and smoother 3D model.

Ideally, you should get as much overlap from one picture to the next as possible. Around 80% overlap is a good rule of thumb from one image to the next sequentially. By overlap, I mean that every two or three consecutive images should share at least one feature such as an eye or a nose.

As soon as you have reached the maximum number of images and have reached a reasonable level of coverage around your face, you'll be greeted with the interface shown in *Figure 11.8*:

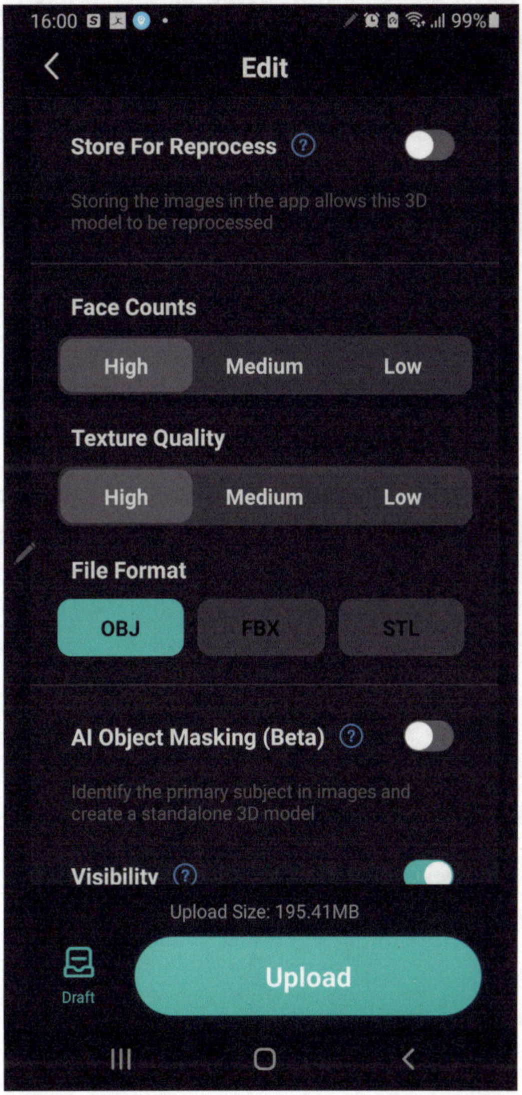

Figure 11.8: The upload screen

In this interface, you'll see the following options:

- **Face Counts**: The number of polygons used to create the 3D model. Choose **High** to ensure the MetaHuman plugin has enough geometry to work with (you don't need to worry about producing very dense geometry as MetaHumans are designed to work with very high-density meshes in terms of polycounts).
- **Texture Quality**: KIRI doesn't produce massive texture maps and if you've managed to work with a MetaHuman in Unreal Engine, then you'll have no problem with the highest quality texture map created by KIRI. So, choose **High** again.
- **File Format**: While Unreal Engine can import both OBJ and FBX file formats, the FBX format has been reported to have longer processing times; Epic Games recommends OBJ for the plugin to work quickly, so choose **OBJ**.

When you have made your selections, hit the big **Upload** button. The upload process depends on the speed of your internet connection; if your connection is intermittent, expect problems as you may have to repeat the upload process. Once your photos have been successfully uploaded, you'll see the following message:

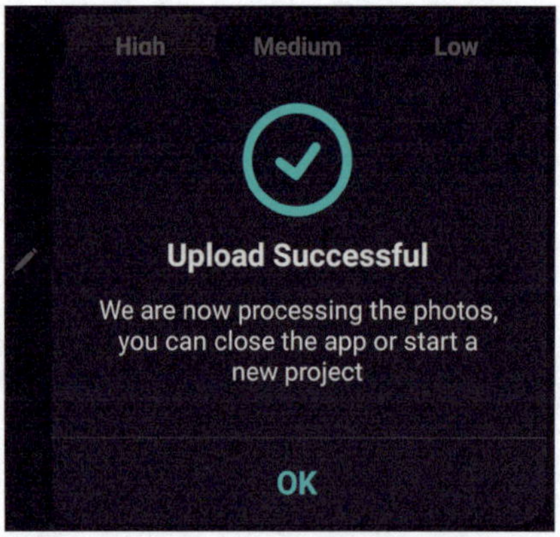

Figure 11.9: Upload Successful notification

A couple of factors need to be taken into consideration for the processing time of your photos. Because the processing is being taken care of by servers in the cloud, your upload will most likely have been put into a queue. So, if there's a lot of traffic, you'll need to hang tight for a few minutes. You'll be prompted if your job has been put into a queue or has started processing and you can check on the status of it within the app.

Once the process kicks in, the model is created alarmingly fast. When it's finished, you can open it up to inspect the model. In *Figure 11.10*, you can see a model of me. I know that you're probably distracted by how angelic I look, so I'll just say briefly that from start to finish that whole process from taking the photos to getting a usable 3D model only took around 10 minutes.

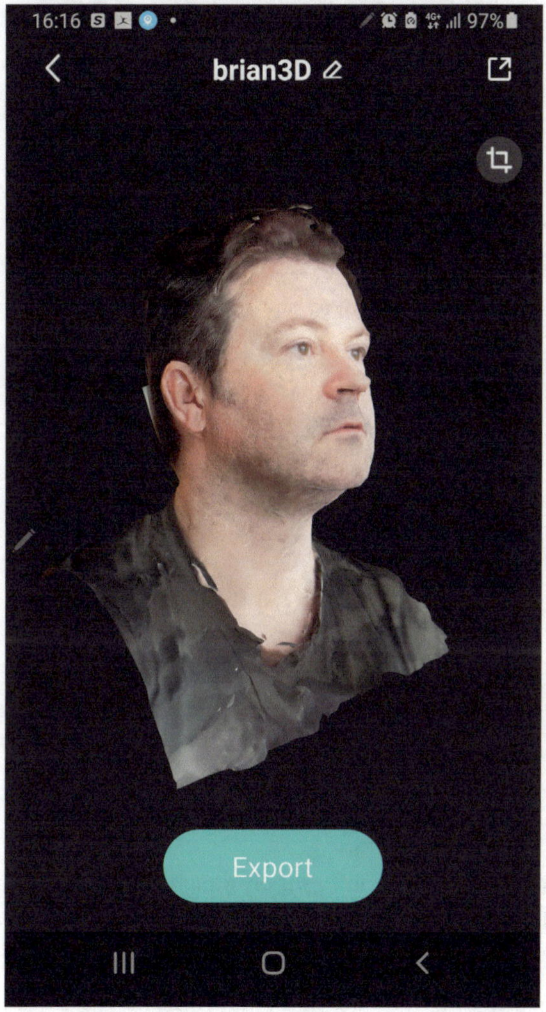

Figure 11.10: 3D scan result

The next step couldn't be simpler. Just hit the **Export** button, which will take you to this screen:

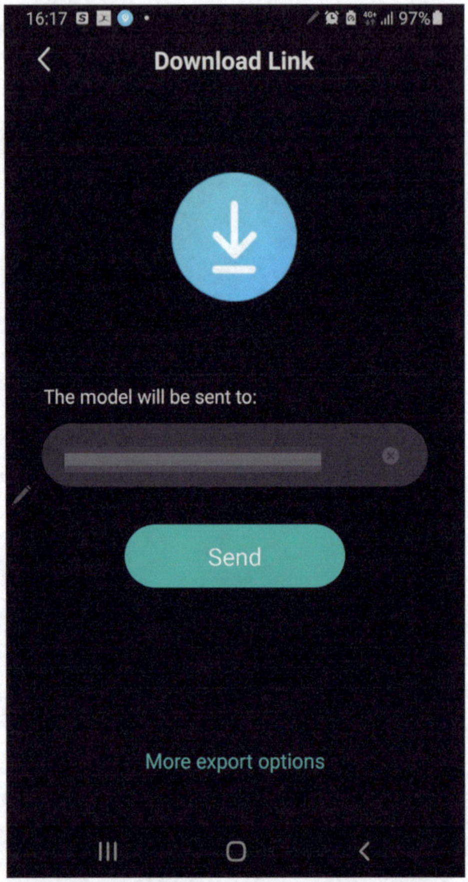

Figure 11.11: Sending your exported model

In *Figure 11.11*, you are given the option to supply an email address. Once provided, hit **Send** to receive a download link to your model. It will come in the form of a `.zip` folder containing both the OBJ of the mesh and a JPG for the texture map. Make sure to unzip the folder before continuing.

In the next section, you will bring your face mesh into Unreal Engine.

Importing your scanned mesh into Unreal Engine

With Unreal Engine open, go to the **Content** folder and create a new folder inside it called `FaceMesh`. Inside the **FaceMesh** folder, right-click and select **Import to Game/FaceMesh**. This will bring up the import dialog box, as per *Figure 11.12*, where you'll see the JPG (on the left of the figure) and OBJ files (on the right):

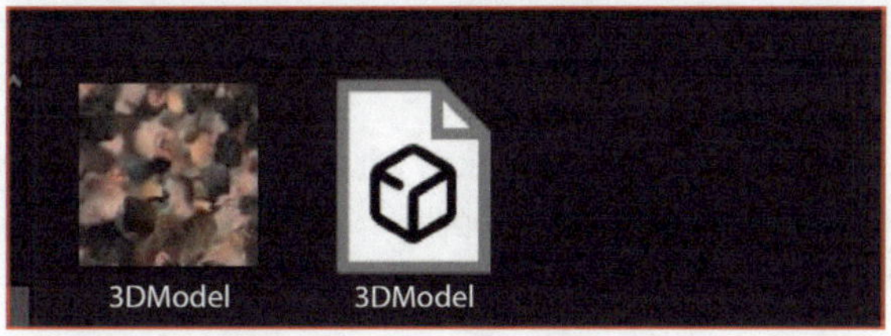

Figure 11.12: The JPG and OBJ files

You just need to click on the **3DModel** OBJ file, then hit **OK**.

This will open up **FBX Import Options**, as per *Figure 11.13* (this may seem odd as the file is an OBJ file, but this is correct):

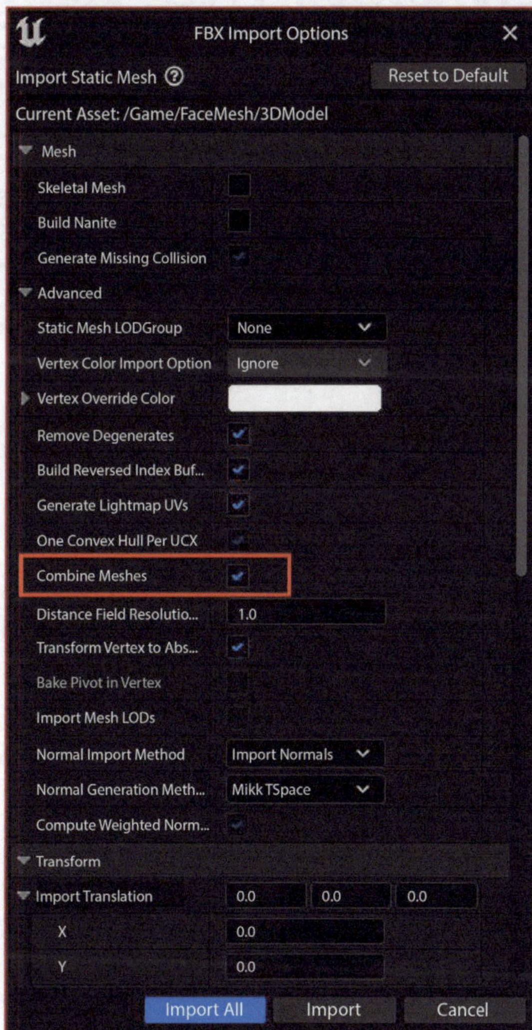

Figure: 11.13: Import mesh options

Make sure you have ticked **Combine Meshes** to ensure the model is imported as just one singular mesh. This is the only option that needs to be changed. Then, click on **Import All**.

It will take a moment to import. You will most likely get an error log dialog box saying there are issues in the smoothing group, but this is completely normal so don't be alarmed. If it happens, it will occur at the end of the import process so there is no action to be taken.

Once imported, as seen in *Figure 11.14*, there are three assets in the **FaceMesh** folder: the model, the shader, and the texture map, which automatically created the shader.

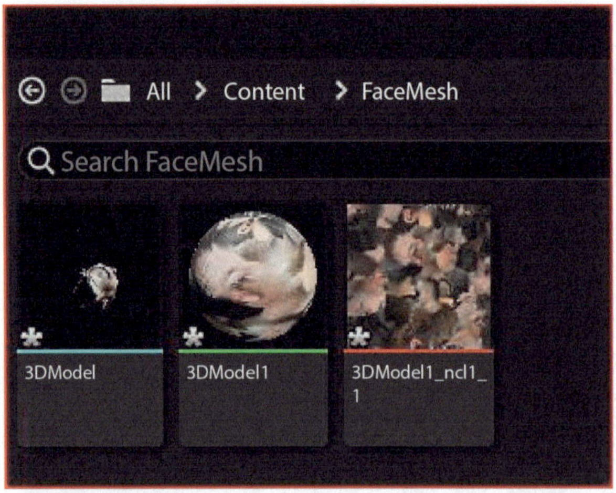

Figure 11.14: The imported assets

Now, right-click inside the **FaceMesh** folder, navigate down to **MetaHuman**, and click on **MetaHuman Identity**. This will engage the new Mesh to MetaHuman plugin you installed into the engine at the beginning of this chapter.

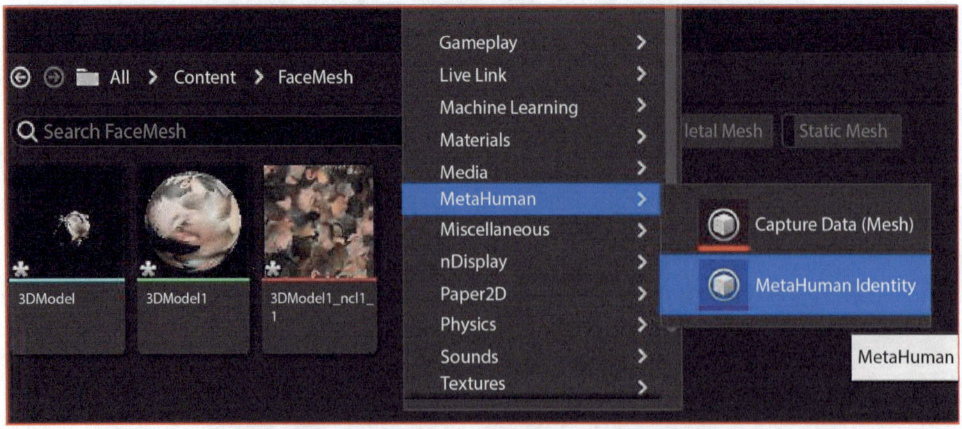

Figure: 11.15: Creating a MetaHuman Identity Asset

By clicking on **MetaHuman Identity**, you will create a MetaHuman Identity Asset, which is required to use the 3D scan you just imported.

Now, double-click on the **MetaHuman Identity** icon once it is created within **FaceMesh**. MetaHuman Identity, as seen in *Figure 11.16*, has a relatively simple interface that consists of four main functions.

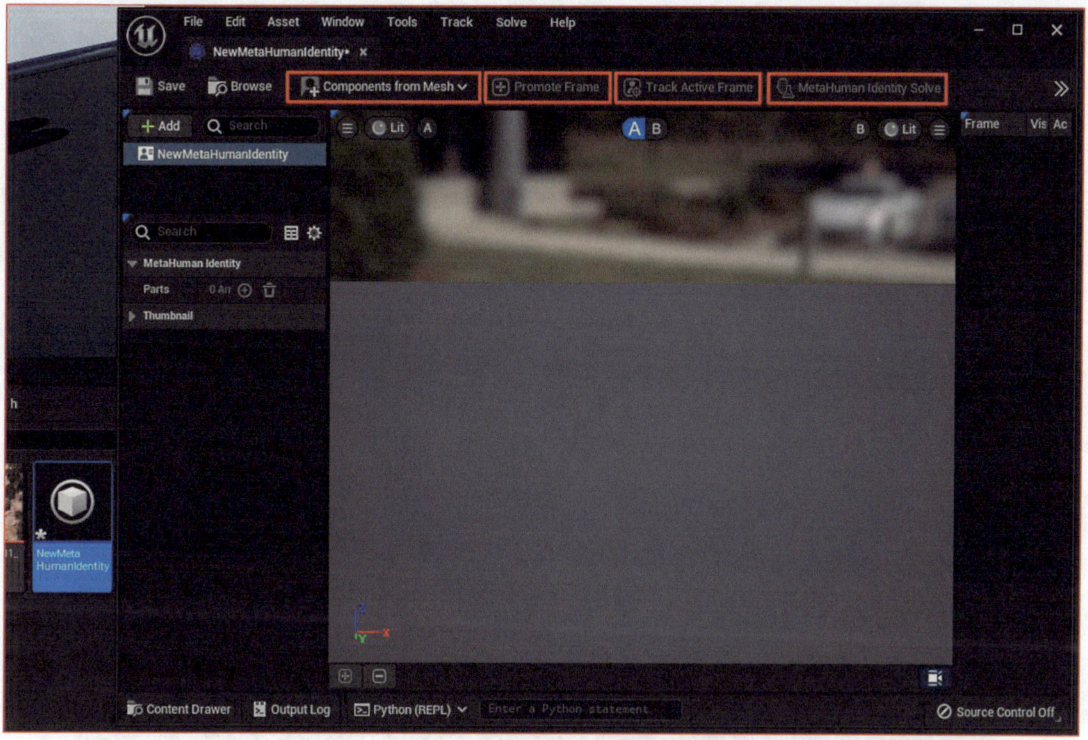

Figure 11.16: The MetaHuman Identity interface

Highlighted from left to right, the functions of the MetaHuman Identity interface are:

- **Components from Mesh**: Where we bring in the mesh that we imported into the engine earlier
- **Promote Frame**: Where we set up a viewing angle of our mesh for MetaHuman Identity to use as a reference for where key features such as the eyes, nose, and mouth are
- **Track Active Frame**: Where MetaHuman Identity uses a facial recognition algorithm to determine key facial features from the new face mesh
- **MetaHuman Identity Solve**: Where the magic happens, creating a MetaHuman that is aligned to the proportions of the new face mesh

Note that I have highlighted each of the four functions in *Figure 11.16*. The far-left function, **Components from Mesh**, is the only one that is active. The rest are inactive as each is dependent on the previous one to work, working as a series of steps that we must follow in order.

We will now go through these four functions:

1. Click on **Components from Mesh** and choose your model:

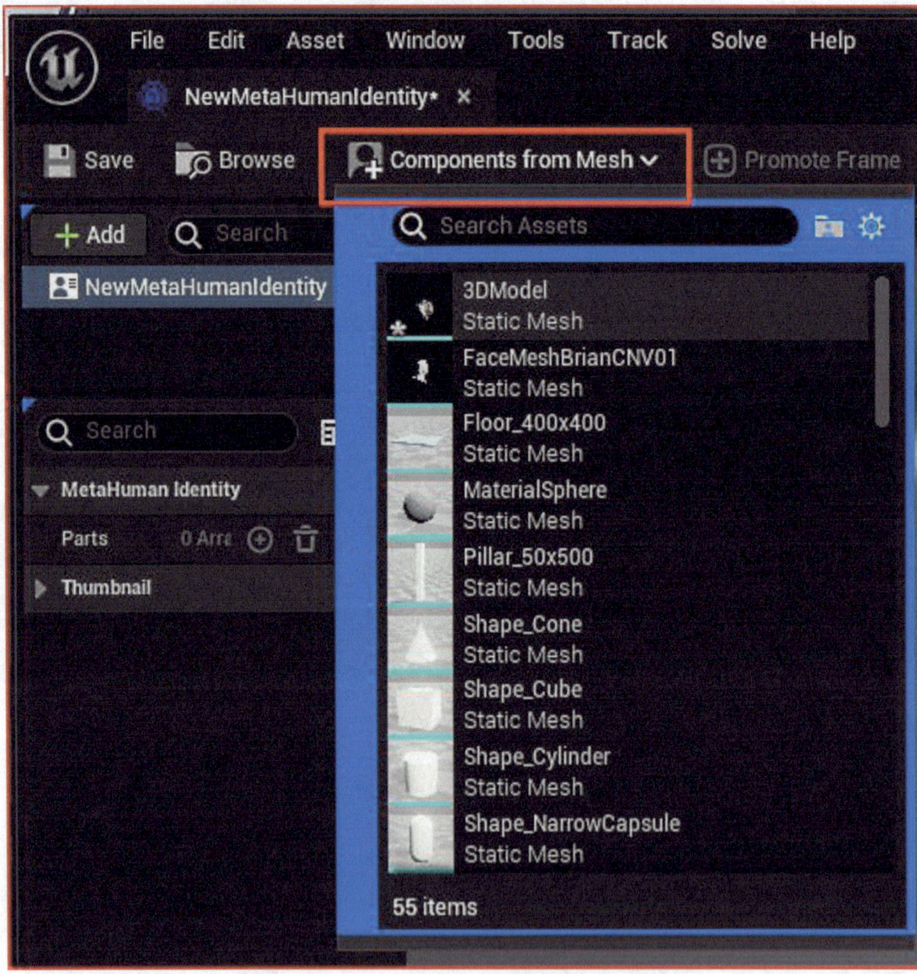

Figure 11.17: Adding your scanned mesh

Then use the *F* key to center your model, and use the rotate gismo with the *E* key to make your model face forward.

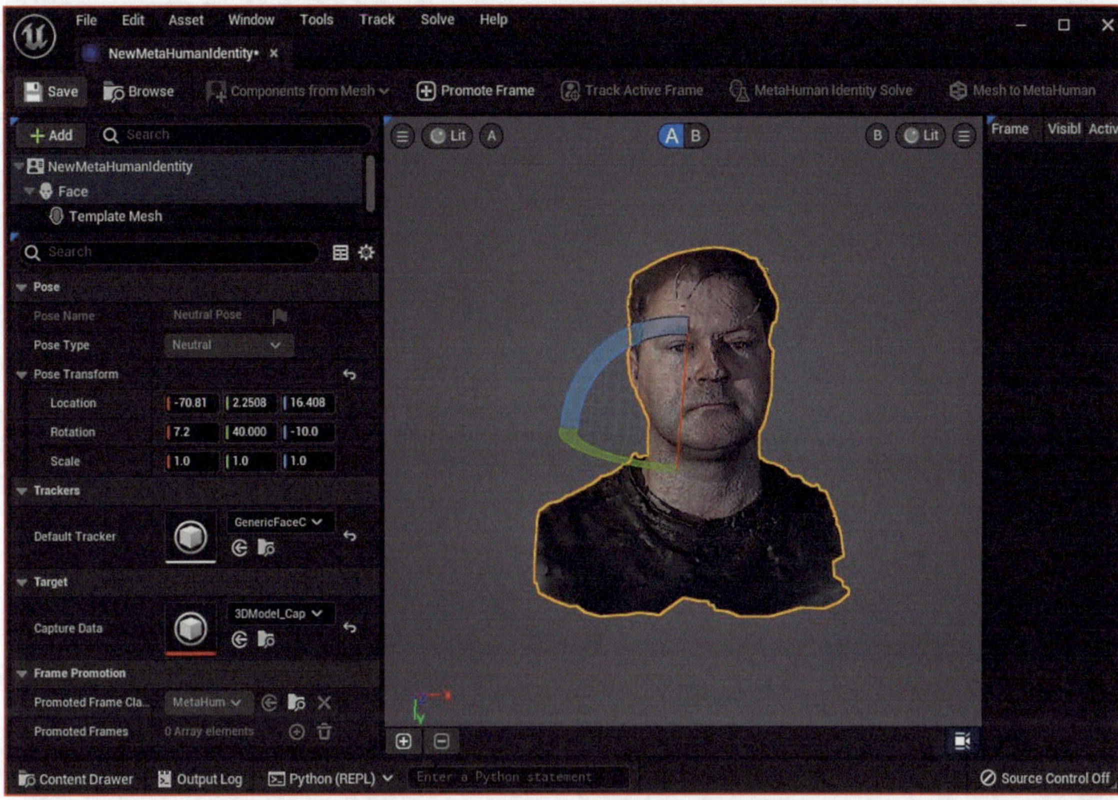

Figure 11.18: Rotating the model

2. When you are happy with the positioning of the face mesh, click on **Promote Frame** to save the angle.

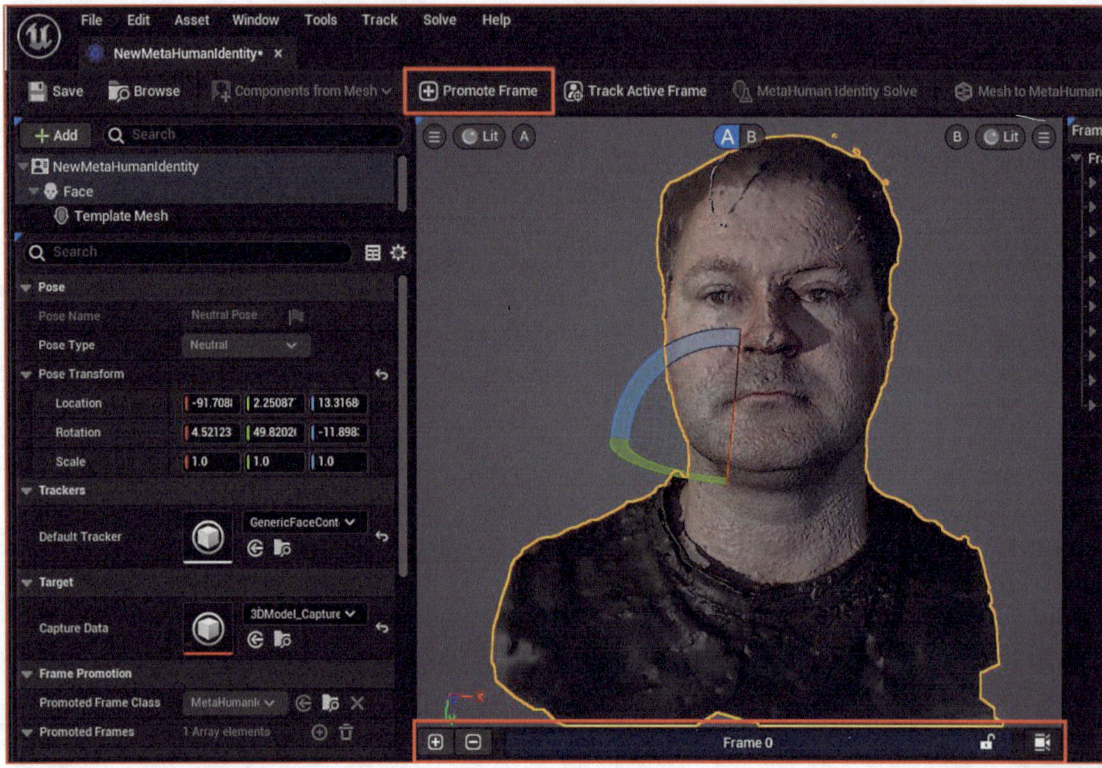

Figure 11.19: Promote Frame

If you take a look at *Figure 11.19*, you can see that under the viewport we now have a promoted frame titled **Frame 0**. This tells us that a frame has been created that will be used as a reference. You can create additional frames by clicking on the camera icon (in the bottom right), which will allow you to get a new angle. Then, you need to click on the **Promote Frame** button again. However, for the purpose of this chapter, let's keep things simple and just use **Promote Frame** once.

3. Moving on, we need to make sure that the face mesh can be properly tracked. Click on the **Track Active Frame** button, as highlighted in *Figure 11.20*.

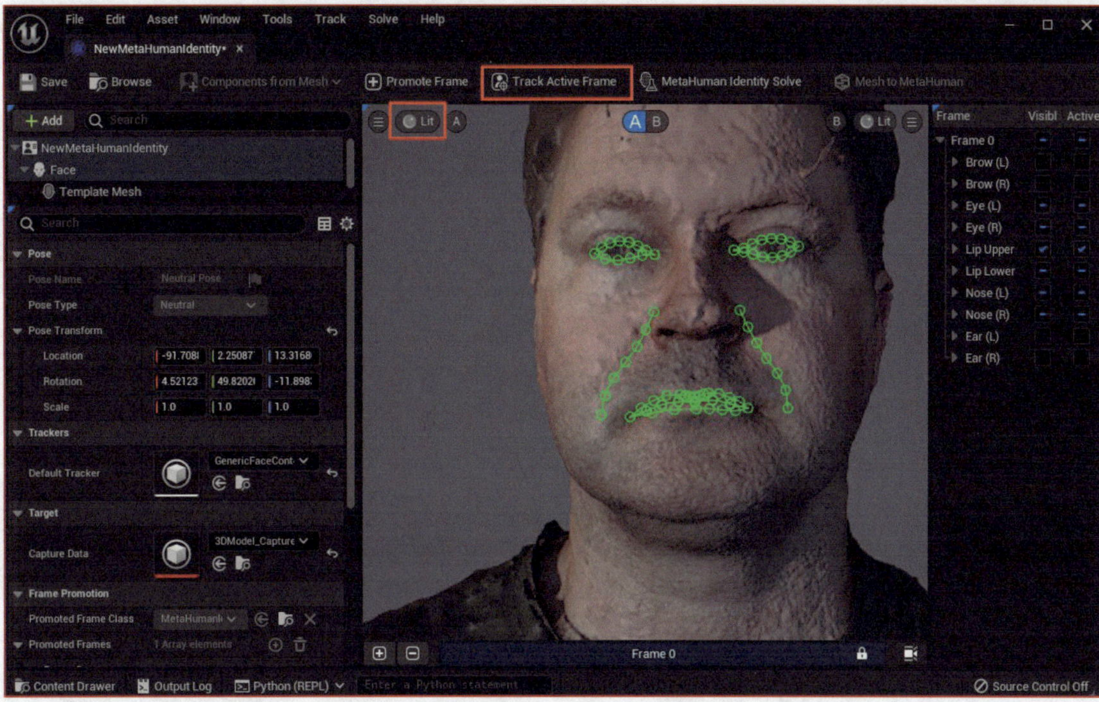

Figure 11.20: Track Active Frame

The MetaHuman Identity tool tracks the facial features that it sees. To make sure it's doing a good job, I suggest you toggle between **Lit** and **Unlit** in the viewport marked in *Figure 11.20*. In general, it does a great job at identifying the eyes and the mouth, which is enough to get you a really good likeness to your face scan.

4. Next, we need to create a body type for the new MetaHuman. Take a look at *Figure 11.21*. Select **Body** and then choose a body type close to your own.

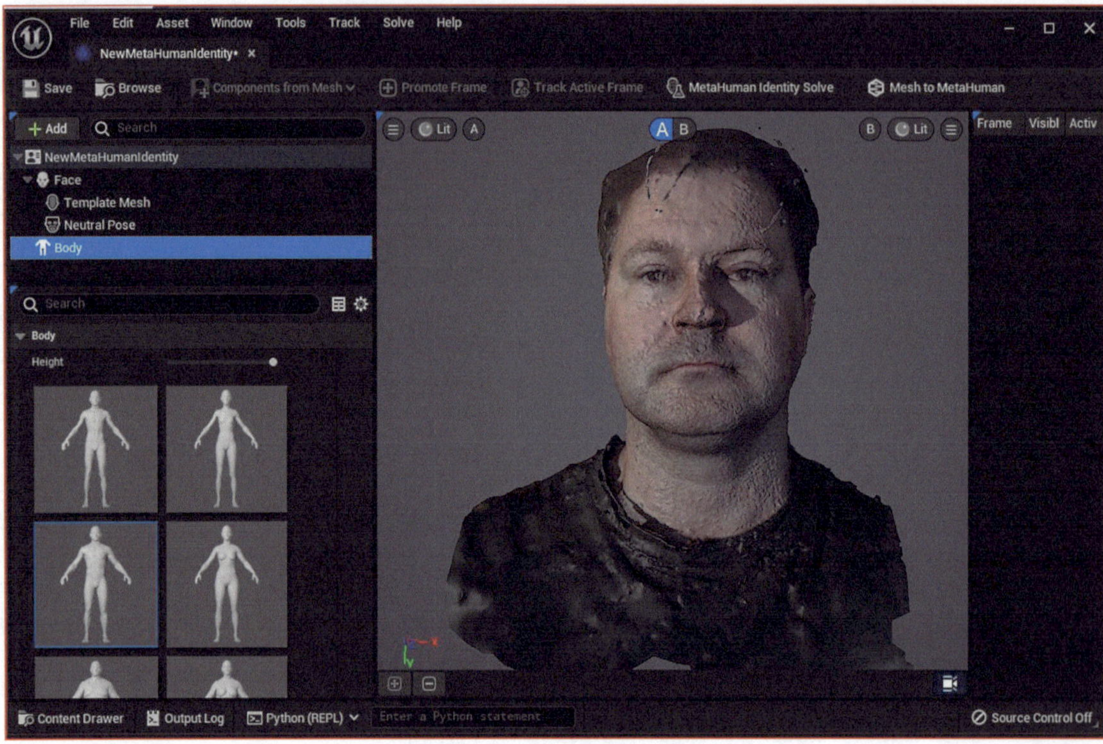

Figure 11.21: Choosing a body

5. Now, we need to process the new mesh shape from the face mesh scan. Click on **MetaHuman Identity Solve**, as per *Figure 11.22*.

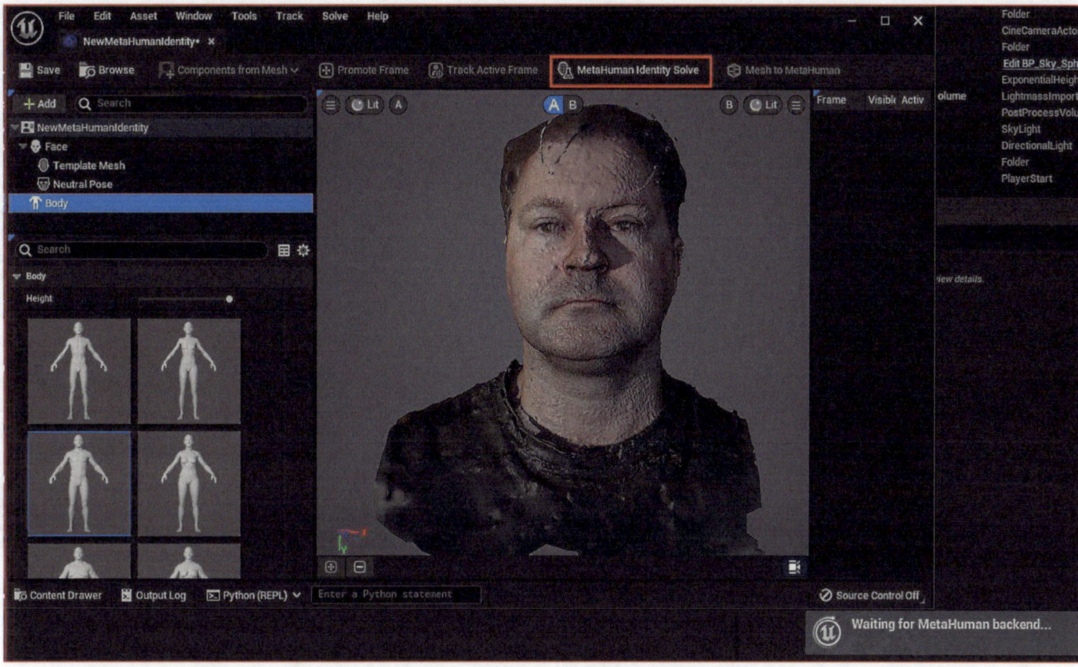

Figure 11.22: Waiting for MetaHuman backend…

You'll see a prompt in the bottom right of the screen saying **Waiting For MetaHuman backend….** This is because the processing will take place on the MetaHuman Cloud as it creates a MetaHuman Solution.

6. The process of waiting for the backend can take a few minutes, but as soon as it has completed, the **Mesh to MetaHuman** button will be available to select, as shown in *Figure 11.23*.

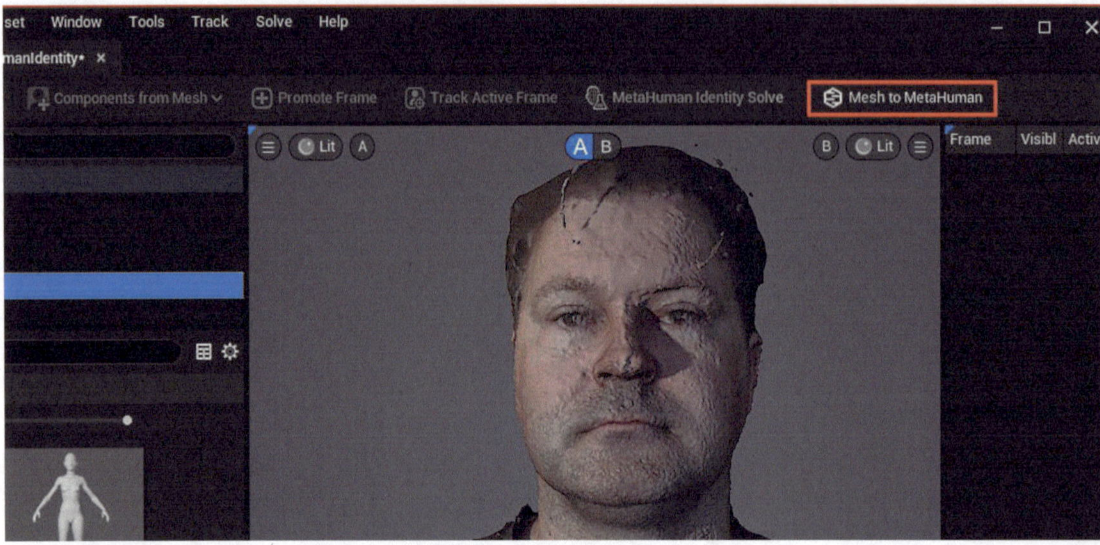

Figure 11.23: The Mesh to MetaHuman button

7. Once selected, you will get a **Mesh to MetaHuman** pop-up dialog box, as per *Figure 11.24*. Just click **OK**.

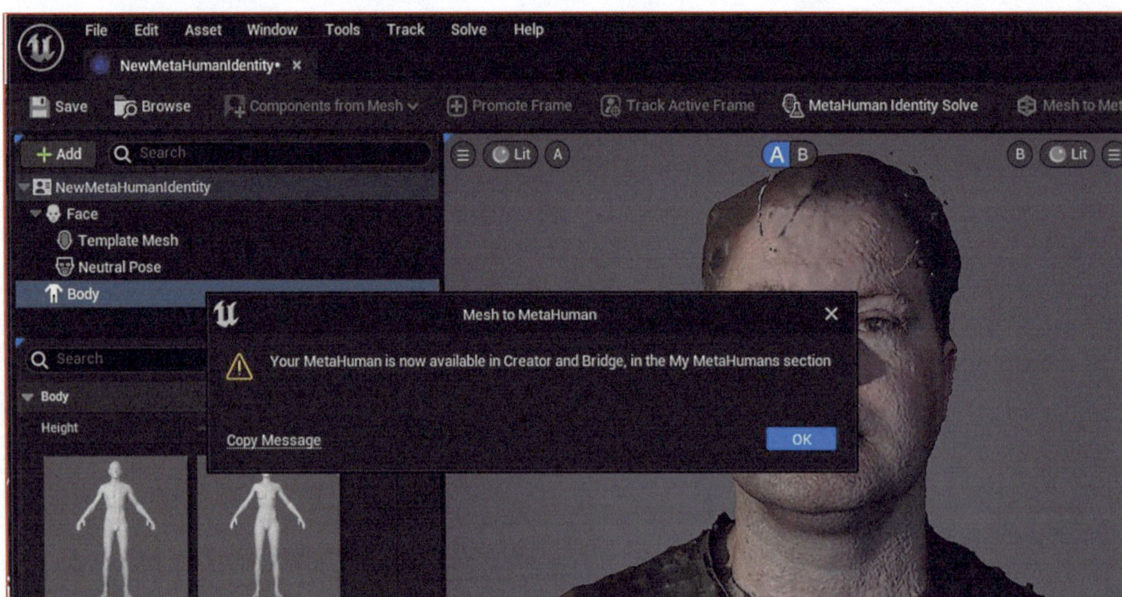

Figure 11.24: Your MetaHuman is now available

At this point, we can't see the progress of the Mesh to MetaHuman plugin because the processing takes place in the cloud. More specifically, we need to go to the MetaHuman Creator online tool to see the result.

In the next section, we will go over to Quixel Bridge, which can be accessed from your **Content** folder or the standalone Quixel Bridge application. We are using Quixel Bridge to gain access to our new MetaHuman so we can make adjustments with the online MetaHuman Creator.

Modifying the face mesh inside the MetaHuman Creator online tool

Once you have opened up Quixel Bridge, navigate to **My MetaHumans**. There you will see a new black-and-white icon. As per *Figure 11.25*, the icon indicates that this MetaHuman was created with the **Mesh to MetaHuman** plugin. Click on the black-and-white icon and navigate to the **Start MHC** button.

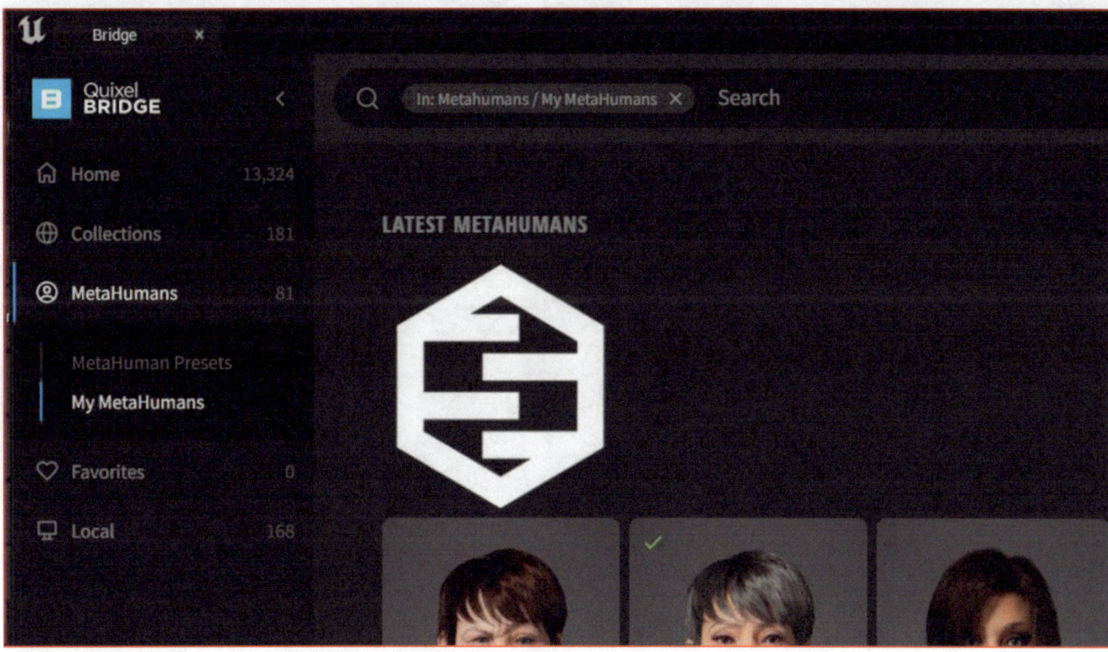

Figure 11.25: MetaHuman Identity icons

You will be taken to the familiar MetaHuman Creator online application featured in *Chapter 2*. As you can see in *Figure 11.26*, the MetaHuman has no skin and it is somewhat distorted. Most notably, the upper head protrudes unnaturally. The reason for this is that the face mesh scan that was created using the KIRI Engine app also scanned my hair; the MetaHuman Identity solver couldn't determine what the hair actually was, resulting in skin tissue instead of hair.

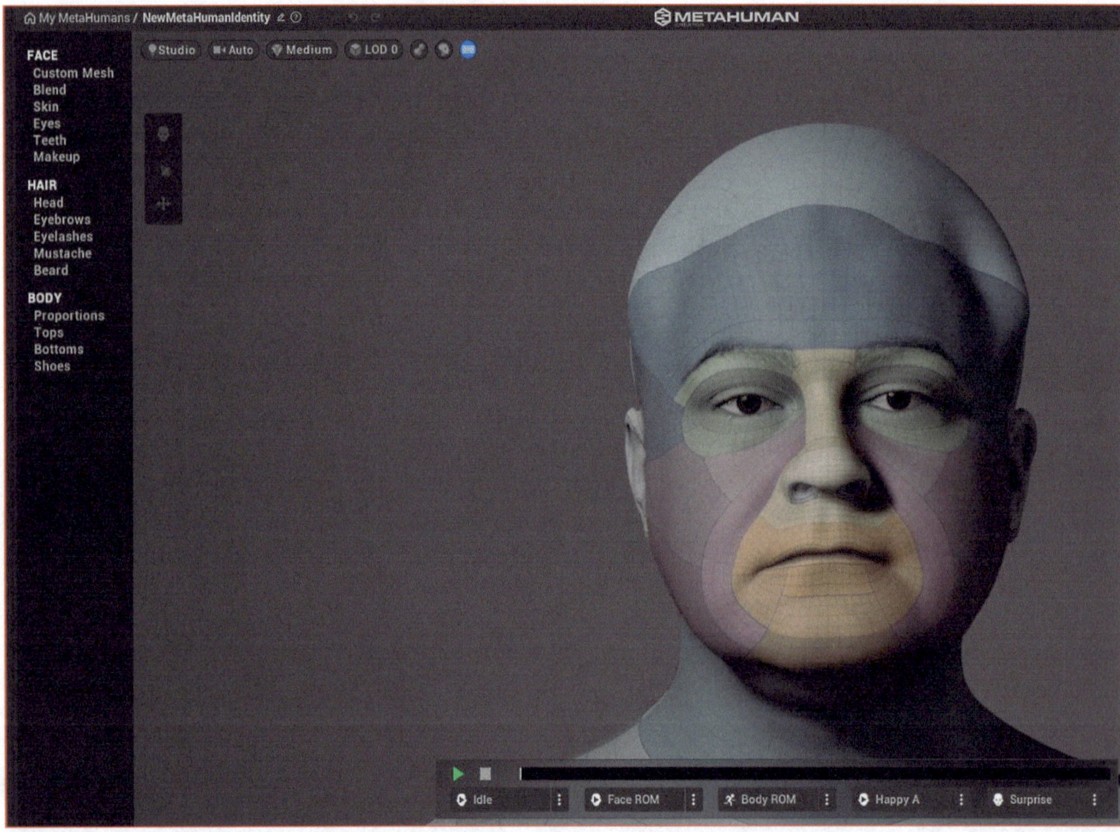

Figure 11.26: MetaHuman Creator with the face scan

There is an easy fix to the hair issue. Click on the **Custom Mesh** option under **Face**, as per *Figure 11.27*.

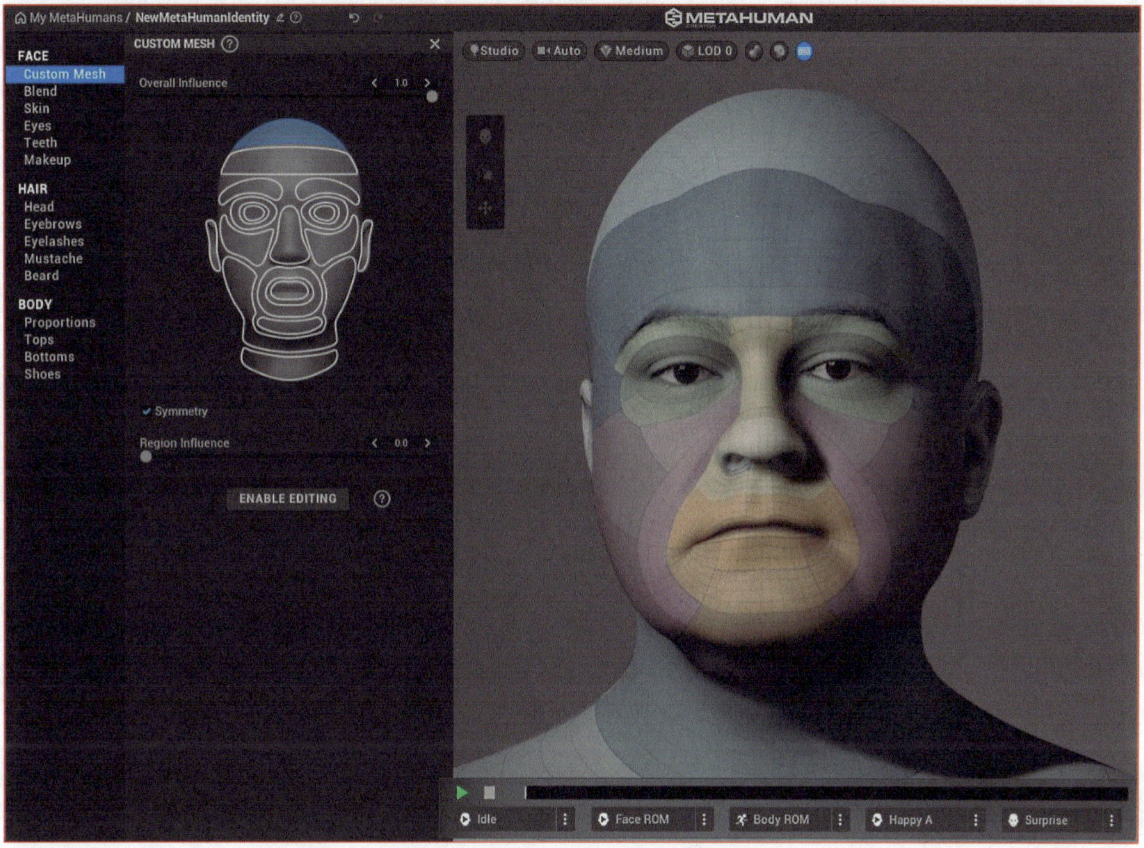

Figure 11.27: The Custom Mesh tool

If you look at the face thumbnail on the left, it is split into various components that correspond to the color-coded components on my face on the right.

Take note of the **Region Influence** slider too, which I have reduced down to *0*. This means that the MetaHuman template determines the shape of that part of the mesh rather than the face mesh created by the KIRI Engine scan. When you compare *Figure 11.26* and *Figure 11.27*, you can see the difference – the former has a much lumpier head than the latter.

If you wish to make further edits, you can click on the **ENABLE EDITING** button to fine-tune the mesh. However, I urge you to first refine your scanning technique to get a better result and use the **ENABLE EDITING** option as a last resort.

> **Note**
>
> Higher-quality photographs will get you a better result. In this example, a smartphone under less-than-ideal lighting conditions contributed to distortion issues. Using a DSLR in a small studio setup with a blank background and very soft light would give superior results. In addition, making use of a polarizer filter to further remove any reflection would be an added bonus.

Now, let's move on to the skin. The texture map and shader we gained from both the KIRI Engine scan and the subsequent import to Unreal Engine have been lost. This is a good thing. MetaHumans have an incredibly powerful skin shader that responds to lighting in Unreal Engine very realistically that we will take advantage of instead.

So, click on **Skin** as shown in *Figure 11.28*, and then click on the **ASSIGN** button to assign a skin color.

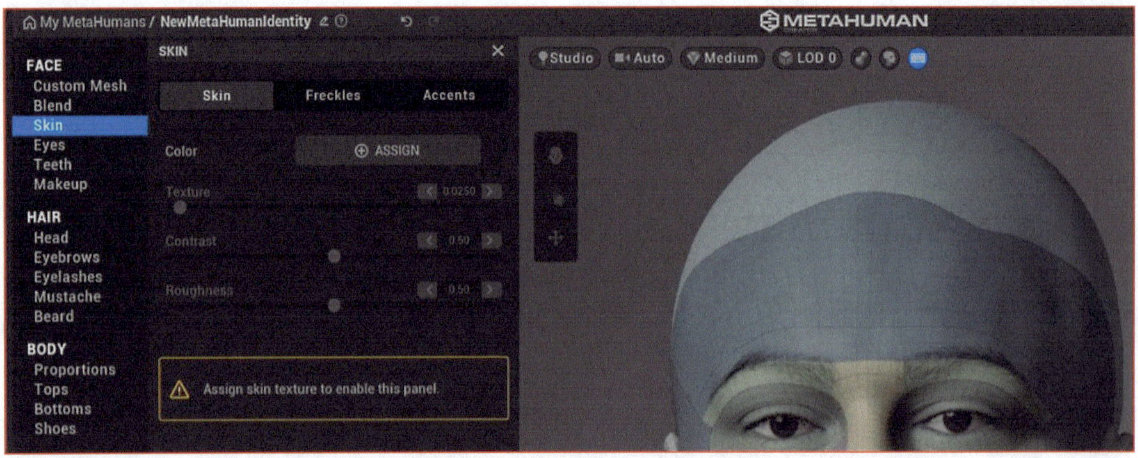

Figure 11.28: Assigning a skin color

Instantly, this will give us skin colors with all the shader attributes that come with MetaHumans. We now have the same level of skin control with our custom face scan that we had when we were first creating our MetaHuman back in *Chapter 2*:

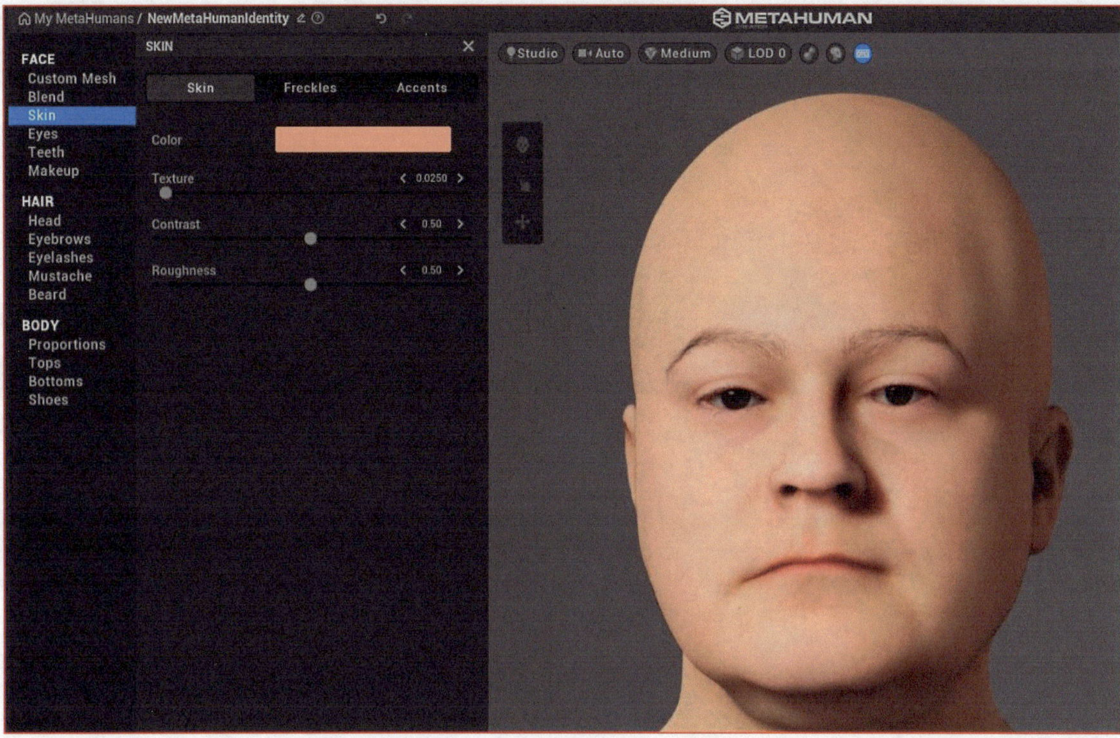

Figure 11.29: Editing the skin

You can also see from *Figure 11.29* that the default lighting gives us a somewhat soft lighting result. As taking photographs with KIRI Engine in soft lighting is preferred, using the default lighting in MetaHuman Creator would be helpful for matching the skin tone of our original photographs.

To get a better sense of whether your model is working, add some hair that is similar to your own, as I did in *Figure 11.30*:

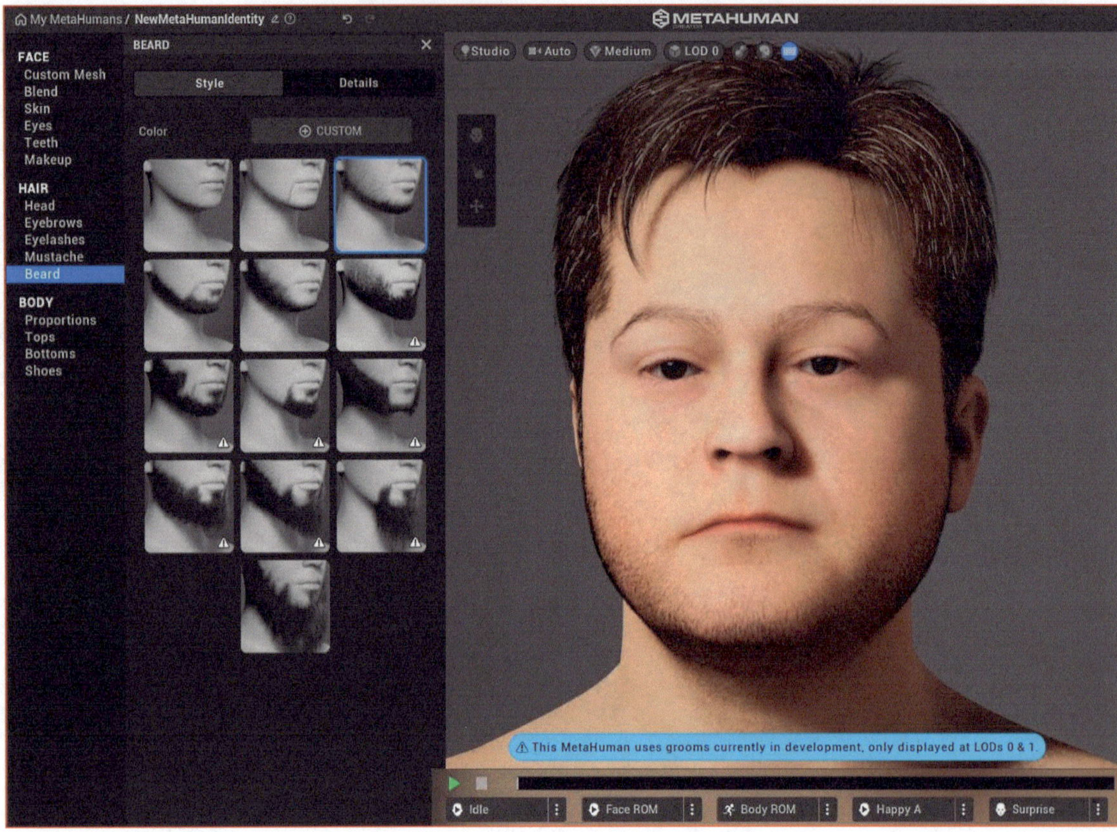

Figure 11.30: Adding hair

Because MetaHuman Creator constantly saves your MetaHuman automatically, you can come back to this at any time. You can also add your new MetaHuman with the custom face mesh into your project at any time using Quixel Bridge.

You can spend a lot of time modifying your custom MetaHuman and the time that you should spend on this really depends on what your end goal is. If you're looking for a perfect likeness, you have all the move and sculpt tools in MetaHuman Creator along with all the photographs used with KIRI for reference to achieve greater realism.

Summary

In this chapter, we learned about a fantastic extra feature that can be used for creating characters that share a likeness with real people. We covered the process of downloading and installing the Mesh to MetaHuman plugin, before moving on to using the photogrammetry KIRI Engine. After that, we imported the KIRI Engine face mesh and made use of the MetaHuman Identity plugin, learning how to get a custom face mesh working inside MetaHuman Creator and how to refine it and fix issues.

Effectively, this chapter was a bonus chapter that delved into a new tool that was made available during the process of writing this book. It is a very powerful new tool that has the potential to not only create reasonable likenesses for digital character doubles but also, with some extra effort, provide very realistic results for digital doubles.

In addition to using 3D scans of people, you may find yourself scanning sculptures, or repurposing other 3D models such as fantasy characters or even toon-like characters. The possibilities are endless.

And that's the end of this book! We have covered a lot of ground here, which is rather an understatement when you think about the technology and innovation we have embraced throughout these pages.

It was my intention, as an artist and filmmaker, to bring together a guide for other artists and filmmakers to follow and enjoy. Many of you will be well versed in CGI and animation and many will be novices at the beginning of your journey. Either way, you now have a step-by-step guide on how you can create your own visions, animations, and entertainment with technology that until recently was exclusive to major animation studios!

Index

A

B

C

O

P

Q

R

S

Other Books You May Enjoy

If you enjoyed this book, you may be interested in these other books by Packt:

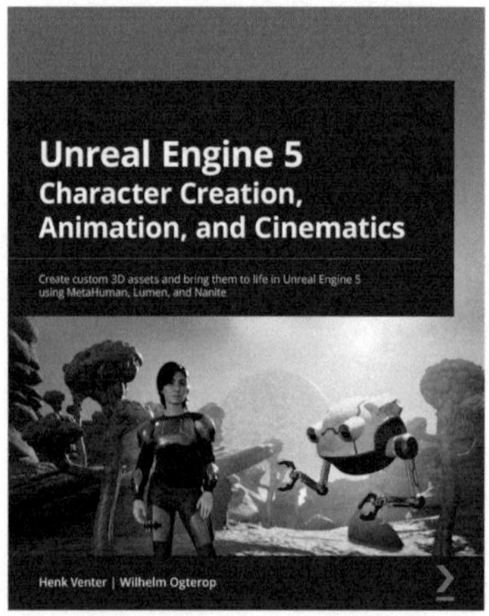

Unreal Engine 5 Character Creation, Animation, and Cinematics

Henk Venter, Wilhelm Ogterop

ISBN: 978-1-80181-244-3

- Create, customize, and use a MetaHuman in a cinematic scene in UE5
- Model and texture custom 3D assets for your movie using Blender and Quixel Mixer
- Use Nanite with Quixel Megascans assets to build 3D movie sets
- Rig and animate characters and 3D assets inside UE5 using Control Rig tools
- Combine your 3D assets in Sequencer, include the final effects, and render out a high-quality movie scene
- Light your 3D movie set using Lumen lighting in UE5

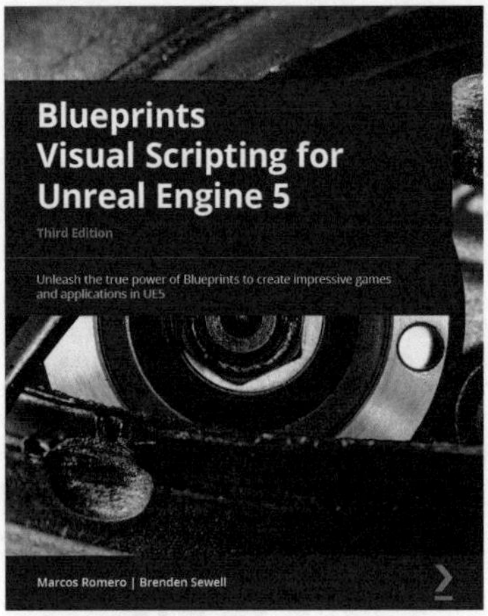

Blueprints Visual Scripting for Unreal Engine 5 - Third Edition

Marcos Romero, Brenden Sewell

ISBN: 978-1-80181-158-3

- Understand programming concepts in Blueprints
- Create prototypes and iterate new game mechanics rapidly
- Build user interface elements and interactive menus
- Use advanced Blueprint nodes to manage the complexity of a game
- Explore all the features of the Blueprint editor, such as the Components tab, Viewport, and Event Graph
- Get to grips with OOP concepts and explore the Gameplay Framework
- Work with virtual reality development in UE Blueprint
- Implement procedural generation and create a product configurator

Packt is searching for authors like you

If you're interested in becoming an author for Packt, please visit `authors.packtpub.com` and apply today. We have worked with thousands of developers and tech professionals, just like you, to help them share their insight with the global tech community. You can make a general application, apply for a specific hot topic that we are recruiting an author for, or submit your own idea.

Share your thoughts

Now you've finished *Reimagining Characters with Unreal Engine's MetaHuman Creator*, we'd love to hear your thoughts! Scan the QR code below to go straight to the Amazon review page for this book and share your feedback or leave a review on the site that you purchased it from.

`https://packt.link/r/1-801-81772-3`

Your review is important to us and the tech community and will help us make sure we're delivering excellent quality content.

Download a free PDF copy of this book

Thanks for purchasing this book!

Do you like to read on the go but are unable to carry your print books everywhere?

Is your eBook purchase not compatible with the device of your choice?

Don't worry, now with every Packt book you get a DRM-free PDF version of that book at no cost.

Read anywhere, any place, on any device. Search, copy, and paste code from your favorite technical books directly into your application.

The perks don't stop there, you can get exclusive access to discounts, newsletters, and great free content in your inbox daily!

Follow these simple steps to get the benefits:

1. Scan the QR code or visit the link below:

   `https://packt.link/free-ebook/9781801817721`

2. Submit your proof of purchase
3. That's it! We'll send your free PDF and other benefits to your email directly

Made in the USA
Monee, IL
13 September 2026

63137523R10197